THE PRICE OF INDIFFERENCE

The Price of Indifference

Refugees and Humanitarian Action in the New Century

ARTHUR C. HELTON

A COUNCIL ON FOREIGN RELATIONS BOOK

OXFORD
UNIVERSITY PRESS

OXFORD
UNIVERSITY PRESS

Great Clarendon Street, Oxford OX2 6DP

Oxford University Press is a department of the University of Oxford.
It furthers the University's objective of excellence in research, scholarship,
and education by publishing worldwide in

Oxford New York

Auckland Bangkok Buenos Aires Cape Town Chennai
Dar es Salaam Delhi Hong Kong Istanbul Karachi Kolkata
Kuala Lumpur Madrid Melbourne Mexico City Mumbai Nairobi
São Paulo Shanghai Taipei Tokyo Toronto

Oxford is a registered trade mark of Oxford University Press
in the UK and in certain other countries

Published in the United States
by Oxford University Press Inc., New York

First published 2002

British Library Cataloguing in Publication Data
Data available

Library of Congress Cataloging in Publication Data
Helton, Arthur C.
The price of indifference: refugees and humanitarian action in the new century/
Arthur C. Helton.
p. cm.
Includes bibliographical references and index.
1. Refugees—Government policy. 2. Emigration and immigration—Government policy.
I. Title.
JV6346.H44 2002 362.87'56—dc21 2001058067

ISBN 0-19-925030-8 (hbk.)
ISBN 0-19-925031-6 (pbk.)

3 5 7 9 10 8 6 4 2

Typeset by Newgen Imaging Systems (P) Ltd., Chennai, India
Printed in Great Britain
on acid-free paper by
Biddles Ltd, Guildford and King's Lynn

Foreword

More large-scale violence. More innocent people forced to flee their country and become refugees. More innocents displaced from their homes within their own country. That is the source of migrants' stories these last ten years. The situation has put an enormous burden on the international community, on governments and on US leadership in particular. Arthur Helton, a renowned expert on these matters, tells this story and tells us in practical terms how we can make the plight of refugees and displaced persons less horrible. This is a book for people who both feel the tugs of humanitarianism and want to know what can be done to turn humanitarian impulses into practical actions.

A good deal of what Mr. Helton has to say comes back to American leadership. To clear the path for humanitarian relief, the United States has been often called upon to intervene militarily in a crisis, risk American lives, and help organize international action. The enormity of the humanitarian problem and the prominent role of the United States has often catapulted refugee and displaced issues to the top of our national policy agenda—where it belongs.

In this book, Arthur Helton presents a sweeping review of the last decade's twists and turns in refugee policy and humanitarian action more broadly. This includes the crises in Bosnia, Cambodia, East Timor, Haiti, Kosovo, Rwanda, and Somalia. No one before Helton has examined all these crises in such depth, systematically discussing them in a lively and engaging style. Informed by the insights of recent literature on the subject, Helton's book goes a step further by proposing a new rationale for reform and concrete steps for action. He clearly identifies the shortcomings of existing policy and institutional mechanisms which are often too reactive and politicized to respond effectively to refugee emergencies. He does not merely expose the deficiencies of current policies and institutions, but also develops concrete proposals for reform which will help decision-makers formulate a new workable refugee policy.

In particular, Helton recommends the establishment of two new agencies—1) a US Agency for Humanitarian Action (AHA) and 2) an intergovernmental mechanism for Strategic Humanitarian Action and Research (SHARE). At the national level, AHA would help enhance contingency planning within the US government and improve policy coordination in international operations, including between the military and civilians. At the international level, SHARE, an intergovernmental expert entity, would allow like-minded states jointly to address humanitarian issues and foster pro-active refugee policies.

A study of exceptional depth with a compelling human quality, Arthur Helton's book makes a valuable contribution to the debate on the complex legal, political and moral dimensions of humanitarian emergencies. I am convinced that by providing a new vision and a much needed strategic direction to US and international decision-makers, this book will contribute to better policymaking.

Leslie H. Gelb
President, Council on Foreign Relations

Preface

The research for this book has spanned much of my professional life. From representing Haitian boat people incarcerated at the Brooklyn Navy Yard in 1981 in New York, to interviewing displaced Serbs from Kosovo residing in Belgrade in 2001, refugees have taken me on a remarkable professional journey. But the inquiry achieved a degree of rigour over the past two years, during which time I undertook a focused study of refugee policy as a Senior Fellow at the Council on Foreign Relations. This particular study took me to Africa, Asia, Europe, and the former Soviet Union. I have read thousands of pages and I have interviewed hundreds of government officials, representatives of international organizations and of NGOs, as well as spoken to many experts as well as refugees and displaced persons. I owe debts of gratitude to them all for making time for me.

The product of this inquiry is a book about how policy pertaining to forced migration should be conceived and managed in the broader context of humanitarian action. It is, in that sense, a book about the foreseeable future, drawing particularly upon the experience of the past decade.

At the Council on Foreign Relations, I am especially grateful for the guidance I received from Les Gelb. Larry Korb and David Kellogg provided valuable advice as well. Steve Friedman, who chaired my Council Study Group, was extremely helpful, as were the members of the Study Group: George Biddle, Kenneth Cain, Roberta Cohen, Barbara Crossette, Bob DeVecchi, Shep Forman, Taryn Higashi, Francis James, Steve Kass, Radha Kumar, Ren Levy, Bill Luers, Princeton Lyman, Elizabeth McKeon, Pat Nash, Herb Okun, Michael Oppenheimer, Jay Paxton, Jack Rosenthal, Enid Schoettle, George Sherry, Jim Sikes, Ted Sorensen, Tom Weiss, Maureen White, and Ari Zolberg.

On the Council staff, I am most grateful to Eliana Jacobs, my research associate, and Marie Jeannot, my assistant, who were indispensable to this project. Also, several interns assisted us, notably Dessie Zagorcheva, James Weatherill, and Anita Butera. I am very appreciative as well of the *pro bono* research assistance of Terry Eder-Kaufman and the law firm of Curtis, Mallet-Prevost, Colt & Mosle.

It is impossible to list all those who helped me directly or indirectly in the preparation of this book. Among those who were helpful, I count Mort Abramowitz, Ken Bacon, Geneviève Bador, Omar Bakhet, Martin Barber,

Rick Barton, Chloé Baszanger, Mats Berdal, Linda Besharaty, Werner Blatter, Rachel Bronson, Jagdish Bhagwati, Nellie Chan, Arne Piel Christensen, Nat Colletta, Jeff Crisp, Tom Crosby, Ralie Deffenbaugh, Marika Fahlen, Pat Weiss Fagen, Erika Feller, Bill Fuller, Theo Gemelas, Matt Gibney, Guy Goodwin-Gill, Martin Griffiths, Raymond Hall, Mort Halperin, Udo Janz, Soren Jessen-Petersen, Sidney Jones, Allan Jury, Mukesh Kapila, Jeff Kaplan, Mats Karlsson, Kevin Kennedy, Irene Khan, Roger Kubarych, Gil Loescher, Susan Martin, Gerry Martone, Kim Maynard, Stan McChrystal, Margaret McKelvey, Dennis McNamara, Doris Meissner, Rick Messick, Michael Moller, Ambler Moss, Koki Muli, Jochen Münker, Kathleen Newland, Binaifer Nowrojee, Bill O'Neill, Bob Oakley, Peter Osnos, Amit Pandya, Elena Popovic, Mike Peters, Joseph Rees, Gideon Rose, Jim Ross, Barney Rubin, Rick Ryscavage, Andy Schoenholtz, Steve Segal, Bill Smyser, Hansjoerg Strohmeyer, Fred Tipson, Amina Tirana, Volker Türk, David Victor, Ruth Wedgwood, Jean-Noel Wetterwald, and Monette Zard.

Some passages in this book originally appeared in the *International Journal of Refugee Law*, *International Migration Review*, and *SAIS Review*, published by the Oxford University Press, Center for Migration Studies, and Johns Hopkins University Press, respectively, as well as in a forthcoming book on humanitarian action published by Baywood. I appreciate the permission to use them here.

The Office of the United Nations High Commissioner for Refugees, most particularly the Centre for Documentation Research, Department of International Protection, and the Evaluation and Policy Analysis Unit, were very generous with information. UNHCR provided critical logistical support in the course of my research travels as well.

There were several essential supporters of this project. The Oxford University Press and the Council on Foreign Relations added important value as publishers. The support of the Open Society Institute, particularly its Chairman, George Soros, and its President, Aryeh Neier, as well as the Ford Foundation, made this project possible. My wife, Jacqueline, was supportive throughout this endeavour.

But while many helped me, the responsibility for this work is solely mine.

Arthur C. Helton
New York
January 2002

Contents

Abbreviations

CIREFCA	International Conference on Central American Refugees
CIVPOL	Civilian Police
CPA	Comprehensive Plan of Action
DHA	United Nations Department of Humanitarian Affairs
DPKO	Department of Peacekeeping Operations
ECHA	Executive Committee for Humanitarian Affairs
ECHO	European Community Humanitarian Office
ECOSOC	United Nations Economic and Social Council
ECOWAS	Economic Community of West African States
ERC	Emergency Relief Coordinator
EU	European Union
FAO	Food and Agriculture Organization
IASC	Inter-Agency Standing Committee
ICRC	International Committee of the Red Cross
IOM	International Organization for Migration
MSF	Médecins Sans Frontières
NATO	North Atlantic Treaty Organization
NSC	US National Security Council
NSPD	National Security Presidential Directive
OAU	Organization of African Unity
OCHA	United Nations Office for the Coordination of Humanitarian Affairs
OECD	Organisation for Economic Cooperation and Development
OFDA	USAID's Office of US Foreign Disaster Assistance
OHCHR	Office of the UN High Commissioner for Human Rights
OSCE	Organization for Security and Cooperation in Europe
OTI	Office of Transition Initiatives
PDD	Presidential Decision Directive
PRM	US State Department's Bureau of Population, Refugees, and Migration
UNAMET	United Nations Mission in East Timor
UNDP	United Nations Development Programme
UNDPA	United Nations Department of Political Affairs
UNDPKO	United Nations Department of Peacekeeping Operations
UNHCHR	United Nations High Commissioner for Human Rights
UNHCR	United Nations High Commissioner for Refugees
UNICEF	United Nations Children's Fund
UNMIK	United Nations Mission in Kosovo
UNPROFOR	United Nations Protection Force

UNRWA	United Nations Relief and Works Agency for Palestine Refugees in the Near East
UNTAC	United Nations Transitional Authority in Cambodia
UNTAET	United Nations Transitional Administration in East Timor
USAID	United States Agency for International Development
WFP	World Food Programme
WHO	World Health Organization

Introduction

This is a book about refugee policy. As reflected in the experience of the past decade, the current system for humanitarian action is in disarray. Policy mechanisms both within and among governments are not equipped to address humanitarian catastrophes. The inadequacy of current policy responses is clearly reflected in the tensions between military and humanitarian action in Afghanistan in the course of a new multilateral anti-terrorist campaign after attacks in the United States in September 2001.

This book thus urges that policy be reconceived and reorganized in order to better address the needs of uprooted persons in more proactive and comprehensive ways. In charting this path, the book maps and evaluates the continuum of responses available to decision makers to manage humanitarian emergencies involving forced displacement, and urges reforms that account for the interests of states.

Why do refugees matter? 'Refugees matter because they are there', answered Richard C. Holbrooke, then the Permanent Representative of the United States to the United Nations, when we spoke in October 2000. Holbrooke, who has been associated for many years with refugee advocacy and assistance activities, was direct. 'How can the world turn away from people made homeless by political evil?' Apart from the dead, they are the most obvious victims of political disasters, which the world simply cannot ignore. Holbrooke also detailed the various costs of international indifference. Protracted exile produces radicalization, such as in the Gaza Strip. Dealing appropriately with the displaced is 'not cheap', he allowed, but the consequences of not dealing with them in a timely fashion are even greater, leading to increased expenditures later and the creation of political instability. Political and strategic considerations are often intertwined refugee crises, but the primary motivation in the eyes of this seasoned diplomat and peace broker is pragmatic compassion: refugees matter because they are there.

Over the past decade, the world has witnessed a distressing number of political catastrophes that have created vast numbers of refugees and internal exiles. Terms such as 'ethnic cleansing', 'failed states', 'humanitarian intervention', and 'humanitarian evacuation' have entered the policy lexicon. These problems transcend humanitarian issues and involve a broader political context which both creates the problems and constrains the ability of policy-makers to deal with them effectively. Basic concepts of national sovereignty and human rights are juxtaposed in new, dynamic relationships.

Refugee emergencies have often surprised foreign policy decision makers and military leaders. Crises over the past decade in Bosnia, East Timor, Iraq, Kosovo, and Rwanda are emblematic. Humanitarian catastrophes in these settings have complicated and, indeed, shaped policy responses in unanticipated ways as they were forced onto decision-making agendas. It is clear that humanitarian action has become an important feature, indeed sometimes a central aspect, of the new national security agenda.

The pace of such crises may increase or decrease over the next decades. But it hardly matters. Whether more or less frequent, humanitarian catastrophes surely await us, and they will affect more people and be more complicated than those that have occurred in the past. Humanitarian action will appear on the front pages of the world's major newspapers for the foreseeable future. This era is characterized by new efforts undertaken by outside governments and international organizations to protect and assist people before they have had to flee across a national border. This potentially intrusive approach, a new feature of the post-cold war era, is reflected in the attention given now to internal exiles as well as efforts to help civilians in the midst of conflicts. The motivations for this new activism, of course, are not always benign. States are less welcoming of new arrivals at a time when asylum seekers are bereft of ideological value. But these endeavours to contain refugee emergencies have introduced new complexities, which are examined in detail in this book. Whatever the motivations, whether selfish or altruistic, more effective humanitarian action will redound to the benefit of both individuals and states.

The end of the cold war has been accompanied by heightened expectations of those officials who confront humanitarian crises that 'something be done', and decision makers come under pressure to produce 'immediate deliverables'. It is simply not workable to counsel 'doing nothing', even though action can often lead to disappointment and unmet expectations, which may be unrealistic in any event. This book identifies the repertoire of available policy options, including exceptional episodes of forcible humanitarian intervention and audacious efforts of state building in connection with refugee return.

The thinking and literature concerning responses to refugee crises have yet to catch up to the new realities that have emerged over the past decade. To address this gap, this book tells the recent refugee story, explores the implications for decision makers, and offers policy prescriptions to address the new challenges. How to make policy more responsive to the needs of the uprooted, including internal exiles, and how to achieve more effective coordination and institutional arrangements are central themes. The book surveys the available refugee policy tools and discusses how they have been used and under what circumstances they might work, or work better, in the future. It is clear that increasingly calibrated responses will be necessary for effective international humanitarian action.

Refugees have become enmeshed over the past decade in evolving notions of humanitarian action, and this book takes an integrated approach to the problem of human exile. It uses the term 'refugee' in a broad generic sense, and with specific legal connotations where indicated. In addition, terms such as 'exile', 'forced migration', or 'forced displacement' are used to signify the full range of forced population displacements, whether internal or external, whether within or outside of the ambit of the UN refugee treaties.

The argument in this book proceeds inductively from an examination of why refugees matter to recent experiences and policy responses, and on to proposals for re-conceiving and reorganizing policy to address refugees as a constituent element of humanitarian action linked to broader issues of foreign affairs. The book is aimed at a policy audience, but is designed to appeal to both general and expert readers, with a research base comprising interviews, reportage, readings, documentation, and analysis. Recommendations are interwoven throughout the text, but discussions of broad policy reforms are concentrated in Chapters 7 to 10.

In Chapter 1, 'Why Refugees Matter', broad questions are posed and answered about the nature of the refugee problem and the meaning of dealing with displacement. The implications for policy makers in the new century are particularly examined in the context of broader notions of humanitarian action.

Chapter 2, 'The Last Decade's Refugee Story', provides a chronology of events over the past decade. Many of the forces driving policy over the past decade are the same as before, but some are new and unique. In this chapter, policy responses are reviewed to determine what worked and what did not work, with a view to assessing what might work in the future and under what circumstances.

New efforts to deal with forced migration are examined in Chapter 3, 'Humanitarian Action and New Complexities in Refugee Protection: The Former Yugoslavia', and Chapter 4, 'Variations on State Building and Refugees: Myth and Reality', through notions of humanitarian intervention and state building endeavours. The former Yugoslavia is treated first in this inquiry as the situation over the past decade that provoked the most innovations in refugee policy. Other significant cases involving refugees during this period—Cambodia, Haiti, and East Timor—are then examined in order to identify broad implications for future humanitarian action.

The case studies in these two chapters explore the dilemmas faced by policy makers as they attempt to build or strengthen governance structures, functioning economies, and benign civil societies, particularly in connection with refugee repatriation, reintegration, and rehabilitation in societies in crisis and transition. While the particulars evolve over time, the cases profiled illustrate enduring dilemmas in humanitarian action. The essential lesson from those cases is that expectations must be modest with a focus on specific achievable elements in post-crisis transitions. This includes realistic efforts in multi-faceted international operations to introduce the basic rule of law as a threshold measure of human security.

There is a broad context for policy responses relating to forced migration. Chapter 5, 'Surmounting Indifference: Refugees and the New Statecraft', discusses the legal framework in which decision makers organize refugee responses. The problem of internal displacement is treated specifically. The relationship of sovereignty and humanitarian intervention is addressed, including in Africa, and newly evolving capacities in Europe are treated. Broad trends relating to the international movements of people are taken into account.

Particular policy tools are surveyed and analyzed in Chapter 6, 'Varieties of Refugee Concern: The Beginnings of a Policy Toolbox'. The chapter opens with a vision of refugee arrangements in Africa. The policy options then reviewed include asylum, temporary protection, humanitarian evacuation, humanitarian transfer, resettlement, in-country protection and processing, safe areas, security zones, regional safe havens, humanitarian corridors, orderly departure programmes, protecting and assisting internally displaced persons, voluntary repatriation, and safe/imposed return. Sequencing and combinations in the use of the policy tools are examined. Approaches are discussed to resolve problems relating to protecting aid workers in the midst of conflict.

Basic dilemmas regarding the organization of policy at the international level are addressed in Chapter 7, 'International Bureaucracy and the Debasement of Mercy'. This includes an examination of the interactions between governments, the United Nations and other international organizations, as well as non-governmental organizations (NGOs). Relations between civilian humanitarians and the military are also addressed with a view to encouraging greater understanding of their respective roles and more effective collaboration. A recent innovative effort to address the relationship of emergency relief to societal development is examined. Basic reform is proposed for consolidating the components responsible for humanitarian action within the UN system in order to better manage the international humanitarian policy process.

Special attention is given to the making and implementation of US government policy as the US is a key player in international humanitarian action. Chapter 8, 'Reaction and Inattention within the US Government', proposes institutional reforms to increase the effectiveness of responses. A new separate civilian Agency for Humanitarian Action (AHA) under the authority of the Secretary of State would enhance both contingency planning, including among military and civilian humanitarian interlocutors, and policy coordination on issues such as contributing to threshold law-and-order components in complex international operations.

Possible policy futures are modeled in Chapter 9, 'Imagining Better Refugee Policy', based on the themes of containment, international cooperation, and proactive policy. Scenario analysis is used to illustrate how external factors could affect new directions in humanitarian action. The scenarios are not intended to be predictions, but rather are heuristic devices designed to provoke thought. The chapter closes with a discussion of likely and desirable policy outcomes, including fostering a greater degree of international cooperation on issues of forced migration.

The driving forces relating to international refugee responses over the past decade are recapped in Chapter 10, 'Achieving Comprehensive and Proactive Refugee Policy'. Limitations on the work of the United Nations High Commissioner for Refugees are treated specifically. A new intergovernmental mechanism for Strategic Humanitarian Action and Research (SHARE) is introduced in order to foster proactive policy, and the possible structure and functions of this proposed entity are detailed. SHARE would be a new expert resource situated outside of the UN system for the use of like-minded countries and international institutions. The contours of this new entity are synonymous with the current gaps in international humanitarian action.

The past decade shows that there is no single answer to the problem of human displacement. Rather, it is a task of humanitarian management, involving a clear-eyed assessment of the problem and the needs of the uprooted, as well as the varied interests of states and the realistic possibilities for reform. These are the prerequisites for a refugee policy which avoids paying the price of indifference.

1

Why Refugees Matter

Refugees matter. They matter for a wide variety of reasons rooted in human experience and international relations. The grim plight of refugees increasingly commands attention by the international community. Refugees are a product of humanity's worst instincts—the willingness of some persons to oppress others—as well as some of its best instincts—the willingness of many to assist and protect the helpless. Refugees also matter to states. They can be weapons or threats; they can be trophies or embarrassments. In personal terms, we care about refugees because of the seed of fear that lurks in all of us that can be stated so simply: it could be me.

Ruud Lubbers, a former Dutch Prime Minister who was appointed in 2001 to be the United Nations High Commissioner for Refugees, answered the question by emphasizing that 'each and every single human being matters'. Refugees have to be given the capacity to live and to participate in society in a genuine democratic fashion. 'It's about dignity', Lubbers said, 'and a just society.' If the international community does not address these issues successfully 'then we will pay the bill in political instability later'. This is particularly so in an interconnected world in which 'peace has to be won all the time'. Lubbers was blunt; while prognostication is always a difficult endeavour, those who accept a world in which Africa spirals downward and Europe prospers clearly 'do not know the future'.

Perhaps refugees matter most because they represent graphically the uncertainties and fears of coping with the future. Refugees are chronic features in the human experience. Today, they are the flesh-and-blood personification of the chaos and insecurities that we confront in the new century which now seems so suddenly fraught with danger. They are a manifestation of instability in international relations. If we could fast-forward to the middle of the twenty-first century, we might well be able to look back and see that episodic fear of attacks and disorder and coerced population displacements were among the defining attributes of this new century.

The term 'globalization' is often used to refer to the transnational movements of goods, services, and capital. The movement of people is frequently neglected as an important aspect of globalization. But the mixing and unmixing of populations will fundamentally shape individual lives and communal identities in the new century. The characteristics of populations in Europe and North America, for example, will inevitably change in a variety of ways such as race, ethnicity, language, and religion. Economic consequences, both general growth and specific job losses, will flow from these changes. Refugees will be a coerced dimension of these evolving societies. How we deal with the discrete issue of the forcibly displaced will say much about our capacity to deal with this new reality.

Refugees are drenched in human values. As an idea they are in the realm of philosophy and theology. Refugees force us to be witnesses to the indignities and deprivations they have suffered at the hands of persecutors. They signify the cruelty and degradation that tyrants can visit upon their people. Their humiliation and loss is manifest.

They are at the same time both invisible and storytellers. Refugees are neither seen nor heard, but they are everywhere. They are witnesses to the most awful things that people can do to each other, and they become storytellers simply by existing. Refugees embody misery and suffering, and they force us to confront terrible chaos and evil.

Refugees produce, as well, an almost irresistible impulse to help. This charitable response begins deeply within those who witness the pain and loss suffered by the uprooted, and sometimes it becomes an overwhelming urge. Electorates in wealthy democracies now are able to witness such tragedies in their own homes through the media, and they demand that their leaders do more, do it better, and do it more quickly, in order to deal with these distressing images and circumstances.

Refugees are perhaps the ultimate transitional figures. They are leaving and have lost a permanent home. Refugees inspire us by reason of their loss as well as their ability to rise above that loss and to re-establish their lives. Some are wasted in their exile, and others triumph. There is something noble and enduring about the ability of people to reconstitute themselves and begin again after suffering such deprivation. Refugees thus can be a source of hope and a flesh-and-blood reflection of a tenacious life force.

Refugees of course, have ancient origins, and the notion of fleeing across borders is as old as the evolution of international borders and the nation-state system itself. Since that time, refugees have mattered to states. The flight of the Huguenots from France in 1685, giving rise to the term 'refugee', is an early example of how a population displacement was produced by a state-building process. A somewhat more recent example is the flight of Palestinian refugees in 1948, producing a lingering legal and political conundrum that continues to frustrate prospects for peace in the Middle East, as well as the largest exile population in the world, some 6 million persons.[1]

The bipolar world that emerged after the Second World War affected many aspects of life and society around the world, including refugees. During the cold war, refugees were often adjuncts to ideological confrontation. Repatriation from the West was tantamount to endorsing the totalitarian system that had emerged in the Soviet Union, and the option of refugee return became unthinkable. Rather, both sides encouraged defectors. Those who sought asylum from one side or the other became trophies in the ideological contest of the day. Confrontations over Cuba as well as proxy contests waged in Afghanistan, Angola, Cambodia, El Salvador, Ethiopia, Nicaragua, and elsewhere involved refugees as a central feature.

The cold war affected responses to refugee and migration emergencies in fundamental ways. The era was dominated by the image of the Berlin Wall, a literally concrete effort to physically contain would-be asylum seekers in the East. The analytical framework was simple: a zero-sum game between East-West antagonists.

As the cold war receded, national interests became more differentiated and regionalized. The decade of the 1990s was the starting point for the adoption of a number of policies by Western governments designed to discourage asylum seeking and to contain refugees in territories proximate to their home countries. These policies became hallmarks of a group of highly capable states which utilized technology and other resources in an effort to frustrate the arrival of uninvited exiles in the name of migration control, an enterprise now tinged with new fears of terrorism and the effects of anarchy abroad.

Refugees can be an external political resource to states to the extent that they have fled from their home countries and are situated in places of asylum where they may be encouraged to engage in home-country politics or conflicts. Encampments near borders provide bases for refugee warriors to launch incursions into their home states. The Afghan Mujahedeen in Pakistan, which began a long trajectory that led to the brutal Taliban regime in Afghanistan, and the Contras in Honduras were but two examples during the 1990s. Refugee populations became buffers between Thailand and invading Vietnamese forces in Cambodia. Nor is the size of the refugee population by itself a measure of its consequence.

[1] United Nations High Commissioner for Refugees, *The State of the World's Refugees: Fifty Years of Humanitarian Action* (New York: Oxford University Press, 2000), 21.

In the United States, a celebrated case in 2000 involving the return to Cuba of a six-year-old Cuban boy enraged political factions and resulted in mass demonstrations in Miami and Havana: a clear legacy of the cold war.

The end of the cold war reduced the ideological value of refugees in the eyes of states. More often now they are seen as potential migration threats that may cross an international border without permission and adversely affect nearby countries. For example, the internal displacement of nearly 2 million persons in Colombia has been noted by US officials. Today, 25 million would-be refugees from conflict are found within their home countries. A new strategy of containment is emerging, this time championing migration control and not ideology.

Refugees have also become intertwined with notions of humanitarianism and human rights. Even the most hardened foreign policy realists in the West accept as important national interests the promotion of democracy and human rights around the world. A willingness to try to address the causes of flight in the home countries of would-be refugees has thus emerged over the past decade, and this is an innovation in international responses. While interventions may no longer, with the end of the cold war, risk escalation and retaliation by the antagonists, a basic question has emerged. What should the criteria be for such international involvements in situations where a conflict could cause displacement or already has produced refugees? Selectivity in intervention is evident. Access to assist needy populations within countries is often problematic and can be very dangerous, including for relief workers.

Refugees and displaced persons inhabit the fault lines of the raging debates about the efficacy of humanitarian relief and development assistance. Humanitarians are increasingly dispirited by perversities and unintended consequences in the provision of aid. Does relief to suffering populations prolong conflict? Does aid create dependency and harm indigenous cultures and societies? The uprooted are frequently the reality in which these concerns play out.

Over the past decade, refugees have continued to be prominent in the activities of states. In 1991, after Iraq had suffered defeat at the hand of a US-led coalition of forces, Saddam Hussein's troops began a brutal campaign of repression in northern Iraq against its Kurdish population. The vast displacement that ensued was designed both to rid Iraq of political undesirables and to cause a political crisis in Turkey. The coalition forces were not to be defeated in this fashion, and 'safe areas' were established under the authority of a UN Security Council resolution and ultimately enforced by air power in the northern and southern parts of Iraq. When fighting among Kurdish factions resulted in Iraqi forces advancing into the north in 1996, the United States evacuated those Kurds, some of whom had worked closely with its Central Intelligence Agency.[2] The skirmishing over population displacements that played out in northern Iraq is an ongoing international chess match between the United States and Iraq.

Conflict in the former Yugoslavia in the 1990s highlighted refugees as consequences, and instruments of war and state building, particularly in Bosnia and Herzegovina, and then in Kosovo. As the Socialist Federal Republic of Yugoslavia broke apart, new nations began to form, and the dynamics of displacement were destructive. The efforts to build new identities reflected the imperative of demography. 'Ethnic cleansing' became the term of the day, and efforts were made to assert territorial control by either expelling or relocating populations.

In Kosovo, the vast displacement in 1999 of ethnic Albanians by the forces of Slobodan Milosevic, the president of Serbia, rendered them virtual weapons of war. When the United States and its allies became concerned that the air campaign to force Serbian troops out of Kosovo might not bring a speedy favourable resolution to the conflict, NATO countries began to resettle refugees who had fled to Macedonia in order to ease inter-ethnic tensions there. This generosity was animated at least in part by feelings of embarrassment in the capitals of the countries conducting the air war which had precipitated the expulsions. A conflict initially justified by the prospect of repression actually resulted in massive displacement, which then became a tactical dimension and an objective of the war. Humanitarian and military action converged and became virtually inseparable.

Africa is awash in refugees and internally displaced persons—over 13 million at the end of 2000[3]—many of whom are homeless by virtue of prolonged conflicts in places like Angola and Sudan. Africa was also the venue for a singular humanitarian catastrophe of the past decade: the 1994 genocide in Rwanda, and the vast displacements produced when refugees of the Rwandan Patriotic Front invaded from Uganda. Militarized border camps harbouring refugee warriors became endemic in this setting. The inability of international organizations or governments to determine who among those displaced was deserving of protection and who was guilty of genocide caused all exiles to be lumped together. This led ultimately to Rwanda's decision in 1996 to attack and break up

[2] See the website of the Federation of American Scientists, Military Analysis Network. At: http://www.fas.org/man/dod-101/ops/pacific_haven.htm, visited on 24 May 2001.

[3] US Committee for Refugees, *World Refugee Survey 2001* (Washington, DC: US Committee for Refugees, 2001), 15.

the threatening encampments in eastern Zaire—now the Democratic Republic of the Congo. A brutal inter-state war in the heart of Africa followed.

The breakup of the former Soviet Union in 1991 produced armed conflicts, including ethnic confrontations, which displaced hundreds of thousands of individuals. But the largest movement of persons after the collapse of the Soviet empire was the return to Russia of over 3 million Russophones and ethnic Russians from nearby countries. In the vacuum produced by the dissolution of empire, Russia argues for international assistance to control migration by persons from outside of the region who are seeking to travel onward to western Europe. At the same time, the Russian government monitors the treatment of 'compatriots' in nearby countries in a bid to gain foreign policy leverage, seizing for this purpose upon a domestic law concept of 'forced migrant'.

Elsewhere in that region, a number of the conflicts which emerged, particularly in the Caucasus countries, remain unresolved, occasioning continued and chronic displacement. Uprooted populations in places like the Republic of Georgia serve as an obstacle to peace and repatriation, and are a continuing source of instability in the region.

Refugees thus matter for individual reasons as well as for reasons of state. Population movements thread through the ongoing debates over human rights and national sovereignty. But refugees matter differentially, in the sense that official responses are likely to remain selective and tailored to the interests at play in different displacement situations. Even more deeply, the problem of refugees and the ways it is dealt with provide important insights into the modern dilemmas of statecraft that characterize the new century.

Refugees are a powerful idiom. They signify loss in a variety of ways: loss of their homes, positions in society, and normal lives free from threat. We can never know what voices and great minds have been silenced through arbitrary displacement. Refugees are the personification of sudden life reversals and imposed change with all the attendant agony and despair. They reflect failures in governance and international relations. Whether they are styled as indicators, causes, or consequences, refugees by their existence have a deeper and more profound meaning. They raise basic doubts about the ability of people to live together.

Refugees thus personify human insecurity, a rather abstract term fashionable at the outset of the new century in development policy circles. The concept comprises notions of poverty, exploitation, tyranny, and other harms. Refugees are a real manifestation of the injustice and misery associated with these broad categories of deprivation.

But refugees not only evoke the images of the world's losers, they frighten the world's winners as well. When they cross international borders and present themselves in countries that are better off, whether by virtue of enjoying relative economic prosperity or circumstances of peace and stability in which people can pursue normal lives, some people become afraid. This forced movement of people has profound effects both on the ordinary citizens of receiving states and on communities within those states, or sometimes even on those states themselves.

Change is almost always painful, and ordinary people may be afraid that they will lose jobs or privilege, or, perhaps most fundamental of all, their identity in societies that are being changed irrevocably by the arrival of newcomers. Compassion leading to calls for help is one response to refugees. But the arrival of uninvited people in need can also exacerbate fears of difference and cultural confrontations, a point not lost on politicians in democratic countries. The terrible evil which produces refugees can be insulated from remedy by an indifference that arises from personal insecurity. Even if attributable to other factors within a society, this worry may nevertheless be aggravated by the arrival of internationally homeless persons. Threats to identity and other fears can battle with compassion and the impulse to help evoked by refugees.

The common thread, then, is fear: fear that gives rise to refugee flight, fear that but for good fortune one could be a refugee oneself, and fear that keeps people from offering haven to those in need. The combinations and permutations of insecurity that emerge in particular situations shape fundamentally the policy responses, whether generous or grudging. In the new century, ordinary people, intellectuals, and decision makers will increasingly grapple with this personification of fear, instability, and failure.

Even where generosity appears to have triumphed, decision makers can be motivated by guilt or revenge associated with refugees, such as the abandonment of wartime allies. This was a key factor, for example, in the very ample Indo-Chinese resettlement programme of the 1980s and 1990s. Demands can give rise to a sense of obligation to deal with the needs of such individuals. In these circumstances refugees sometimes are, indeed, beyond charity, in the sense that responses to them are informed by political calculation or a sense of unwelcome responsibility.

Insecurity can also permeate the responses of communities, or even states, to refugee emergencies. Concerns about loss of political power can frustrate refugee return. Take as an example Srebrenica, the site of a terrible massacre in 1995, where Serb inhabitants later refused to seat a Bosniak mayor elected by displaced persons and refugees who have yet to return. The political careers of leaders can be put at risk, as illustrated in the case of the prospect of nearly 500,000 Iraqi Kurds arriving in Turkey in 1991, or the influx of over 200,000 Kosovars in Macedonia in 1999. In rare circumstances, the very life of a nation might be put at risk in terms of broad-scale refugee return: witness the stalled negotiations over Cyprus, or the more recent negotiations concerning Israel and a Palestinian state over refugee repatriation.

Refugees as weapons of war became a starkly clear dimension of the Kosovo conflict, which virtually became a refugee war. The measure of winning or losing was whether or not 800,000 Kosovar refugees would be able to return home. Refugees in this case rescued the NATO alliance which surely would have fractured, absent the massive displacement and the sense of responsibility associated with that outcome by reason of the NATO air campaign. Perhaps ironically, refugees were the glue that kept the Alliance together.

The notion of a refugee policy toolbox is attractive to decision makers. There is no one single remedy to deal with humanitarian emergencies. It is largely a question of managing well the combinations and sequence of responses. This act of humanitarian management will be a gauge for how successfully policy makers will address the wide variety of governance challenges in the new century. The stakes are high. The way that we deal with refugees will necessarily reflect how well we deal with other manifestations of chaos in society.

In the new century, there will be more people, more population movements, more displacement—both internally and internationally—and more demands for effective responses by the relevant authorities, whether they be international organizations or governments. Demands will be made of humanitarian relief capacities that are under-resourced and inadequate. Emergency assistance is invariably deployed reactively, creating a customary mismatch of relief and need, at least in the early phases of the international response, and often thereafter.

But the conventional approaches of the recent past, seeking to contain the problem or intervening to solve it, are likely to be insufficient to deal with this new reality. Containment involves writing off people in need and sacrificing them to larger objectives which serve to justify indifference. The 1994 genocide in Rwanda is the prime example of not dealing effectively with a massive humanitarian catastrophe, an outcome for which a US president and a UN Secretary-General have apologized. But larger objectives are now more difficult to discern in the post-cold war era. The prospect of retaliation by one of the protagonists against an interloper affiliated with one side or the other currently provides little counterweight for political leaders who face demands by an aroused citizenry to answer the message of misery communicated by refugees. What sometimes seems like abstract objections based on territorial sovereignty are viewed as cynical efforts by evildoers designed to let them get on with the carnage. Decision makers today are less likely to be able to sustain policies which consign populations to deprivation and death in the absence of compelling countervailing constraints.

Nor is a diplomacy of coercive or forcible means likely to be sustainable. The impetus to help will quickly run up against limits on resources and differing political interests. Priorities will emerge and involvements will become selective; witness Chechnya, where the response was meagre and exclusively humanitarian in character. The reality is that people, not just refugees, matter differently in the ways that states calculate their interests. This produces discriminatory outcomes that are justified publicly on grounds of limited resources and theories of sovereignty. This ugly truth will almost never appear in the statements of decision makers in developed states, but will increasingly become featured in the speeches of politicians in developing countries. The widening gap between the haves and the have-nots will make humanitarian involvements, ranging from human rights monitoring to material assistance and military deployments, increasingly an object of debate between the states and peoples in the developed and developing world. Wrangling over privilege and justice will be a hallmark of humanitarianism in the new century.

Neither containment nor intervention is a lasting solution to refugee problems. More attention will have to be given to developing a preventive orientation and a greater degree of international cooperation if refugee responses are to be more workable and enduring. New comprehensive and proactive approaches will be needed to make humanitarian action more supple and effective in this era.

A preventive orientation would seek to contribute over time either to mitigating the structural causes of displacement—for example, poverty or widespread human rights violations—or, perhaps more feasibly, to addressing the proximate causes of displacement. Operational and tactical approaches to deal with crises are oftentimes difficult to formulate. But there are simply too few people and too little time spent on investing policy responses with a preventive approach. Prevention should be a normal objective in crisis situations where feasible, whether in advance of, during, or after the upset. Staff and time should be explicitly devoted to this end. Put another way, there should be centres for preventive action within and outside of government, including in the humanitarian sector, which address crisis situations as they emerge, play out, and dissipate. Only by investing resources in thinking about and addressing these questions in specific situations can we expect real progress.

International cooperation to share the risks of insecurity has faltered in this human dimension. It is not just a question of sharing dislocated people, known as 'burden sharing' by refugee-policy devotees. Success in this realm depends on a broader appreciation of sharing all aspects of crisis situations, taking into account the interests and incentives in each circumstance. There is no one-size-fits-all template. This means that resources must be devoted to understanding the political, economic, social, and cultural aspects of critical situations, preferably in advance of crisis. In this sense, prevention and cooperation are interrelated. Efforts to achieve risk sharing in relation to likely or emerging crisis situations should be fostered initially at the sub-regional and regional levels around the world, with the ultimate ambition to achieve a global understanding and a universal framework that has sufficient flexibility to address the nuances of particular situations.

Refugee policy today, perhaps like foreign policy more generally, is often characterized by surprise and bewilderment. The need to better prepare for effective reaction is recognized, as are tentative efforts to engage in contingency planning in order to learn to expect the unexpected. Big ideas have become small problem-solving efforts in the post-cold war era, and policy makers are more akin to managers in a broad international political process. This is the new landscape for humanitarian action.

I remember an admonition by the late Ernest Gellner after he had taken me on an extraordinary walking tour one cool autumn evening a few years ago in Prague. I had bemoaned the negative forces of nationalism as a cause of ethnic conflict in countries in the Soviet Union and former Yugoslavia. Gellner, a renowned scholar of nationalism, corrected me. 'Nationalism is negative only in the same sense that gravity is negative', he replied. The question is one of political leadership and management. Policy-relevant scholarship might suggest approaches, but the issues are fundamentally managerial. 'There are no disciplines', he asserted, 'only problems.'

The small idea is that there is no single answer, no single tool or even formula or combination of tools to deal with a particular situation. It is to a great extent a question of nuance and timing as well as effective and expert humanitarian management. But the big idea is that, by solving refugee problems and dealing with the fears and insecurities that both give rise to refugees and animate refugee responses, policy managers may begin to deal better with the insecurities that characterize the new century. This would require the institutionalization of preventive approaches and effective forms of international cooperation. In this fashion, from time to time we may be able to avoid or minimize the traumas associated with human displacement and refugee flight: among the terrible scourges of our time and, in a very tangible way, the price of indifference.

2

The Last Decade's Refugee Story

This was a decade of extraordinary human displacement. As the relational structure imposed by the cold war waned in the 1990s, refugees became an important feature of the new era. Grand policy designs devolved into specific problems for which solutions must be found and managed. A few highlights follow.

In the 1990s, new conflicts broke out, particularly in connection with the dissolution of the Socialist Federal Republic of Yugoslavia and the Union of Soviet Socialist Republics (USSR). Ethnic and internal conflicts which produced displacement emerged as key features of the decade. Older proxy conflicts abated, particularly in Central America and Africa, leading to the return of millions of refugees. New international arrangements were forged to address issues of displacement and their underlying causes in Central America and Asia. Crisis followed crisis in a seemingly accelerated fashion, and the policy responses over the past decade contain largely undigested lessons which have yet to be learned.

The last decade's twists and turns in refugee policy began with the Kurdish crisis in northern Iraq. After a US-led coalition of forces had driven Iraqi forces out of Kuwait, an uprising occurred in both the north and the south of Iraq. Saddam Hussein's military attacked, seeking to put down the insurrection with force, and prompting some 450,000 mainly Kurdish people to flee to the Turkish frontier. Another 1.3 million Kurds fled to Iran, giving it one of the world's largest refugee populations. In addition, 70,000 Iraqis, mostly Shiite Muslims, were displaced from their homes in the south of Iraq.[1]

Television crews, assigned to cover the Gulf War, captured the exposure and suffering of the Kurds in the mountains of northern Iraq. Turkey refused to admit asylum seekers at its frontier, and instead supported the creation of a 'safe haven' for Kurds inside northern Iraq. On 5 April 1991, the UN Security Council adopted Resolution 688, which provided the justification for a

[1] United Nations High Commissioner for Refugees, *The State of the World's Refugees: Fifty Years of Humanitarian Action* (New York: Oxford University Press, 2000), 212.

US-led operation to establish a security zone in northern Iraq.[2] Troops mainly from France, the United Kingdom, and the United States carved out the territory. Later that April, the Iraqi government and the United Nations signed a memorandum of understanding concerning the delivery of humanitarian assistance in the safe zone. A small contingent of UN guards was deployed to protect the relief effort.

A stalemate ensued and as the winter approached hard shelters were constructed at considerable expense to ward off the cold, a new feature in the management of refugee affairs. Previously such arrangements had generally been made in tropical climates where sheets of blue plastic could suffice to create shelter. Humanitarian workers and soldiers worked side by side in unprecedented ways in this setting. One institutional product of this international effort was the creation of the Department of Humanitarian Affairs in the UN Secretariat to promote coordination among UN agencies.

The safe zones in northern and southern Iraq have been expanded and continue to be enforced by air power. But squabbles ensued among the Kurdish factions, and in 1995 and 1996 troops from Iran, Iraq, and Turkey became embroiled in military operations in the zone in the north. As of 2002, the north remains a dangerous place outside of Iraq's jurisdiction, but under threat, and without formal autonomy.

Other crises soon followed the resumption of history after the end of the cold war. In 1991, the first incidents occurred in what proved to be a very violent breakup of Yugoslavia. The process of dissolution began when Slovenia and Croatia both declared independence. Croatia, with a population of over 500,000 Serbs, experienced outbreaks of serious violence. Serb paramilitary fighters seized control of much of Croatia's territory, 'ethnically cleansing' these territories and precipitating massive displacement.

In 1992, the war spread to Bosnia and Herzegovina, and later beyond, with catastrophic consequences, as detailed later in this book. When Bosnia declared its independence in March 1992, Serbia sided with the Serb minority of this ethnically diverse former Yugoslav republic. Sarajevo, the Bosnian capital, was surrounded by military forces and placed under siege. Serb forces conquered most of Bosnia and drove Muslims from the major towns and cities. By June 1992, some 1 million persons had been displaced.

In early 1993, fighting broke out between Bosnian Croats and Bosnian Muslims. By the time the fighting ended in December 1995, 2.5 million people had been displaced: an estimated 1.3 million internally and some

[2] UN Security Council Resolution 688: Iraq (5 April). At: http://www.un.org/Docs/scres/1991/scres91.htm

500,000 into neighbouring countries. In addition, approximately 700,000 had become refugees in western Europe, about half of these in Germany.

The limits of humanitarian action were tested and, indeed, exceeded in the former Yugoslavia. Humanitarian assistance became a substitute for a firmer political and military response by the international community. UN peacekeepers were deployed to protect the relief effort. Safe areas such as Srebrenica were created by Security Council resolution, but shortly thereafter overrun, and thousands of Muslim inhabitants were killed.

The complexion of the conflict changed when, in mid-1995, successful military action by the Croatian army—Operation Storm—coupled with a NATO bombing campaign prompted a ceasefire. Negotiations produced the Dayton peace agreement, signalling the launch of an effort by the international community to build the state of Bosnia and Herzegovina. Refugee return became and remains an essential measure of the success of this ambitious but uncertain developmental effort.

The next stage of the crisis in the former Yugoslavia occurred in February 1998, when Serbian security forces intensified operations against the Kosovo Liberation Army in that separatist province. The crackdown resulted in the displacement of an estimated 175,000 people by September 1998. Diplomatic initiatives followed, and a large international mission was deployed under the auspices of the Organization for Security and Cooperation in Europe (OSCE) to verify a ceasefire and partial troop withdrawal. But this response was overtaken by events. Escalating conflict, including an infamous massacre of 45 Kosovar Albanians by Serb forces in Racak in mid-January 1999, and the failure of peace negotiations in Rambouillet, France, in February 1999 set the stage for the hitherto unthinkable: a war involving great-powers in Europe.

On 24 March 1999, without the benefit of a UN Security Council resolution, NATO commenced an air campaign against the Federal Republic of Yugoslavia, including targets in Kosovo. When the air strikes began, there were an estimated 260,000 internally displaced persons in Kosovo, as well as some 70,000 Kosovar Albanian refugees and displaced persons in the region. Another 100,000 Kosovar asylum seekers were present in western Europe.

An even larger humanitarian catastrophe followed with the killing of thousands of Kosovar Albanians and the uprooting of some 800,000 Kosovars. Of these, approximately 426,000 fled to Albania, 228,000 to the former Yugoslav Republic of Macedonia, and 45,000 to Montenegro.[3] The United Nations High Commissioner for Refugees (UNHCR) was roundly criticized

[3] UNHCR, *State of the World's Refugees*, 234.

for lack of preparedness in the face of this sudden unexpected displacement. Macedonia temporarily closed its border with Kosovo at the beginning of April 1999, denying entry to tens of thousands of Kosovars for fear of exacerbating political instability. The international community launched a novel humanitarian evacuation programme. Almost 96,000 Kosovar refugees were relocated from Macedonia in an effort to relieve political and inter-ethnic tensions there.[4] The repatriation of refugees and displaced persons became a central war aim for NATO.

On 9 June 1999, as the NATO alliance was finally beginning to come to terms with a possible ground invasion, Serbian forces formally accepted a peace plan requiring their withdrawal from Kosovo, the return of all refugees and displaced persons, and the deployment of a UN mission under Security Council authorization. Repatriation was unexpectedly swift. By the end of 1999, 820,000 Kosovars had returned, placing great pressure on a budding UN transitional administration in Kosovo.[5] At the same time, approximately 200,000 Serbs and other minorities left Kosovo under pressure from ethnic Albanians, going mainly to Serbia and Montenegro.[6] The prospects for their return remain bleak in 2002.

The former Yugoslavia was the crucible for perhaps the widest variety of refugee policy innovations over the past decade, as detailed elsewhere in this book, and the record is decidedly mixed. But perhaps the greatest single humanitarian challenge of the decade was posed by the refugee crisis in the Great Lakes region of Africa after the Rwandan genocide in 1994. The daunting nature of the challenge was occasioned both by the magnitude of displacement and by a poisonous context of insecurity and injustice.

Rwanda has been a place of ethnic crisis and confrontation for many years. But the death of President Juvenal Habyarimana of Rwanda and President Cyprien Ntaryamira of Burundi in a mysterious aircraft crash on 6 April 1994 signalled the start of a well-orchestrated genocidal attack by extremist Hutus on the Tutsi population and Hutu moderates. Upwards of 800,000 people were killed between April and July 1994.[7] Warnings were ample, yet a multilateral UN peacekeeping force was reduced from 2,500 to 250 as the genocide unfolded.

In response, fighters with the Rwandan Patriotic Front, who themselves had been refugees in Uganda, invaded and gained control of most of the country in a matter of weeks. International action was limited to a brief

[4] Ibid, 239. [5] Ibid, 241.

[6] Stephen Glover, 'How We're Aiding The Ethnic Cleansers', *Daily Mail* (UK) (26 February 2000). See also 'Ethnic Albanians urged to stop threatening Serbs in Kosovo,' *CNN* (7 October 1999); and 'Daily Abuses Dismay NATO Troops,' *USA Today* (2 August 1999).

[7] UNHCR, *State of the World's Refugees*, 246.

French military intervention, discussed later in this book, which sought to assist the displaced Hutu. Over 2 million Hutus fled the country, establishing threatening camps in Zaire—renamed the Democratic Republic of Congo (DRC) in May 1997—and in Tanzania. The failure to avert the genocide and the ensuing refugee catastrophe laid the foundation for an expanded war which brought down President Sese Seko Mobutu, and which now involves the armies of five countries and several non-state armed groups in central Africa.

The camps in the DRC were a dangerous amalgam of fighters and civilians. They quickly became a potential spawning ground for renewed attacks upon Rwanda, a recurring phenomenon in Africa and elsewhere. Also, many of those seeking refuge had been involved with either the armed forces of Rwanda or Hutu militia groups, and some were fugitives of justice who had committed genocide.

Conditions in the ramshackle encampments were harsh. In July 1994, cholera and other diseases broke out, killing tens of thousands in Goma. The host government was asked by UNHCR to provide camp security. But its incapacity and ultimately its unwillingness to play this role, coupled with the failure to separate the armed elements from the civilian population, meant that the camps continued to pose serious security threats to Rwanda. The Security Council considered the deployment of multinational military forces on two occasions in the mid-1990s to deal with the refugee crisis. No mission was deployed, however, and the Rwandan army answered the security threat by attacking the camps in October 1996, breaking them up and pursuing fleeing refugees into the DRC.

Some refugees returned to Rwanda; others were forced back, even from traditional asylum states such as Tanzania. Thousands more fled deeper into inaccessible forests in the DRC and beyond. Large numbers died as a result of the hardship of dislocation, while others were reportedly killed by military combatants. Throughout 1997, efforts were made by UNHCR to locate and rescue fleeing refugees for return to Rwanda.

Indeed, the enforced return of refugees to Rwanda became a hallmark of the region in late 1996, and UNHCR was criticized for acquiescing in coercive return, a violation of the duty under international law not to return a refugee to a place where he or she might experience persecution.

Apart from the Great Lakes region, the continent of Africa was, and indeed is likely to remain, a site for humanitarian crises. Over the past decade, old conflicts abated, new ones arose, and a variety of international actions were attempted. A summary of some of the key events follows.

In January 1991, the overthrow of President Siad Barre signalled a descent into clan-based conflict in Somalia. Massive internal displacement resulted, and the misery was compounded by drought and famine. By mid-1992 some 2 million people had been uprooted, including some 400,000 who fled to Ethiopia and over 200,000 who went to Kenya.[8] Hundreds of thousands of Somalis perished before the first UN peacekeeping troops arrived in April 1992 to oversee a ceasefire between the warring factions.

A cross-border operation under UN auspices was launched from Kenya in September 1992 in response to the humanitarian crisis. At that time, I travelled in north-eastern Kenya with Arne Piel Christensen, who then headed the Danish Refugee Council. We followed a convoy of relief trucks across the border into Somalia and watched as food was unloaded and systematically stolen. The feeding site we visited further inside Somalia was far from being an oasis in that arid clime. Instead, it was a mobbed and dangerous concentration of desperate people who had gathered among the thorn bushes. Insecurity was palpable.

In December 1992, President George H. W. Bush deployed 28,000 US troops as part of what was to become a 37,000-strong UN force. The initial objective was to address the needs of famine victims. Robert Oakley, then US special envoy to Somalia, explained the justification for this international initiative. At the time, the Administration of George H. W. Bush was being criticized for doing too little on Bosnia and also for not doing enough in Africa. The Somalia deployment addressed both points, although it was 'primarily a humanitarian intervention', Oakley allowed. Indeed, it is perhaps as close as the world has come over the past decade to a military deployment for mainly humanitarian reasons, at least at the outset.

In 1993, the United Nations took charge, and the objective of the UN peacekeeping mission evolved into a very intrusive effort to reconstitute Somalia. The UN force, some 20,000 strong, came from 27 countries, including US troops which operated with considerable latitude. Confrontations escalated between the UN mission and a Somali warlord, Mohammed Farrah Aidid, with a series of open clashes that culminated in the shooting down of two US helicopters in October 1993. But political support in the US for this deployment was soft. The Clinton Administration sought to use the UN to pursue humanitarian goals, which it sought to direct, but it had not made the case to the American people to justify the investment of treasure and blood. As a result, the death of 18 US soldiers and the spectacle of dead soldiers being hauled through the streets of Mogadishu prompted the abrupt withdrawal of US troops. In this instance, the so-called CNN effect led to the disengagement of all US and European forces, which had left

[8] UNHCR country information about refugees. At: http://www.unhcr.ch/world/afri/somalia.htm

Somalia by March 1994. All remaining troops departed by the end of March 1995. Somalia remains synonymous with the notion of a failed state, and the crowning failure of 'nation building', a term from which many western politicians and military leaders recoil.

Elsewhere in the Horn of Africa, after more than a decade of war which had forced Ethiopian refugees into Somalia and Sudan, rebel forces captured Asmara, the Eritrean capital, in May 1991, paving the way for Eritrean independence in 1993. Shortly thereafter, rebel forces entered the Ethiopian capital, Addis Ababa, the Ethiopian army collapsed, and President Mengistu Haile Mariam was ousted. But a conflict between the two newly independent countries in May 2000 produced substantial new displacement. In 2001, some 97,000 refugees and 1 million internally displaced persons were returning to their homes as a result of ongoing peace negotiations.[9]

Conflict waxed and waned in other places in Africa. The war in Mozambique ended in 1992 after 16 years. After decolonization, the Mozambican conflict had become a cold war proxy contest. By 1992, approximately 1.7 million Mozambican refugees were being hosted in neighbouring countries, with 1.1 million alone in tiny Malawi.[10] There was also a vast internally displaced population. Significant costs were borne by host countries, with adverse effects on the local economy and environment. Reintegration as well as mine clearance and awareness efforts under UN auspices sought to pave the way for refugee return. The rehabilitation accomplishments, however, were badly undermined by severe flooding in Mozambique in 2000.

Repatriation prior to elections was an approach frequently used by the international community over the past decade. In Namibia, in 1989, over 40,000 Namibians returned from Zambia, Angola, and a number of other nearby countries.[11] Though not without tension and despite some conflict between the South West African People's Organization (SWAPO) and South African forces, elections were held in November 1989 after the refugees returned. SWAPO won easily and formed the first independent government in Namibia. However, Namibians continue to confront difficulties in finding work and achieving economic self-sufficiency.

[9] US Committee for Refugees, *World Refugee Survey 2001* (Washington, DC: US Committee for Refugees, 2001).

[10] UNHCR, *State of the World's Refugees*, Mozambique. At: http://www.unhcr.ch/sowr2000/ch05.pdf. See also UNHCR country information at: http://www.unhcr.ch/world/afri/mozambiq.htm

[11] Dierks, Klaus, 'Chronology of Namibian History'. At: http://www.klausdierks.com/Chronology/131.htm See also: http://www.klausdierks.com/chronology/references.htm

Many other developments over the past decade in Africa presented humanitarian challenges. War in Liberia displaced 1.2 million people, sending many to poor, remote locations in Guinea, Côte D'Ivoire, and later Sierra Leone. Life was grim for the displaced who remained inside Liberia. These conflicts in west Africa were fuelled by competition over resources and the proliferation of small arms, creating nearly 1 million refugees. A regional peacemaking force, led by Nigerian troops and under the auspices of the Economic Community of West African States (ECOWAS), was deployed in 1990. A fragile peace in Sierra Leone broke down after a UN peace operation deployed there in October 1999, and came under attack when it replaced the original cohort of regional peacemakers. A ceasefire negotiated in November 2000 again raised hopes for peace. In 2001, some 500,000 refugees and 670,000 internally displaced persons remained uprooted by fighting in the sub-region.[12]

And then there are chronic conflicts, such as Angola or Sudan, convulsed by long-standing civil wars. The cycle of conflict in Sudan seems frustratingly perpetual, with the most recent outbreak in 1983.[13] In the 1990s, civil war continued and relief experts were forecasting that hundreds of thousands would starve to death. Efforts by international and private organizations to assist a vast internally displaced population in the south were often hindered by the authorities in Khartoum. Sudan hosts both refugees and some 4 million internal exiles. Apart from occasional diplomatic forays, which have proven up to this point to be unsuccessful, international humanitarian endeavours have focused on providing relief assistance through channels such as the UN's Operation Life Line Sudan, headquartered in Kenya.

Outside of Africa, there was also much disquiet elsewhere in the world over the past decade. The dissolution of the Soviet Union in December 1991 resulted in massive population movements prompted by conflicts as well as the return of ethnic Russians and Russian speakers to the Russian Federation. From 1989 to 1996, approximately 9 million persons had moved within or between the countries of the former Soviet Union. The number of asylum seekers in western Europe from the region increased, but the vast majority of those forced to migrate stayed within the region. Unresolved conflicts, discrimination, hardship, and social and economic decline continue to characterize the region. Inter-ethnic and separatist conflicts in the southern Caucasus region, including the Armenian-Azerbaijani conflict over

[12] *Towards a Comprehensive Approach to Durable and Sustainable Solutions to Priority Needs and Challenges in West Africa*, Report of the Inter-Agency Mission to West Africa, UN Doc. S/2001/434 (2 May 2001), Sect. D. 56.

[13] UNHCR, *State of the World's Refugees*, 115.

Nagorno-Karabakh, and the conflicts in Georgia relating to Abkhazia and South Ossetia, produced hundreds of thousands of uprooted people. At the same time, civil war in Tajikistan prompted the flight of hundreds of thousands more.

The northern Caucasus region was particularly a site of conflict-induced forced displacement. As of 1992, tens of thousands of Ingush people were expelled from North Ossetia to neighbouring Ingushetia. Later in the decade, fighting and large-scale displacements in and around Chechnya, first in 1994–5 and again from September 1998, resulted in much hardship and were accompanied by substantial loss of civilian life.

The international community envisaged a preventive and early-warning role in the former Soviet Union in relation to forced displacement. UNHCR sought to implement its concept of 'preventive protection', involving humanitarian presence that permitted early warning and advocacy of international humanitarian standards and technical assistance. Furthering this approach, the UN agency, in conjunction with the International Organization for Migration and OSCE, after consultations with governments, sought to develop a framework for donor action under the aegis of a 1996 migration conference concerning the Commonwealth of Independent States (CIS), an assemblage of twelve successor states of the USSR. A comprehensive perspective involving institution building was envisaged in order to infuse into policy making a genuinely preventive approach to avert forced displacement. This multilateral effort, however, played out in mostly unimaginative ways and thus attracted relatively modest donor contributions in the name of prevention. Difficulties in the region continue to frustrate international donors, who are seeking strategies that are both affordable and effective.

The past decade sorely tested the capacity of the international community to respond to forced displacement. An important venue for innovation was Central America. The peace process which emerged in the late 1980s began to bring an end to civil conflicts in El Salvador, Guatemala, and Nicaragua which had forced more than 2 million people to flee their homes. In 1989, as the cold war waned, the combatants and other stakeholders joined together under the rubric of an international conference on Central American refugees—CIREFCA, an acronym from the Spanish—to address issues of repatriation and development. Refugees themselves from both El Salvador and Guatemala began to return without international assistance.[14]

Reconstruction under the CIREFCA process was a key component to peace building. Toward this end, international organizations, namely UNHCR and the United Nations Development Programme (UNDP),

[14] UNHCR, *State of the World's Refugees*, 121–5.

worked to address the needs of returning refugees and displaced persons, taking somewhat different approaches to ease the integration of returning refugees and displaced persons.

The 1991 Cambodian peace accords were another product of the tectonic political shifts that followed the end of the cold war. The withdrawal of Vietnamese forces from Cambodia in 1989 brought an end to fighting, and a peace process emerged in 1991. A UN transitional authority was deployed under Security Council authorization with broad powers, and an ambitious effort at state building ensued. Eventually, $US 1.7 billion was expended and a staff of 22,000 deployed, including 15,000 peacekeepers and 3,600 civilian police from more than 40 countries.[15]

Refugee repatriation was a key element of the peace plan, and between March 1992 and April 1993 more than 360,000 Cambodians were returned from Thailand prior to an internationally supervised election.[16] Promotion of indigenous NGO activities, explored later in this book, turned out to be an important by-product of this international endeavour. Targeted development projects were again initiated in order to ease re-integration, although any enduring effect is now difficult to discern.

In perhaps the most ambitious effort yet at refugee burden sharing, a plan was negotiated in 1989 between countries of origin, asylum, and resettlement relating to exiles from South-east Asia. The 1989 Indo-Chinese refugee conference sought to staunch an outflow of asylum seekers, particularly Vietnamese boat people, that exceeded the willingness of nearby countries to provide asylum in their territories. The countries of asylum resisted providing temporary stay unless offers of resettlement could be guaranteed by third countries, notably Australia, Canada, and the United States. This deal was struck initially at an international conference in 1979 as a humanitarian response to the legacy of the Vietnam War. The follow-on 1989 conference introduced the remedy of examining individual asylum seekers under international refugee-law criteria, and provided for the return of those denied status, including enforced return.

The arrangements for Indo-Chinese refugees represent an extraordinary measure of generosity in resettlement. More than 3 million people fled their countries over nearly a quarter of a century, of whom some 2.5 million found new homes elsewhere. But there were losers as well. Some 500,000 were obliged to return to their home countries.[17]

[15] Security Council Resolution 717: Cambodia (16 October) and Resolution 718: Cambodia (31 October).

[16] UNHCR, *State of the World's Refugees*, 145.

[17] UNHCR, *State of the World's Refugees*, 98–9.

There were some unusual role reversals which led to innovations in refugee policy over the past decade. For example, the United States, traditionally a country of resettlement, was challenged repeatedly as a country of asylum by the arrival in the territory of persons seeking refugee protection. The efforts to deal with Haitian boat people were illustrative. The US programme to intercept and return Haitian boat people, initially conceived in late 1981, was refined and expanded following the September 1991 *coup d'état* that ousted Haitian President Jean Bertrand Aristide. After temporarily halting the interdiction programme, US officials resumed the policy of return, but instead of Haiti they were taken to the US naval base in Guantanamo, Cuba, to have their claims determined.

In May 1992, President George H.W. Bush ordered that all interdicted Haitians be returned summarily to Haiti without any inquiry into possible claims that they would be persecuted. In June 1994, President Bill Clinton instituted a new but short-lived procedure to deal with intercepted Haitians. Hearings on refugee protection claims were to be carried out on a United States naval ship anchored off the coast of Jamaica. The number of Haitians picked up and waiting for refugee interviews, however, grew so rapidly that the US ended the on-board effort and relocated the Haitians again to Guantanamo.

Prompted by the prospect of the continuing migration and refugee crisis, a US-dominated multinational force was deployed in Haiti in September 1994 in order to oust the Haitian military junta. President Aristide returned and thereafter a multilateral effort, led once more by the US, was undertaken to begin a state strengthening effort, involving at its core the creation of a new national police force, an initiative examined later in this book. Most Haitian asylum seekers were then returned to Haiti, although some were allowed into the United States. In 2002, developments in Haiti are worrying and raise the prospect of another migration and refugee crisis.

The last decade ended with a conflict relating to an independence struggle in East Timor. After a 1999 pro-independence vote, Indonesian security forces and affiliated militia instigated a campaign of violence and arson against the civilian population. This led to mass displacement into West Timor and even beyond. A UN-authorized military deployment, led by Australia, re-established security and, in October 1999, the Security Council created a transitional authority in East Timor to assist in the building of a new state, an effort profiled later in this book. An estimated 250,000 East Timorese fled to West Timor, some of whom remain under pressure from militia elements which continue to resist independence.[18] This highly

[18] 'East Timorese Refugees Face New Threat,' *Human Rights Watch* (30 March 2000).

volatile mix on the border provided the setting for the brutal killing of three UNHCR workers in September 2000. East Timorese continue to trickle back as the state-building effort continues.

The prevailing directions of international humanitarian action are well reflected in the experiences of the past decade, and even earlier. The new policy directions that have been taken produced mixed results which in many instances failed to relieve hardship and save lives. Initiatives were invented and re-invented, and policy responses reverted to a largely reactive mode. Humanitarian crises continue to fester in several places in Africa. At the same time, a dire situation in Afghanistan risked becoming a humanitarian catastrophe as a result of military action there by United States forces in retaliation for horrific terrorist attacks in New York and Washington DC on 11 September 2001. At the outset of the twenty-first century, the policy debate is driven by selective apathy and creeping trepidation.

3

Humanitarian Action and New Complexities in Refugee Protection: The Former Yugoslavia

'State building' is the term used here to describe efforts by the international community to construct or fortify societies riven by crisis in order to, among other things, encourage the repatriation and reintegration of refugees. In its most recent iteration in East Timor, this has come to mean ensuring security, establishing a justice system, achieving a minimum provision of public services and infrastructure, creating a sustainable civil administration, and managing the transition to democratic governance. These complex efforts which address forced population displacements, while increasingly prevalent over the recent past, have resulted in uneven outcomes. This chapter examines the ambitious endeavour to build new states upon the conflicted dissolution of the Socialist Federal Republic of Yugoslavia.

Not all state-building efforts concern refugees. However, over the past decade, these initiatives have often been associated with finding solutions to the needs of refugees for new permanent homes. Refugees have been both a cause and a consequence of conflicts, which have been addressed by peacekeeping operations, peace-building efforts, and even ambitious attempts to directly undertake civil administration in newly emerging states. The military has been an instrumental component of such complex international missions. Refugee repatriation and re-integration programmes have thus been components of peace operations. Despite the mixed record, the international community is likely to resort to this approach again in the future, and a premium will be placed on making such endeavours more effective.

As experience has accumulated over the past decade, several basic questions have loomed. What are the constituent elements of state building in post-crisis settings? Related to this point is the question of the appropriate measures of success. Is stability a sufficient criterion, or merely a necessary precondition to achieving the more ambitious outcome of a society imbued with justice and tolerance, and enriched by economic development? What are the appropriate benchmarks and the necessary sequence of initiatives required to achieve progress? What is an appropriate period for international involvement? How should international actors in such operations interact with the indigenous authorities and the host community in order to hand over governance responsibilities to them? These are the issues that are addressed in this chapter and the chapter that follows.

The former Yugoslavia has provided a real-time crucible in which to mix new refugee policy responses. The delivery of humanitarian assistance in the midst of armed conflict, creation of putative safe areas, and arrangements for temporary relocation and stay abroad were chief among the innovations over the past decade. Ultimately, the refugee protection question was subsumed by the evolution of peace and conflict and ongoing efforts to construct new successor states. Refugee return and re-integration have emerged as key elements of this process.

The last decade's experience teaches that expectations should be modest. International operations should be able to achieve basic security relatively quickly. However, sustained engagement is necessary if such efforts are to contribute usefully to broader political and economic transitions. Serious planning and effort are necessary to hand over responsibilities to local entities. But as currently configured, the United Nations, and the international system more generally, are simply not equipped to meet even modest expectations. Enhanced international capacities will be needed if this new feature of humanitarian action is to be a serious option for decision makers.

To address the need for new capacities, this book proposes the establishment of a new intergovernmental mechanism for Strategic Humanitarian Action and Research (SHARE), discussed in detail later in this book. This organization would develop situation-specific strategies for reconstruction and rehabilitation in post-crisis settings. This would include establishing the basic elements of a justice system compatible with human rights standards which can contribute usefully to indigenous structures.

In terms of organization, SHARE would have a small corps of experts and expertise from governments, international organizations, and the independent sector. Together, working groups would formulate strategic plans, develop doctrine, and compile lessons on state building in post-crisis settings which would be archived for guidance in future operations. SHARE would be a resource to governments and international organizations. Intergovernmental sponsorship would enhance political legitimacy as well as provide a secure funding base. But more on this proposal later.

THE ROLE OF THE MILITARY

The United States military has sometimes been asked over the past decade to engage in the craft of state building in settings where refugees and displaced persons were returning to their homes. This has included deployments in connection with international operations in Bosnia and Herzegovina, Haiti, northern Iraq, and Kosovo. Perhaps the most experienced officer in the United States Army who has dealt with these issues is Major General John Abizaid, who commanded US forces in each of these settings. For those reasons, he has a lot to say about how such endeavours have been undertaken.

Würzburg, Germany, is the home of the United States Army's First Infantry Division, the 'Big Red One', which was under General Abizaid's command when we met in July 2000. Würzburg itself is a university town that has been eclipsed by the frenetic prosperity of Frankfurt, about 90 minutes away by train. It is a city that sits on the edge of Germany's wine country. It is also a city that in some sense history has passed by, as it is no longer ground zero in the East-West confrontation embodied by a divided Germany.

General Abizaid has the demeanour of a corporate manager in a camouflage uniform. His headquarters office has a no-nonsense decor. While adorned with military decorations and certificates, the office is modestly appointed. But it has the busy air of the nerve centre for a US army division which has been involved over the past decade in a wide range of humanitarian deployments around the world.

General Abizaid got right to the point: 'We will have more of these ahead of us', he said, speaking of military deployments in connection with humanitarian emergencies. 'As wired as the world is, we can't turn our back on humanitarian crises; we can't allow them to happen', he added. This is, in his view, a new reality of United States military missions.

Reflecting on a decade of experience, General Abizaid suggested that the international community has learned how to do certain aspects of this work. It knows how to address immediate security issues. The military is able to expel an opposing army and suppress guerrilla activities. Civilian humanitarian agencies are able to address immediate humanitarian needs. What is missing is what Abizaid called 'everything in between'. This includes bringing stability and sustainable peace to a setting. The immediate objectives he explained were to 'stop the dying and let people come home, and these objectives should not be downplayed. But what then?'

General Abizaid cited Kosovo as an example, explaining that NATO was able to expel the Serbian army and prepare defensive positions in the event that they tried to return. UNHCR deployed humanitarian relief effectively and there were no deaths resulting from lack of material assistance among the displaced Kosovars. But he criticized the inability to get the 'angry young men' back to work quickly. Most particularly, he was critical of the decision to preclude the majority from governing Kosovo. He thought that efforts to exclude the Kosovo Liberation Amy (KLA) were heading in the wrong direction and seemed destined to result in confrontation. He compared the situation with that of northern Iraq, where specific tasks, including policing functions, were given to the Kurdish factions; the UN police deployment there, he noted, was 'a joke'.

Indeed, in Abizaid's view, UN civil police deployments have been dismal failures. He recalled that during the occupation in Germany and Japan after the Second World War indigenous police forces were kept and, while fanatics were weeded out, those local forces were used to maintain law and order in the immediate aftermath of the occupation. The efforts in Kosovo to exclude the KLA from this function was in his view a fatal flaw. 'You cannot hold a local population responsible for security if you give them nothing to secure', he explained. Moreover, there was a need to build institutions and revitalize the local economy, a prerequisite to both local and foreign investment. He cited the example of Bosnia, which had become virtually a ward of the international community.

The use of the military in state building endeavours, of course, is not new. After the Second World War, the forces of military occupation in Germany and Japan had civil affairs components that undertook the responsibilities of civil administration. More recently, efforts have been made to mount comprehensive international responses in settings where state structures were weak—Haiti—or non-existent—Kosovo, East Timor—or were reluctant to accept international direction—Cambodia, Bosnia. These different circumstances clearly call for differently calibrated international involvements. But in each of these settings, the need to address issues of law and order has been urgent.

General Abizaid favours a 'lead nation' model, like the US-led coalition of the willing in northern Iraq. In other instances where the UN would be in charge, the organization would clearly have to be strengthened to play an effective role. As it stands now, he explained, no one can answer the following questions: 'Who is in charge? Who has the authority for each component of the international response?' He attributed this weakness to lack of resolve on the part of important states, including the inability of political leadership to rise above the immediate short-term need to get the story of a crisis 'off the news screens, off of CNN'. Politicians are willing to say 'yes' he noted, but not to do what is necessary. Expedient short-term approaches to deal with immediate problems are not good enough, he emphasized.

A basic issue in his mind is whether governments will 'bear up under the pressure' and permit a stronger UN to undertake these responsibilities. Abizaid is unsure of the answer. Above all, he emphasizes the importance of bringing local actors into the effort, perhaps after an initial internationally imposed period of martial law.

In Abizaid's experience, international efforts are often uncoordinated and full of 'frictions' because of the variety of elements involved, particularly at the outset of a comprehensive international deployment, and because there is no functional chain of command or clarity of purpose throughout such efforts. Fundamentally, he found missing a genuine strategic framework for designing international responses in such situations.

There are, Abizaid said, three erroneous assumptions which have animated such international efforts. The first is that military force equals security, which is not the case because military force can address only immediate security issues; longer-term internal security matters frequently dictate success or failure in achieving stability. The second is that early elections equate with democracy. He saw this point illustrated well in Bosnia, where elections were in his view too early, resulting in the consolidation of the power of nationalist parties that continued to jockey for position. The third is that security equals economic prosperity, which he found has never been achieved in the international deployments in which he has been involved.

General Abizaid put forward a sobering description, and perhaps a self-fulfilling prophesy. The lack of capacity at the international level has meant that responses have been driven by crises. As a consequence, political leaders have lurched from crisis to crisis. The outcomes have generally been disappointing, leading, in turn, to a failure to invest in building any further capacity to respond to crises. This results in a vicious circle of unpreparedness.

He also suggested why the system worked in this way. The problem is that such an audacious effort must be a success or a failure. If, for example, Kosovo goes bad, who is to blame? The lack of accountability and unclear lines of authority have meant that success was likely to be elusive. But what better protection could there be for those involved in such situations with 'a high risk of failure' than having no clear accountability?

Kosovo is 'not over', according to General Abizaid; neither is Bosnia, and there are lurking crises in the Middle East and Africa, which he believes will be difficult to ignore. The international community's response in the past has been to muddle through. But the future world is going to demand more, and according to General Abizaid, 'muddling through is just not good enough'.

BOSNIA AND HERZEGOVINA

Muhamed Sacirbey, who was the UN representative of Bosnia and Herzegovina when we met in July 2000, was an accidental diplomat. An investment banker who was born in Sarajevo and who migrated to the United States in 1967 as a child, Sacirbey was stunned when the war began in April 1992. War was unthinkable to him because Bosnia was so 'ethnically harmonious'. After Bosnia applied for UN membership in May 1992, he agreed to become the first UN representative, a position he held until he resigned in December 2000, interrupted only by a brief stint as the Bosnian foreign minister in 1995.

On the issue of state building, Bosnia is failing, according to Sacirbey. We had 'pretty good institutions' and a 'functional state' when the cease-fire under the 1995 Dayton peace agreement took effect. But the way the Dayton accord has been implemented has resulted in people being brought into government who have 'no commitment to the state' and, indeed, who are 'dedicated to destroying the state'. Bosnia in this sense has been de-evolving since 1995 into more and more of an artificial entity. 'Dayton in its implementation feels like a defeat', he sighed.

Sacirbey is angry with the international community, which he calls derisively 'Carl Bildt and company'—Bildt being the first High Representative nominated at the London Peace Implementation Conference in December 1995 to oversee international rehabilitation efforts in Bosnia. The lack of accountability and naivety of international actors in Bosnia is infuriating to Sacirbey. It is a normal humanitarian impulse, he allowed, to try to be neutral in dealing with warring parties. But to attempt to equate the sides in Bosnia, he said, was an arrogant and a dangerous assumption where one side—his—believed in the rule of law, and the others did not. There is a basic contradiction between humanitarianism and international state building in Bosnia.

Sacirbey mused wistfully about the contrast with the outcome in Kosovo, where, he noted, the UN had taken sides. The state was handed on a plate to the ethnic Albanians, he explained. In contrast, Bosnia was a reflection of a kind of new colonialism.

Muhamed Sacirbey's office, located in a high-rise building next to the UN, had a sparse and unsentimental look. In July 2000, the focus of his attention was Serbia and Montenegro, and the mission had been a de facto opposition headquarters, providing technical assistance for the Montenegran representative to the UN.

The walls of Sacirbey's office were bare except for two photographs: one of him as a football player at Tulane University; the other of him with Bosnian President Alija Izetbegovic, when they were together attending a Tulane football game during a break from the negotiations in Dayton. This was an act of 'self-assertion' as Sacirbey put it, to go to the game in contravention of Richard Holbrooke's peace-negotiating imperative.

Sacirbey said that one of the most important lessons he learned from football was the need to spend time sitting on the bench as a reserve before starting in a game. But this enduring sports wisdom may also be a lesson for Bosnia. How should the international community prepare Bosnia for statehood and the ensuing 'game' of international relations among the community of sovereign states? Currently, the Bosnian state is consigned to the status of being a seemingly perpetual ward of a High Representative.

Political fortunes can change quickly in transitional settings. In September 2001, financial police in Bosnia levelled charges of economic fraud against Sacirbey.

The conflict

From the inception of clashes in June 1991 in Slovenia and later Croatia, the conflict in the former Yugoslavia became synonymous with the generation of refugees and displaced persons. Indeed, the conflict revolved around episodes of 'ethnic cleansing', employed to achieve the strategic objective of altering the demographic composition of ethnic groups in new states. This was a qualitative change. Refugees were not the by-product of conflict, they had become the very objective of the conflict.

In June 1991, Slovenia and Croatia declared independence, and war ensued in Croatia, resulting in a UN-brokered ceasefire and the deployment of UN peacekeepers. The UN located its headquarters in Sarajevo in an attempt to stave off the prospect of conflict there. The gambit, however, failed. In February 1992, Bosnia declared independence and Bosnian Serbs immediately proclaimed a separate state. The fighting spread, and Bosnian Serbs began a siege of Sarajevo in April 1992.

It was in Bosnia that the strategy of humanitarianism evolved most clearly, providing assistance to meet the basic needs of internally displaced persons and war-affected populations in lieu of a comprehensive political and security framework. Peacekeepers were deployed to protect the delivery of aid, although not necessarily to protect the individuals in need of assistance. This sometimes resulted in a frustrating minuet involving UNHCR truck convoys loaded with humanitarian assistance which would be stopped at Bosnian Serb checkpoints and turned back before they were able to reach needy populations. United Nations peacekeepers often stood on the sidelines and watched due to their limited mandate. During this period, the siege of Sarajevo slowly wrung the life out of that city, and Bosnia became an emblem of the international community's impotence and lack of commitment to address issues of immorality and injustice.

Bosnian Serbs ultimately seized approximately 70 per cent of the territory, and Bosnian Croats and Muslims—or 'Bosniaks', as the Muslims prefer to be called—began fighting over the remaining 30 per cent. In April and May 1993, the Security Council declared six 'safe areas' for Bosnian Muslims in Bihac, Gorazde, Sarajevo, Srebrenica, Tuzla, and Zepa. The UN also imposed a no-fly zone over Bosnia that NATO planes began to enforce.

The siege of Sarajevo continued, and, in February 1994, 60 people were killed and some 200 were wounded when a mortar shell exploded in a downtown market place. In the face of threats of air strikes by NATO, Bosnian Serbs withdraw heavy guns from around Sarajevo in return for an arrangement to deploy Russian peacekeepers under UN auspices. The conflict continued and in late 1994 Serbs detained groups of peacekeepers: a tactic replicated in 1995. The UN-declared safe areas were shelled, including an incident in May 1995 in Tuzla where 71 people were killed and over 150 injured. Serb forces increased the shelling of Sarajevo and other safe areas, after which UN hostages were released. Serb forces then overran Srebrenica in July 1995 and 20,000 Muslim women, children, and elderly were expelled to Tuzla, where they reported atrocities. Approximately 8,000 Muslims were counted as missing from Srebrenica and are presumed to have been killed.[1]

Later in July, Serb troops occupied Zepa, resulting in the flight of additional thousands of civilians. In August 1995, NATO threatened air strikes to protect the safe areas. Later that month, Croatia launched a massive assault on rebel Serbs in the Knin area—Operation Storm—capturing most of it in four days. More than 180,000 Serb civilians fled. NATO planes launched air strikes to silence Serb guns around Sarajevo, and the Serbs shelled Sarajevo in response. Sarajevo airport, which had been

[1] 'Conflict in the Balkans: 8,000 Muslims Missing', *New York Times* (15 September 1995).

closed since April 1995, re-opened in September. Croat and Muslim forces advanced in central and western Bosnia, achieving roughly an equal apportionment of territory with Serb forces.

In October 1995, the warring parties agreed to a ceasefire, and peace talks opened in Dayton, Ohio, resulting in a peace agreement which was signed formally in Paris in December. A separate Erdut agreement followed concerning eastern Slovonia and surrounding areas, which was administered by the United Nations. But, in relation to Bosnia, the UN Security Council transferred all peacekeeping duties to NATO, which was authorized to deploy 60,000 troops in a multinational military force, the implementation force (IFOR). In December 1996, IFOR was replaced by the Stabilization Force (SFOR), which is currently deployed in Bosnia and Herzegovina. The ceasefire was accompanied by new displacements when thousands of Serbs fled from the burning suburbs of Sarajevo, carrying their possessions. In January, the UN-sponsored airlift ended; the siege of Sarajevo officially ended a month later.

Sarajevo

I actually saw very little of Sarajevo on my first visit to the city in May 1993. I had borrowed a helmet and flak jacket from colleagues at the office of the International Rescue Committee (IRC) in Zagreb, Croatia, and I arrived in Sarajevo on a C-130 cargo plane operated by the US military.

We moved quickly to a sheltered area at the airport and boarded an armoured personnel carrier, which made its way past shattered homes and overturned automobiles along the front line to the headquarters of the United Nations Protection Force (UNPROFOR) at the PTT—telephone—building in Sarajevo. It was on this route in January 1993 that a deputy prime minister of the Muslim government had been executed by Serb soldiers in the presence of French peacekeepers. We were met at UNPROFOR headquarters by an IRC representative who drove us, sometimes at breakneck speeds, past 'snipers' alley', to a house the agency used in Sarajevo. Of course, there was no water or electricity; Sarajevo had been under siege for over a year.

The UN Security Council asserted jurisdiction over the airport at Sarajevo in June 1992. The airport was a key installation during the conflict. It was the main portal to the conflict for journalists, diplomats, and aid workers in the course of the war. It was also the point of entry for what turned out to be the longest humanitarian airlift in history. The airport was badly damaged in the fighting and was fortified by sandbags.

The plane on which we arrived took a circuitous route to avoid flying over hostile forces, and dived steeply to a landing. The engines were kept running as we departed in order to ensure a quick turn around, as snipers hidden in rows of broken houses frequently plied their trade across the airport runway.

I received a military-style briefing from Fred Cuny, a high-profile aid worker who later lost his life in Chechnya, who at that time was attempting to restore Sarajevo's water supply. I had agreed to come to Sarajevo at Cuny's suggestion, in order to give a talk on refugee repatriation to the Bosniak government. Amila Omersoftic, who was responsible for refugee issues in the government at that time, explained in 2000 that a focus on the hoped-for future repatriation was meant to bolster the 'mental health' of the inhabitants of Sarajevo. Looking back, she particularly praised Cuny's work and that of the IRC, which she contrasted to UNHCR which she found to be 'very arrogant'. My talk in Sarajevo was held at the Holiday Inn hotel, which, while badly damaged, remained open during the war and which became the base for many foreign journalists and others visiting Sarajevo during that period. Several hundred people were in attendance and the talk was uneventful, save for a brief interruption by sirens warning of shelling in the city.

In the evening, we chatted with Cuny and his colleagues as we watched sniper tracer bullets play over the city, punctuated by an occasional burst of a mortar shell. Needless to say, this was a night of fitful sleep for me, and I awoke early after dawn. Birds were chirping and occasionally there was the crackle of small arms fire on what would be a fine spring day. The prospect of refugee repatriation seemed to me incongruous in a situation in which normality and the rule of law were remote dreams.

Seven years later, in August 2000, Sarajevo was open for viewing. War damage had been extensive and was still visible in many places. The broken glass in windows had long since been replaced, and there were a few conspicuous new construction projects, such as a dark purple apartment house near the airport that the city of Barcelona had refurbished as a contribution to a sister Olympic city. Workers were also putting the finishing touches on an opulent new mosque financed by Saudi Arabia and located on the way from the airport to downtown Sarajevo.

The suburbs from which Serbs had fled en masse in the early days of Dayton's implementation were relatively untouched. My driver, Damir, took me on a tour of Sarajevo and its environs, and showed me the building near the airport where he had served as one of the city's defenders during the war. He explained the lack of destruction in the

Serb suburbs thus: 'We had no artillery.' De-mining projects were still under way in these areas, however, and some Serbs were returning, particularly the elderly.

UNHCR initially coined the phrase 'protection by presence' as a way to explain how its deployment of staff and programmes of humanitarian assistance in Bosnia were to assist some of those at risk in the conflict. Some years ago UNHCR dropped this term. This is perhaps not surprising in a situation where upwards of 200,000 individuals ultimately perished.

As many commentators have noted, the provision of humanitarian assistance in the midst of conflict in Bosnia constituted a kind of alibi, and a substitute for the failure to mount a robust political or security response. This is particularly the view of José Mariá Mendiluce, who in December 1991 became UNHCR Special Envoy for the Balkans. Mendiluce, who left UNHCR in 1993 to run for election to the European Parliament, remains proud of the extraordinary airlift to provide relief to the besieged city of Sarajevo. But he also remains agonized by the UN's failure to protect the safe areas which had been declared for Bosniaks. Indeed, aid in Bosnia was not just a substitute for political will, it was highly politicized in its own right. This is perhaps necessarily so in a conflict where assistance would help the victims, mainly Bosniaks, and undermine the objectives of the victimizers, mainly Bosnian Serb nationalists and fighters. While there were abuses on all sides of the conflict, military capabilities and the fortunes of battle resulted in most of the abuses being perpetrated by the Serb side. Nevertheless, the deployment of UN forces to safeguard the delivery of aid compounded the question of neutrality and impartiality in the eyes of both antagonists and allies. Humanitarianism in Bosnia was a highly charged political act.

Nevertheless, humanitarian involvement in Bosnia clearly 'made a difference' in the eyes of a young UNHCR protection officer who worked there during the war, and who is now posted at the agency's headquarters in Geneva. Yet she acknowledged that the work of the agency, its 'preventive protection' approach in particular, undermined the right to asylum in neighbouring countries. Protection work in such settings became an exercise in 'bullying tactics' used against the local authorities, she said, with evacuation as the main tool of protection. While this outcome—evacuation—was greeted with mixed reactions by some officials in national capitals as promoting the objectives of ethnic cleansers, in the field there was no ambiguity: evacuations saved lives. 'Our presence sometimes simply delayed the inevitable', said this UNHCR protection officer. She was certain, however, that 'we did save people's lives in a sense that some who did not move we learned later were killed, and some who were evacuated we found later as refugees'. She said that if she were sent into such a situation now, based on her experience, she would begin promoting evacuation much earlier than had been the case in Bosnia.

Mendiluce also emphasized the difference made by the evacuation under UNHCR auspices of some 30,000 persons in the course of the conflict. The author of two best-selling books in his native Spain which were inspired by his tenure with UNHCR, Mendiluce noted that the agency worked closely with the media in Bosnia to get the story of abuses publicly reported. This was a departure for a humanitarian agency for which caution and discretion are thought to be necessary to secure access to needy populations.

The Bosnian conflict resulted in 1.2 million persons fleeing abroad, mainly to countries of the former Yugoslavia and western Europe. An additional 1.3 million persons were internally displaced in Bosnia.[2] This is out of a pre-war population of a little over 4 million people. As of May 2000, a total of 356,308 refugees are estimated to have returned from abroad, and 309,633 persons displaced within Bosnia have returned to their homes. Approximately one-quarter—143,380—of these returns have been to areas where the individuals in question would constitute members of an ethnic minority. Some 100,000 minority returns are projected for 2001.

According to UNHCR, at the end of 2000 over 300,000 refugees from Bosnia still require new permanent homes, and over 800,000 persons displaced within Bosnia have not yet been able to return to their homes. Of these, 473,500 are in the Federation of Bosnia and Herzegovina, and 336,000 are in the Republika Srpska, the two entities created under the 1995 General Framework Agreement for Peace in Bosnia and Herzegovina (Dayton).[3] Clearly, much remains to be done in terms of refugee solution.

Those Bosnians who returned from abroad often were not able to return to their pre-conflict homes. Instead, they became internally displaced, and sometimes were locally settled or relocated to places where they belonged to a majority ethnic group. In this fashion, local authorities encouraged relocation to secure control over territory and to prevent minority returns by installing groups of people in housing belonging to

[2] 'Bosnia and Herzegovina: Population Profile and Figures', Global IDP Database, Norwegian Refugee Council. At: http://www.idpproject.org

[3] UNHCR country reports at http://www.unhcr.ch/world/euro/seo/croatia.htm

different ethnic groups, a practice referred to by UNHCR as 'hostile relocation'.

In addition, so-called 'war taxes', the practice of imposing penalties and fines on those who were abroad during the conflict, have been assessed against those who would return. Difficulties by returnees in obtaining identification documents also continue to frustrate access to social services, health care, and other public services.

Asylum countries in western Europe introduced complications by impatiently withdrawing their offers of temporary protection to Bosnians once the conflict had abated. In 1998, for example, Germany established return programmes based on the lifting of temporary status and provision of financial assistance in order to encourage return. In July 2000, an estimated 1,000 Bosnians returned to Tuzla under a repatriation grant scheme organized by officials in Berlin. Tuzla, however, had little or no absorptive capacity. Nevertheless the German authorities continued the repatriation programmes despite UNHCR's cautionary note that non-voluntary return to Bosnia was 'not appropriate'. In 2000 some 1,237 Bosnians were forcibly repatriated, most—979—from Germany.[4]

The current High Representative, Wolfgang Petritsch, has declared 2001 to be a new critical period for minority return, which he views as essential to state building. As of June 2001, UNHCR had registered nearly 90,000 persons for return to minority circumstances over the past 18 months. Yet funds are needed for the construction of some 15,000 houses. Also, the local legal and administrative frameworks to promote and facilitate repatriation remain incomplete. Some 190,000 houses still must be returned to their pre-war owners.

The conflict in Bosnia was displacement by design. Demographic re-alignment was a war aim in Bosnia, a circumstance which has profound implications for state building and refugee return. Population displacement and movement were designed to assert control by one or another of the combatants in Bosnia. After Dayton, perhaps the primary instrument for this unmixing of people was the continued use of wartime property legislation respecting apartments, particularly in cities and towns. Property rights in Bosnia were a major factor in state building. This led the drafters of the Dayton peace agreement, in Annex Seven, to abolish discrimination relating to property which could inhibit the return of refugees and displaced persons, particularly to areas in which they would be members of a minority group. Wartime property legislation

[4] US Committee for Refugees, *World Refugee Survey 2001* (Washington, DC: US Committee for Refugees, 2001), 205–6.

had given what amounted to preferences for residences on ethnic grounds. This was particularly the case in the urban areas in which flats and socially owned property were up for grabs.

These wartime property enactments were thus among the arsenal of weapons that the nationalists used to continue battling for dominance in Bosnia. Under Dayton, previous inhabitants were to be restored to possession or given compensation. But the efforts of the Commission for Real Property Claims (CRPC), established under Annex Seven to unravel discriminatory property arrangements, could be no stronger than the Dayton accord itself. The work of the CRPC has burgeoned. By the end of May 2000, it had accumulated 220,280 claims for houses and apartments in Bosnia. However, only 27,202, or 12 per cent, of the claimants have actually repossessed their property.[5] At this pace, implementation would take another 15 years.

The situation overall is one where nationalist parties and ethnic extremists who waged the war in Bosnia continue to manipulate legal and administrative structures in an effort to pursue their war aims of separation in the formal confines of the emerging Bosnian state. Obstruction by the authorities and security problems are still evident in both the Federation and Republika Srpska, including menacing demonstrations by Croats and Serbs. The UN oversees unarmed international police who seek to monitor and train local police. They do not have arrest authority or the capacity to suppress incidents of public disorder. The UN mandate does not extend to the judiciary, which is overseen by the High Representative.

The custodians of Dayton have over the past five years searched for an effective state-building strategy. Early elections, however, seemed to fortify the nationalist parties on all three sides. The local authorities were able to obstruct many initiatives, leading the international community to mount a more aggressive effort, reflected in the investiture in the High Representative of the so-called 'Bonn powers', named after a meeting of the Peace Implementation Conference in Bonn in December 1997. These prerogatives included the power to dismiss obstructing local officials and impose legislation. With the arrival of Wolfgang Petritsch, who has been High Representative since 1999, a more aggressive international approach emerged.

To deal with the ways in which the ethnic parties in Bosnia have used property legislation to frustrate repatriation, the High Representative in

[5] Accession of Bosnia and Herzegovina to the Council of Europe: Progress Review # 11 (28 July 2000), 10. At: http://www.oscebih.org/humanrights/pdf/assess-july.pdf

October 1999 imposed a new regime of property legislation in order to facilitate return. A month later, in November 1999, Petritsch dismissed 22 public and housing officials who had obstructed the implementation of the property legislation. Another 15 officials were dismissed in 2000. It remains to be seen whether the politics of imposing laws and dismissing officials will become more complicated with additional rounds of local elections which have buttressed the position of local authorities.

Petritsch has decided on a three-pronged approach: seeking to strengthen common state institutions in Bosnia, promoting minority refugee return, and economic reform. These three broad objectives are being pursued, however, in a climate of diminished expectations and resources by donor countries.

According to Petritsch, neither Serb nor Croat politicians in Bosnia aspire to a common state. Instead, they seek separation. The Bosniaks desire an 'exclusive state'. The efforts to harmonize these disparate perspectives will clearly dictate the outcome of state building in Bosnia. The task is further complicated, in Petritsch's view, by the absence of an understanding of the rule of law or the role of civil society in Bosnia.

Residential property law arrangements have emerged once again as a key target for international action. The imposition by the High Representative of a new property law regime in late 1999 changed the legal framework in Bosnia for post-conflict property claims. There have been a flood of requests for repossession and return of property. Even the Human Rights Chamber established under Annex Six of Dayton estimates that some 80 per cent of 5,000 cases pending in 2000 pertain to property claims. The issue is simple. A refugee or displaced person cannot return to his or her home if it is occupied by someone else. Nor can the interloper leave without becoming homeless if he or she does not have premises to go to, and sometimes these are illegally occupied as well or have been destroyed.

An international strategy of evictions to implement laws awarding possession of housing to prospective returnees has become a priority. As the new head of OSCE's human rights department noted in July 2000, her brief is 'evictions, evictions, evictions'. The High Representative's reinvigorated programme to target property law issues is based on an exacting implementation of the law, irrespective of various humanitarian arguments often raised against reoccupation. A countrywide effort throughout Bosnia to enforce the law in a standardized fashion is envisaged. Elected officials are to be pressured in a variety of ways to comply with international decisions. Ultimately, judicial reform and further legislative enactments will be required.

The notion is that prioritizing property law issues will encourage individuals to pursue their self-interests in order to secure their premises and return, even as members of ethnic minorities in majority population areas. This is a new approach: re-mixing people through property law arrangements. Undoubtedly, the nationalist parties will seek to obstruct this approach and the confrontation will sharpen between the High Representative and the international community on the one hand, and the local political power structures on the other hand. This highly targeted approach contrasts with the variety of past efforts that have been pursued by international actors, and reflects a new resolve. It is an act of both desperation and re-commitment, with the statehood of Bosnia hanging in the balance.

But state building in Bosnia is a slow and plodding process. In answer to my question as to whether such initiatives should have been taken years earlier by other High Representatives, Petritsch said 'absolutely'. Six years after the Dayton Peace Agreement, passions in Bosnia were cooling, in part due to the concerted efforts of the international community. Thomas Miller, the US Ambassador to Bosnia and Herzegovina, has reduced the endeavour to a list of ten categories on which he issues periodic report cards to visiting dignitaries. Miller has the kind of direct and no-nonsense demeanour that seems to get the attention of local officials in the region. His ten Dayton 'benchmarks' range from military issues, to which he gives his highest score, to corruption, which gets the lowest score. The return of refugees and displaced persons are among those issues he scores in the middle. When we spoke in 2000, Miller had caused some $75 million in US government aid to be directed to projects relating to returning refugees, the largest single national donation to repatriation-related projects. The approach is one of 'muddling along', and while Bosnia is not yet a state it is 'on the road to that end', said Miller optimistically.

There is cause for a measure of cautious optimism. The municipal elections in 2000 had loosened the grip of the nationalist parties, particularly in the Federation. Also, changes in leadership in Croatia coupled with the NATO attack on Serbia had underscored to Bosnian Croats and Serbs that their future lay with a functioning Bosnian state. This perception is likely to be buttressed by the ousting and arrest of Slobodan Milosevic. Increased return of refugees to minority areas was one indication of this qualitative shift in the situation in Bosnia.

Major-General Ronald Adams, the commander of SFOR, had a somewhat darker assessment when we spoke in August 2000. Adams was frustrated with the international civilian response, a frustration echoed as well by some civilians with the military. When Adams arrived in Bosnia in September 1999, he asked whether there was a 'game plan'. 'No one could tell me what was the strategic plan', he complained, beyond achieving a 'multi-ethnic society'. A planner by profession, Adams needed more in order to prioritize and assign tasks to a military force being reduced from 60,000 troops initially to 20,000, and he prepared a five-year plan addressing and benchmarking issues such as the economy, judicial reform, corruption, and human rights. The civilian internationals, however, were 'lukewarm' towards the effort, reinforcing Adams's assessment that they did not believe in planning and were totally reactive. There is no real accountability in the civilian international institutional framework in Bosnia. 'If something goes wrong with the economy or judiciary, who is responsible? I know the answer for the military', he emphasized.

Adams was concerned about the tendency of civilian authorities to call upon SFOR in undisciplined ways, saying that he was 'sick and tired' of being asked as a first recourse to provide services that others could easily provide, such as snow and ice removal, firefighting, or the delivery of water. He espouses a 'tough love' approach designed to wean the civilian authorities, both international and local, off unnecessary reliance on SFOR. Of course, in a life-threatening situation, or where security crises erupt, 'we are there', he affirmed.

Minority returns are increasing as are the associated security incidents, although the latter may be growing at a somewhat slower pace. Nevertheless, such incidents are a primary focus of SFOR's attention. Adams totally rejects any suggestion that the US contingent in SFOR is not robustly patrolling Bosnia, citing comparative patrol statistics relating to other contingents.

The multinational character of SFOR presents unique challenges. Forces from 35 nations, including Russia, are involved in this NATO-plus deployment, making the act of communicating itself a critical challenge. In addition, the reality is that the national contingents relate to their national capitals, and the mission is thus constrained by having 35 different political agendas. Consensus has been difficult to achieve on issues such as the configuration and interrelationship of the three Bosnian armies. 'My job is more political than military', Adams explained.

Adams is concerned that the Bosnia operation was not well thought-out and suffered from poor policy implementation. As he reflected upon the mission it was 'very frustrating', yet 'very worthwhile', he allowed. His ultimate judgment, however, on whether the military should be involved in 'nation building' missions was curt: 'hell no.'

On the other hand, the breadth of the societal engagement of SFOR was embraced by Lieutenant-Colonel Michael Knop, a German tank battalion commander who serves as deputy commander for a civil-military coordination programme—'CIMIC' in NATO doctrine—which has teams specializing in subjects such as the economy, democratization, rule of law, and displaced persons. He describes himself as a 'manager' of such activities, which are clearly related to state building. Knop served in the humanitarian intervention in Somalia, and he considers such missions to be likely in the future. Indeed, he is pleased by this prospect. Because of such deployments, he noted, recent opinion polls in Germany have put the army just behind Amnesty International in terms of popularity.

This civil-military programme in Bosnia is designed to fill a vacuum in administration until a civilian authority is established. The purpose of the programme is to undertake projects which can be handed over to local authorities and civilians. This approach distinguishes it somewhat from the US Army's normal civil affairs function, which consists largely of reserve elements that implement projects entirely by themselves. In operations such as those in Bosnia, as the military operations wind down it takes time for civilian authority to emerge. Civil affairs fills a gap in the transition from the security phase, in which the military is dominant, to the reconstruction phase, in which civilians must take the lead. For example, in Germany after the Second World War, civil affairs ran the country, Knop noted, 'And we probably should have done the same thing here'. According to Knop, such assistance can promote good community relations and reduce tensions, which also have force-protection consequences. Nevertheless, in Bosnia, the pace of the transfer from military to local civilian authority is slow. In Knop's words, it will take 'a very long time to make progress' sufficient for the institutions of Bosnia to 'act like a common state'.

When we spoke in October 2000, Richard Holbrooke, then US ambassador to the UN and tireless negotiator of the Dayton peace agreement, said Bosnia is the classic 'glass half full or half empty' dilemma. Some progress on minority refugee return was evident to him in a recent visit to the region. But 'ethnic separatists' were still victimizing the population, and places like Srebrenica, the site of the notorious massacre of Bosnian Muslims by Serb forces in 1995, seemed to him to have been left out of the modest and uneven process of rehabilitation. Nor does he think that Wolfgang Petrisch has been sufficiently aggressive as High Representative. European diplomats are just too 'polite' and process oriented, he argued, suggesting that Petrisch should disenfranchise the committed separatists and remove them from public life.

Dayton was a bad peace to end a horrible war. The long-term prospects for the emergence of a functioning Bosnian state are decidedly uncertain. The slow pace of progress was underscored by the Federation ombudsmen: Vera Jovanovic, Esad Muhibic, and Branka Raguz. Representing all three ethnic groups, the ombudsmen officials, who had worked together effectively since January 1995 addressing such issues as discriminatory property provisions, graphically represent the possibility of a multi-ethnic Bosnia and Herzegovina. When I met with them in Sarajevo in August 2000, they were concerned with the way privatization efforts were being undertaken: 'The nationalist parties are looting the country.'

Issues of justice and reconciliation are inextricably intertwined in the emerging Bosnian state. Jakob Finci, a lawyer and the elected head of the Jewish community in Sarajevo, emphasized the need for a mechanism to promote reconciliation. 'Everyone in our country is a victim, but no one is ready to take responsibility', explained Finci, former head of the national Soros Foundation in Bosnia and Herzegovina.

It is by reason of the thinking and deeds of people like the three ombudsmen and Jakob Finci that Bosnia may ultimately become a rights-respecting democracy. The international community cannot substitute for the commitment of such indigenous visionaries, but perhaps it can better identify and support them as they undertake their labours of change. This is the kind of astute and patient resolve that should have been followed from the outset in this audacious endeavour.

The environs of Sarajevo

Trnovo is south of Sarajevo in the mountains on the road to Gorazde. Before the war, Trnovo was inhabited by 6,991 persons: 68.5 per cent Bosniaks, 29.5 per cent Bosnian Serbs, and 2 per cent Bosnian Croats.[6] Trnovo town was the administrative centre of the municipality with a population of 2,099, of whom 51 per cent were Bosniaks. The rest of the population lived in villages. Intense fighting during the war destroyed many houses, factories, and much infrastructure. Civilians fled the area, finding shelter in nearby places under the control of their ethnic minority. During the conflict, Bosniaks moved mainly to Sarajevo and Bosnian Serbs to Pale.

Under the Dayton accord, Trnovo was divided into two administrative units: Federation Trnovo, which is part of the Sarajevo Canton with the

[6] Census Data for Bosnia-Herzegovina, Yugoslav Census Bureau. At: http:// tweedle-dee.ucsb.edu/~kris/bosnia/demographics

city hall in Djeici village, and Republika Srpska (RS) Trnovo, which is split into two parts. The current population of RS Trnovo is estimated to be 1,642 Bosnian Serbs, two-thirds of whom are displaced persons from Sarajevo.

We drove from Sarajevo to Trnovo in an unmarked UNHCR car in August 2000. Our driver explained that the agency had a few unmarked cars in order to avoid provoking hostile reactions from local people on journeys into Serbia and Montenegro. UNHCR suggested the visit to Trnovo because of the unique cooperation between the mayors of the divided municipality. Other municipalities reflected greater progress on issues such as minority returns.

The drive to Trnovo reintroduced me to the scenic beauty of the former Yugoslavia as the road snaked between mountains. When we arrived in Trnovo town, we stopped initially to visit an elderly Bosniak baker of some local repute, who had fled along with his wife to Sarajevo during the conflict. The baker had returned when UNHCR reconstructed his destroyed house at a cost of approximately $10,000. UNHCR no longer had a shelter reconstruction programme, and a proliferation of agencies under the aegis of the Refugee Return Task Force of the Office of the High Representative meant that it was no longer clear who was responsible for such work. UNHCR had submitted housing reconstruction projects to the Stability Pact for Southeastern Europe, but they had not yet been funded.

The baker, however, had a different problem. He had been living in his newly constructed house for the past four months, subsisting on a pension from the Sarajevo canton of approximately $120 per month that was paid up only until last March. He had been promised funding by some unremembered NGO to repair a stove which had been damaged during reconstruction in order to resume operating his bakery. But the money had not been forthcoming.

During our drive, we stopped and stood with the mayor of RS Trnovo, Cedo Mandic, and watched as an encamped family repaired their broken house. Mandic reported that six Bosniak families had returned; and others were in the process of returning. Reconstruction projects, however, were in 'stagnation'. The mayor said that in general he tried to avoid evicting illegal occupants of houses in order to avoid ethnic confrontation and homelessness.

The mayor of Federation Trnovo, Dervo Aljovic, had visited the returned Bosniaks and confirmed that they had not been harassed or intimidated. He also said that the Trnovo towns were likely to cooperate on extending electrical power to the Federation side, as electricity to outlying villages had been disrupted during the conflict. The biggest obstacle to return in his view was the absence of jobs. He urged international support for the reconstruction of a nearby carpet factory in order to provide employment to both Bosniaks and Bosnian Serbs.

If the factory was not reconstructed, people would likely leave for good, Aljovic predicted. Rehabilitation, he opined, 'depends on the international community. Our destiny is not in our hands. Practically, we have a kind of protectorate. Others are responsible for us'. But international largesse is not always very effective. The mayor told us of ten houses that had recently been constructed in Federation Trnovo with financing from the European Union for the return of Bosnian Serbs, but the houses stood empty as there were no takers.

The visit to Trnovo was sobering. The two mayors did, indeed, profess the kind of cooperation that would be needed for reconciliation in Bosnia. But five years after Dayton, the results of the international community's endeavours were so modest as to be almost negligible. Half-done jobs and waste characterized the efforts. The local authorities were passive and dependent.

The state of Bosnia and Herzegovina is very much a work in progress. While there is some measure of hope by reason of new international strategies, a positive outcome is far from certain. Indeed, as we drove back at the end of the day to Sarajevo over a rough back road past several ruined villages, state building seemed to me to be a curiously inapt and premature label for the endeavour in Bosnia.

KOSOVO

Dennis McNamara is a veteran humanitarian who has become a state builder, a role he clearly relishes. When we met for our conversation in 2000, he had just finished a one-year stint in Kosovo. There, he ran the 'humanitarian pillar' of the UN mission, which is now winding down, signalling the end of emergency assistance. McNamara, an intense New Zealander, is no stranger to international efforts to fortify transitional societies, having directed the human rights component of the UN mission in Cambodia in the early 1990s. His assignment in Kosovo over, he was about to start a new assignment with the UN in Geneva, working on efforts to coordinate international responses to internal displacement. McNamara has since taken a senior UN position in East Timor.

The passion of our conversation contrasted sharply with its setting, the pleasant expanse and panoramic view of the Manhattan skyline from the

UNHCR representative's office at the UN. McNamara had worked for UNHCR since 1975. He spoke frankly and in a rapid-fire manner, loosing a torrent of thoughts about Kosovo. His cascade of commentary reflected an overall feeling of deep frustration.

According to McNamara, the 'in-built contradictions in the UN mission are fundamental'. The wide-ranging responsibilities of the mission—political, military, human rights, and humanitarian activities—produced, in his words, 'enormous tensions'. As an example, and somewhat at variance with General Abizaid, he noted that the need on the political side not to alienate the de facto local authorities had resulted in a failure by the UN and others to denounce atrocities committed early in the mission against Serbs and Roma people by the victorious KLA. McNamara thus took issue with Abizaid's counsel to incorporate the KLA into local security arrangements. The silence of the international authority created an atmosphere of ethnic impunity which continues to haunt Kosovo today. By late June 2000, the political tide had turned, and a desire to get the Serbs to the table led to an agreement between the UN and the Serb National Council, which in turn provoked a boycott by Hasim Thaci and his supporters of the territory's joint administration.

Yet, in McNamara's view, the UN provides the only viable framework for such international efforts. Bodies such as OSCE are highly politicized, and a trend to turn to the military undermines the application of neutral humanitarian principles, he noted. But if the UN is to play this role responsibly, it must be able to say 'no' to powerful states. At a minimum, the UN must insist upon conditions for involvement in peace-building efforts. Otherwise, as in Kosovo, the UN simply has to accept the terms dictated by important member states if it is to remain relevant to their concerns. The result is what McNamara called the 'abysmal' history of UN peacekeeping.

The flaws McNamara described are magnified in new multi-faceted peace-building efforts. Instead of turning to civilian agencies, governments increasingly use military forces which are neither transparent nor accountable in the ways that they operate—an observation the military sometimes makes of civilian humanitarians—and which often are used inappropriately to undertake directly humanitarian work such as refugee return or societal reconstruction. While the military is often uncomfortable in this role, 'the policy guys love it', said McNamara. Governments also increasingly enlist NGOs that they support with earmarked funds in lieu of contributions to multilateral organizations. This is a form of privatization in the name of efficiency, according to McNamara, a trend which is on the rise, with the attendant problems of coordination and politicization.

McNamara's prognosis for Kosovo is bleak. 'It is an ongoing crisis in every sense of the phrase', he said, with ethnically motivated killings occurring regularly. A monthly update issued in June 2000 by UNHCR listed 24 incidents of violence committed against minority group members. While it was appropriate to reduce the massive humanitarian relief efforts in Kosovo, McNamara is convinced that there will be a long-term UN civilian and military presence. The rehabilitation of this war-torn country has barely begun, and the civil administration is 'desperately flawed' and not well managed, in McNamara's assessment. This includes everything from policing to garbage collection. Resource shortages and inadequate personnel policies have undermined the UN's effectiveness. The 'foolish efforts' to force refugees back to the dangerous flash point of Mitrovica were emblematic of a failed approach, in his view. The mismatch between the mission's capacity and the evolving reality in Kosovo is redefining the end state for the UN in Kosovo. We no longer talk about 'reconciliation or multi-ethnicity', McNamara said, now we talk about 'coexistence and tolerance'.

The ultimate question, of course, is whether even this is an unrealistic objective. Can the international community impose tolerance in Kosovo?

The evolution of conflict

The Balkans crisis achieved high relief in Kosovo. After 1987, when Slobodan Milosevic rose to power in Yugoslavia, approximately 1.8 million ethnic Albanians in Kosovo were increasingly subject to political repression. Measures were imposed aiming to eliminate the political, legal, and cultural indicia of the Albanian community. In March 1989, Milosevic stripped the province—at that time 90 per cent ethnic Albanian—of its autonomy. Serbia took over control of police, defence, and economic activities. In 1990, Albanian language newspapers and radio stations were closed down, and teaching in the Albanian language was prohibited. Over 80,000 Albanians working in the public sector were dismissed from employment.[7]

Elections in May 1992 favoured Ibrahim Rugova, who began a strategy of non-violent opposition to Belgrade. Informal parallel political and social structures began to emerge in Kosovo. As Serb forces began a campaign of ethnic cleansing in Bosnia, the United States warned the Serbian authorities that it would use force if they attacked Kosovo. By the

[7] Noel Malcolm, *A Short History of Kosovo* (New York: New York University Press, 1999), 347.

the autumn of 1997, the KLA began killing Serbian police officers and Albanians remaining loyal to the Federal Republic of Yugoslavia. Serbian security forces responded to these provocations with a brutal counter-insurgency campaign through mid-1998, which displaced 350,000 persons.[8] The OSCE approved the deployment of 2,000 monitors for Kosovo in October 1998. Settlement discussions were punctuated by scattered incidents of daily violence.

In January 1999, 45 ethnic Albanians were slain by Serbs outside the village of Racak.[9] After political negotiations in Rambouillet, France, failed in February 1999, a NATO bombing campaign began on 24 March, and systematic episodes of ethnic abuse and uprooting in Kosovo by Serbian forces followed. The conflict displaced nearly 1 million people in or from Kosovo, and killed several thousands of persons before the bombing campaign ended in June 1999.[10]

Perhaps the most striking features of the humanitarian emergency in Kosovo were the speed with which it evolved and the ways in which its twists and turns were not anticipated by those planning the international intervention. Military planners profess not to have anticipated the vast external displacement orchestrated by Serbian forces after bombing began in the spring of 1999. Humanitarian agencies had accumulated a certain amount of materiel, but the amount was wholly insufficient to meet the numbers of those who fled to Albania and the Former Yugoslav Republic of Macedonia in the course of the NATO bombing campaign.

The planning deficiency was described in a review of US government humanitarian programmes concluded in late 1999.

> U.S. policy makers, intelligence officers, regional experts and humanitarians, along with their counterparts in other NATO member countries, failed to predict until just several days before the bombing campaign that Serb forces would systematically expel Kosovars. Instead, the prevailing worst case scenario was that one million Kosovars would be displaced internally, prohibited from exiting, and remain largely inaccessible, in the context of an ongoing air war and a NATO determination not to launch a ground invasion. . .
>
> As the air war unfolded, NATO suddenly found itself shouldering a massive humanitarian project. Once Serbian forces induced the mass expulsion of Kosovars, NATO unexpectedly added to its core objective of degrading Serbia's

[8] 'NATO Force is to Monitor Kosovo Pact as Yugoslavia Steps Back from Brink', *Wall Street Journal* (14 October 1998), A19.

[9] 'Policeman Slain and 2 Hurt at Scene of Kosovo Massacre', *New York Times* (20 January 1999), A3.

[10] United Nations High Commissioner for Refugees, *The State of the World's Refugees: Fifty Years of Humanitarian Action* (New York: Oxford University Press, 2000), 234.

military capacities, the protection of IDPs [internally displaced persons] and the return of refugees safely to their homes. Yet there had been no pre-planning for NATO involvement in humanitarian operations in neighbouring states. For the initial period, the humanitarian agenda was overwhelming due to: the extreme rapidity of events, the colossal scale of the exodus, the depth of uncertainty regarding circumstances inside Kosovo, and the strategic risk that mass refugees posed to Macedonia and Albania.[11]

When Macedonia expressed concerns about being overwhelmed, 'humanitarian evacuation' programmes, which were in the nature of relocation and resettlement efforts abroad, resulted in some 96,000 Kosovar Albanians being temporarily placed or resettled in several Western countries.[12] As military and humanitarian planners began to prepare the refugee camps for the winter, Serbian forces withdrew in June 1999 under the terms of a military technical agreement, and NATO forces entered on the ground. The rush of Kosovars back into Kosovo again caught repatriation planners off guard, and many of those displaced had returned before the UNHCR was able to initiate registration procedures and organize an assisted return by buses.

The relations between the US government and UNHCR were a particularly sore point in the Kosovo crisis, as the US humanitarian review noted.

While the U.S. clearly led the NATO military campaign, on humanitarian matters we preferred that UNHCR play the lead role, with the U.S. in a supportive role. To an important degree, this humanitarian calculation served U.S. interests, given UNHCR's mandate and its broad acceptability as the appropriate body to manage international support to refugees. Also, given Congressional criticism of the preponderant USG [US government] share of NATO military contributions, a comparable USG lead commitment on humanitarian requirements would likely have complicated our efforts to win Congressional support for the emergency supplemental that addressed, among other things, Kosovo emergency programs.

However, our multilateral humanitarian approach created vulnerabilities. We were deeply reliant on UNHCR's cooperation and performance to achieve our core objectives, versus relying upon our own bilateral efforts. Subject to conflicting guidance from other nations, and struggling with weakened capacities at field and headquarters levels, UNHCR was only partially responsive in critical periods to U.S. interests. For instance, in the days leading up to the bombing, UNHCR did not accede to our appeals to prepare for a major refugee outflow far

[11] US Department of State, *Interagency Review of U.S. Government Civilian Humanitarian & Transition Programs* (Washington, DC: US Department of State, January 2000), Annex 1, Sect. 1. At: http://www.gwu.edu/~nsarchiv/NSAEBB/NSAEBB30/index.html

[12] UNHCR, *The State of the World's Refugees*, 239.

in excess of UNHCR's 50,000 person planning figure (admittedly our proposed 300,000 figure still fell far short of eventual demand.) . . .

Our frustration in shaping UNHCR's response to U.S. interests resulted in part from inherent limits to U.S. power: we did not have much choice but to rely heavily upon UNHCR, given our limited direct operational capacities.[13]

Perhaps the overarching lesson from Kosovo was the need to bring together military and humanitarian actors earlier in the planning and implementation of international responses. How to do this, of course, raises many complications. The 2000 review emphasizes the point.

It was not until the Kosovo Coordination Council was formed after the onset of the bombing campaign that a senior civilian humanitarian figure was empowered to lead our humanitarian agenda, including the military components of relief efforts. Had accountable and consistent senior humanitarian leadership been incorporated early on into senior Administration deliberations, we might have seen superior contingency planning for, and later management of, the refugee outflow.[14]

The review found specifically that humanitarian planners were isolated 'from key information on military planning for the Kosovo operation [which] limited its usefulness in developing effective humanitarian contingency planning'.[15]

The humanitarian consequences of military action and the impact of a humanitarian catastrophe on military capacities are important lessons from Kosovo, with serious implications for the relevant bureaucracies. There is a growing recognition that policy planning structures in NATO and within the US government and military, for example, need to be restructured to better integrate humanitarian and military perspectives. This is apart from the relations between military and political structures on the one hand, and military forces and civilian humanitarian actors outside government on the other. These communities must necessarily remain somewhat distinct given their different ultimate responsibilities; as a former Médecins Sans Frontières official put it, the former to kill as an act of state and the latter to save lives. But there are coincident interests as well. This new foray into humanitarian action provides the military with a new legitimacy in public opinion.

The political framework in Kosovo that has emerged under United Nations auspices with the support of the European Union, OSCE, and

[13] US Department of State, *Interagency Review*, Annex 1, Sect. 4.

[14] US Department of State, *Interagency Review*, Annex 1, Sect. 2.

[15] Ibid.

UNHCR continues to play out. Retaliation and reverse ethnic cleansing have driven out approximately 200,000 non-Albanians, Serbs, and Roma, most of whom have relocated to Serbia.[16] Civil administration under the United Nations is evolving slowly. Diplomats and policy makers draw upon the experience in Bosnia and continue to call for multi-ethnic society; and yet, at the same time, observing the increasing ethnic homogeneity in Kosovo, they search for ways of managing separation, including considering territorial partition.

Kosovo is likely to prove the exception rather than the rule for robust international responses to complex humanitarian emergencies. Refugees became virtual weapons of war. Kosovars were uprooted and driven out by Serbian forces who sought thereby to achieve some tactical advantage with respect to technologically superior NATO forces. The swift and massive unanticipated repatriation created a vacuum and an opportunity for political consolidation on the ground by the KLA after the withdrawal of Serbian forces and before the arrival of the UN mission. The informal power structures that have evolved continue to vex the emerging United Nations civil administration.

Pristina

We crossed the border from the Former Yugoslav Republic of Macedonia to Kosovo in the early afternoon on 21 March 2000. The delays at the airport in Skopje and at the Blace border crossing were predictable, and I was anxious to get to Pristina. My driver, Sokol, an ethnic Albanian who had remained in Kosovo during the terror of 1999 and who was now employed by UNHCR, did his best to make up the time, speeding down the narrow, two-lane highway to Pristina.

As we drove into Kosovo, there was just the first hint of spring. This had been one of the harshest winters in Sokol's memory, a point reinforced by several international aid workers whom I interviewed later. As we passed over the hills on the road to Pristina, it began to snow furiously, emphasizing the reluctant loosening of winter's grip over this conflicted land.

We arrived at the outskirts of Pristina and navigated several traffic jams, comprising a jumbled mix of four-wheel-drive vehicles adorned with the emblems of the world's various humanitarian organizations, and a bevy of private cars with no licence plates. Pristina was bursting

[16] 'Nato Overseas Ethnic Cleansing in Reverse', *The Tampa Tribune* (5 August 1999), 19.

at the seams with returned refugees and displaced persons, including many from surrounding villages which had been destroyed, as well as the many varieties of international agency staff that have customarily been deployed during the humanitarian 'gold rushes' of the past decade. We stopped at the UNHCR headquarters, which was located in a building that had served previously as the headquarters of an extremist Serbian political party before the withdrawal of Serbian forces in 1999.

Kosovo is the battlefield site of a major victory of NATO. The return of refugees became a central war aim during NATO's bombing campaign that began in March 1999. The Kosovars who rushed back in June after the withdrawal of Serbian forces felt victorious and deeply angry. They regarded the victory as theirs after a decade of repression and 'humiliation', a word often used by those seeking to explain the retaliatory actions of ethnic Albanians. Vengeance was theirs, and a rash of killings of Serbs and other minorities followed. The summer of 1999 was the occasion for political infighting among various Kosovar factions, particularly those headed by Ibrahim Rogova and Hasim Thaci, who sought to position themselves in the power vacuum before the UN civil administration had become fully operational.

The United Nations Mission in Kosovo (UNMIK), established in 1999 under UN Security Council Resolution 1244, created four 'pillars' of activities to re-establish Kosovo. The first pillar was 'humanitarian' activities led by the UNHCR, which immediately confronted the oncoming winter. In March 2000, UNHCR was consolidating its operations and planning a phased withdrawal.

The second pillar was the United Nations itself, which is responsible for the civil administration of Kosovo. The third pillar of UNMIK is headed by the OSCE, which was given the responsibility of 'institution building', including the legal system. The fourth pillar on economic reconstruction is being handled by the European Union, although the distribution of funds for physical reconstruction was delayed at the outset due to the complexities of EU tendering procedures.

The use of the term 'pillars' is somewhat of a misnomer in describing the UN mission in Kosovo. Some of the activities of UNMIK came early in the sequence of tasks, such as humanitarian aid and threshold human security. Others proceed more slowly, such as economic and social rehabilitation. Indeed, the structure supported by these four 'pillars' is hardly uniform, and is more akin to a cubist painting than a classical façade.

The arrangement puts a high premium on coordination, always a scarcity in multi-faceted international humanitarian deployments in such emergencies, and raises important issues about lack of accountability.

Responsibility is difficult to pin down in such a complicated structure. Mandates overlap, activities are duplicated, and difficult tasks go unaddressed. If everyone is responsible, then no one is responsible.

UNMIK clearly faced a daunting set of challenges in its early days in 1999. The OSCE's Kosovo Verification Mission had withdrawn before the bombing campaign began in March 1999. After much of the population had been uprooted and then had returned, and with the KLA beginning to establish itself politically, little remained of the parallel structures that Kosovars had established as resistance structures over the course of the past decade. After the rush back to their homes in June, self-appointed elements among the Albanian factions began to occupy municipal offices and act as the de facto local authorities in an attempt to consolidate power.

From the outset there was a pervasive lack of human security, with impunity for crimes, particularly against minorities. This inspired a debate about the role of the military in policing, which featured the reluctance of the Kosovo Military Force (KFOR) to undertake this role. This debate was followed by the OSCE's establishment of the Kosovo police service, with 15 per cent minority membership, perhaps the most multi-ethnic local institution in Kosovo. A police training facility was opened, and by March 2000 the first few classes of graduates had been deployed. These unarmed police apprentices are ultimately to constitute a new indigenous police force. However, this local police force was still a sufficiently rare sight in March 2000 to prompt my driver to note the unusual sight of a dark-blue-uniformed policewoman walking in the streets of Pristina. Some 20 per cent of these apprentice police are women, an unprecedented innovation in Kosovo.

There were also grave abuses in the early days against minorities, notably against Serbs and Roma people. These included intimidation, threats, attacks, and killings. Many Serbs fled their homes, which were then occupied by ethnic Albanians. The abuses have continued, and while the pace of departure has lessened the situation was aptly described by an OSCE representative at a meeting in Pristina in 2000. We are witnessing, he said, 'a kind of an exodus on a low scale'.

The main effort to secure law and order was in the form of 'static security', by which is meant the round-the-clock, seven-days-a-week guarding of vulnerable persons and places. In March 2000 I visited the village of Urosevac/Ferizaj, where some 20 elderly Serbs remained scattered around the town in their flats. Many had already sent their children elsewhere. The village, in the US sector, was also the site of a UNHCR field office, which was scheduled to close in the course of the agency's consolidation of operations. According to the UNHCR protection officer, a quiet but intense young Japanese woman and former journalist, 'if KFOR left they [the Serbs] would be killed'. The village is a stronghold for Hasim Thaci, however; and the UNHCR head of office, a retired British army major, believed that incidents were not likely because they would invite a deployment of international police and troops.

On the drive out of Urosevac/Ferizaj I noticed a poignant juxtaposition which seemed to me to capture the human-security dilemma in Kosovo. Near the town square, an Orthodox church stood immediately next to a mosque. I asked why, given the passions of the victorious Kosovars who were an overwhelming majority in the village, the church had remained untouched. Many other religious edifices in Kosovo had been damaged or destroyed. The UNHCR's representative drew my attention to the fact that Greek soldiers had been deployed and were guarding the church on a continuous basis in order to prevent its destruction.

One of the central issues presented in the early days of the Kosovo mission was securing the rule of law as a prerequisite to refugee repatriation and other efforts to revive the economy and rehabilitate society. This included not only police but also laws—both penal and criminal—courts, and prisons. But the effort was not going well. A drafting effort by the local legal community had produced a penal code that lawyers at OSCE found deeply flawed and biased against minorities. One young OSCE lawyer, an American who had worked on similar issues in Bosnia, suggested that a model international criminal code was needed for such occasions.

The state of the judiciary in Kosovo in March 2000 was even more problematic. According to Sylvie Pantz, a French investigating judge who had joined UNMIK to develop the judiciary in early November 1999 after a stint with the prosecutor's office at the International Criminal Tribunal for the former Yugoslavia in the Hague, the laws of Kosovo were simply an adjunct to the conflict. 'They use laws like weapons', explained Pantz. At the outset of UNMIK, there was considerable dispute over the applicable law, with ethnic Albanians insisting upon using the law as it stood in 1989 when they were largely ousted from public life by Serbian authorities in Belgrade. An international judge and prosecutor had been assigned to Mitrovica to handle minority cases out of a concern that ethnic Albanian judges would be unwilling, because of threats, to punish ethnic Albanian defendants, or would unfairly punish minority defendants. Proposals were under discussion to establish a court with international personnel for ethnic and war crimes, and in March 2000 a dozen more lawyers from the United Kingdom had been promised to adjudicate pre-trial release cases. Pantz explained that ethnic Albanian defendants were released even if they had committed serious offences, but that minority offenders were detained irrespective of the likelihood that they might abscond or pose a danger to the community. The prison outside Prizren was to be refurbished, although it was already filled to near-capacity in 2000.

One of the hidden issues that had begun to emerge concerns residential property rights. Issues relating to commercial property and privatization are still distinctly in the future for Kosovo. In terms of residential property, at the outset of the bombing campaign in March 1999 there were concerns that anything less than a complete withdrawal of Serbian authorities would produce a war of property laws like that which has occurred in Bosnia and Herzegovina, where such laws have been used to promote ethnic separation. An aristocratic young German lawyer was handed the property policy file when he arrived late last year in Pristina, reflecting both the difficulty that his superiors had understanding the importance of the question and the uncertainty of how to address such highly technical issues in this complicated context.

The property issues in Kosovo turned out to be different from those in Bosnia in the sense that, when the ethnic Albanians prevailed, they began to evict minorities—Serbs and Roma—and illegally occupy their homes. Housing and property offices have been established by UNMIK to provide mechanisms to clarify rights and resolve disputes among residential property owners. Modelled on an international property commission formed in Bosnia under the Dayton peace agreement, the Kosovo effort may in fact have the consequence of fortifying majority interests and diminishing minority rights, according to a British lawyer responsible at OSCE for its implementation. UNHCR's protection officer in Urosevac/Ferizaj noted that property claims have already emerged as perhaps the main category of human rights complaints made by minorities in Kosovo.

My visit to Kosovo in March 2000 also illuminated graphically the banality of state building. Upon arriving in Pristina, I witnessed an interagency discussion about the payment of utility bills. Bills for water and electricity services in Kosovo had not been sent for several months, depriving UNMIK of very substantial revenues. The meeting participants discussed exemptions from paying bills that might be claimed by impoverished minority members, and there was much criticism about the lack of arrangements for minorities who do not generally enjoy freedom of movement in Kosovo. Would KFOR, for example, provide military escorts for minorities to go to municipal centres to apply for exemptions? But such centres do not even exist in each municipality. The payment procedure proposal which has been made by the United Nations (pillar two) was vigorously criticized by representatives from UNHCR (pillar one) and OSCE (pillar three) who were responsible for minority protection. This squabble among the pillars was reflective of the differing perceptions of roles and the difficulties of coordination.

The conundrum in Kosovo is compounded, of course, by the lack of an end-state objective in terms of national independence. The meaning of the term 'substantial autonomy' in the UN Security Council Resolution 1244 is not self-evident. Is it to mean independence? Or does it mean autonomy as a province within a sovereign Yugoslavia? Ethnic Albanians insist on the former and eschew the latter. The uncertainty of Kosovo's ultimate status is pervasive and permeates the institutional arrangement, and this ambiguity is only likely to be deepened in view of Slobodan Milosevic's ousting and removal to the War Crime Tribunal in The Hague in 2001.

The Kosovo assemblage of pillars suffers from multiple personalities. First and foremost, is the mission one of state building? The answer is: sort of. The differing views of the responsibilities of the various international actors produce an incoherence that will make it difficult for the mission to succeed. Is UNMIK a dictator? Well, the notion that the UN mission is a protectorate would have profound implications. In the words of an experienced Canadian OSCE official who had served previously in Bosnia: 'In a quasi-protectorate, the protector should make the decisions.' But the dilemma is clear. As a young ethnic Albanian programme officer at the local Soros Foundation puts it: 'It is hard to rule in someone else's land.' The UN mission was surprised in March 2000 by an Amnesty International report critical of UNMIK's response to the violence in Mitrovica. While UNMIK has formal executive authority, in some sense it continues to shy away from accepting responsibility for that supreme role.

If UNMIK is not a dictator, is it then a referee, seeking to build a bridge between contending parties? Sometimes. While some progress has been made on disputes among the Albanian factions from time to time, these incremental successes do not translate into agreement on the deeper conflicts between Albanian and minority populations, notably Serbs and Roma people. UNMIK has not been able to play a broker's role in these more conflicted circumstances. Instead, UNMIK has adopted a monitoring role on minority issues. An inter-agency Minority Task Force has been established, and UNHCR and OSCE have together produced several reports that contain a mind-numbing litany of minority abuses. In December 1999, OSCE produced a 329-page catalogue of human rights violations by ethnic Albanians during June–October 1999. This is really akin to what NGOs do: 'witnessing', where public reports are issued to shame perpetrators.

Is the ensemble of cast members of international agency workers I met in Kosovo the new state builders? Again, sort of. One young lawyer whom I interviewed at the OSCE headquarters acknowledged, somewhat ruefully, 'we are state building'. Yet, as he also admitted, 'all of us feel some discomfort at being dictators'. Another even more seasoned OSCE representative was more direct, urging international institutions to develop a set of 'technical arrangements' which are 'divorced from politics' and which can be applied in situations such as Kosovo. He gave as an example elections, which he thought could be outsourced as a technical exercise.

Kosovo in 2000 was populated with hundreds of international agency workers, mostly men and women in their mid-20s to mid-30s, many of whom have been involved in deployments in Bosnia, Cambodia, Haiti, and now Kosovo. After the hard winter, some are looking forward to working in East Timor once their short-term contracts expire. They are a human resource that international organizations have not yet figured out how—or whether—to nurture and retain. They constitute a kind of informal and somewhat inefficient roster of persons who are summoned shortly after the UN Security Council resolves to act and international institutions are requested to deploy in situations of fragile peace.

Pristina encore

Pristina was as crowded when I visited in October 2000 as it was in March; refugees and displaced persons continue to swell the city's population. Satellite television dishes had sprouted like mushrooms on most buildings as we drove on this pleasant autumn day from the airport. 'We are hungry for information', explained Sokol, who again was my driver. The streets of Pristina were still filled with a myriad of four-wheel-drive vehicles advertising various international agencies and NGOs. The red and white vehicles of the UN's international police had been joined by the white cars of the blue-uniformed Kosovo Police Service, whose personnel could be seen at several intersections directing traffic. More cars with licence plates were in evidence, at least in Pristina. A good deal of construction could be observed, financed to a great extent by money from Kosovars abroad as well as the wealth associated with the deployment of the UN mission. This spurt of building is largely unregulated, and uncontrolled construction is proving dangerous to curtail. A local architect who was working on a project to demolish illegally built buildings was shot and killed by unknown assailants in September 2000.

UNHCR was no longer an UNMIK 'pillar'. The office had been scaled down, and Eric Morris was the new UN Humanitarian Coordinator for Kosovo. Morris reported both good news and bad news on the humanitarian front. The good news was that small numbers of Serbs, a few score, were returning to minority areas in Kosovo. Returnees explained that conditions in Serbia were deprived and difficult. Morris was urging UNMIK to assist these returns on a priority basis, notwithstanding the UNHCR headquarters' general advice that conditions were not conducive to safe return. His advocacy apparently paid off. In August 2001, UNHCR organized the return of 54 Serbs to Kosovo under KFOR escort.[17]

Morris's bad news was that a significant number of Kosovars, perhaps 30,000 or more, would still be living in tents in the winter of 2000–1. Indeed, the next day I visited a group of Roma encamped in tents near a junk yard in north Mitrovica. Emergency shelter arrangements were still needed to assist these and the others in Kosovo who remain homeless and without adequate shelter.

The evolution of local administration in Kosovo will clearly be a benchmark of UNMIK's progress in handing over authority on a variety of municipal affairs. One striking feature is a bizarre reversal of responsibilities in Kosovo. This is graphically illustrated by a sign I saw in Pristina on which the European Union took credit for garbage collection. Yet local municipal councils are obsessed with national politics, and local mayoral candidates run for election on passionate platforms espousing national independence.

Several Kosovar city managers expressed particular frustration with the failure of the UN mission to devolve responsibilities. One suggested that in some instances local authorities were not ready to take on the responsibilities, but that in other instances UNMIK officials were reluctant to cede the authority and acted like 'little kings' in the way they conducted themselves. The city managers found the pace of devolution to be clearly unsatisfactory as province-wide elections loomed in November 2001.

An unusually public squabble among UNMIK's pillars was occasioned by the release in October 2000 of a report by OSCE (pillar three) on the

[17] 'Kosovo: First Group of 54 Serbs Repatriated', *UN Wire* (14 August 2001). At: http://www.unfoundation.org/unwire/index.as.

criminal justice system under UN civil administration (pillar two).[18] OSCE has a legal systems monitoring unit which is part of its human rights staff, and which was assigned a reporting responsibility under the authority of the UN Secretary-General's 12 July 1999 report on the implementation of Security Council Resolution 1244. The OSCE report undertook an exacting survey of the operation of the UNMIK judicial system during February 2000, addressing the ambiguities of the applicable law, practices relating to arbitrary arrest and detention, appointment of defence counsel, lack of impartiality in court decision-making, and low priority in prosecuting sexual offences. The report found the system woefully deficient in these areas and made numerous recommendations for reform. UN experts have privately called the efforts to construct a judicial sector in Kosovo a 'disaster'; the difference is that OSCE went public.

UNMIK Department of Justice Co-head Sylvie Pantz, however, mounted a spirited defence. 'No one would deny where we need to go', she said. But she called the OSCE report 'unrealistic' and a 'luxury'. The question has to be put in context. As the OSCE report itself noted, the Kosovo criminal justice system had to be built from scratch, with a new legal framework and new personnel. The court infrastructure was poor, and the level of knowledge of human rights law is low among the available local judges, prosecutors, and defence lawyers. As of September 2000, 405 judges and prosecutors and 724 support staff were working in Kosovo's judicial institutions in a system that had grown larger than the one that had existed before the 1999 conflict.[19] To address the problem of ethnic pressures being placed on judges and prosecutors, especially in cases involving minority members, twelve international judges and five prosecutors were being appointed as of October 2000. But these appointments were not in numbers or circumstances sufficient to ensure impartial justice, according to OSCE.

UNMIK has established a working group to examine the OSCE report with a view to implementing appropriate reforms. OSCE is part of the group, although its participation is limited to staff who give technical advice, and excludes staff involved in judicial monitoring who might be compromised through their participation in relation to the ability to produce another report. Senior UNMIK officials have learned an entirely different lesson from this dispute. 'We won't do that again', one of them said, referring to the OSCE monitoring arrangement in the mission structure.

[18] 'Kosovo: A Review Of the Criminal Justice System, 1 September 2000–28 February, 2001'.

[19] United Nations Interim Administration Mission in Kosovo, *The Justice System of Kosovo* (UNMIK-Administrative Department of Justice, 9 October 2000), 2.

The OSCE report controversy raises important issues concerning judicial functions in UN peace operations. At least three distinct issues are bound up in the debate. First, immediate human security must be achieved in a post-crisis setting. Second, broad issues emerge concerning justice relating to serious violations of human rights and humanitarian law committed in the course of the conflict. How to address questions of justice in a peace process requires a delicate balance of considerations that are being addressed or that have been addressed in places like Argentina, Cambodia, Chile, El Salvador, former Yugoslavia, Indonesia, Rwanda, Sierra Leone, and South Africa. The justice and peace issues in these settings are intertwined, demanding contextual responses.

The third issue involves finding an approach to building a sustainable judicial system, an objective of indefinite duration. This is an ambitious endeavour involving entities such as the World Bank and the UNDP in the context of broader country development strategies.

One lesson from Kosovo seems clear. The absence of a judicial mechanism as an adjunct to a UN peace operation in order to address immediate issues of insecurity can threaten the viability of the operation over the short term and scar it over the longer term. The impunity that characterized the early days of the mission compromised its effectiveness and resulted in loss of life, abuses, and mass displacement. It continues to inhibit minority return and the achievement of peaceful coexistence. The UN obviously needs a new capacity to address such issues in the future.

The justice system dispute reflects a broader coordination challenge. The UNMIK pillars argue chronically with each other. Nor is UNMIK fully in the control of Bernard Kouchner, the first Special Representative of the Secretary-General, said Richard Holbrooke in 2000, when he was the US ambassador to the UN. Holbrooke favours more ad hoc arrangements such as the Office of the High Representative in Bosnia.

Kosovo remains an incomplete project. A classic dynamic is already evident: interest in, funding for, political engagement in, and opportunities for getting things done are fading fast as the international response moves from the emergency phase to longer-term development-related activities. Whether Kosovo succeeds or not, of course, will depend largely upon the nature of the mix of these endeavours over the next several years. In the words of an OSCE official, 'we need a few successful examples' of state building in order for the international community to continue these endeavours. But if the international community cannot marshal sufficient clarity and capacity to build something akin to a benign state in Kosovo—and such an outcome seems unlikely—then new measures of success will have to be articulated for such efforts in the future.

Political developments and dilemmas

October was a cruel month for Bernard Kouchner, Special Representative of the Secretary-General, who from July 1999 to January 2001 led UNMIK. He was succeeded in 2001 by Hans Haekkerup, a former Danish Minister for Defence, who in June 2001 proposed a new constitutional framework for the region, with Kosovars running health, education, economic, and local policy. The UN would be in charge of justice, law enforcement, revenue collection, and the Kosovo Protection Corps. Negotiations among the factions continued after provincial elections in late 2001. Haekkerup resigned and was replaced in early 2002.

At the outset of my meeting with Kouchner in Pristina in October 2000, he began by making reference to the fact that he had just been passed over by the Secretary-General that week for the post of High Commissioner for Refugees in favour of Ruud Lubbers, former Dutch Prime Minister. But the roots of Kouchner's distress were deeper.

The election in Yugoslavia of Vojislav Kostunica earlier in October was surely a 'triumph of diplomacy', acknowledged Kouchner. But it also posed a dilemma for Kosovo. The world's attention had shifted. Just that morning, the Norwegian government had notified Kouchner that it was re-allocating funding for a banking project from Kosovo to Serbia. This was only the beginning of a predictable rush to Belgrade by governments, NGOs, and international organizations. Given UNMIK's bureaucratic budgetary cycles, experts say that there would be no substantial funding impact before 2002. But the dapper and renowned humanitarian had a warning. 'Do not forget the Kosovars', said Kouchner, who warned that inattention by the international community could result, at a minimum, in 'terrible hardship' or in the worst case even serve to 're-start a war'.

Kouchner, who paints pictures with words and gestures, was animated as he walked around his expansive office in the course of our conversation. He felt that the international shift of attention would only accelerate the growing alienation of the ethnic Albanian majority from the UN, which he predicted would increasingly be seen as 'part of the problem', obstructing the Albanian quest for independence. He also expressed irritation with some of the criticisms that had been levelled against UNMIK by what he called 'the watchers', particularly criticisms by Médecins sans Frontières (Belgium) and the International Crisis Group, both organizations which he had helped to create.

He was somewhat more accepting of the complaints from the ethnic Albanians, Serbs, and others who were jockeying for political position in the run up to the first municipal elections in October 2000. OSCE reported that Ibrahim Rugova's party received 58 per cent of the vote and former guerrilla leader Hasim Thaci's party received 27 per cent. Rugova's party won most of the contested municipalities. Kouchner, who would leave shortly after the municipal election, said that his basic objective was to put the contending parties together and get them to talk and ultimately to coexist peacefully. Indeed, UNMIK could be described as more of a peace process than a state-building endeavour, a characterization reinforced by UN Resolution 1244, which stops short of advocating independence for the province. 'Missions like UNMIK are the diplomacy of tomorrow', said Kouchner.

Kosovo was considered by many to be 'mission impossible'. Kouchner was reflective on this point. 'We did not know it was impossible', Kouchner explained, 'so we did it.' Of course what the 'it' is has yet to be determined, a question only complicated by political developments in Serbia.

We ended our meeting as a German diplomat entered Kouchner's office. Kouchner asked him whether there was news from Berlin; he nodded. I saw the look of apprehension in Kouchner's face as I exited. He was plainly fearful of receiving more bad news.

Serbia

The Bogovadja youth camp, opened by the Red Cross in 1939, is located approximately 70 kilometres southwest of Belgrade. Bogovadja's sprawling grounds have served as a refugee reception centre since 1991. The facility reminded me of several communally-owned resorts that I had visited in the former socialist East. No longer were they summer camps for vacationing youth and families, at least exclusively. Rather, such facilities have become collective centres for displaced persons and refugees in a region beset by a series of armed conflicts over the past decade.

At the time that I visited Bogovadja, there were 70 refugees living there from Bosnia and Croatia, mostly old people with a smattering of children and youths. The administrator of Bogovadja, Jovo Knezevic, was himself a refugee from Croatia who had been a high-school geography teacher in Split. He fled to Serbia after the Croatian army's 1995 campaign had ousted Serb forces. 'I have lived the horrors of war' he explained. Knezevic sees as his goal at Bogovadja giving people 'some sense of normal life'.

We met with a group of refugees in a large, dimly lit room at the camp. Many were elderly people; one woman was blind, and an old man used crutches. None of the refugees we spoke with expected that they could return in the foreseeable future to their homes in either Bosnia or Croatia. Nor did any believe that they had any prospects of resettlement abroad, although some others had left the camp for the United States and Canada over the past several years. A 30-something Bosnian Serb woman explained that she was afraid her children would be harassed or harmed if they returned to Bosnia, a sentiment echoed by others.

Others explained that those who went back were mainly old people who expected to receive pensions upon return. They were willing to repatriate, at least if they had houses to which they could return. Many homes are damaged or destroyed, or are now occupied by other persons. Jobs are scarce for those returning. The reality, of course, is that many refugees will not return home. Their future, if such a benign term could be used, was in Serbia.

It was instructive to hear what was on their minds. The refugees grew animated as they raised and discussed citizenship and property rights problems. Some were worried that by accepting citizenship in Serbia they would cut off their rights to houses they owned in their home countries. Others described restrictions on the sale or renting of property. Several mentioned that they were hopeful of improvements in the situation because of the new government in Belgrade. But overall the mood was sombre. 'I was born in the wrong time' said Knezevic, aged 35 years, who explained that the last ten years of his life had simply been lost to conflict and its aftermath.

We left Bogovadja as daylight dwindled on that cold winter evening for our return to Belgrade. 'He must see us as some kind of aliens', one refugee woman in her mid-30s with young children said to my interpreter as we left. While she said it in a joking manner, it was clear that she was embarrassed and ashamed of the situation in which she found herself. As we travelled in the dark over the sparsely travelled road, it seemed to me that the refugees at Bogovadja reflected accurately the essence of the refugee condition: the pain and anguish of being between homes.

Belgrade

It was a cloudy and dreary day in January 2001 when our plane descended to the Belgrade airport. As we landed, I noticed the browns and greens of the farm fields and the orange tile roofs of the houses. This contrasted sharply with the broken houses I had seen just a few months earlier landing in Sarajevo. Nor were there very many passengers, again in contrast to the glut of foreigners I had witnessed travelling to Pristina. But this is changing: NGOs are arriving and beginning to implement international programmes. 'We are all starting to duplicate', said one foreign NGO official who had arrived in December 2000, referring to the burgeoning needs assessments and funding proposals being prepared.

I was last at the Belgrade airport in 1993, at a time when it had been closed by reason of sanctions imposed by the international community. I had then arrived on a UN flight from Zagreb to an aerodrome that was eerily quiet. Economic sanctions had not yet bitten deeply; everything was available then in Belgrade's shops. But conditions quickly deteriorated.

In January 2001, the airport was open and the effects of the sanctions regime were waning. My interpreter, Biljana, a 20-something student just finishing her study of English literature at Belgrade University, explained that ordinary people had coped with the intervening economic deprivation by holding several odd jobs in the shadow economy. But conditions were improving. Gas prices were finally falling, and cars were on the streets again. Young people are no longer looking to leave the country at the first opportunity.

We drove from the airport past the selective damage caused by the NATO air campaign: the ruined former Communist Party headquarters and destroyed military and police buildings. But precision in war had its limits, and my driver, Dejan, could not help showing me the destroyed Chinese embassy, which the Central Intelligence Agency has admitted mistakenly targeting during the 1999 air campaign: an explanation summarily disbelieved by my young, anti-Milosevic driver and interpreter.

This was a moment of high political drama in Belgrade. Carla del Ponte, the Swiss prosecutor at the international tribunal in The Hague responsible for the trial of war crimes in the former Yugoslavia, was coming to Belgrade to discuss the surrender of indicted war criminals such as Slobodan Milosevic. In anticipation, the Hyatt hotel was filled to capacity with diplomats, journalists, and security personnel. The diplomatic chatter at the hotel, however, could not mask the quiet desperation and anger of Serbia's displaced.

Indeed, Serbia is a land of exiles. According to UNHCR, over the last decade approximately 500,000 ethnic Serbs fled to the Federal Republic of Yugoslavia (FRY) comprising Serbia and Montenegro, coming from Bosnia and Croatia in the course of fighting.[20] In addition, approximately 200,000 ethnic Serbs and others, including Roma people, fled from

[20] 'Reversal of Fortune: Serbia's Refugee Crisis', US Committee for Refugees Website. At: http://www.refugees.org/world/articles/serbialead_rr00_1.htm

Kosovo to the FRY largely as a result of pressure and 'reverse ethnic cleansing' which occurred after the NATO air campaign ended in June 1999 and Serbian forces withdrew.[21] This opened the way for victorious and vengeful ethnic Albanians to rush back to their homes.

Most of Serbia's refugees and displaced persons live in the homes of local families, although, according to UNHCR in early 2001, 50,000 were accommodated in over 600 collective centres located throughout the FRY.[22] These dislocated persons must fend for themselves in an environment of impoverishment and scarcity caused at least in part by a series of economic sanctions imposed by the international community in an effort to dislodge Milosevic.

These exiles are a tangible manifestation and result of Serbia's loss of a series of armed conflicts that accompanied the breakup of the Socialist Federal Republic of Yugoslavia. Military setbacks in Croatia, Bosnia and Herzegovina, and Kosovo have brought successive waves of refugees and internally displaced persons to Serbia as well as to the much smaller republic of Montenegro. Finding new or old homes for these dislocated people will surely be a measure of a broader political settlement in the complicated political setting of the Balkans.

A basic question is where these exiles will have their permanent homes. Will they return to their previous homes or will they assimilate into the places where they currently reside? The outcome depends upon such matters as citizenship arrangements as well as possession of houses that were destroyed or that are occupied by others or compensation for their loss. Politics and money are the customary constraints.

The authorities in Belgrade in 2001 see many challenges ahead in order to solve the problems of refugees and displaced persons. They are adamant that international assistance will be needed to address these problems. The official position of the new government is that refugees and displaced persons should be able to return to their places of origin as long as conditions are conducive to return. This means a guarantee of security and, in many instances, provision of accommodation, as the houses of many individuals have been destroyed or are currently occupied by members of other ethnic groups in Bosnia, Croatia, and Kosovo. However, the repair and rebuilding of damaged and destroyed houses is expensive, and would require substantial sums from the international community. Such largesse, however, is unlikely to be forthcoming.

[21] US Committee for Refugees, 'Country Report: Yugoslavia', Worldwide Refugee Information. At: http://www.refugees.org/world/countryrpt/europe/yugoslavia.html

[22] UNHCR Branch Office Belgrade, 'Collective Accommodation of Refugees and IDPs in FRY' (1 January 2001).

At the federal level, the issue of refugees and displaced persons has important implications for national security and stability in Serbia. This point has been underscored by Milo Djukanovic, President of the Republic of Montenegro, who emphasized that Montenegro's generosity to refugees—approximately 14,400 refugees were housed in 73 collective centres, according to UNHCR in early 2001—should be considered as a point in favour of it being able to pursue national independence. Djukanovic complained that Montenegro's future should not be held hostage to the unresolved status of Kosovo. But western governments are not very sympathetic, instead worrying about the instability that could be engendered by the unravelling of the federation. If Montenegro goes, then what about Kosovo? Or what about the partition of Macedonia? Whether Djukanovic's trajectory of self-determination will lead to further conflict in the Balkans is a question with an uncertain answer. But it is not at all clear that an arrangement for even a high degree of autonomy would be acceptable to Montenegrans, who in April 2001 split nearly evenly on a pro-independence vote. Once the forces of nationalism and ethnic identity have been unleashed, they are difficult to control. A bubbling insurgency by ethnic Albanians in Macedonia, which in July 2001 had resulted in displacement affecting over 100,000 persons, is but a recent illustration of this all too customary pattern over the last decade.

Serbia has already made some progress in facing its international challenges, according to Goran Svilanovic, the new federal minister for foreign affairs. Svilanovic, whom I have known for several years, was previously an opposition political leader who played an important role in the dramatic demonstrations on 5 October 2000 which brought down Milosevic. I sat with Svilanovic in a spacious meeting room in the foreign ministry in January 2001. He noted with satisfaction that the FRY had accomplished much in the repair of relations with nearby countries, NATO countries, and various international organizations. This new cooperative approach had been rewarded with pledges of foreign aid, and there is now a hope that the Stability Pact for South Eastern Europe could actually become a reality. But issues such as the status of Kosovo and Montenegro and an Albanian insurgency were vexing problems. The war-crimes issue was looming large with the visit of the prosecutor from The Hague, and Svilanovic had to end our meeting to attend President Kostunica's first meeting with Carla del Ponte.

Svilanovic noted as we ended our conversation that the refugee issue presented a very delicate question in the current political climate in Serbia. 'They can turn nationalistic very easily', he warned of this exile population. This sentiment was shared by Rasim Ljajic, the new federal minister of national and ethnic communities, with whom we met in the monumental federal building where this small new ministry is located. Refugees can be good fodder for political radicalization.

The point was underscored as well by William D. Montgomery, the US Ambassador in Belgrade, who had worked previously in Croatia and on Bosnia peace issues. He drew upon these experiences in discussing the implications of refugees and displaced persons in the region: 'Every place I have been it's the refugee folk who are the most extreme nationalists and who make it hard for governments to move toward reconciliation.' Having lost everything, they are not willing to accept concessions and they stridently oppose a political settlement. They are needy and can drag down the already traumatized host society. 'Most leaders here believe Kosovo will be lost', said Montgomery, 'but they do not want to be responsible.' The displaced from Kosovo make it even harder for leaders to address the issue. And it is not clear that there are very many enlightened politicians in any event. 'Very few leaders care about these folk in the region', Montgomery explained; the main response to refugees and displaced persons in his view has been 'lip service'.

Steps at the federal level are being taken to address the refugee issue by amending the FRY citizenship law in order to permit persons to acquire the citizenship of other countries without compromising their FRY citizenship. Svilanovic explained that the new federal interior minister had pressed forward with this initiative. This could provide some assurance to individuals who are afraid that by taking citizenship they may forfeit property rights. However, negotiations are not yet under way between the countries in the region on issues relating to the return of properties or compensation for their loss. Conferral of citizenship may also ease the process of integration of refugees and displaced persons in Serbia, although many of those in collective centres will also need substantial amounts of material assistance.

But the real action relating to refugees and displaced persons, who account for nearly 10 per cent of FRY's population, is at the republic level. The burden of dealing with these individuals will thus fall most heavily upon Gordana Metkovic, the new Serbian minister for labour and social issues. Metkovic's office is located in a dilapidated building, which on the morning we met in January 2001 was thronged by people looking for various kinds of help. We retired to her small office and its no-nonsense decor, sitting around a table where she spoke frankly about the challenges ahead of her.

Trained as an economist, Metkovic knows that she has an impossible job. Under the new citizenship law, the first refugees will have been granted FRY citizenship in 2002. She projected that by the end of 2001 there may be no more refugees, at least technically, if they have accepted FRY citizenship. While this may be an overly optimistic projection, the trend is clear and the policy consequences are significant. Many of these new citizens are likely to be people in need of social assistance, particularly most of the nearly 35,000 refugees who live in authorized collective centres, as well as some others who, while not presently housed in such centres, are vulnerable and needy. These likely social cases will comprise older and disabled people, including people who will not have access to sell their property back in Bosnia or Croatia. Special micro-financing schemes from donors may be appropriate to facilitate integration, Metkovic noted, as long as local people are not excluded from such benefits.

But internally displaced persons from Kosovo will be 'a huge problem', she allowed. Many of those from Kosovo still believe they can go back and, indeed, are planning to go back, unlike refugees from Croatia or Bosnia. The policy of the Milosevic regime was to maintain those from Kosovo without status, thereby manifesting a continuing claim upon the province.

According to Metkovic, 'it would be a disaster' for FRY if the international community reduces its support for refugees and internally displaced persons upon the expectation that the needs could be addressed by local resources expended on behalf of new citizens. The numbers of likely cases may be a bit uncertain, but they would clearly overwhelm FRY's frail social safety net. There is simply not sufficient money in the government budget to deal with the needs of such vulnerable individuals, or even to raise the inadequate salaries of ministry workers. Nor does any inter-governmental framework yet exist in the region to coordinate issues of property and pensions, a critical gap in Metkovic's view. The result, she said, is 'openly speaking, my problem'.

What then will be the impact on the future of Serbia? The transition of the Serbian government is fragile, and the authorities must ask for help. Metkovic believes and hopes that the international community will not 'turn its back on us'. But, citing a Serbian proverb, she noted that it was possible that she 'was being optimistic to the point of stupidity' about the future.

Uncertainty characterizes the assessments of civil society actors about the Serbian transition. Otpor, or 'resistance', is a student and youth movement that aspires to be a political party. An impromptu visit to its headquarters in Belgrade on a chilly, sunny day in January 2001 revealed a frenzy of triumphal activity in the post-Milosevic era. The headquarters, located in a prime location in downtown Belgrade, was donated by the mother of one of its members.

Otpor achieved a high public profile when it actively organized mass student demonstrations over the last months of the Milosevic regime. Their slogan, 'He is finished', adorned not only the hallways of nearby Belgrade University but many other public areas around the city in the crucial days leading up to the 5 October 2000 uprising. Pedrag Lecic, at age 25 years, is one of the elders at Otpor, which now counts among its members many high-school students. Lecic said that Otpor planned to support the new government and to give it 100 days to accomplish something, during which time it would make no comment. Thereafter, if Otpor was unsatisfied, it would go public. But the role of this expression of people power in the future of Serbia is decidedly uncertain.

The more established elements of civil society that had functioned even under Milosevic's rule are similarly unsure of the future. Sonja Licht, a short, plump woman with an intense demeanour, is the board president of George Soros' Open Society Fund in Belgrade. Licht harbours both optimistic and pessimistic thoughts. Her optimism is fuelled in part by the fact that key actors from the alternative civil society are moving into the mainstream. This is happening at all levels, she explained, from the leadership of federal ministries to municipalities. Indeed, the local Soros Foundation is focusing funding on the training of new municipal authorities. 'We want to do it now because it is the time', she explained. But while she was gratified to see pro-democracy advocates move from 'outside to inside' in the government, it was important that the foundation remain independent. 'We will play the same role as we played earlier in terms of supporting an alternative civil sector', she vowed. According to Licht, this should involve supporting projects such as independent media and policy think tanks. She is optimistic because she believes that new people in authority understand that they are 'lagging behind so much' and that they must learn the lessons from other countries in the region in order to accomplish an accelerated transition in Serbia. Licht also believes that the human resource capacity is good; expatriate experts are returning to help and there is no resentment of them on the part of those who stayed.

Ambassador Montgomery joins Licht in her optimism. 'Very good people are involved in the government', he said, and 'bright young people are coming back', providing good potential for rapid progress and economic reform. 'I am an optimist', allowed Montgomery.

Licht's pessimism is perhaps more fundamental. For the new government in Serbia, it will be 'easy to make mistakes' in this very complicated transition, she explained. The economy is in shambles with an estimated 50 per cent unemployment rate, higher than that confronted by any other transitional country in the region. Even a simple safety net for vulnerable people may not be affordable.

Put another way, will Serbia over the next several years look more like Poland or Romania? The uncertainty and instability concerning Kosovo also figured in her pessimism. Serbia's transition clearly will be very hard.

The Serbian displaced

The Serbs displaced from Kosovo in 1999 are angry and despairing. How they are treated, and how their futures are secured or not by local officials and the international community, will influence dramatically the prospects of reconciliation in the region more generally.

I visited internally displaced persons at Pansion Avala outside Belgrade in January 2001. The facility had been a restaurant and resort until it was converted into a collective centre under contract with the local authorities. The restaurant area had been subdivided to accommodate the 117 displaced persons who were in residence.

We met with a group of displaced persons in the foyer of the former restaurant. The inhabitants of Pansion Avala were from a company town in Kosovo with a factory that produced rubber belts for coal mines. They had fled in June 1999 after Serbian forces withdrew. Perhaps the common element of their lives was a feeling of excruciating boredom. Mainly, they watch television and play cards. Their children attend local schools through high school. During the summer, some of the men are able to obtain part-time employment building houses.

All of those assembled said that they would like to return, but could not return at this time. They said they would be in danger if they went back and, in any event, their homes had been destroyed. They had no idea how long they would have to call Pansion Avala their home. Nor were they particularly happy with the local authorities who had promised to give them houses, a promise they did not keep. Some reported hostility and bias on the part of locals.

Many of the displaced with whom I spoke were clearly angry and full of rage. 'We left houses one thousand times better than here' said one man, who also complained that the displaced were paid very small sums for any work that could be found. They thus wait sullenly for charity.

For the first and only time during my visit the anger of these people was directed at me. They blamed the United States: 'What if we came and threw you out of your homes?' they asked. I had to acknowledge that I would be angry too if I had been bombed. 'All we do is wait for US forces to withdraw so that we can go back', said another. 'We are judged as war criminals; no Albanian is accused, only Serbs.' 'The Albanians are the problem and the Americans are the ones to blame', said an elderly woman bitterly. The anger in this meeting was palpable.

We then drove to a nearby construction company where a number of internally displaced persons had taken up residence in the workers' barracks of the company. We initially met two elderly women, dressed in traditional black garb, who explained that they had fled Kosovo in June 1999 and had lived first in private homes where they had paid rent. Conditions were better in the unauthorized haven to which they had moved in March 2000. Here they had their own bathroom, paying 70 Deutschmarks—approximately $35—a month in rent.

We then went to a large communal room where a dozen or so young families gathered. These are persons who should have been at the beginning of productive careers and who now found themselves dislocated and wasted in this setting. People with property, prospects, and lives were reduced to being non-productive, marginal, and socially invisible. They accepted this fate with surprising equanimity, perhaps in part due to the philosophical reflections of Jeremic Rajko, aged 38 years, the man who hosted us.

Rajko explained that he did not blame Albanians for his plight. In January 1999, while working as an automobile part importer in Kosovo, he and his family had been ambushed and severely wounded as they were sitting in a car. However, Albanians rescued and took him to a hospital where he received care for his injuries. After this incident, his fear became unbearable and he left with his family for Belgrade.

Rajko said he was not angry with Albanians, because an Albanian had saved his life. But it will be difficult for Serbs and Albanians to become reconciled, he conceded. 'Lots of blood has been shed', and it would take many years for things to be forgotten. He was sympathetic to Albanians who had been excluded from public life in Kosovo by Serbian authorities since 1990. He did not blame the Albanians but rather the Serb politicians and the previous regime, which had mistreated the Albanians. His spark of empathy, however, was doused by the disagreement of virtually all of the others present during our conversation who, while polite, made it clear they were firmly of an opposing view.

This reminded me of a crossroads moment at Pansion Avala. As we were gathered in the foyer of what used to be that resort restaurant outside of Belgrade, the intensity of the anger that was mounting in our discussions was dissipated momentarily by the laughter of small Serb children playing just outside in the snow. The displaced may, indeed, be a lost generation in Serbia. But those children seemed impervious to this tragedy. The answer to the question of whether they can remain apart or whether they will be drawn into the cycle of resentments and ethnic animosities will likely chart the future of peace and conflict in the Balkans.

4

Variations on State Building and Refugees: Myth and Reality

As discussed at the outset of Chapter 3, state building has been an important feature of many international operations which have involved refugees. This chapter opens at the beginning of the 1990s with the peace agreement concerning Cambodia and the ensuing repatriation of over 300,000 refugees from Thailand. Treated then is Haiti, where a refugee emergency in 1994 was the occasion for a US military deployment and subsequent efforts to fortify governance in Haiti, presumably to minimize the prospect of a similar crisis in the future. Finally, at the close of the decade, a crisis in 1999 in East Timor galvanized an international effort to secure refugee return and manage the emergence of a newly independent state in Asia, which this chapter discusses as well. Policies to address forced migration are a key feature of each of these case studies.

Modesty in expectation remains the leitmotif for these examples of international humanitarian action. The international efforts in Cambodia, Haiti, and East Timor add to the weight of the evidence from efforts in the former Yugoslavia. There is a need for reform both in the substance of policy and in how it is organized. These new international involvements have proven messy, complicated, and difficult to quit. Policy needs to be more proactive so that international cooperation and a preventive orientation animate refugee responses. And new capacities are needed within and among governments as well as international organizations if these new state-strengthening objectives are to be seriously pursued in the future.

CAMBODIA

Prior to my visit to Phnom Penh in September 2000, the largest Cambodian city I had ever visited was the sprawl of Site 2, a camp inhabited by some 170,000 Cambodians located just over the border in Thailand. In fact, when I met with Dr Lao Mong Hay, Executive Director of the Khmer Institute of Democracy (KID) in Phnom Penh, he remembered me from a visit to Site 2 in late 1988. The Khmer Institute of Democracy had been founded by the election component of the United Nations Transitional Authority in Cambodia (UNTAC). KID is an NGO which is highly dependent upon international donors, including a number of foreign foundations.

In Site 2, Dr Lao had been the head of the human rights unit of the Khmer People's National Liberation Front (KPNLF). One of his main activities had been the translation and distribution among the camp's inhabitants of the 1948 UN Universal Declaration of Human Rights.

I sat with Dr Lao, a pleasant, scholarly looking man in his nicely appointed office, and we discussed the legacy of UNTAC. He credited UNTAC with facilitating NGO work during its tenure. Dr Lao noted that international pressure remains the principal source of protection for the human-rights NGO community in Cambodia. It is our 'insurance', he explained.

He expressed some optimism in our discussion, saying that past elections had tended to loosen the grip of authoritarian political parties, and he anticipated this trend to continue. However, the social dysfunction of Cambodia was evident. He related a recent conversation with a senior government official who explained that one ministry has 1,400 employees on paper but only 70 employees showing up for work on a regular basis. He was also concerned about recent human rights trends. Vigilante killings of petty criminals were particularly upsetting to him, and had caused him to write to government officials. The authorities are now more responsive to popular opinion, he allowed, but the sense of accountability is embryonic. 'I have lost a bit of my optimism', Dr Lao said.

Cambodia's recent history has been turbulent, involving political intrigue, revolution, and genocide. It was drawn into the Vietnamese war in 1970 with the occupation by Vietnamese forces of north-eastern Cambodia and incursions and bombing by US forces. When the United States pulled out of Vietnam in 1973, conflict between the Khmer Rouge (KR) and the government intensified, resulting in the triumph of the KR in 1975. The reign of the Khmer Rouge was brutal; an estimated 1–2 million Cambodians died as a result of overwork, disease, starvation, and outright killing. Cambodian society was devastated.

In December 1978, Vietnamese forces invaded Cambodia and thousands of refugees fled to neighbouring countries, mostly Thailand. During the period from 1975 to 1979, virtually the whole of Cambodia's urban population and a large portion of those living in the rural areas were displaced or relocated. Repatriation and refugee solutions thus became central to the state-building endeavour in Cambodia.

The UNHCR did not assume responsibility for the border population in this highly politicized and militarized situation. Initially, United Nations Children's Fund (UNICEF) and the International Committee of the Red Cross (ICRC) provided assistance to these displaced populations. In 1992, a new organization, the UN Border Relief Operation (UNBRO), was created to coordinate the provision of food and other services to the border camps.

The camps were separated along the lines of the political factions which administered specific camps. A major offensive by the Vietnamese army in 1984–5, including shelling of the camps, caused the encampments to be relocated to sites further inside Thailand. During the 1980s, these camps became highly militarized and politicized fixtures of the Cambodian resistance.

The end of the cold war created new possibilities in terms of refugee repatriation to Cambodia. In 1989, Vietnam withdrew its forces under the terms of a UN-brokered peace process, with the intense involvement of China, France, the United States, and several countries of the Association of South East Asian Nations. Two years later, in October 1991, the Phnom Penh administration, members of the opposition alliance, and representatives of various governments met in Paris and signed a comprehensive political settlement of the Cambodia conflict. Under the terms of the settlement, Cambodian sovereignty was formally vested in the Supreme National Council, a twelve-person body led by Prince Norodom Sihanouk, on which four Cambodian political factions were represented.

The former communist Phnom Penh regime was represented by the Cambodian People's Party (CPP). The three insurgent factions were the Khmer Rouge, the Khmer People's National Liberation Front, which was represented by the Buddhist Liberal Democratic Party (BLDP), and the royalist *Front uni national pour un Cambodge indépendent neutre pacifique et coopératif* (FUNCINPEC). Pressure on Hun Sen from the Vietnamese, who had lost Soviet assistance, coupled with Chinese pressure on the Khmer Rouge led to the settlement. The KR effectively withdrew from the arrangement shortly after the formal signing, but lost the support of China and progressively Thailand.

Cambodia in 1992 began hosting a UN peacekeeping operation with unprecedented powers. UNTAC's mandate was comprehensive and intrusive, requiring that it supervise the disarmament and the demobilization of armed forces, and organize and conduct elections. UNTAC was to have 'direct control' of areas of governmental activity and to 'supervise and control' the police, coordinate the return and re-integration of refugees and displaced persons, and undertake social rehabilitation.

In practice, UNTAC's actual powers varied greatly. This was due to continuing low-level conflict, a failure to disarm any of the Cambodian factions, and the mission's limited influence on some of the basic structures in the legal system empowered to safeguard the rule of law. At that time, there was virtually no tradition of organized NGO activity.

The return of the border population formed an integral part of the peace agreement. UNHCR was requested by the UN Secretary-General to be the lead agency for the operation and to take over the management of UNBRO. With the establishment of UNTAC, in the beginning of 1992, UNHCR became the repatriation component of UNTAC.

Given the human rights catastrophe that had befallen Cambodia, it seemed appropriate that the mission have a human rights component. However, the rights unit was small and given low priority within the broader mission. Early on, the handful of personnel who staffed the human rights component, which was led by Dennis McNamara from UNHCR, recognized that encouraging the development of local NGOs would be crucial to handing over responsibilities at the end of the mission term. While this was not a primary objective of the mission overall, it was ardently, if not always effectively, pursued by this small group within UNTAC. The human rights component offered financial, technical and administrative assistance to emerging local human rights NGOs, particularly those present in Phnom Penh.

The centrepiece of UNTAC's work from 1991 to 1993 was a technically impressive election. Yet, when UNTAC announced that the royalist FUNCINPEC party and its ally the BLDP had won the election, the incumbent CPP immediately rejected the results, threatening civil war in the eastern part of the country if it was not allowed to retain power. A political settlement was brokered by the king in which there would be a 'two headed' government, led by co-Prime Ministers Norodom Ranariddh (FUNCINPEC) and Hun Sen (CPP). Effective control of the government, police and the military, particularly at the local level, remained with the CPP. In 1997, Hun Sen, who had retained control of large elements of the armed forces, revisited the power-sharing arrangement and unleashed his forces against FUNCINPEC in a violent and bloody *coup d'état*. Hundreds of persons were killed or disappeared.

In late 1993, the human rights component of UNTAC was merged with the UN Centre for Human Rights; this later became the Office of the UN High Commissioner for Human Rights, which in 2000 employed

71 expatriates and Cambodian nationals in Phnom Penh. UNTAC created a trust fund for human rights education programs in Cambodia, which continues to be a source of financing for local NGOs.

There were two refugee repatriations in Cambodia over the past decade. The first repatriation of refugees and displaced persons began on 30 March 1992, and ended 13 months later, in time for the election under the peace agreement. Some 370,000 refugees who returned from the camps of Thailand, and another 150,000 internally displaced persons, were assisted.[1] The electoral imperative behind the settlement necessitated a swift return, which made planning difficult in certain respects. One of the hardest problems encountered involved the plan to provide all returnee families with housing and a two-hectare plot of arable, mine-free land located in the area of their choice. As it turned out, despite early estimates based on satellite photography, it became clear that not enough land was available for returnees in the country's northwest, where most of the refugees registered to return.

Consequently, four alternative assistance packages were developed. The most popular, which was eventually selected by some 85 per cent of the returnees, was a cash grant of $50 per adult and $25 per child paid on arrival in Cambodia. That UNCHR was able to switch plans in the midst of the repatriation operation demonstrated flexibility, but at a price. According to a 1993 UNHCR evaluation of the operation, the 'credibility' of the operation was 'compromised' in the eyes of the refugee population.

The use of cash grants also contributed, to some extent, to the growth of urban poor in Phnom Penh, according to Mu Sochua, the government's Minister of Women and Veterans Affairs. Sochua, who established one of the first NGOs in Cambodia after a stay in the United States, explained that the large homeless population now present in Phnom Penh had been created by a variety of factors, including refugee return. In Cambodia, the poorest of the poor are landless. As confirmed in a 2001 UNHCR draft evaluation, the adjustment from a land to a cash grant programme at levels not sufficient to buy land destined a disproportionate number of returned refugees to be part of Phnom Penh's urban poor.[2] Of course, the alternative—further stay in the austere border camps—would also have taken its toll. Sochua also faulted UNTAC for not sufficiently addressing women's issues in the context of the refugee

[1] United Nations High Commissioner for Refugees, *The State of the World's Refugees: Fifty Years of Humanitarian Action* (New York: Oxford University Press, 2000), 145.

[2] See UNHCR, Geneva (forthcoming, 2001).

operation. The 'high score' UNHCR gave itself in its initial evaluation of the first refugee repatriation thus has to be tempered to some extent.

During the first repatriation, UNHCR and UNDP entered into a cooperative arrangement to establish the Cambodia Area Rehabilitation and Regeneration Project (CARERE), which was designed, in part, to address re-integrative assistance and to begin developmental activity. This effort was modelled on a well-regarded Central American precedent. In Cambodia, however, the effort faltered. 'Assistance and development activities should not be confused', said Scott Leiper, Program Manager of CARERE in Phnom Penh. 'Quick impact projects are not sustainable and are not development', he asserted.

The second refugee repatriation concerned the flight of over 46,000 asylum seekers to Thailand in 1997 and 1998 following the CPP *coup d'état*.[3] The refugees came from several specific places in Cambodia, and the displacement persisted until national elections were held in July 1998, when the remnants of the Khmer Rouge surrendered to the government. In the first part of 1999, UNHCR organized the return of some 36,000 refugees from camps in Thailand.[4] An evaluation by the agency underscores the critical issues of land rights in the second repatriation as a significant political factor which affected the prospect of lasting resettlement.

UNHCR identified the 1990s as the decade of repatriation; but it was also the agency's decade of re-integration experimentation. This activity, one step along the continuum from relief to development, has proved vexing to those seeking to ensure that return is enduring. Based upon experiences in Latin America, UNHCR in Cambodia deployed 'quick impact projects' comprising some 80 projects concerning infrastructure, such as roads, wells, and schools, and involving some 50 implementing partners in relation to the first repatriation. Additionally, some 'small-scale projects'—as UNHCR now prefers to denominate such efforts—were initiated in relation to the second, more recent repatriation from Thailand to Cambodia. In October 2000, UNHCR ended its field operations in Cambodia.

The experience in Cambodia illustrates that the 'gap' between relief and development is not so much a lacuna in a continuum, as it is a completely different conceptual notion. Relief agencies look at quick impact projects as a way to build confidence among returnees and assist them in

[3] US Committee for Refugees, 'Country Report for 1999: Thailand'. At: http://www.refugees.org/world/countryrpt/easia_pacific/1999/thailand.htm

[4] Ibid.

being accepted back by local communities by providing resources to both groups. Such a focus on specific populations and geographical areas, however, is alien to development planners who look broadly at societal sectors and seek to take longer-term perspectives. Returnees and places of return are largely irrelevant to this analysis. Agencies and experts thus largely talk past each other in this discussion.

It may be only now, long after the demise of UNTAC, that there is sufficient stability to make significant progress on development objectives and government accountability. More effort should be invested in developing innovative approaches to confidence building and assisting in avoiding conflicts and tensions in the immediate aftermath of refugee return. Returning refugees in this regard should be seen as human resources for state building.

The most tangible legacy of UNTAC was its contribution to the growth of the NGO sector, which has blossomed over the past several years. UNTAC created an environment in which NGOs in Cambodia could feel reasonably secure in undertaking activities that previously would have been impossible. The human rights NGOs in particular are relatively high-profile and in many ways a leading aspect of civil society. However, other NGOs involved in social services, development, and policy analysis have also emerged in Cambodia. Nevertheless, virtually all of the NGOs are deeply dependent upon international funding sources, whether through multilateral or bilateral channels. Those that have achieved a measure of sustainability have done so because they have created income-generating activities such as selling publications or renting equipment. In this fashion, the NGO sector has also became associated with entrepreneurial skills and activities, and the persons involved in these endeavours represent human capital for Cambodia's future.

The NGOs remain a tangible manifestation of the continuing interest of the international community in Cambodia. Funding of local NGOs, for example, has been an important component of US government support for democratic development in Cambodia. But it is not yet a fully sustainable sector. Oftentimes, Cambodians move from NGO to NGO as they become dependent upon internationally supported structures that remain vulnerable in the impoverished environment of Cambodia. These NGOs are therefore a kind of a greenhouse-nurtured group of entities that may wither if the international community withdraws. Yet, as Thomas Hammarberg, a Swedish diplomat and until 2000 Special Representative of the Secretary-General for Human Rights, told me, a community of indigenous human rights advocates has developed that will be important for the future whatever happens with respect to support from the outside.

A recent controversy involving the human rights NGOs illustrates both their effectiveness and their vulnerability. Some of the most effective local NGOs, as members of the Cambodian Human Rights Action Committee, on 15 August 2000 issued a press release concerning 'the disappearance and killings of about 30 people in May 2000', which it alleged 'were committed by the sub-operational military of the Sonul district, Kratie province'.[5] On 29 August the Minister of National Defense issued a counter-statement denying the involvement of the military in any such killings and threatening to bring a lawsuit against the human rights groups for defamation. Retracting its statement in some respects, the Action Committee released a further statement on 1 September 2000, seeking to clarify the claim. A contemporaneous speech by Hun Sen and press statements from senior government officials severely criticized the Human Rights Action Committee, causing activists to fear an impending governmental crackdown. Two leading activists left the country temporarily out of concern for their safety.

The Cambodian human rights groups agonized over apparent missteps in this dispute, and squabbled a bit among themselves on how to rectify the situation. One prominent human rights leader noted the absence of any supportive public statements by the UN human rights office, and even opined that it would be better for the UN to have raised such a sensitive political and sensitive case with the authorities.

The controversy reflected both the increased advocacy proficiency of the local human rights groups and their vulnerability to official criticism. Human rights violations have littered much of Cambodia's recent past, and are a continuing problem. The prospect of repression is just below the surface in the minds of many of those who are leading the human rights movement in Cambodia.

The record of UNTAC is mixed. The mission helped to create an environment where local NGOs and a combative press could flourish, a strategy that perhaps the international community should have pursued even more directly by enhancing the human rights component in the broader strategy of the UN mission. An organization dedicated to marshalling the expertise of state building, like the SHARE model discussed later in this book, could elaborate such a strategy. UNTAC can clearly take some credit for assisting the development of local NGOs in Cambodia, but they remain largely tied to international largesse and protection, and could disappear if the international community reduced its involvement in Cambodia.

[5] Cambodia: Amnesty International Report 2001'. At: http://web.amnesty.org/web/ar2001.nsf/webasacountries/CAMBODIA?OpenDocument

What then should be UNTAC's measure of success? The election was impressive, but the results were undone by political machinations. The repatriation was effective over the short term, but may have produced unforeseen adverse consequences as well in terms of increasing the numbers of the urban poor. International institutions continue to struggle with the re-integration of refugees. Phnom Penh benefited economically, but the provinces have not reaped similar benefits. The government is still not accountable to the people, and official wrongdoing goes unpunished. Now, $3 billion and a big international effort later, Cambodia fundamentally remains an impoverished and a lawless authoritarian state that will not become a democracy any time soon.

Yet Cambodia has achieved some measure of peace, although communal elections in 2001 and the prospect of national elections in 2003 have caused some observers to worry about polarization and instability. As one international aid worker noted: 'Hun Sen is a poor loser.' A spate of attacks upon human rights workers, the bullying of human rights NGOs, and recent political violence and killings may signal a deteriorating situation.

In socio-economic terms, Cambodia remains desperately poor. The per capita income is $274 and health indicators reflect high levels of infant mortality and low life expectancy.[6] An outcome of impoverished stability would not be very palatable for those in the international community who still seek to justify the effectiveness of such multi-faceted UN endeavours. Yet this 'winning ugly' outcome may be the most realistic scenario for Cambodia's foreseeable future.

HAITI

> 'We feel deceived, with a capital 'D'.'
>
> From an interview of an NGO activist at a training seminar in Port au Prince in June 2000 in response to a question about assessing the effects of the UN mission in Haiti.

Our drive in 2000 up the serpentine road to the Convent of the Sisters of Wisdom (*Soeurs de la Sagesse*) was a relief from the crowds of pedestrians and traffic jams on the road through the Carrefour section of Port au Prince and past the slums of Cité Lumière and Cité Liberté. The dusty

[6] CIA, 'Cambodia'. World Fact Book (2000). At: http://www.cia.gov/cia/publications/factbook/geos/cb.html

browns of the heaps of small buildings and shacks were abruptly transformed into lush green flora. The beautiful grounds of the convent brought to mind what a Haitian woman once said to me: 'Mothers tell their children to become nuns or priests. They live well.'

After we entered the convent complex, we stood for a moment on the veranda admiring the deep blue waters of the outer bay of Port au Prince. When we entered the building, we walked into an ongoing meeting for local Haitian activists organized by the National Coalition for Haitian Rights, one of the premier human rights groups working in Haiti.

The role of the international community in Haiti was the subject of this meeting. Approximately 30 representatives of NGOs from all around Haiti were arrayed around the room in the middle of the morning, listening intently to an animated lecture on the destructive effects of the structural adjustment programmes of the World Bank and the International Monetary Fund. The presentation was a kind of populist rant, interlaced with Marxist slogans. It was not long before 'globalization' was invoked in terms reminiscent of protests in Seattle and Davos, and explained to those assembled as a conspiracy to exploit the peasantry. Deepening socio-economic misery was the result, it was argued, and the forced migration of Haitians an outcome. There was an element of irony in this denunciation. On the ride through Carrefour I had noticed several advertisements for 'internet connectivity' and 'cyber cafes'. Indeed, the newest accessories of the relative handful of prosperous Haitians are the cellular telephones they now carry, including the organizers of this training session. After a brief break for refreshments, the session participants reconvened to a bout of dancing to a song that they had composed with the pointed refrain: 'Forget the IMF.'

Haiti, a former French colony, occupies the western third of the island of Hispaniola, west of the Dominican Republic, and has a population of approximately 8 million persons, out of which 1 million or more live in its capital, Port au Prince. Haiti is desperately poor. About 80 per cent of the population lives in abject poverty; 85 per cent of the population is illiterate.

Haiti became independent in 1804 after a successful slave revolt: a singular event in the history of this human evil. The United States has had a long-standing and somewhat controversial involvement in Haiti. Claiming to restore stability, US troops invaded and occupied Haiti during 1915–34. Interestingly, during this period the United States controlled Haiti's finances, and established and administered public health and public works projects as well as supervised routine governmental affairs. In Haiti's provinces, US Marine Corps commanders actually served as civil administrators. The intrusive role played by the United States in Haiti during this period stands in stark contrast to the trepidation expressed today by many international organizations involved with modern state-building efforts in places such as Bosnia, East Timor, and Kosovo.

The more recent political history of Haiti is no less rife with political intrigue and turmoil. In the 1950s, Haiti saw the rise of a brutal dictator, François Duvalier (Papa Doc) who, after declaring himself president for life, was succeeded in this position in 1971 by his son, Jean Claude (Baby Doc). The mid-1980s was a period of particular turmoil in Haiti, with mass demonstrations against high unemployment, poor living conditions, and lack of political freedom. Brutal attempts followed to suppress protest. A succession of military regimes ruled Haiti after the departure of Baby Doc Duvalier in 1986, which was orchestrated by the United States.

On 16 December 1990, in what was widely reported to be the first free election in Haiti's history, a leftist Roman Catholic priest, Jean-Bertrand Aristide, won the presidency in a landslide victory. Aristide was the leader of a broad network of grass-roots organizations, the 'Lavalas' (flood) movement. When he took office in February 1991, he immediately announced the reorganization of the Haitian army. This commitment to the primacy of civilian government was fateful. In September 1991, President Aristide was deposed and the Haitian military forced him into exile.

The military targeted Aristide's supporters and killed more than 1,000 of them over the two-week period following the *coup d'état* in 1991. During the ensuing reign of terror some 400,000 persons were displaced abroad and internally.[7]

The involvement of the international community changed in response to the military takeover. In September 1992, an Organization of American States (OAS) civilian presence was established with 18 observers. The mission was deployed without vehicles, communications, office space, or even a signed agreement with the de facto authorities. The Haitian military argued that the presence of the mission was illegal, and stated that the security of its members could not be guaranteed. As a result, the OAS mission members were effectively confined to their hotel for several months.

In November 1992, the UN joined the OAS, and in March 1993 a joint international civilian mission to Haiti (MICIVIH) was deployed under the authority of the UN General Assembly. The mission encountered a hostile military-dominated regime, as well as sceptical political parties and NGOs. In this period, serious human rights violations were widespread.

[7] UN Commission on Human Rights, 'Situation of Human Rights in Haiti' (January 1996). At: http://www.unhcr.ch/refworld/un/chr/chr96/country/94-hti.htm

The mission was part of a broader international political strategy designed to address the crisis before a political settlement had been reached. In this connection, the mission had a mandate to monitor and report on rights violations, thereby either to help suppress the incidents by its presence or to encourage international attention and action to deal with the abuses.

The joint international mission established a presence in all of the regions of Haiti within six weeks after arrival. Its mandate was to verify respect for human rights in Haiti, with particular attention to the rights to life, integrity and security of the person, personal liberty, and freedom of association and expression. The mission had to cope with poor infrastructure, abysmal roads, and poor telephone communications. These difficulties were compounded by the effects of the embargo and delays in the procurement of vehicles, laptop computers, and other equipment.

In June 1993, the UN Security Council imposed a fuel and arms embargo and froze Haitian assets abroad. In July, the Haitian military agreed at Governors Island in New York harbour to let Aristide return to Haiti in return for the lifting of the embargo. However, when the deadline for his return passed on 30 October 1993, naval vessels from the United States, with ships from Argentina, Canada, and France, were deployed to enforce the embargo.

The UN mission size fluctuated from a high of 220 in October 1993 to a low of 70 in July 1994.[8] In October 1993, mission observers were temporarily evacuated for security reasons. One Haitian human rights activist recalled of that event: 'We felt that we were being abandoned.' While MICIVIH returned, the UN mission was finally expelled in July 1994.

Ian Martin, the head of the human rights component of MICIVIH, is certain that, as the human rights situation deteriorated in 1994, public reports of the mission figured prominently in the policy deliberations of decision makers, including in the reversal of the US government policy of intercepting and summarily returning Haitian boat people directly to Haiti. President Clinton was said to have quoted from the mission's report in October 1994 in which an Aristide supporter is said 'to have been beaten, and killed with a machete; his face was then sliced off with the machete'.

Ian Martin sees human rights as a separate and distinct but interrelated sector in crisis and post-crisis UN missions. Human rights discussions can sometimes be somewhat theoretical. In Haiti, rights activities were part of the international institutional strategy to respond to the crisis. 'A human rights presence on the ground can improve the

[8] See OAS/UN, MICIVIH, 'International Civilian Mission in Haiti'. At: http://www.un.org/rights/micivih/first.htm

prospects for negotiation', Martin explained when we discussed the issue in 2000. The integration of a rights perspective into a broader political framework can produce dilemmas, but on the whole Martin believes that an integrated approach with the director of a UN human rights mission reporting to a special representative of the UN Secretary-General is 'generally a plus', depending on the personalities, of course. 'The risk is to become marginalized and isolated . . . [or] compromised and corrupted', said Martin. 'Human rights people want it both ways', desiring perhaps unrealistically to be both pure and effective.

According to Martin, the UN human rights mission in Haiti from 1995 onwards built ties with indigenous NGOs which have had a positive legacy. He noted better official mechanisms of accountability and the growth of indigenous NGOs and civil society. 'Some things have made a difference; there is some progress, built slowly and painfully.' Nevertheless, perhaps the single most enduring improvement in Haiti, he allowed, was the destruction of the Haitian army as an instrument of popular repression.

A critical factor in the formulation of US policy was the impact of Haitian refugees who were making their way in small boats to southern Florida. Since the early 1970s, Haiti's identity has been closely linked to migration, whether for political or economic reasons, frequently a combination of both. During this period, Haitian boat people became a testament to state repression and failure, and the bodies of victims periodically washed up on Florida beaches. In 1981, US government detention and high-seas interception programmes were initiated in order to forestall the arrival of Haitian boat people.

There was a corresponding appreciation within the Haitian government of the impact of the Haitian refugee crisis on the United States. 'We understood that this was a powerful card to play against the *coup* leaders', confided a Haitian who had served as a diplomat during this time in the foreign ministry. He acknowledged that it was not clear whether the Haitian government could actually do much to promote the departures, or whether the Haitian military could do much to stem the tide of boat people. 'They were leaving from all over Haiti', he explained. However, he clearly appreciated that the growing haemorrhage of refugees in 1994 was a factor that galvanized an aggressive US response.

After the 1991 *coup*, over the next several months, more than 38,000 Haitians attempted to reach the United States in rickety little boats.[9] Early

[9] US Department of State, 'Background Notes: Haiti' (March 1998), released by the Bureau of Inter-American Affairs. At: http://dosfan.lib.uic.edu/ERC/bgnotes/wha/haiti9803.html

in 1991, the Administration of President George H. W. Bush requested various Caribbean and Central American nations to host Haitian asylum seekers. While Belize, Honduras, Jamaica, Trinidad and Tobago, and Venezuela agreed to provide temporary refuge to small groups of Haitians, these diplomatic efforts ultimately failed mainly because the authorities of those countries did not want them and feared that they would never go home. Eventually, more than 12,000 Haitians encamped at the US naval base at Guantanamo, Cuba, and the US military declared the base full to capacity.[10] Some 10,500 of the Haitians interdicted after the 1991 *coup* were found by US authorities to have a credible fear of persecution and were allowed to enter the United States to apply for asylum.[11]

In May 1992, President Bush ordered the Coast Guard to return Haitians intercepted at sea forcibly without the need for prior inquiry into whether they might be persecuted upon return. The Coast Guard then stopped 31,400 Haitians, a number which fell to 2,400 in 1993. In 1994, however, it rose again to 25,000 after a change in screening policy (discussed below).[12] The UNHCR protested, asserting that the Haitian interdiction programme amounted to *refoulement*—forcible return of a refugee to a place of possible persecution—in violation of the UN refugee treaties.[13]

The political crisis in Haiti persisted throughout the early 1990s, prompting Haitians to flee overland to the Dominican Republic or to attempt a dangerous journey by sea. President Bill Clinton had pledged during his campaign that he would allow boat people to come to the US. As the presidential inauguration approached, word came that boats were being built for 200,000 Haitians to take to the sea after his inauguration. Clinton then quickly announced in January 1993 that his Administration would continue to return Haitian boat people directly to Haiti.

In 1994, the US policy response to Haitian asylum seekers changed once more. On 4 April, President Aristide, while in exile, unilaterally rescinded the 1981 agreement with the United States which purported to allow the interception of Haitians found at sea. One month later, on 8 May, President Clinton announced that Haitian boat people would be interviewed to determine whether or not they should receive refugee

[10] 'White House Statement on Haitian Migrants'. At: http://bushlibrary.tamu.edu/papers/1992/92052400.html. See also Department of Defense News Briefing (25 October 1994). At: http://www.defenselink.mil/news/Oct1994/t102594_t1025asd.html

[11] UNHCR, *State of the World's Refugees*, 177. See also Peters, Philip, 'Fair Welcome for the Haitians', *Washington Times* (29 March 1998). At: http://www.adti.net/html_files/imm/HIATIWT.html

[12] UNHCR, *State of the World's Refugees*, 177.

[13] This proposition is discussed in Chapter 5 below.

protection, estimating that approximately 10 per cent would receive asylum. All others were to be returned to Haiti.

By late June, boat people leaving Haiti had overwhelmed US capabilities to screen their claims on board a designated ship. In response, the Clinton Administration announced on 5 July that the Guantanamo Bay naval base would be used as a safe haven, where about 20,000 Haitians were ultimately held.[14] UNHCR, working with US officials, obtained expressions of interest from Suriname, Belize, and several island nations of the eastern Caribbean to accept Haitian asylum seekers temporarily. Panama agreed to accept up to 10,000 Haitians for temporary stay. But no broader arrangements were made.

Domestic political debates in the United States significantly influenced the ways in which the US government's Haitian refugee policy evolved. In particular, the congressional Black Caucus in 1994 began to agitate against the policy of summarily repatriating Haitians. Randall Robinson, a noted African-American civil rights activist, began a high-profile hunger strike in April 1994, protesting against the repatriation policy. He ended his fast only after the summary return policy was ended in May 1994. The US government at this time began to consider seriously the use of force in Haiti.

In July 1994, as a result of US advocacy, the United Nations Security Council in Resolution 940 authorized 'all necessary means' to restore democracy in Haiti. Within the US government, two plans were prepared for invasion: one based on an 'opposed entry' or armed resistance by the Haitian army, and the other based on a 'permissive entry' or the surrender of the Haitian army. A last-minute diplomatic mission by former President Jimmy Carter, Senator Sam Nunn, and US Army General Colin Powell secured the acquiescence of the Haitian military in a US occupation, even as troop transports were in the air. On 19 and 20 September 1994, US forces, together with a small contingent of troops from various Caribbean Community and Common Market (CARICOM) countries disembarked at Port au Prince and began deploying throughout Haiti.

The difficulty in shifting from the forcible entry to the permissive entry plan complicated the deployment, as many of the troops designed to support the heavier option continued to flow into Haiti and were re-tasked to support permissive entry. Following the arrival of 21,000 US troops, President Aristide returned to Haiti in October 1994.

[14] UNHCR, *State of the World's Refugees*, 177.

The mission of Operation Uphold Democracy was described in a 1995 Joint After Action Report by the US military as:

> . . . to protect US citizens and interests, designated Haitians, and third country nationals; to create a secure environment for the restoration of the legitimate government of Haiti; to conduct operations as required to preserve civil order in Port-au-Prince (at a minimum) and elsewhere as required by emerging events; to provide technical military assistance to the Government of Haiti (GOH); and, on order, to pass responsibility for military operations to the United Nations Mission in Haiti (UNMIH).[15]

With respect to the last point, on 31 March 1995, US forces were placed under the nominal control of Mr Lakhdar Brahimi, Special Representative to the Secretary-General of the United Nations. Upon President Aristide's return, the UN mission was to have a comprehensive mandate, working closely with international financial institutions and integrating UNDP into its efforts to build a functioning state. The human rights component of the mission continued its work with a broadened mandate, including monitoring elections, institutional development—police, prisons, and the judiciary—and local capacity building—NGOs. The mission became increasingly involved in training and technical assistance. Monitoring and reporting were related to institution-building activities in a bid to increase respect for human rights, lay the foundation for the rule of law, and promote the democratic process.

The most recent US military involvement in Haiti produced much reflection. A study conducted under the auspices of the National Defense University on the inter-agency and military-political dimensions of Operation Uphold Democracy in Haiti, asserts at the outset that '[b]y most measures, the Haitian intervention was a success'. The assessment pointed to three factors to support this proposition: 'decapitating' the military dictatorship, restoring the elected president to Haiti, and turning the operation over to UN control in six months. 'All of these were accomplished in good order in which there were very few casualties among either the US forces or the Haitian population.'[16]

Despite the assertion of success, however, the study noted several weaknesses in the US government's capacity to respond to such

[15] United States Atlantic Command, *Operation Uphold Democracy: Joint After Action Report* (JAAR) (Norfolk, VA: June 1995), 3.

[16] Hayes, Margaret and Wheatley, Gary F., *Interagency and Political-Military Dimensions of Peace Operations: Haiti, A Case Study* (Washington, DC: National Defense University, Institute for National Strategic Studies: Directorate of Advanced Concepts, Technologies, and Information Strategies, 1996), 25.

emergencies. For example, US military planners were surprised when their civilian counterparts were not ready immediately to undertake state building programmes. The study noted that there is no US government doctrine that integrates the military component of a complex humanitarian operation with the civilian agencies responsible for assistance. 'Economic assistance operations are not real time because USAID (US Agency for International Development) contracts everything out', said one participant in the National Defense University workshop. This assertion, of course, understates the challenge of civilian development specialists, virtually the remaking of societies.

On the issue of military-NGO relations, the study noted an oft-reported assessment over the past decade:

> ... the workshop recognized that the military and civilian private voluntary organizations (PVOs) have not learned to work together, particularly in developmental programs. Doing so is constrained, *inter alia*, by a real suspicion of one another. One military participant observed, 'We were viewed with complete suspicion by the PVOs because they were concerned about compromising their neutrality. That point of view took us a while to understand. We finally made some progress at the grassroots level. We assisted them when they asked for something or told us what they needed.'[17]

In Haiti, military operations other than war, or 'MOOTW' in military jargon, produced several lessons that seem obvious in hindsight:

> Units operating in a permissive environment require special tactics and training in the use of nonlethal agents for clearing. Grenades and automatic weapon fire are usually undesirable for clearing a room in MOOTW. Covert movement and Night Vision Devices are hampered by traffic lights, vehicular traffic, civilians and dogs in an urban environment ...
>
> In MOOTW the attitudes of the population can be the single largest factor in determining the success of the operation. Psychological Operations act directly on these attitudes and played a significant and continuing role in Operation Uphold Democracy. Openness can build better press relations, and effective press relations can help get the message out ...
>
> The JTF [Joint Task Force] needs a single point of contact for HCA [Humanitarian and Civil Assistance] on the CINC [Commander in Chief's] staff. The CINC should consider establishing a Civil Affairs and Humanitarian Assistance (CA/HA) Coordination Center or Cell during MOOTW. The roles and responsibilities of CA reservists assigned to the CINC staff must be defined.[18]

[17] Hayes and Wheatley, Interagency and Political-Military Dimensions, 40.
[18] United States Atlantic Command, *Operation Uphold Democracy*, 42, 51, 53.

This bureaucratic language cannot mask completely the deep disjunctions between military and civilian humanitarian perspectives in such operations.

In a manner reminiscent of the earlier occupation of Haiti, US Army Reserve civil affairs officers deployed in 1994 and assumed posts in almost every Haitian ministry, and special operations forces undertook civil administration responsibilities throughout the countryside. The National Defense University study noted: 'The complete collapse of local security and police forces was not anticipated.'[19] The need for policing, however, was not accompanied by enabling doctrine, and there was a hiatus which produced a law and order vacuum before international police monitors and indigenous replacement police forces were organized. Indeed, given the security gap, international police were issued side arms in a departure from past practice. The need for a more formal inter-agency planning process was emphasized in the study in order to avoid 'haphazard and incomplete' planning and implementation in inter-agency missions in the future. Presaging later operations in places like Kosovo, the study noted: 'political[-]military planning for civilian agencies needs to parallel military planning, but in lesser detail and with flexible adjustments.'[20]

The Clinton Administration's 'success' in Haiti was the subject of much partisan wrangling. Clinton Administration officials noted the accomplishment of the restoration of democracy. But a Republican-dominated Congress sought to impeach that assertion, including through impugning the good faith of former President Aristide in his quest to rule Haiti. But as the political crisis in Haiti deepened, the Administration and Congress both grew concerned that problems in Haiti could affect the United States and impinge upon its own presidential elections and transition in 2000.

The United States provided the impetus for the international institutional response in Haiti. At the behest of the United States, the UN General Assembly agreed to establish a new international civilian support mission in Haiti (MICAH), with a mandate only until February 2001. According to one UN staff person, the new mission was deployed 'because the Americans want it' and are willing largely to pay for the deployment. As a result, after an initial delay MICAH was funded from US accounts with approximately $20 million in a bureaucratic sleight of

19 United States Atlantic Command, *Operation Uphold Democracy*, 44.
20 United States Atlantic Command, *Operation Uphold Democracy*, 51.

hand without the need for formal agency re-programming or congressional consultation.

MICAH was given a one-year technical assistance mandate dealing with the justice, human rights, and police sectors. The capacities of local NGOs were to be strengthened as well. Given the time needed to recruit and deploy staff, the mission had in reality only some five to six months in which to work until it was withdrawn on 6 February 2001, one day before the inauguration of newly re-elected President Aristide.

The peaceful transfer of power in January 1996 from Jean-Bertrand Aristide to President René Preval marked a historic first in Haiti, providing a glimmer of hope that the nascent democratic system could provide long-term stability. That glimmer, however, has begun to fade in the eyes of many Haitians, whose lot has not improved after audacious promises by the international community. At the same time, increased incidents of random criminal activity and police excesses feed popular suspicions that, while leaders may change, practices remain the same.

Haiti is once more embroiled in an 'ongoing crisis', in the words of a UN expert. While support for continued international engagement is diminishing, the spectre of a new refugee emergency is looming once more. Society has become fractured and polarized. In June 2000, rock-throwing protesters in Port au Prince disrupted traffic and blocked roads with burning barricades. The protesters demanded the immediate publication of the results of Haiti's parliamentary and municipal election held in May. Unofficial results had indicated a landslide victory for the party of former President Aristide, but their accuracy was questioned by independent election monitors. International donor resources are being withheld because of the refusal of the Haitian government to recount the votes.

Aristide and the opposition have continued to squabble. In June 2001, six members of a minor opposition party were arrested on treason and terrorism charges. At that time, approximately 50 Haitians are reported to have sought refuge in the Dominican Republic, alleging political persecution by Aristide supporters.

Collin Granderson, a Trinidadian diplomat and a former director of the OAS-UN international civilian mission in Haiti, analyses the current political crisis and violence in Haiti as a product of the absence of any genuine 'dialogue'. Granderson, who led the UN mission from 1993 to 2000, noted that the quality of leadership and institutional development has been 'slow and uneven'. The international community, moreover, has had 'highly unrealistic expectations'. While progress has been modest, Granderson noted reforms in the security forces, greater accountability, freedom of expression, and political pluralism. Indeed, in

June 2000 Port au Prince was ablaze with banners, posters, and graffiti relating to recent parliamentary elections. Nevertheless, much more needs to be done on the capacity of government structures and NGOs, and the international community needs to remain engaged. Such initiatives, moreover, must cope with deep frustrations. As Granderson puts it, while there is a 'Haiti fatigue' evident in the international community, there is also 'international community fatigue' evident in Haiti.

The turmoil in Haiti has a number of indicators. There are reports of widespread police abuse and scattered political killing. The crime rate is rising, and boat departures are increasing. Official structures have difficulty in coping with the problems. A backlog of criminal cases has developed in the courts. Accusations of corruption are widespread. The police have been implicated in more killings in disputed circumstances in recent years, and the judiciary has increasingly come under pressure from external forces seeking to undermine its independence and impartiality.

The potential for a migration or refugee emergency in Haiti remains high and could be unleashed quickly by a sudden political or economic crisis. According to a UNHCR protection officer in September 2000, at least 2,000 Haitians had left Haiti by boat since January. An internal draft UNHCR contingency plan estimates that some 24,000 Haitians could flee for political reasons in a crisis.

Questions of human security in Haiti loom large. An early response, the organization of the Haitian National Police (HNP), is perhaps the most tangible legacy of the UN mission. Prior to the US intervention, the Haitian police had been an instrument of repression. It had its origins in the infamous *Tonton Macoutes* that Papa Doc Duvalier had organized to help secure his dictatorship. The international civilian police mission was deployed in conjunction with an effort to replace the indigenous police force in order to fill a vacuum in law and order created when US troops arrived in 1994 and the indigenous police force was disbanded. Advisory services were provided through international police monitors, and later in March 1995 under the United Nations Civil Police Mission in Haiti, which on 21 February 2000 comprised 219 officers from ten countries who were stationed in Haiti.

The Haitian National Police represents the first truly civilian, national security force in Haiti's 200-year history. Organized under a law enacted in October 1994, HNP candidates, including a few women, began training in January 1995. The application process was very competitive and the candidates received four months of instruction on a variety of subjects concerning law, investigations, and policing. Instructors came from Canada, France, Norway, and the United States.

But the police in Haiti have come under a variety of new pressures, which may substantially reduce their ability to enforce the law: a troubling prospect in the current political turmoil. An increase in criminal activities associated with the drug trade and gang violence committed by offenders who have been deported after residing for many years in Miami and elsewhere in the United States are only two aspects of the challenge. An important part of the problem concerns the HNP itself. The HNP has fewer than 4,000 police in 2002, down from a high of 6,000. Those who remain work twelve-hour shifts seven days a week. While their hours have increased, their pay has been reduced to the equivalent of about $250 a month.

The Petionville branch of the HNP is housed in a slightly dilapidated building; its peeling white paint reflects the early stages of neglect. The police station overlooks a plaza dominated by the Catholic church of St Peter. Petionville, an enclave of relatively prosperous Haitians, is located on the hills above the steamy impoverishment of Port au Prince. It is relatively luxurious duty for the police. But in 2000 there are signs of trouble brewing even in Petionville.

'We are the victims', explained Jean-Marie Jean-Rose, a pleasant and earnest 29-year-old policeman at the Petionville station who lives with his parents in Petionville. 'We were told we would be able to be professionals, but we are being squeezed by long shifts and low pay. Many police have quit.' Jean-Rose, who has been a policeman for five years, had studied to be a civil engineer. He had hoped to pursue his engineering studies after joining the police, but had been disappointed because of lack of time and opportunity. 'Some police leaders with less education try to limit our advancement', he explained. Similar sentiments were echoed by police stationed elsewhere in Port au Prince.

Perhaps the most revealing insight into the deteriorating morale among the Haitian police came from Pierre—not his real name—a 29-year-old officer in a special 350-person rapid reaction and crowd control unit stationed near the National Palace in Port au Prince. Pierre declined to give his last name out of fear that his superiors might discipline him for what he was about to say in 2000. The members of this special unit are adorned in light grey paramilitary uniforms and drive around in ominous-looking black land cruisers. The government had sought to invest the unit with an *esprit de corps*, but Pierre said that he had been 'deceived' by the twelve-hour daily shifts and reductions in pay. However, his main concern was the way that his pro-Aristide neighbours had 'targeted' him as a representative of the government. Three officers in his unit had been killed recently under mysterious circumstances, and he was now planning to move his residence. He believed that the police had been given instructions not to interfere with certain political activities, citing as an example the violent demonstrations in June 2000 in Port au Prince over parliamentary election results. However, he said that he found the political situation very difficult to understand. Pierre, who had studied economics at the university level for two years, said that he planned to quit the police force as soon as he could find another job.

Patrick Rene, the Inspector General of the Haitian National Police, in 2000 was the senior official in the Haitian government responsible for investigating complaints of police abuse. Rene's office is located in a sprawling hill-top mansion which had belonged to a former notorious *Macoute*. According to Rene, a lawyer, the HNP has become 'more professional', although he acknowledged that it was experiencing 'lower morale', particularly after the twelve-hour shifts were introduced in 1997 and 1998. He admitted that 'corruption' existed in the HNP and that many killings of police were likely attributable to the involvement of those killed in 'illicit activities', such as the burgeoning trade in drugs which are trans-shipped through Haiti. A statistical report provided by Rene reveals that, from November 1995 to March 2000, 75 police officers had been 'assassinated' or killed on duty and one had been 'poisoned'; ten had committed 'suicide'. The HNP was the *avant-garde* of reform in Haiti, but as a measure of success this state-strengthening legacy of the UN and OAS missions is increasingly vulnerable. Over the long term, it is doubtful that the HNP can exist in a vacuum and remain impervious to destructive dynamics in the surrounding society, and Haiti is once more a society in crisis.

There has been some progress in police and prison reform efforts in Haiti. The Haitian judicial system, however, is characterized by systemic weaknesses, according to a July 2000 UN report, which found lack of independence and failures of due process.[21] The successful prosecution of the police chief and some senior officers for murders committed in May 1999 in Kafou Fey causes some commentators to be hopeful. Convicting a sitting Haitian police officer for a serious crime was a first, but the sentences imposed—three years of imprisonment and $1,180 in fines—were relatively light.

The police and prison bureaucracies were eliminated and rebuilt from scratch after the return of President Aristide. The judiciary, on the other hand, is largely populated with personnel who were already

[21] UN Doc A/55/154, p. 8.

in place, and who are imbued with customs, traditions, and values derived from an earlier time. Political influence and corruption are rampant, in the eyes of UN experts. Also, some donor efforts have clearly gone astray. The US television news programme *60 Minutes* in 1999 profiled a USAID project that had largely wasted $1 billion on ineffectual efforts to enhance the Haitian judicial system. The Haitian authorities do not conceal their anger with the international community's efforts.

Camille Leblanc, Haiti's Minister of Justice and Public Security, returned from his studies in France in 1986 after Baby Doc Duvalier's departure. A successful private lawyer and civil rights advocate, Leblanc founded a lawyers' association, which offered free legal services to indigent persons. He has also published compilations of laws in Creole for the use of the poor. Leblanc took the risky route of defending supporters of President Aristide who were prosecuted after the 1991 *coup*. Given the looming crisis in Haiti, he joined the government at the request of Aristide in 1999 after rebuffing his overtures twice before.

Leblanc greeted us at his beautifully appointed palatial home in Port au Prince, where we sat in an expansive drawing room. He disputed the UN's assessment about the failures of the justice system. 'Because Canada, France, and the United States invested so much money in the Haitian National Police, they have to say that it is working very well', he explained. 'They blame the failures on the justice system. No one wants to admit that they have failed.' The justice system in his view has become a 'scapegoat for donors'. But he was not uniformly negative. He cited the work of a magistrates' school as evidence of progress, and he noted that a discrete programme in 1997 by the Canadian government to build court facilities had been 'extremely positive'. Resource limitations and low morale are facts of life for the judiciary, he noted, and corruption is endemic. But Leblanc was philosophical: 'a society in perpetual crisis cannot make progress.' Nor is the international community the answer. 'MICAH is failing before it has started', he observed in 2000.

Indigenous human rights NGOs in Haiti are not yet capable of performing the monitoring and reporting role envisaged by MICAH, according to UN officials there. But the NGO community has grown and obtained 'some results' with human rights education, according to Pierre Esperance, who runs the Haiti office of the National Coalition for Haitian Rights. When the people know the limits of the authorities' power, and the authorities know they know, human rights violations are reduced, he explained. Esperance knows what he is talking about. On 8 March 1999, he was shot and seriously wounded as he was driving near his Port au

Prince office. The assailants have not yet been apprehended. Esperance received new round of threats in March 2000. He continues his work but says, 'I have to be careful.'

Overall, the legacy of the UN mission in Haiti is at best mixed, in the eyes of NGO activists. Jocelyn McCalla, the New York-based director of the National Coalition for Haitian Rights, credited the UN human rights mission with having helped the local NGO sector. There had been 'very small steps' taken, and the NGOs were 'better organized'. Nevertheless, he saw many lost opportunities, with the UN having failed to build the capacity of local NGOs who could then step in after the mission departs. We need 'sustainability in the area of human rights', he said. There should be less dependence on the international community and more self-reliance. A strong civil society sector is a prerequisite, according to McCalla, who added optimistically: 'It's not too late.'

Approximately $3 billion has been committed by international donors to establish democracy and improve the socio-economic situation in Haiti. Yet Haiti remains deeply troubled. The future of democracy there is uncertain, and crushing poverty afflicts the vast majority of the population. The Haitian National Police, the UN mission's most tangible legacy, is slowly disintegrating. The NGO community is embryonic and fragile. An organization such as SHARE, discussed in detail later in this book, could have developed plans for an integrated approach to reform the justice system and sought to better harness the energy of the independent sector.

Decision makers desirous of concrete change must take heed of what many Haitians have called their 'Haitian reality'. The UN civilian mission had ambitious plans for Haiti. But the reality was sobering. In 2000, a Haitian school teacher, who worked as a translator for the UN, assessed the UN effort, saying 'they just scratched the surface'. It takes a very long time and constant effort, and we court disappointment if we think that there are quick fixes. The efforts of the UN mission in Haiti teach a simple lesson: that the expectations related to state-strengthening endeavours must be astutely realistic and modest. They also must be anticipatory and preventive in their orientation if they are to help avert a new refugee emergency.

EAST TIMOR

On the eve of the first anniversary of the 30 August 1999 vote, approximately 100 human rights workers gathered for a buffet meal organized by the UN human rights office at one of the new restaurants that cater to foreigners in Dili, the capital of East Timor. The dinner commemorated the local staff members of the United Nations Mission in East Timor (UNAMET) who had been killed in the violence that followed the balloting. The UNAMET staff of 700 had been augmented to nearly 4,000 to monitor the 1999 election.

It was a steamy evening in Dili, and we sat around tables under dim neon lighting open to the night air. The guest speaker was Ian Martin, who had served as the Special Representative of the Secretary-General and head of UNAMET.

Martin was clearly happy to be back in Dili. While he noted the many destroyed buildings, he was most impressed by the 'faces of people'. The 'biggest and most satisfying difference I observe is their smiles', he explained. In his address, Martin described the chronology of UNAMET's work to register voters and oversee the balloting in August 1999. He portrayed the agony he felt in addressing the difficult decisions of when or whether UN personnel should be evacuated as the violence escalated. When the decision was finally taken to withdraw UN staff in Dili, UNAMET evacuated its local staff as well to Darwin, a first for a UN mission. This point was not forgotten by the East Timorese people, who cheered Martin when he spoke the next day at the official commemoration of the 30 August vote.

UNAMET was a mission with a cause: to organize and facilitate an independence vote. Its staff included many persons with established interests in East Timor who had a commitment to seeing its dream of self-determination realized, according to Francesc Vendrell, who as head of the Asia section of the UN's Department of Political Affairs had selected the mission members. UNAMET was administered by the Department of Political Affairs at the Secretariat. Vendrell was the architect of UN involvement in the negotiations concerning East Timor and the driving force for the ballot.

For Vendrell, who subsequently became a special envoy for the Secretary-General's in Afghanistan, UNAMET was one in a series of missions in which human rights objectives were dominant. Indeed, Vendrell is perhaps the person most responsible for promoting human rights elements in peacekeeping operations, and he cited earlier UN missions in El Salvador, Guatemala, and Haiti as precedents. One can see these UN deployments as 'progressive', said Vendrell, since 'now a human rights component is required in missions'. On the other hand, he allowed, they are 'retrogressive' in the sense that often human rights components are still regarded as an afterthought, albeit a necessary one, in international deployments.

The subsequent United Nations Transitional Administration in East Timor (UNTAET) mission was much larger than UNAMET, and it was assembled with haste and a much broader set of responsibilities associated with state building. Mission members had relatively little knowledge of East Timor, rendering UNTAET's mission commitment and morale comparatively more mixed. UNTAET is administered by the Department of Peacekeeping Operations at the UN Secretariat in New York.

It was clear at the commemorative dinner in Dili in 2000 that Martin had been devastated by the loss of the lives of his local staff in UNAMET. Such missions are led by human rights generals who must come to terms with the prospect of loss of life where human right deployments are at the leading edge of international action. It obviously helps to believe in the cause, and Martin admitted to thousands of onlookers at the official ceremony on 30 August 2000 that the day of the ballot was 'the most rewarding day of our lives'. The evening before, however, he was a bit more reflective in that dimly lit restaurant: 'The biggest question is was it all worthwhile? This is a question to be answered by the people of East Timor.'

Under International Administration

The flight from Denpasar, Indonesia, to Dili was an international departure, reflecting the new status of East Timor. It had the feel of a commuter flight for international officials, journalists, aid workers, and off-duty peacekeepers. This was the week of the first anniversary of the independence vote. Sergio Vieira de Mello, the head of UNTAET and de facto governor of East Timor, boarded the plane just before take-off and was seated in the first row. The other passengers were a polyglot group from nations around the world on their way to this international project to rehabilitate a devastated East Timor. As the flight progressed, many of the passengers nearby pulled out thick files and began preparing for the next week of work in East Timor, a tiny island located south of the Equator 1,300 miles east of Jakarta and 150 miles northwest of Darwin, Australia.

Approaching the first anniversary of the independence vote, Dili conveyed a sense of anarchy and a chaotic exuberance. The anarchic dimension was reflected well by the Darwinian state of automobile traffic. Traffic lights were not working and signs went hardly noticed as drivers jockeyed for position on the few streets of Dili. A few traffic officers went through the motions of directing vehicles, to scant effect. From the airport we drove warily to the container ship which would be my home for the next week. We passed many devastated buildings still standing empty after the destruction of a year ago.

Massive security deployments were evident near the civilian police headquarters and other strategic locations. The first anniversary of independence was considered to be a possible target for the anti-independence 'militias' who had sacked Dili after the vote and then fled to West Timor where they continued to harass would-be returnees.

The sense of anticipation and excitement relating to the forthcoming anniversary of the independence vote was manifested by the Congress of the National Council for Timorese Resistance (CNRT), an umbrella group of East Timorese political parties which had been meeting since 20 August. The president of the CNRT, Xanana Gusmao, and its vice-president, Nobel peace prize co-laureate José Ramos Horta, were deeply involved in the increasing complexity of East Timorese political life. They had just announced their resignations from the CNRT, only to reconsider them at the urging of the hundreds of CNRT delegates present. The strongest political party under CNRT's umbrella, Fretilin (Frente Revolucion Elria Do Timor Lese Independente), was bidding for more influence. Indeed, Fretilin won 55 of 88 seats in the 2001 constituent assembly elections.[22] Swirling in the political discourse were issues such as the future official language of East Timor—whether it should be Portuguese, Tetun, English, or Indonesian—and differences between younger political leaders and more established ones who had been in exile during the Indonesian occupation.

The 'frozen' politics of 1975, when the independence movement was born in violence in East Timor, casts a long shadow. UN political analysts noted the relative immaturity of the East Timorese political debate. It was a kind of extended electoral campaign, with the September 2001 parliamentary elections to be followed by the drafting of a constitution. The first president could very well be Gusmao, a former commander of the Timorese guerrilla force (Falintil). This is so notwithstanding the fact that he had stepped back from public life when the CNRT was dissolved in June 2001.

A 'civic education campaign' is needed, one UN analyst noted. The context is a highly political culture fostered in resistance to acute repression. The consultative council established by UNTAET was neither fully representative nor democratic in the sense that it was subject to an absolute veto by the UN. But the process of consultation and deliberation was

[22] 'East Timor: Constituent Assembly Inaugurated; New Cabinet Delayed', *UN Wire* (17 September 2001). At: http://www. unfoundation.org/unwire

designed as a 'training ground' for democracy, presenting a basic dilemma for the international community: is it possible to impose from the top down a bottom-up democratic tradition?

The question of refugee return was important to Vieira de Mello, who saw the issue in security terms. The existence of refugee camps just across the border in West Timor could serve as a recruitment resource and breeding ground for an insurgency of those opposed to independence for East Timor. The camps were thus a major security threat to East Timor and the elimination of those camps and the dispersal of the associated concentrations of disaffected populations on the border were a high priority.

Vieira de Mello was also extremely concerned about the increasing sophistication and abilities of the militia elements which had infiltrated back into East Timor. Intelligence reports indicated that there were more such elements over the border in West Timor, and it was clear to him that investments were being made in their training and ability to make such incursions, which sometimes had deadly consequences. Two UN peacekeepers were killed in fire fights in 2000.

Vieira de Mello noted that the mission in East Timor was unlike any other UN mission. Here, he had complete control, including over the military. However, when I asked him whether he could order the military to undertake various actions, he answered with only a qualified 'yes'. In such a multinational force, national capitals had an effective veto. In particular, he cited the example of a militia element that he had wanted to attack in the Portuguese sector. This had not yet happened because Lisbon was concerned that its soldiers would return in body bags.

Evolution of the Mission

There are many external influences at play in East Timor. When Indonesia declared independence from the Netherlands in 1945, East Timor remained a Portuguese colony. When Portugal surrendered its colonies, violent conflict broke out between contending indigenous political factions, a division still evident today. Indonesia then invaded in 1975 and occupied East Timor.

The United Nations Security Council in Resolution 383 of 22 December 1975 called upon 'the government of Indonesia to withdraw without delay all its forces from the territory' of East Timor, and further urged 'the government of Portugal as administering power to cooperate fully with the United Nations so as to enable the people of East Timor to exercise freely the right to self-determination'.[23] In the late 1980s, guerrilla resistance shifted to an *intifada*-type urban uprising, which led in 1991 to over 250 demonstrators being killed or wounded by the Indonesian army in a massacre at the Santa Cruz cemetery in Dili.[24] International attention followed in 1996, when Catholic Bishop Carlos Ximenes Belo and resistance leader José Ramos Horta jointly received the Nobel Peace Prize. Insurgent activities continued and escalated in East Timor in the latter part of the 1990s.

A change of government in Indonesia in 1998 created new political possibilities in the region, and in August 1998 diplomats from Portugal, Indonesia, and the United Nations began discussions. Indonesia proposed granting wide-ranging autonomy to East Timor. The territory would first be given the option of agreeing to autonomy within Indonesia. If that were rejected, however, the province could become independent.

From January 1999 onward, militias supported by the Indonesian army began to engage in a growing campaign of violence in East Timor as part of a campaign to influence the outcome of the vote. A framework agreement on 5 May 1999 between Portugal and Indonesia entrusted the United Nations with the organization and conduct of the referendum. On 7 May, the Security Council mandated UNAMET to conduct a 'popular consultation' on the acceptance or rejection of a framework for autonomy for East Timor within the Republic of Indonesia. The agreement had three phases: first was the run-up to the balloting, second was the period in which the election results would be acted upon by the Indonesian parliament, and third was the time when an international peacekeeping force would be deployed. The Indonesian security forces would be the guarantor of security until the international force was in place.

The 'popular consultation'—in effect a referendum on independence—took place in a climate of escalating violence on 30 August 1999. UNAMET registered 451,792 potential voters, and on the day of the vote, defying the intimidation, nearly 99 per cent of the registered East Timorese turned out to cast their vote. More than 78 per cent—344,580—voted to reject autonomy, thus beginning a process of transition to independence.[25]

The voting was marred by militia violence and the killing of UN poll workers. Following the announcement of the ballot results, the militia began a rampage throughout East Timor, destroying buildings and city centres in Dili and elsewhere. Hundreds of people were killed in the

[23] The text of Resolution 383 is at: http://www.un.org/documents/sc/res/1975/75r384e.pdf

[24] UNHCR, *State of the World's Refugees*, 236.

[25] Ibid.

campaign of violence, and 540,000 people out of a population of 880,000 were either internally displaced or became refugees in West Timor.[26] The Indonesian military and militias began rounding up East Timorese and transporting them to West Timor. The majority of residents lost their houses, possessions, and savings. The UN immediately announced that it was withdrawing from East Timor. The evacuation was delayed, however, by the presence of some 1,500 East Timorese who had taken shelter at the UN headquarters compound. The UN staff left in the early hours of 14 September, taking the locals with them.

A UN Security Council mission visited Jakarta and Dili, and the Secretary-General worked to rally support among member states for deployment of a multinational force. Indonesia initially resisted calls to allow a peacekeeping force in East Timor, but as a result of outside government pressure it agreed on 15 September to accept such a force. The Security Council authorized the International Force for East Timor (INTERFET) to restore peace and security under a unified command structure led by Australian forces.

The wanton destruction began to subside only with the arrival of the multilateral force on 20 September, in the face of which the Indonesian militia and army withdrew. But East Timor was completely destroyed. Over the preceding three weeks, 70 per cent of public and private buildings were rendered unusable.[27] A variety of services, systems, and institutions were disrupted, such as water, electricity, telephone and telecommunications, public services, health and hospital services, banking, business, and the police. East Timor was plunged into a catastrophic pre-modern situation.

The path to this catastrophe describes the limits of international action. The architecture of the framework agreement raised concerns from the outset about the prospect of deteriorating security, particularly after the 30 August ballot. There were many warnings that pro-Indonesia militia forces would engage in violence if the vote favoured independence, but observers were surprised by the severity and duration of the violence and by the 'scorched earth' policy which followed the announcement of the results of the ballot.

Much remains to be done, of course, by the international community in East Timor. But one lesson that can be drawn is the importance of more intrusive engagement by the international community in early

[26] UNHCR, *State of the World's Refugees*, 237.

[27] 'East Timor's Scourge Serves Time on His Patio', *The New York Times* (16 May 2001), A4.

phases of negotiating the political framework as a preventive strategy in such situations. While held under United Nations auspices, the negotiations over East Timor were conducted primarily between Indonesia and Portugal. A more proactive involvement by Australia or the United States in this phase might have helped to insert provisions in the agreement to encourage more robust security guarantees, including the prospect of a pre-emptive international deployment, which in turn may have helped to avert the abuses that then occurred.

But it is far from clear whether this lesson is learnable. According to one Portuguese diplomat familiar with the negotiations, the UN Secretariat had attempted to identify specific benchmarks for security in the course of negotiation. What was missing was the 'political will' to introduce such specifics into the negotiations. Security deteriorated as UNAMET began to register voters and oversee the count, but the framework had been fixed: Indonesia was the guarantor of security. The wholesale violation of this guarantee finally galvanized the international intervention led by Australia.

At the outset of the emergency, a large-scale humanitarian relief effort was undertaken by the United Nations, and increasing attention was given to the voluntary repatriation of the approximately 250,000 East Timorese who had initially fled to West Timor and elsewhere.[28] To finance the relief effort, a consolidated inter-agency appeal for $199 million was launched on 27 October 1999. UNAMET re-established its headquarters in Dili on 28 September, and on 19 October Indonesia formally recognized the result of the consultation. Shortly thereafter, on 25 October, the UN Security Council by Resolution 1272 established the United Nations Transitional Administration in East Timor (UNTAET) as a multi-dimensional peacekeeping operation responsible for the administration of East Timor during its transition to independence. UNTAET was to be supported by approximately 11,000 personnel, including 9,000 troops, and it was given full executive authority over administrative, legal, and judicial matters in East Timor. Sergio Vieira de Mello, the UN's Emergency Relief Coordinator, was chosen by the Secretary-General to administer East Timor.

UNTAET's mandate consists of providing security and maintaining law and order throughout the territory, establishing an effective administration, assisting in the development of civil and social services, ensuring the coordination in the delivery of humanitarian assistance as well as rehabilitation and development assistance, supporting capacity building

[28] UNHCR, *State of the World's Refugees*, 237.

for self-government, and assisting in the establishment of conditions for sustainable development. Military operations were handed over from INTERFET to UNTAET on 28 February 2000.

The mandate of UNTAET gave the Special Representative of the Secretary-General complete administrative, legislative, and judicial authority. Three 'pillars' were established: military, humanitarian and governance, and public administration. Benchmarks were established for the transitional administration: ensuring security, establishing a credible system of justice, achieving a minimum reconstruction of public services and infrastructure, establishing a civil administration that is financially sustainable, and managing a political transition to independence, including the adoption of a constitution and democratic elections.

From the beginning, UNTAET worked with the CNRT umbrella of East Timorese political parties, along with other East Timorese leaders on the National Consultative Council (NCC). By August 2000, the NCC had already approved 31 regulations which serve as the legal basis for governance and administration in East Timor. Humanitarian assistance was delivered to the devastated country's population in coordination with local CNRT representatives working at the sub-district level. In Dili, the CNRT organized working groups that corresponded to the sectoral activities of the UN mission.

This governing structure was revised in July 2000 because of concerns that it was not representative of East Timorese society and not transparent in its deliberations. The restructured effort was designed to give more responsibility to a wider range of East Timorese. Internally, UNTAET has formed a new cabinet structure with eight cabinet members, four Timorese, and four international staff. The NCC was replaced by a new 33-member, all East Timorese National Council, with members from all segments of East Timorese society selected by Vieira de Mello.

The international community proved to be relatively proficient at providing humanitarian relief. In East Timor, the humanitarian sector is 'perhaps the area in which most progress has been made to date', said Vieira de Mello in his 27 June 2000 report to the UN Security Council. The UNTAET humanitarian pillar was consolidated with the governance pillar at the end of 2000.

But even the humanitarian response faced difficulties. An external review of the humanitarian operation conducted in May 2000 found several weaknesses. The absence of a clear exit and transition strategy posed complications when NGOs proposed to move from emergency to longer-term development activities. But, in the absence of functioning governmental structures, UNTAET asked NGOs to remain to undertake these responsibilities for an unspecified period of time. The gap between relief and development was manifested in a particularly sharp way in this setting with the absence of functioning state structures.

Initially, there was an effort to use NGO standards—the Sphere Project, a collection of indicators created by a consortium of NGOs—and the Red Cross code of conduct to ensure quality control in humanitarian responses. However, there was no monitoring of the application of these standards, and no evidence was found that humanitarian actors reviewed their activities in light of the principles. These standards remained essentially a statement of good intentions and not operational criteria for agencies in East Timor.

The evaluation of the consolidated appeal process in East Timor demonstrated that, while the process had some utility for donors, it was less attractive to international agencies and NGOs. The appeal was a static planning document. NGOs were particularly disappointed, and those who did not receive funding under the process stated that they would not participate again.

Nor was there a framework agreement established between UN agencies or international NGOs that worked with local entities to ensure East Timorese participation. While language barriers and lack of qualifications were significant constraints, efforts to incorporate East Timorese obviously will be crucial to a successful hand-over of UNTAET's administration and the facilitation of the process of state building.

State building is not possible without a measure of security. As CNRT vice-president José Ramos Horta emphasized when we met in August 2000, East Timor's greatest need is 'security, security, security'. The deployment of peacekeepers heralded an initial measure of security. However, new security concerns have been created by renewed activities by pro-integration militias that had infiltrated into East Timor from West Timor, coupled with the precarious situation of the remaining refugees in West Timor who are subject to intimidation by militia elements.

Upwards of eight militia groups with 100 to 150 members had infiltrated into various regions of East Timor in 2000. According to Vieira de Mello, militia fighters arrested in East Timor had provided information that there were significant forces present in West Timor. Former East Timorese militias are reorganizing with 'the help of rogue elements of the Kopassus', the Indonesian military intelligence service, and, according to Vieira de Mello, 'it appears that militias are better coordinated now than they were a few months ago and seem to be operating under unified command in West Timor'. This assessment about more capable militia activities in East Timor was shared by US Ambassador to Indonesia Robert Gelbard, and Lieutenant-General Boonsrang Niumpradit, a Thai officer and the UN force commander in East Timor.

Nevertheless, there are continuing pressures from troop-contributing governments to reduce the peacekeeping force. According to Gelbard, the United States has a small 20-person contingent which rotates, bringing differing expertise into the setting as needed. Recently, for example, combat engineers were rotated to undertake activities related to infrastructure rehabilitation. Ultimately, the plan is for the former guerrilla force, Falintil, to become a key part of the defence force for East Timor.

Lieutenant-General Niumpradit had been in East Timor for five weeks when I met with him in 2000. Niumpradit, who attended the United States Military Academy at West Point, New York, has achieved some measure of fame in Thailand by virtue of the unusual character of his assignment. This is the first command by a Thai general of such a mission. He was very comfortable with his assignment, explaining that the Thai military, unlike military forces in countries like the United States, were accustomed to undertaking development-related activities to help poor people. Nevertheless, the challenges of commanding a multinational force were similar to those in other peace-building operations. Twenty-four countries were contributing troops to the multinational force in East Timor with some 7,800 troops. According to Niumpradit, it was impossible to move troops from one sector to another without permission from national contingent commanders, who reported directly to their home capitals.

The refugee return issue has become situated squarely in the environment of insecurity in East Timor. The UNHCR established a presence in West Timor in October 1999. As of July 2000, approximately 80,000 to 130,000 persons who had fled from East Timor remained in camps and other shelter arrangements in West Timor.[29] The absence of precision in the number of refugees was due to the lack of access by international agencies to survey the population.

Security concerns were echoed by the Indonesian Minister for Foreign Affairs, Alwi Shihab, in a speech in Jakarta in August 2000. He noted that, beyond the humanitarian dimension, charges of intimidation and violence committed by armed individuals against refugees, problems between them and the local population, and cross-border issues presented a bundle of serious security questions. In terms of magnitude, the foreign minister explained in 2000 that, of the 200,000 refugees in West

[29] Ibid.

Timor, about 130,000 were left in West Timor.[30] Shihab asserted that constraints on return went beyond questions of security in the camps, and included lingering doubts about the quality of security and prospects for economic survival if the camp inhabitants chose to repatriate to East Timor. For that reason, he opined, the shortcomings in resolving the issue were not exclusively the responsibility of Indonesia, but must be shared by others, including UNTAET. Indonesia has said that it would close the camps that are closest to the borders, but has urged the establishment of transit camps both in West Timor and East Timor to deal with those who wish to move. Shihab called in his speech for international assistance to implement this plan.

On the refugee return question, René van Rooyen, Regional Representative for UNHCR, noted that the Indonesian government had promised a variety of measures to remedy the militarization of camps in West Timor, but 'had done nothing'. He was 'very pessimistic' that real progress would be made on these issues. He feared that if international pressure were brought to bear on Indonesia there could be a panic reaction 'to bring in the troops'. This could have catastrophic consequences, in his view. However, a representative of the Jesuit Refugee Service (JRS) noted that 42,000 East Timorese had returned in November 1999 without serious problems. JRS as well as the UN civilian police have been seeking information from UNHCR about where returnees are relocating within East Timor in order to work with the local population to prevent violence upon return.

My conversations in Dili in August 2000 had been preceded by ominous signs of insecurity for humanitarian workers. Earlier that month, three UNHCR workers had been severely injured in an attack in West Timor by militia elements, and UNHCR had suspended its operations. This incident followed a series of incidents beginning in June 2000, which resulted in a decision in August by UNHCR and the International Organization for Migration to suspend repatriation activities in West Timor. The question of whether to resume operations was at the time of my visit a topic of intense debate between political figures and humanitarians. Gelbard and Vieira de Mello urged that operations not be resumed in order to have leverage with Indonesia on the issue of security. But UNHCR wants to 'play humanitarian again', said Gelbard, who ultimately proved to be tragically right. UNHCR resumed operations in West Timor on 29 August, and one week later three UNHCR international staff

[30] 'Remarks by H. E. Dr. Alwi Shihab Minister for Foreign Affairs of the Republic of Indonesia on the Question of East Timorese Refugees in West Timor'(Jakarta: Department of Foreign Affairs, 15 August 2000).

were brutally murdered by militia elements in Atambua, West Timor, prompting the refugee agency to withdraw all of its staff from West Timor.

An internal UN review examined the process by which the decision was made to resume activities in West Timor on 29 August. The review report was critical of the fact that, despite the obvious political sensitivity, there was no single UNHCR official within the region with exclusive and sole responsibility for decisions affecting programmes and staffing in both East and West Timor. The review found further that, while there were no clear warnings of an impending attack, too many UNHCR staff were present in West Timor, and that a 'serious error of judgment' had been made when, in view of the indications of insecurity of the situation, UNHCR officials did not insist on the evacuation of staff to the local Indonesian army compound in Atambua.

UNHCR'S Staff Council disagreed with the conclusion of the internal review that, 'short of a serious security incident', the agency probably could not have remained out of West Timor. 'If three UNHCR staff almost being killed does not qualify as a serious incident, then what would?' This was a reference to the earlier physical attack on staff. The Staff Council concluded that no UNHCR staff should have been present in Atambua on 6 September.

In September 2001, an Indonesian court sentenced six men to prison terms from 10 to 20 months for the UNHCR staff killings.

Reports of hunger among the refugees in West Timor followed the withdrawal of international assistance. Since the UNHCR withdrew, a trickle of East Timorese refugees have continued to return on their own from West Timor, reporting continuing control and intimidation by militia elements.

An IOM registration exercise in 2001 which indicated that 97 per cent of East Timorese refugees wished to stay in Indonesia was denounced as a 'sham' by José Ramos Horta. In September 2001, UNHCR and IOM agreed to resume helping refugees return to East Timor, with UNHCR insisting on security guarantees before re-establishing operations in West Timor.[31] Approximately 2,500 refugees returned in the first week of September 2001.[32]

While the security issues are immediate, perhaps the greatest long-term challenges UNTAET faces are in the responsibilities of governance

[31] 'West Timor: UNHCR Wants Security Guarantees Before It Returns', *UN Wire* (17 September 2001), 8. At: http://www.unfoundation.org/unwire

[32] 'West Timor', 9.

and public administration. These tasks includes establishing a system of justice, physical reconstruction, creating an East Timorese administration, and managing a successful political and economic transition.

A reconstruction trust fund was established for East Timor, administered by the World Bank. The fund received $47.2 million in 2000 and will run for three years.[33] An implementing organization, the Community Empowerment and Local Governance Project, provides block grants to communities in consultation with local elected councils. A small enterprise project seeks to revive the local economy and create jobs by providing lines of credit to small and medium-size businesses. These are 'totally unprecedented' approaches in terms of the 'new Bank', said a World Bank representative in Dili. 'We have never worked so quickly in the history of the Bank.', he said.

But dissenting voices can also be heard. Vieira de Mello noted in his June 2000 report to the Security Council that, because of slowness in disbursements, reconstruction was the 'most exasperating area'. Gelbard noted that both UN and World Bank have been very slow. USAID through its office of transitional initiatives had provided funds to create approximately 25,000 jobs. It had initially wanted to use the funds to support local NGOs, but Gelbard insisted that job-creation receive priority.

Land rights issues have surfaced as a significant challenge in state building in East Timor. This is somewhat different from Bosnia and Herzegovina, for example, where housing as opposed to land rights issues were a key ingredient of state building. In East Timor, according to one UN official, it is clear that land rights questions could spawn future conflicts if an adequate mechanism is not put into place to resolve disputes between contending claimants. In this regard, UNTAET has taken steps to reconstruct the housing registry, which was almost entirely destroyed after the independence vote in August 1999. In addition, a special panel in the national court system will address disputes. Informal mechanisms of mediation and arbitration are also envisaged to handle the majority of disputes. But the land and property rights component of UNTAET is relatively small. 'Those responsible for organizing missions do not really understand the issues concerning property rights,' said this UN official.

The demand for justice in East Timor is deeply felt in the population. At issue is justice for past serious human-rights violations, including the

[33] For information on the activities of the Trust Fund for East Timor (TFET) see: http://www.worldbank.org/eap. See also TFET, *Progress Report* (East Timor Rehabilitation and Development, Donor's Council Meeting, Portugal. 21–3 June 2000).

violations that occurred after the August 1999 vote. But militia leaders have also insisted that pro-independence abuses be addressed as well. A tribunal for serious crimes has been established to investigate and possibly bring to trial at least some of the 74 relatively low-level militia members who are presently in custody in East Timor, although progress has been slow. Because of the impracticality of organizing a large-scale tribunal in a setting in which there is virtually no existing legal system, a truth and reconciliation commission is envisioned to deal with lesser offences.

In 2000, Indonesia launched investigations of 25 suspects who may be brought to trial there for offences relating to the violence after the August 1999 vote. In July 2001, a former militia member was sentenced to 15 years of imprisonment for murdering a local UN staff member in 1999 post-election violence. But many East Timorese are doubtful that high-ranking Indonesian officials will ever be convicted. The justice issue is particularly important in relation to refugee return. While the individual motivations of the remaining East Timorese in West Timor are difficult to ascertain, some may well be concerned about the prospect of vigilante justice.

More generally, building a justice system in East Timor has proved to be a challenging endeavour. Law and order is in the mandate of a UN civilian police (CIVPOL) mission which was scheduled to have 1,600 members. According to Ross Grimmer, the deputy head of CIVPOL, when we spoke in August 2000, of the 1,300 international police deployed, about 600 are simply 'pairs of boots'.

Grimmer, a Canadian assistant commissioner with 34 years of experience as a policeman, was deeply frustrated with the UN mission. He found himself 'surrounded by incompetents' and 'mission groupies' who are engaged in a form of mission shopping, moving from one UN deployment to another. 'It looked easy at the beginning', he said, 'but there was no plan.' The international police recruits do not understand the people in many instances, said Grimmer, and the police academy which has been established is mere 'window dressing'. He was concerned that the local police recruited will have but subsidiary roles in relation to defence and security forces affiliated with Falintil.

Grimmer, who earlier had been chief of the CIVPOL office in Bosnia, said that the tasks in East Timor should have been 'easier than in the Balkans'. Nevertheless, there are basic problems in the practice of policing in the mission. Grimmer, a proponent of community-based policing, found himself at odds with his boss who advocated a more hierarchical form of command and control policing. Grimmer, who was close to retirement when we spoke, was pointed in his criticism, 'I was not allowed to do what I know how to do.'

Building a judiciary is an even more daunting task in a setting where there are no judges and just a handful of persons trained as lawyers. Given the limited time and resources, UNTAET is focusing efforts on training and the dissemination of standards of conduct on issues of independence of the judiciary and the legal profession in East Timor. Judicial operations are themselves embryonic. UNTAET has retained full operational control over the prisons. But donors are somewhat hesitant to make contributions to build prisons, and the correctional services in Australia and New Zealand have supported those efforts on a bilateral basis.

In August 2000, there were a total of 188 persons in the two operating detention facilities in East Timor. Space was available for another 57 individuals. Among the detainees were eight juveniles and two women. The lack of alternatives to incarceration was bemoaned by Grimmer. He noted, for example, that the two women in question likely did not belong in detention. One woman, under duress from her husband, had killed her baby, which had been conceived by another man. The other, apparently disturbed, had killed her 100-year-old father by hitting him on the head with a rock. Neither offence, in Grimmer's view, justified incarceration.

On the broad question of transition, many at UNTAET echoed the words of a senior official with the UN mission who had had extensive involvement in northern Iraq and the Balkans, who said that state building in East Timor should be 'relatively easy'. There is a clear end state—independence—and the interlocutors are cooperative. But the absence of a democratic tradition in East Timor and a paucity of local human resources complicated matters. A constitutional commission is planned to engage the East Timorese in the drafting of their constitution. But the head of UNHCR's office in Dili, a Singaporean, was not sanguine. 'We do not think in individualistic terms', she says, 'Asians seek the protection of leaders.' In terms of politics, she noted that this is still the honeymoon and that future elections may well polarize the situation.

East Timor is likely to be considered the paradigmatic test case for international state building. It will be regarded as either easy or difficult, depending on how success is measured in terms of the ambitions of the international mission. If the objective is to provide basic security and lay the groundwork for a minimally functioning state after many years of patient massaging by international organizations and financial institutions, it may be a success. But if it is to leave with the sustainable architecture of a new state in place, it is likely to be regarded a failure. Whatever the characterization, the strategies and programmes employed will leave another layer of silt on the floodplain of international responses which could clearly have been better refined and informed by prior responses. But such is the state of the international system, and having a better capacity to learn lessons is one of the principal rationales for the creation of a new international entity on Strategic Humanitarian Action and Research, or SHARE, which is discussed later in this book.

The Hand-Over

Sergio Vieira de Mello looked tired when I joined him early in the morning for the ride to the cathedral for the 8 a.m. mass on 30 August 2000. Vieira de Mello, who set up the UN mission in Kosovo, is widely regarded as one of the most effective senior officials in the UN system. His work in East Timor has demanded all of his time and more as the Special Representative for the Secretary-General and head of UNTAET. This day, 30 August, was the first commemoration of the independence vote, a day that will surely be East Timor's Independence Day.

It was already oppressively hot as we approached the cathedral, and a large crowd was gathering. We made our way to the front of this airy and imposing structure where Vieira de Mello took a seat next to the Australian Foreign Affairs Minister, Alexander Downer, who was also in attendance. The mass was celebrated by Bishop Carlos Ximenes Belo, Nobel peace prize co-laureate with José Ramos Horta. Bishop Belo expressed heartfelt appreciation to the United Nations and the international community. His call for peace, justice, and reconciliation was short on detail, leaving to others the delicate dance needed to achieve these interrelated objectives.

In the midst of the service, Xanana Gusmao entered, to a chorus of murmurs, having just been elected president of the CNRT at its first annual congress, which had just concluded that morning after much debate and some small measure of political intrigue. Despite the political infighting that had preceded the election and which continued thereafter, Gusmao seemed at that moment to be destined to be the first president of an independent East Timor.

After the mass, we proceeded to the Santa Cruz cemetery, the site of the notorious 1991 massacre in Dili. There, Horta made a short statement and flowers were laid. We then drove to the harbour side in front of the governor's office—now UNTAET's headquarters—where dignitaries threw flowers into the sea, commemorating the loss of life that had accompanied the 1999 independence vote.

A series of speeches followed in front of the UNTAET headquarters. The Australian Foreign Minister used the occasion to announce a commitment to construct a parliament building in Dili for East Timor. I learned later that the Portuguese government had also proposed a public works project which included the construction of a parliament building. These competing pledges reflect well a central problem in state building: international donors can construct the buildings to house democratic institutions, but fostering a democratic tradition is much more difficult. For his part, US Senator Tom Harkin, sponsor of the first congressional resolution in 1975 demanding the withdrawal of Indonesia from East Timor, gave a long speech, extolling the virtues of democracy. Getting from here to there, though, will surely be the fundamental challenge in East Timor.

The day was clear and a pitiless sun beat down from a brilliant blue sky, which served as a colour-coordinated background for the UN flag flying in the breeze over the governor's house. Thousands of East Timorese in attendance were folding copies of the UNTAET newspaper, *Tais Timor*, into hats to find shelter from the sun. The speeches ended at midday, and we adjourned to a private luncheon hosted by UNTAET.

For the East Timorese, the party was and is just beginning. On 30 August it lasted until past midnight, featuring a variety of songs and entertainment. The spectacle was visible and the music could be heard from an impromptu cocktail lounge on the deck of the towering container ship which had been moored in downtown Dili and which provided accommodation to many international visitors, including me. Impatient for independence, the Timorese are pushing for more authority from the UN despite the absence of an indigenous capacity. The test will be whether the UN mission leaves in place at least a rudimentary set of governance tools as it begins to wind down in 2002.

As I watched the entertainment, an image came back to me from the mass earlier in the day. Several pews had been reserved at the front of the cathedral for dignitaries and the heads of several international organizations present in East Timor. Many of these foreign notables, however, were absent; many were on home leave in late August, and others had departed early because of security concerns. As a result, there were several open pews. As the mass began, East Timorese began to move to the front to occupy the places of the absent internationals. Perhaps this will be my most enduring image of that day of commemoration and celebration: without much by way of design, the people of East Timor are beginning to replace the international community in the building of a new state.

5

Surmounting Indifference: Refugees and the New Statecraft

Why should decision makers care about anticipating and responding to forced migration emergencies? First and foremost, as discussed previously, they should care because there is a moral imperative to assist persons in need. Nor is this simply a question of charity. It is in the clear national interest of states such as the United States to promote a stable and moral world, one in which peace and respect for human rights are pervasive and firmly rooted. Increasingly, ethical values are recognized to be significant dimensions of foreign policy. Achieving human security for others is a way to ensure our own human security. The enhancement of human dignity is thus a proper subject of statecraft.

As decision makers invariably come to recognize, humanitarian emergencies are intertwined with political and social considerations which inform responses. There are many examples. Perhaps the most discrediting aspect of the international response in Bosnia in the early 1990s was the use of humanitarian assistance as an inadequate substitute for firm and direct political and military measures, which materialized only later. Indeed, displaced persons and refugees have often been caught in the vortex of strategic interests, such as the Mujahadeen fighters in Pakistan who made war upon the Soviet-based regime in Afghanistan, or the Khmer Rouge in Thailand who forayed into Cambodia to attack the Vietnam-backed regime in the 1980s. In 1999, the return of Kosovar refugees became a specific war aim of NATO and, indeed, its basic measure of success. The failure to anticipate the humanitarian catastrophe in Kosovo still haunts political and military planners.

In addition, refugee emergencies have tangible spillover effects. By definition, refugees go from their home countries to another country. The growing internal displacement in Colombia, for example, could affect many countries in the Americas.

Refugees can also present specific national security threats. The UN Security Council has now found the prospect or fact of population displacements to pose threats to international peace and security on several occasions. Domestic political impacts can be grave, and the financial costs great. Illustrative are the risks to Turkey in 1991 posed by the arrival at its border of Kurdish asylum seekers from northern Iraq, and the threats to Macedonia in 1999 associated with the arrival of Kosovars.

The bipolar conflict during the cold war discouraged engagement. The end of this conflict both unleashed forces that caused population displacements and made it more likely that international humanitarian action would be undertaken. Now, involvement is more likely because of the absence of the risk of retaliation and escalation by one of the protagonists. Risk-averse decision makers are no longer able to avoid messy complications when confronted with demands by their constituencies that action be taken. While no one becomes the US Secretary of State or National Security Advisor in order to manage responses to refugee emergencies, over the past decade these and other senior decision makers have had to do just that in places like Bosnia, East Timor, Haiti, northern Iraq, Kosovo, and Rwanda. These are new national security and foreign policy agenda items, and a reflection of increasingly malleable concepts of territorial sovereignty.

Indeed, decision makers come under immense pressures to become involved. The media and NGO press relentlessly for something to be done to address the needs of people at risk. Ordinary people become formidable advocates for action. While political leaders may be concerned about the indefinite and protracted character of involvements, they are also afraid of looking bad. The rising expectations of those who have been driven to a point of view in media-saturated societies such as the United States will thus often force an issue of humanitarian action. It is not possible as a matter of either morality or politics simply to stand by in the face of immense suffering. Even intelligence bureaucracies in Western countries have come to maintain atrocities watch lists for political leaders who may have to engage the issues when they move into public discourse. This has institutionalized the CNN effect within governments.

Refugees matter fundamentally because of the way that they challenge policy makers to address the new chaos of the twenty-first century. The many varieties of repression and oppression that are now open for some form of involvement provide a demanding new terrain for decision makers. While the proclivities over the past decade have included a greater likelihood of international involvement in the countries which may produce refugees, an array of conventional instruments remain in the refugee policy tool box. But the tools that we have used to manage humanitarian emergencies must be augmented, refined, and used more effectively.

Policy tools, of course, do not exist in a vacuum. There are several norms and trends which frame the options available to deal with refugee emergencies. These include legal norms and a variety of broad socio-economic trends and policy debates: in other words, the tool chest. To set the context for the examination of specific policy options this chapter discusses international law, internal displacement, humanitarian intervention, sovereignty, and international migration.

LAW AND THE RULES OF THE HUMANITARIAN GAME

The rights and obligations under international law concerning refugees provide a framework structure with many gaps; indeed there may be more gaps than structure in the international legal architecture relating to forcibly displaced persons. States enjoy considerable discretion in terms of policy responses to refugee emergencies. Several approaches have been taken to protect and assist refugees and internally displaced persons over the past decade, with decidedly mixed results.

What, then, are the rules of the game? A tapestry of international law comprising refugee, human rights and humanitarian law articulates the rights of uprooted persons and imposes obligations on states. While the norms declared are broad and treaty-based, the implementing and enforcement mechanisms under these treaties are relatively weak. As a result, there is often a disjunction between refugee rights and realities. This problem is compounded by the fact that refugees matter to states in ways that can result in restrictive policy responses. But the key question is whether these official responses fall within or outside of the ambit of discretion permitted to states under international law.

The United Nations refugee treaties, the 1951 Convention relating to the Status of Refugees, and its 1967 Protocol, which 143 states have signed, are the principal sources of protection for externally displaced persons who meet the treaty definition of 'refugee'. Moreover, there is, in this sense, an international consensus on the notion of who is a refugee. They are defined under the UN treaties as persons who, owing to a well-founded fear of being persecuted for reasons of race, religion, nationality, membership of a social group, or political opinion, are outside of their country of nationality or last habitual residence for stateless persons, and are unable because of such fear to return to that country. Thus, individuals who remain in their home countries and who have not crossed an international border, or individuals who fear harm for generalized reasons such as being caught in the cross-fire of war, are not included in this definition. Also excluded under the UN treaties are those who no longer need protection because, for example, they have returned home or settled elsewhere, and those who are considered undeserving of protection because they have committed certain serious crimes or other heinous acts.

At the regional level, a 1969 Organization of African Unity refugee treaty expands protective coverage to forced migrants who flee conflict and civil disorder. National practices around the world also reflect expanded refugee concepts, particularly in Latin America.

The principal remedy for refugees under the UN treaties is the right not to be returned to a place where an individual may experience persecution. This rule of *non-refoulement* has only limited arguable exceptions based on risks to national security or public safety posed by unmanageable mass influxes. Even in such exceptional circumstances, the treaties recognize that the individual refugee should be provisionally accorded asylum and given the opportunity of travelling onward to another state. Indeed, the principle of *non-refoulement* is considered by many commentators to have become part of customary law, binding even on states which are not signatories to the refugee treaties.

This non-return precept is the foundation of all refugee protection and was a fertile source of protection innovations over the past decade, albeit with mixed results. The crisis-driven border closures by Turkey in 1991 and Macedonia in 1999 occasioned special arrangements for a safe area in northern Iraq and a humanitarian evacuation programme. A resettlement programme for Indo-Chinese refugees in the 1980s and 1990s was inspired by the refusal of nearby states to provide asylum. These multilateral innovations buttress the point that the protection of refugees is to be seen increasingly as an obligation owed by states broadly to the entire international community.

Yet there is no international consensus on the method for determining who a refugee is. The procedures for determining whether an individual meets the treaty definition of the refugee concept are left largely to the discretion of states, as long as minimum standards of fairness and non-discrimination are observed. Many different systems are used around the world, informed largely by countries' legal cultures and traditions.

The refugee treaties also guarantee a variety of civil, economic, and social rights, harmonizing the treatment owed to refugees with that owed to citizens or aliens, depending on the particular provision. Entitlements include the right to property, right of free association, equal access to courts, and legal redress. There are also provisions for employment, adequate housing, public education, assistance, workers' compensation, and social security benefits.

The special needs of refugee women and children, the predominant proportion of the world's refugees, have begun to receive increased attention in the formulation and implementation of policy. These developments have been assisted substantially by NGO lobbying. While standards and guidelines have been promulgated, and staff dedicated to these issues within international organizations and governments, implementation remains uneven.

Refugees have human rights. Indeed, all persons have human rights, including those who have been uprooted, regardless of whether or not they are categorized as refugees. General human rights law thus protects non-citizens to the same degree as all other individuals, with specific express exceptions such as voting in national elections. That we have an internationally recognized category of refugees is due in large measure to the fact that population displacement presented an immense international problem in Europe from the period after the First World War to the end of the Second World War for which solutions were needed. Refugee law was the answer to that discrete problem, but human rights provided an overall legal superstructure.

In post-crisis situations, human rights law provides the foundation of principle for the authorities of a country seeking to rebuild political, social, and economic systems. These guiding principles and rules find expression in the basic human rights instruments, which address such matters as the fundamental rights to life and freedom from cruel and inhumane treatment or punishment. Also included are entitlements respecting freedom of movement and freedom to choose a residence, as well as the fair and equal treatment of all individuals by a country's courts. Freedom of religion, opinion, and expression are also addressed, as is the right of peaceful assembly and freedom of association. A state's obligation to respect these rights is unqualified except for reasons of national security or public order, which may, of course, be precisely the circumstances when respect for international human rights standards is needed most.

International law relating to the conduct of war is another source of protection for the uprooted, including internal exiles. Humanitarian law protects civilian non-combatants in the midst of armed conflict. It is based on international treaties limiting the means of warfare and the methods that the parties to a conflict may employ. Warring parties are thus obliged to distinguish between civilians and combatants, to ensure respect and protection for civilians, and to direct operations only against military targets.

Persons protected under the 1949 Geneva conventions and their 1977 protocols are those who find themselves in a situation of armed conflict, whether international or internal. They are entitled to respect for their persons, honour, family rights, religious convictions and practices, and manners and customs. Protected persons are to be humanely treated and sheltered from acts of violence as well as insults to their dignity, including rape. In situations of international armed conflict, civilians who may face persecution upon return may not be repatriated.

The humanitarian law provisions governing internal armed conflicts are somewhat less well developed. Nevertheless, in these circumstances, violence to life and person, including murder, mutilation, cruel and inhumane treatment and torture, taking of hostages, and infringements of personal dignity are prohibited.

The International Committee of the Red Cross (ICRC), an independent international humanitarian organization expressly referred to in the Geneva conventions, is a key promoter of international humanitarian law and has won the Nobel peace prize on four occasions. ICRC seeks to disseminate the content of humanitarian law and engages in discussions and confidential negotiations based on precepts of humanitarian law. ICRC, which was founded in 1863 to address the situation of wounded soldiers in need of medical attention who were abandoned on the battlefield of Solferino, has been buffeted over the past decade by conflicts in Iraq, Rwanda, Somalia, and the former Yugoslavia. Broader efforts to meet humanitarian needs have also become a key feature part of ICRC's work, and the agency has become a major relief provider. In 2000, ICRC deployed on average 1,250 expatriate staff and 8,000 locally recruited employees in the field, distributing relief supplies in 62 countries, and expended a budget of nearly $600 million.[1] At the beginning of the new millennium, the ICRC has 21 delegations with some 4,000 staff in Africa alone.

The obligations of states under human rights and humanitarian law are implemented at the international level by a variety of monitoring and reporting mechanisms, special rapporteurs, and individual complaints procedures. International criminal courts have been established with jurisdiction to prosecute crimes against humanity and war crimes in Bosnia and Herzegovina, Rwanda, and more recently Sierra Leone, with a global international criminal court likely to become operational in the foreseeable future. But these international mechanisms have severely limited capacities. Enforcement is primarily the responsibility of states, including in the formulation of foreign policy, raising potential for profound conflicts of interests.

THE PROBLEM OF INTERNAL DISPLACEMENT

Internally displaced persons often have specific vulnerabilities by virtue of their immediate proximity to a conflict or because they are targeted by

[1] International Committee for the Red Cross, *ICRC Annual Report 2000* (Geneva: ICRC, 2001), 8, 244–5.

warring factions in civil conflict. Risks include direct physical attacks, sexual violence, forced displacement, forced labour and military service, loss of employment, and denial of access to health care, education, and other basic services.[2] In 2001, some 25 million individuals have been forced from their homes by conflict, but have not yet crossed an international border. Oftentimes the reasons for flight are akin to those which prompt the flight of refugees. As discussed above, because these individuals have not crossed a border they are not covered by international refugee law.

To deal with this growing phenomenon of internal displacement, Francis Deng, the Representative of the Secretary-General on Internally Displaced Persons, oversaw the development in 1998 of Guiding Principles on Internal Displacement, which have been accepted by many UN agencies and NGOs. The guidelines eschew a definition of the category, simply noting descriptively that :

> . . . internally displaced persons are persons or groups of persons who have been forced or obliged to flee or to leave their homes or places of habitual residence, in particular as a result of or in order to avoid the effects of armed conflict, situations of generalized violence, violations of human rights or natural or human-made disasters, and who have not crossed an internationally recognized State border.[3]

This description encompasses a vast population with a wide variety of needs who are found in diverse circumstances; indeed, so varied as to make uniform treatment almost unworkable. For that reason, the guidelines are necessarily quite general in character, drawing upon human rights, humanitarian, and refugee law. They articulate 30 principles relating to protection from displacement, protection during displacement, humanitarian assistance, and return, resettlement and reintegration.

The difficulty of protecting and assisting internally displaced persons raises basic questions about the competence of the international system. The problem can be seen as well as the failure of humanitarian agencies acting within their respective mandates to accept responsibility for this vulnerable population. This was the assessment of Richard Holbrooke, then the US ambassador to the UN, during a visit to Angola in 2000. When he saw needy and similarly situated populations treated differently by international organizations, he posed a basic and an unanswerable question: who is in charge?

[2] US General Accounting Office, *Internally Displaced Persons Lack Effective Protection*, GAO-01-803 (Washington, DC: GAO, August 2001).

[3] 'Guiding Principles on Internal Displacement' (New York: United Nations Office for the Coordination of Humanitarian Affairs, 1998), Introduction. At: http://www.reliefweb.int/ocha_ol/pub/idp_gp/idp.html

Internal displacement has presented a policy coordination challenge for several years. I remember leading a human rights delegation in 1984 which examined the plight of 500,000 conflict-related internal exiles in El Salvador. We found an urgent need for new institutional arrangements to help them. But while this call went unheeded, the issue has persisted. In 1998, the UN Inter-Agency Standing Committee (IASC), described later in this book, recommended various measures to address the issue of 'internally displaced persons'. Under the current system, the Emergency Relief Coordinator, as the Chairman of the IASC, is designated the 'focal point' at UN headquarters for inter-agency coordination of humanitarian assistance to the internally displaced. At the field level, the resident humanitarian coordinator is responsible for coordination of assistance to those who are displaced within their national borders. The IASC working group serves as the forum for consultations on the issue '[i]n order to minimize the risk of duplication of activities and/or to ensure the gaps in assistance to and protection of IDPs [internally displaced persons]'.[4]

The debate on internal displacement was given impetus when Ambassador Holbrooke, upon his return from Angola, suggested that the mandate of the UNHCR be enlarged to address this population. At an extraordinary meeting at the US mission to the UN in January 2000, Holbrooke importuned Mrs Sadako Ogata, then High Commissioner for Refugees, to consider mandate expansion. Holbrooke's call added impetus to a debate, raging for many years, about the responsibilities of the international community to become involved more often in countries in which there are population displacements by reason of crisis. In March 2000, Ambassador Holbrooke made a detailed proposal on the issue. Calling these individuals 'internal refugees' or 'in-country refugees'—terms which cause concern to some in UNHCR who are worried about muddling the agency mandate—instead of 'IDPs', which he considered a 'cold, bureaucratic term', Holbrooke urged greater attention by the international community.

> [T]oday there are twice as many internal refugees as there are those who come under the care of the UNHCR. In Sudan, nearly 4 million people have been displaced as a result of three decades of conflicts; in Sri Lanka, there are over 600,000 displaced people; there are over half a million in Azerbaijan, many of whom live in railroad cars; there are over 300,000 in Burundi; over a quarter million in Russia due to the fighting in Chechnya; and according to most recent estimates, 500,000 in eastern Congo alone . . . [Holbrooke also discussed at some length in his speech the

[4] UN Office for the Coordination of Humanitarian Affairs, *Inter-Agency Standing Committee Recommendations Related to the Review of the Capacity of the United Nations System for Humanitarian Assistance* (Geneva: OCHA, 14 August 1998), Sect. II.21.

1.3 million displaced in camps in Angola]. All told, there are over 20 million internal refugees worldwide.[5]

Calling for more attention to principles of 'predictability', 'accountability', and 'universality', Holbrooke proposed greater engagement by the United Nations system to alleviate this problem. He made the following specific recommendations:

> First, . . . the UN should designate a lead agency for each specific internal refugee emergency, and define much more clearly lead agency responsibilities. I still believe that in many, indeed most cases where protection is the main issue, UNHCR would be the most effective lead agency . . .
>
> Second, in order to facilitate cooperation throughout the UN system, we must encourage all UN humanitarian agencies to designate a point of contact on internal refugees . . .
>
> Third, we must improve our understanding and monitoring of internal refugee emergencies. One possibility would be for the Secretary-General to provide regular, comprehensive reports to the UN General Assembly and the Economic and Social Council on the state of the world's displaced and the nature of the UN's response on a country-by-country basis . . .
>
> Fourth, we must be as clear as we are for refugees, that protection and advocacy are essential elements of assisting internal refugees. Some humanitarian and development agencies still do not see that as part of their mandate, or do not implement it sufficiently in the field.[6]

It is often difficult to separate concerns over bureaucratic turf from substantive concerns in a reform debate. Would a focus on internal displacement undermine principles of asylum abroad? Could UNHCR undertake these new responsibilities on behalf of such a large and diverse population without diminishing its effectiveness in relation to refugees? What are the resource implications? Of course, earlier UN reform efforts have demonstrated that bureaucratic biases can frustrate efforts to consolidate and rationalize UN system activities. Governments may be concerned that the time and energy required to get an agreement among the humanitarian components of the UN system on the question may not be justified. And no one is looking to build a new operational capacity within the UN. Nevertheless, a consensus has emerged, namely, that the status quo is not satisfactory, and that, even if a unified structure cannot be achieved, improvements

[5] US Mission to the United Nations, 'Statement by Ambassador Holbrooke, United States Permanent Representative to the United Nations, Cardozo Law School', USUN Press Release #44(00) (28 March 2000), 2.

[6] US Mission to the United Nations, 'Statement by Ambassador Holbrooke', 4–5.

must be made in practice, taking into account the widely differing circumstances in which internal exiles are found.

One early consequence of Ambassador Holbrooke's 'outburst', as one senior UN official who spoke to me characterized this foray into policy advocacy, was to galvanize further thinking and consideration within the UN system itself. The 1999 IASC policy paper on the issue of internal displacement has been revised to include a mechanism to identify a senior official in each humanitarian emergency who would be accountable for marshalling a response from within the UN system to deal with the needs of internally displaced persons, namely, the person responsible for coordinating the humanitarian response more generally.[7] It is this person's responsibility to adopt a collaborative approach and stitch together a response from within and outside the UN system to deal with the needs of the internally displaced. Whether this is the resident humanitarian coordinator or head of a designated lead agency, the UN will in the future be able to answer Holbrooke's basic question: who is in charge?

Under the current system, however, no guidance exists about how the agencies are to respond. The next question to be addressed then is: 'who will do what?' To address these operational problems the IASC in 2000 established a Senior Inter-Agency Network on Internal Displacement, with focal point persons in the various international organizations involved with the issue. The inter-agency response in several countries was surveyed in 2001 by Dennis McNamara as UN Special Coordinator on Internal Displacement. His mission to Angola, for example, found 'progress in collaboration between the UN system and governmental structures ... [but also found] a need to further strengthen such collaboration ... '.[8] In general, McNamara found serious gaps in the UN and agency humanitarian responses to the needs of internally displaced persons, especially their protection. As a result, the UN Secretary-General approved the establishment within United Nations Office for the Coordination of Humanitarian Affairs (OCHA) of a small, non-operational Unit on Internal Displacement in January 2002, specifically to promote more effective international institutional responses to internal displacement.[9] But NGOs are wary of such a modest solution, and have expressed a preference instead for Holbrooke's

[7] United Nations Office for the Coordination of Humanitarian Affairs, *Protection of Internally Displaced Persons*, Inter-Agency Standing Committee Policy Paper (New York: OCHA, December 1999), Annex B, Sect. A.

[8] UN Special Coordinator on Internal Displacement, 'Senior Inter-Agency Network on Internal Displacement: Mission to Angola, 12–17 March 2001, Findings and Recommendations' (Geneva: 23 March 2001) (mimeo).

[9] US General Accounting Office, *Internally Displaced Persons*, 56–7.

lead agency approach, in which a particular UN entity would take the lead in a specific situation.

Holbrooke, who stimulated the most recent debate, also is not impressed with the OCHA review. While noting that McNamara is a capable UN official, Holbrooke believes that a more significant institutional structural response is required. Recent squabbles over bureaucratic roles between UNHCR, the United Nations Children's Fund (UNICEF), and the World Food Programme (WFP) are 'incomprehensible' to Holbrooke. The heads of the three agencies personally lobbied him in the course of the recent debate on respective roles and delineation of responsibilities regarding internal displacement; a 'pretty sad story', in his view. Ad hoc measures like reviews are devices designed by the UN to remove the pressure for reform. While UNHCR has some problems, in Holbrooke's view, it is still the most capable agency. When I specifically asked whether UNHCR should normally play a lead role in providing protection to 'internal refugees', he was direct: 'of course'.

Whether the bureaucratic adjustments that have been made will result in a significant improvement over the current situation remains to be seen. This will have to be demonstrated in future protection and assistance arrangements for the internally displaced in places like Angola, where problems of security and access persist. Ultimately, as this book argues, more fundamental reform will be required to address this crucial issue.

HUMANITARIAN INTERVENTION: AN EMERGING NORM OR AN ABERRATION?

Humanitarian intervention is a frontier path in international law that was trodden with some frequency over the past decade in refugee settings. But the meaning of the term and the circumstances of such international military deployments remain controversial.

While the state may no longer be opaque, it is far from transparent. And while we now may look into the inner workings of a state for a variety of purposes, whether we then reach in coercively to make changes for humanitarian reasons depends largely on notions of morality and legitimacy as well as capacity and proportionality, all of which may engender controversy. The international responses to circumstances involving forced displacement provide an important context for the evolving notions of humanitarian action.

Scholars inevitably point to 1648 and the Peace of Westphalia as the occasion for the recognition of the supremacy of the nation state in international affairs and the state's absolute territorial sovereignty. Those who negotiated this treaty were undoubtedly motivated more by the devastation and death that had been caused in the name of religion by the Thirty Years War than by effectuating a basic change to the international order. Yet thinkers even now wrestle with the implications of the end of the cold war and globalization for a post-Westphalian perspective.

The issues are presented in sharp relief by the question of humanitarian intervention defined in the aftermath of the Kosovo crisis by Kofi Annan, the UN Secretary-General, as a range of measures which vary according to the degree of coercion utilized and which are designed to influence the ways states address the basic rights and needs of their citizens and other persons under their jurisdiction. Such 'interventions' can include international condemnation, fact-finding missions, use of international dispute resolution mechanisms, humanitarian assistance, sanctions, and the use—or the threatened use—of force.

Terminology is crucial. International lawyers would cite the classical connotation of humanitarian intervention as the proportional use of military force for humanitarian motives. The Secretary-General in 2000 used the term 'humanitarian action' to describe the range of responses to situations of conflict and crisis including the consensual provision of aid. But he urged that in order to avoid confusion the term 'humanitarian' not be associated with military operations. Mindful of the controversy stirred up by his 1999 General Assembly statement about intervention and sovereignty, the Secretary-General noted that while a use of force may be legitimate and necessary in rare cases 'to save masses of people from extreme violence and slaughter . . . [n]o government should fear that accepting humanitarian aid is the first step towards military intervention'.[10]

The notion of calibrating international responses is well supported in the text of the UN Charter. In Chapter VI, Article 33, the Charter provides that '[t]he parties to any dispute, the continuance of which is likely to endanger the maintenance of international peace and security, shall, first of all, seek a solution by negotiation, inquiry, mediation, conciliation, arbitration, judicial settlement, resort to regional agencies or arrangements, or other peaceful means of their own choice'.

Resort to enforcement actions, such as economic sanctions or the use of military force, is contemplated under Chapter VII of the UN Charter in response to a threat to 'international peace and security', a concept which

[10] Annan, Kofi, *Opening Remarks of the Secretary-General of the United Nations,* International Peace Academy Humanitarian Action Symposium (20 November 2000). At: http://www.ipacademy.org/Publications/Reports/Research/PublRepoReseHumAc_body.htm

has been interpreted expansively to include widespread, serious human rights abuses. The repertoire of responses includes mandatory economic sanctions, which permit the UN Security Council to bring coercive pressure to bear on states without recourse to military force. However, experience has shown that general economic sanctions are blunt instruments which, all too often, have substantial negative humanitarian consequences. To address this concern, sanctions may be targeted, such as arms embargoes, travel and international participation bans, or freezing financial assets.

The most vehement debates, of course, concern the use of military force for humanitarian ends, particularly resort to such means without an authorizing resolution from the United Nations Security Council. Among the recent refugee episodes surveyed in this book, Kosovo in particular is grist for these debates. The military air campaign there in 1999 raised troubling questions about the relevance of international law in the conduct of foreign affairs.

The basic international legal framework is the United Nations Charter, which in Article 2(4) prohibits member states from exercising 'the threat or use of force against the territorial integrity or political independence' of another state. Article 2(7) provides that the United Nations shall not 'intervene in matters which are essentially within the domestic jurisdiction of any State' except where enforcement measures are permitted under the Charter. Under Chapter VII of the Charter, the Security Council is authorized collectively to use such 'air, sea or land forces as may be necessary to maintain or restore international peace or security'. Recent practice has broadened this concept, and the language of 'threat to international peace and security' was invoked in Security Council resolutions concerning the repression and displacement of populations in Iraq and Bosnia, as well as the after-the-fact resolution concerning Kosovo.

As lawyers learn, all language contains ambiguities, and the UN Charter is no exception. Not all 'action' such as reports, condemnations, recommendations, or economic sanctions are 'interventions' which involve the 'use of force'. Even the qualification limiting the use of force to those interventions which infringe upon 'territorial integrity' or 'political independence' may not rule out an intervention calculated to address only a humanitarian catastrophe without territorial aspirations or political motivations. Also, the modifier 'essentially' may significantly loosen the bonds of non-intervention in relation to the domestic affairs of a state. Nor does the language of the UN Charter purport explicitly to overrule any prior and presumably now evolving state practices reflecting a limited custom of intervention.

But textual analysis alone is insufficient to answer the fundamental question of whether, apart from an authorized collective intervention under the UN Charter, there are circumstances which legitimize humanitarian intervention without the consent of the sovereign. The issue is important in an era when the Security Council may decline or be unable to address the issue in at least some circumstances.

The protection of human rights as a primary purpose of the United Nations is well reflected in the Charter. Indeed, the human rights movement is premised upon recognition of the legitimacy of international concern over internal human rights violations and has rejected the notion that a state's mistreatment of its citizens is exclusively a question of its 'domestic jurisdiction', at least in so far as such treatment contravenes basic guarantees under human rights law. While this evolution may not specifically authorize a military use of force as distinct from other 'soft' forms of action or economic coercion, it underscores the mutable nature of the concept of national sovereignty in relation to a forcible intervention.

Political theory buttresses the point, as the UN Secretary-General emphasized in his 1999 speech to the General Assembly:

> The State is now widely understood to be the servant of its people, and not vice versa. At the same time, individual sovereignty—and by this I mean the human rights and fundamental freedoms of each and every individual as enshrined in our Charter—has been enhanced by a renewed consciousness of the right of every individual to control his or her own destiny.[11]

Sovereignty is thus synonymous with the responsibility of the state for good governance and to uphold fundamental human rights. A state forfeits sovereignty as a shield against international action, if it fails to uphold the promise of decent treatment. Sovereignty is not a weapon to abet violations of the human rights of a state's inhabitants.

The use of military force to forestall a humanitarian catastrophe ordinarily would have to satisfy the requisites of the United Nations Charter. But given the inherently benign character of the objective and the increasingly available ways, including through NGOs and the mass media, to measure and monitor proportionality and duration of action, United Nations authorization, while highly desirable, might not always be required in rare instances where no other alternatives are available. A norm may thus be emerging in favour of forcible intervention in such exceptional circumstances to remedy widespread and grave harms.

[11] 'Secretary-General Presents his Annual Report to General Assembly', Press Release, U.N. Doc. SG/SM/7136 and GA/9596 (20 September 1999), 1.

An analogy can be found under classical Anglo-American property law. In the common law, commentators have often spoken of a landowner's absolute right to exclude intruders. Yet trespass has been permitted for reasons of both public and private necessity, such as avoiding imminent disaster or serious harm to another person. Even the use of force in connection with such invasions can be justified. Concepts of sovereignty, often invoked by governments in similarly absolutist terms, should be considered qualified as well by instances of vital humanitarian necessity to address widespread and grave harms such as genocide.

There are, of course, crucial follow-on questions: when is such an intervention authorized, and which type of response is appropriate in the circumstances in question? Efforts to state an overly broad substantive rule would likely be unavailing. An overemphasis on conventional *Realpolitik* is likely to lead policy makers into unpleasant surprises: witness Kosovo, where the humanitarian fallout—mass refugee displacement—was disastrous. Indeed, strong states may be drawn to the United Nations as an auspice through which to deploy forces in relatively weak states in order to avert refugee emergencies: witness the US deployment of forces in Haiti in 1994 or the Italian deployment in Albania in 1997. But too much attention to overly narrow notions of national interest or pragmatic feasibilities will be criticized understandably as too selective. Why Kosovo and not Chechnya? Or Sudan?

The tragedy in the Great Lakes region of Africa in 1994 underscores the difficulties of securing international intervention in a place which is deemed to have less strategic value now than during the cold war. The perceived misadventure in Somalia in 1993 was a prescription for immobility by the United Nations Security Council in the face of the genocide in Rwanda. The ensuing inability to separate combatants and criminals from innocent refugees fleeing conflict precipitated aggression against the entire displaced Hutu community, resulting in massive loss of life and a descent into inter-state war.

A search for a set of rules will prove elusive in a situation which is itself an exception to the general rule requiring Security Council authorization and in which one invariable criterion is whether an intervention is feasible. A process that takes into account a variety of factors would be more promising, such as the size of the population adversely affected, the spread and severity of harm or the threat of harm, the existence of less intrusive alternatives, the identification of national interests and values by potential intervenors, and the feasibility of intervention. A calculation involving such factors could inform the choice of the method of involvement, whether soft, coercive, or forcible. While such initiatives have been and are likely to remain selective, considering such factors might help to rationalize the use of such exceptional measures of last resort.

Along these lines, the UN Secretary-General has recently recommended that, in the face of massive and ongoing abuses, the Security Council consider the imposition of appropriate enforcement action taking into account the following criteria: (1) the scope of the breaches of human rights and international humanitarian law, including the numbers of people affected and the nature of the violations; (2) the inability of local authorities to uphold legal order, or the identification of a pattern of complicity by local authorities; (3) the exhaustion of peaceful or consent-based efforts to address the situation; (4) the ability of the Security Council to monitor actions that are undertaken; and (5) the limited and proportionate use of force, with attention to repercussions upon civilian populations and the environment.[12]

Refinement of this proposition, including in the discrete context of forced migration, must await further experiences and analysis. In a bid to garner support for the Secretary-General's concept of humanitarian intervention and action, the Canadian government supported in September 2000 the establishment of an International Commission on Intervention and State Sovereignty, building on earlier analytical work by the Danish and Swedish governments. Chaired by Gareth Evans, former Australian foreign minister, and Mohammed Sahnoun, Special Adviser to the UN Secretary-General on the Horn of Africa and former Special Representative of the Secretary-General on Somalia and the Great Lakes of Africa, the Commission is working with a wide network of advisers and experts to produce a report on the issue in 2001.

THE SOVEREIGNTY DEBATE

The debate over national sovereignty and humanitarian action, while not new, reached a crescendo over the past decade. From northern Iraq in 1991 to Kosovo in 1999, humanitarian concerns were featured as justifications for the use of military force, led in both instances by the United States. The dialogue over sovereignty and intervention is now manifested in several contexts in the UN system. Shifting coalitions of like-minded states drawn from the Group of Seven (G7) big economic powers have in general favoured greater internal involvements—but do not necessarily want to commit to

[12] 'Report of the Secretary-General to the Security Council on the Protection of Civilians in Armed Conflict', UN Doc. S/1999/957 (8 September 1999), 24.

deployments—and several states from the Group of Seventy-Seven (G77) non-aligned states in the developing world have opposed the notion of such involvements—but then often have called for international crisis responses.

This controversy has played out in relation to the politics of protecting internally displaced persons. Francis Deng, a Sudanese scholar and the UN Secretary-General's special representative on internal displacement, had overseen the work of a group of legal experts which prepared guiding principles for the protection of the internally displaced. But as this drafting project sought recognition and implementation within the UN system, increasing discomfort was expressed by some developing states. As a result, in August 2000 the G77 blocked the UN's Economic and Social Council from endorsing Deng's initiative.[13] Another test looms with the efforts to strengthen UN system capacities relating to work on behalf of internal exiles around the world.

The issue was revisited in the November 2000 debate in the UN General Assembly over UNHCR's work. In a departure from recent practice, a recorded vote was requested on the paragraph of the General Assembly resolution concerning UNHCR's involvement with internally displaced persons and the relevance of guiding principles on internal displacement developed under UN auspices. While the paragraph was retained, 30 states abstained, including Cuba, India, and Sudan.[14] The lines have been drawn.

The implementation of the report of the Secretary-General's high level Panel on United Nations Peace Operations issued in August 2000—the Brahimi Report, named after Mr Lakhdar Brahimi, the former foreign minister of Algeria who chaired the Panel—has provided yet another venue for the sovereignty and intervention debate.[15] The report identified many of the critical issues that have vexed recent efforts to deal with humanitarian emergencies. These include: the use of civilian police and related rule of law elements in peace operations; the need for mechanisms to promote justice and reconciliation; the vital importance of disarmament, demobilization, and re-integration programmes involving combatants; the use of 'quick impact projects' to build confidence and address the immediate needs of those who inhabit the international mission area; and the

[13] US General Accounting Office, *Internally Displaced Persons*, 14.

[14] 'Third Committee Winds up Work for Current Session with Call for Respect for Humanitarian Law, Human Rights', Press Release, UN Doc. GA/SHC/3624 (10 November 2000).

[15] 'Report of the Panel on United Nations Peace Operations' (Brahimi Report), UN Doc. A/55/305-S/2000/809 (21 August 2000).

importance of integrating electoral assistance into a broader strategy for the support of governance institutions.

The Brahimi Report was greeted with quiet enthusiasm by the European Union governments, according to ambassador Luigi Boseli, the EU liaison to the UN. The enthusiasm reflects the fact that analogous discussions and developments are under way in Europe. But the response was quiet in order not to antagonize the G77 developing countries which are sensitive to incursions on national sovereignty signalled by new trends of humanitarian action.

By way of illustration, the course of action recommended in the Brahimi Report has fallen foul of the General Assembly's Fifth Committee, charged with approval and oversight of the United Nation's budget. Several recommended posts and the establishment of an analytical unit within the Secretariat to support the work of the Security Council were disallowed ostensibly on budgetary grounds by the Fifth Committee. Some countries complained that the implementation of the report could adversely impact Secretariat staffing, and, during a period of zero budgetary growth, could result in diverting positions from other sectors, notably development programmes. A handful of non-aligned states involved in the Fifth Committee simply 'hijacked' the report implementation process, complained one senior UN official in the Secretariat. He bemoaned the clout exercised by the budget committee, which even many UN ambassadors fail to appreciate.

Peacekeeping reform will continue to be a focus of efforts in the General Assembly, vowed this senior UN official. Indeed, the stakes are high for the bureaucracy. If the UN system is not able to come to terms with the need for more effective peacekeeping deployments, then greater emphasis is likely to be placed on coalitions of like-minded states to undertake these and related activities. In 2001, the United Kingdom supported a series of regional meetings on recommendations to strengthen UN peace operations, including a meeting in Africa where significant support was expressed in favour of strengthening the capacities of both the UN and regional organizations. It remains to be seen whether this effort to go over the heads of permanent representatives in New York will extract peacekeeping reform efforts from this North-South impasse.

The suspicions of developing countries over claims of humanitarian action and intervention are well reflected in the thinking of Kamalesh Sharma, Indian ambassador to the United Nations. India has been a persistent critic of such interventions. This is so despite the fact that India itself intervened in the war that established Bangladesh in 1971, and deployed peacekeeping troops in Sri Lanka in 1987, justifying both undertakings on humanitarian grounds. Sharma referred in passing to the Bangladesh intervention and the plight of 10 million refugees when we met in the opulent Indian mission to the UN in February 2001. But he concluded, 'there is simply no need for the doctrine of humanitarian intervention'. Humanitarian catastrophes and atrocities at a level that would justify intervention necessarily pose inherent threats to international peace and security, in his view, and would be recognized as warranting appropriate action by the United Nations Security Council acting under the Charter.

Nor does Sharma see the strengthening of the UN's capacity to undertake peacekeeping operations as the most important issue on the international humanitarian agenda. A greater emergency is the 'devastation of underdevelopment', he urged, explaining that there is simply 'no game plan for social uplift' on the part of the developed world. Sharma cited the preparation of an international conference on financing development to be held in Mexico in 2002 as more deserving of attention. 'If AIDS is a security threat', he challenged, 'then why not underdevelopment'?

Debates between the haves and have-nots have characterized the life of the United Nations, and they reached new heights in connection with humanitarian action over the past decade. These debates will continue, and inaction may well be the outcome, at least over the short term. But the world's reality will undoubtedly intrude upon the passion of these debates, and aroused populations may simply insist that their leaders find a more effective apparatus to distribute both political and economic justice. If the United Nations proves not to be up to the task, then like-minded states are likely to resort to structures outside of the UN system, including regional structures such as those currently emerging in Europe.

EUROPE AND CRISIS MANAGEMENT

Brussels, a city with its own exquisitely complicated administrative structure, is a fitting setting for the activities of the European Union. With a governance agglomeration of 19 communes, each with its own mayor and council, Brussels has been a place of linguistic and cultural confrontation—Flemings and Walloons, the Dutch and French languages—since Belgium gained independence from Holland in 1830. The often-portrayed Gothic and Baroque skyline of Brussels now features as well the monumental modern structures of the European Union. These include the European Commission—displaced to several sites when the Palais Berlaymont was evacuated in 1992 upon the discovery that it was riddled with asbestos—the

Council of Ministers, and the European Parliament. But it is the political and bureaucratic architecture, not the buildings, from which the true complications arise.

The most recent political milestone in the economic and political harmonization under way in western Europe is the Treaty of Amsterdam, which entered into force in 1999 and further developed the structures created by the Treaty of Maastricht establishing the European Union (EU), which entered into force in 1993. Under the EU's structures, there are three 'pillars'. The first pillar, the European Community, is the province of the Commission—the Euro-bureaucracy—which has the exclusive right to propose policy initiatives on subjects such as development aid and humanitarian assistance. These initiatives are subject to the advice of the European Parliament and the approval of the Council of Ministers, representing the 15 member states. The Commission is responsible for implementing policy.

EU consolidation was limited from the outset. The states that established the Union retained discretion over a common foreign and security policy—the second pillar—and justice and home affairs matters—the third pillar. These subjects are addressed in the framework of intergovernmental processes, although an incrementalist approach was taken with the third pillar on justice and home affairs, which is effectively being slowly integrated into the first pillar—the Commission. This means that the European Commission is becoming more involved with issues such as the consideration of a common asylum policy. Even the need for a common European migration policy is being debated quietly by Eurocrats at the Commission.

Two broad potentially contradictory dynamics are at play in the evolution of governance at the European level. The first is the consolidation of EU structures, reflected by the growth of the Secretariat for the Council of Ministers and the strengthened role of the 626-member European Parliament, which, for example, forced the resignation of Commissioners in 1999 over allegations of corruption. The second trend is the contemplated enlargement of the EU, with perhaps up to 28 member states. These two separate dynamics will clearly take a very long time to reconcile.

Nevertheless, the reference to the Union's foreign policy reflects the notion that a common foreign and security policy is more than the sum of the—sometimes conflicting—national interests and priorities of the member states. The implementation of this common policy involves a new position, the Secretary-General and High Representative, to assist the presidency, which is held by a member state for a six-month term on a rotating basis: France in late 2000 and Sweden in early 2001, to be followed by Belgium and Denmark. While the most recent debate has concerned the development of an EU military capacity, a less noticed bureaucratic innovation may directly affect the EU's capacity to support peace operations: the establishment in 1999 of a policy planning unit.[16]

This unit is situated in the Secretariat of the Council of Ministers under the direction of Javier Solana, a former Secretary-General of NATO, who is the first Council Secretary-General and High Representative. The planning and early warning unit coordinates at the working level with the Commission, which is responsible for the EU's external economic aid and development policies. There is no direct link by this unit with the European Parliament, which has budgetary control over the Commission.

The policy planning unit in the Council's Secretariat monitors and analyses developments relevant to the European Union's foreign policy and security interests, provides assessments and early warning of potential crises, and produces policy papers to guide strategic planning. These papers are internal by nature and promote the convergence of views between member states on key foreign and security policy issues. The policy unit also contributes to the work of implementing the common strategies on Russia, Ukraine, and the Middle East, which have been adopted by unanimity by the European Council in recent years. The adoption of these broad framework documents permits implementing decisions to be taken on the basis of a qualified, as opposed to a simple, majority of the weighted votes of member states. But the common strategies mechanism has not proved to be very useful in fast-developing situations, such as the Balkans, for which no strategies paper has been prepared.

The December 1999 EU Summit in Helsinki included an aspiration for the development, by 2003, of the ability to deploy within 60 days and sustain for at least one year up to 60,000 troops for use in peace operations. This capacity is well on its way to realization, and as of late 2001 a staff of around 130 military officers had been located at the Council Secretariat.

The Helsinki Summit also foresaw the strengthening of the capacity for deploying civilian crisis-management resources in post-conflict settings, including civilian police and legal, judicial, and prison administration personnel. The policy planning unit thus began working on arrangements to deploy civilian police from EU member states in peace operations, a task which has since devolved to a new police planning unit located in

[16] Conflict prevention is a significant agenda item for the European Commission, as reflected in a recent 'Communication from the Commission on Conflict Prevention', COM (2001) 211, issued on 11 April 2001. Discussions are under way on the identification of indicators of imminent crises and on the coordination of aid programmes to address the deeper structural origins of conflict. The prevention issue is also being addressed by OSCE, which in 1991 established a small Conflict Prevention Centre in Vienna to advise its various field missions.

the Council Secretariat with a staff of seven senior police officers as of August 2001.

According to an expert in the Council Secretariat, of the approximately 8,500 police deployed in UN operations in 2000, approximately 3,300 were from EU states.[17] Kosovo alone is the site of 5,000 armed international police with full executive authority to make arrests and enforce the law under the terms of the UN administration there. The difficulties that the EU member states had in marshalling international police to deploy in Kosovo was a key inspiration for the development of this new capacity. There is also a growing consensus in Europe that there will probably be more of these types of security-related crisis responses in the future.

The EU now plans to be able to deploy up to 5,000 police officers in international peace operations—1,000 within 30 days.[18] As of 2001, member states had informally made the commitments necessary to reach these targets, and a first conference of national ministers responsible for police forces is scheduled in November 2001 to formalize the commitments. But, as of August 2001, questions regarding training and financing had yet to be resolved.

While policing issues have received considerable attention, recent peace operations demonstrate that police are ineffectual without a variety of follow-on structures, notably prisons, courts, judges, prosecutors, and defence lawyers. But the thinking on these components is preliminary. The EU member states have agreed to a target figure of 200 personnel for these purposes, but as of August 2001 had not yet broken down this figure in terms of the numbers of judges, lawyers, and prison administrators, or of the array of expertise that should be held in reserve. It is also an open question whether the Council Secretariat or Commission should administer this initiative. The Commission has ongoing rule of law and aid programmes which argue in favour of locating the management of the effort there. In any event, complicated coordination issues will persist for some time at the European level.

On a proposal by the Commission, a rapid reaction mechanism has been established, to be managed by the Commission. This mechanism brings together the relevant components of the Commission to manage a crisis situation, such as Macedonia in 2001. It also is a tool to mobilize funding for crisis responses on an urgent basis over an initial six-month period. But a challenge remains in how to relate this assistance to longer-term

[17] 'Presidency Report on Strengthening the Common European Security and Defence Policy, Presidency Conclusions, Santa Maria da Feira European Council (19 and 20 June 2000)', Appendix 4, Sect. A.1.

[18] 'Presidency Report', Annex I, Sect. III.3(d).

capacity building and development funding mechanisms, which normally take from 12 to 18 months to engage. Framework agreements are contemplated with member states, international organizations, and NGOs to implement crisis management policies. The overarching policy framework was adopted by EU heads of states at a meeting in Laeken in Belgium in late 2001. In 2002, these new EU crisis management capacities are to become initially operable.

There are other regional capacities apart from the EU which are evolving at the European level. In particular, the Organization for Security and Cooperation in Europe (OSCE), a group of 55 governments which includes the United States and Russia, has been involved in police training activities in many settings in the former Yugoslavia. OSCE, for example, administers the police academy in Kosovo. As a result of decisions taken at the 1999 Istanbul Summit in 2001, OSCE launched a rapid recruitment programme designed to insert quickly police and civilian expertise into its field operations. The programme is designed to accelerate the time necessary to recruit personnel for OSCE missions, by a matter of weeks.

Traditionally, OSCE mission personnel are seconded from participating states in response to vacancy notices. Standardized application forms, personnel classifications, and training modules have been developed to facilitate pre-screening by national authorities, who then indicate the number of personnel they are prepared in principle to deploy on an urgent basis—two, four, or eight weeks. Recruitment can concern a wide variety of fields associated with crisis management, including police as well as rule of law and human rights experts. Further screening by the Secretariat in Vienna and the heads of the respective OSCE missions occurs before actual deployment.[19] This new OSCE rapid recruitment mechanism had not been invoked as of August 2001, although internal consideration of the issue was prompted by the prospect of a NATO deployment in Macedonia.

While not solely a European institution, the North Atlantic Treaty Organization (NATO) has also become an important player in responses to complex humanitarian emergencies in Europe. The policy planners and programme staff at NATO, also located in Brussels, are likely to remember the 78-day air campaign in Kosovo in the same terms as senior officials in Washington: they want never again to undertake such an operation. The apparent lack of results near the end of the air campaign caused deep

[19] See website of Rapid Expert Assistance and Co-operation Teams (REACT) programme. At: http://www.osce.org/react

unease at NATO. As one official noted, 'the Alliance came a little closer to coming undone than people would like to admit'.

Having stared into the abyss in Kosovo, NATO officials are understandably cautious in considering whether to undertake future peace-enforcement missions. This hesitancy is apparent in 2001 in the narrow design and early exit advertised—30 days—for a NATO deployment in Macedonia to collect weapons from ethnic Albanian insurgents.

In a quest to be relevant in the post-cold war world, NATO has expanded its mandate to include humanitarian operations. But the implementation of this new authority reflects hesitancy in commitment. Referring to the campaign in Kosovo, one senior official in 2000 noted that, while such operations cannot be excluded in the future, they are not likely to be undertaken. 'Kosovo was probably a one-off engagement', he said. Future NATO operations are instead likely to focus not on peace enforcement but on civil implementation programmes under the authority of a UN Security Council resolution, perhaps in places such as the Caucasus region of the former Soviet Union.

The overarching lesson of NATO's involvement in Kosovo was the importance of integrating humanitarian considerations into planning for military action. NATO is now prepared even to share advance planning documents relating to military action with civilian humanitarian interlocutors. A senior NATO official noted that many international humanitarian organizations have expressed a willingness to participate in such planning endeavours, with the notable exception of the ICRC. NATO has elaborated a broad mandate with respect to humanitarian work. Whether it will develop a robust capacity to undertake this work, however, remains to be determined.

The path trod by NATO to reach its current configuration is worth noting. Since its creation in 1949, NATO has had a civil defence programme. These civil protection programmes evolved in response to natural disasters in Europe as a complement to the United Nations. The Chernobyl nuclear accident in 1986 and a devastating earthquake in Armenia in 1988 underscored the need to strengthen regional capacities in Europe to respond to such disasters. A 1998 Russian proposal to enhance cooperation in disaster relief resulted in the establishment of the Euro-Atlantic Disaster Response Coordination Center (EADRCC). The EADRCC was a focal point for the international response to flooding in Ukraine in 1998, when the UN was preoccupied with the international response to Hurricane Mitch in Central America.

But it was the crisis in Kosovo that brought the EADRCC to the humanitarian centre stage. In June 1998 it received a request for assistance from

UNHCR to move relief items to Albania in response to the initial influx of refugees from Kosovo. As a result, in a surge of activity impressive to the humanitarians 16 flights airlifted 165 tons of relief from Sarajevo to Tirana using cargo planes offered by Belgium and Norway.

Upon the beginning of the NATO air campaign on 24 March 1999, and the ensuing Serbian campaign of forced expulsion of hundreds of thousands of ethnic Albanians, the EADRCC was transformed into a seven days a week, 24 hours a day operation, handling a multitude of tasks. It served as the humanitarian focal point and information clearing house at NATO for both non-NATO bodies and affected countries, including Albania and Macedonia. It also assisted UNHCR, particularly with airlift and transportation, as well as the provision of relief supplies, tents, and telecommunication equipment. EADRCC also helped UNHCR to channel requests to NATO forces and partner countries regarding such matters as establishing refugee camps and increasing humanitarian evacuations of Kosovar asylum seekers to third countries.

While the humanitarian response succeeded in avoiding loss of refugee life, UNHCR was uncomfortable, according to an EADRCC official, suggesting that NATO 'had blown them away' in public relations terms—a proposition that he agreed with—and that NATO had portrayed itself as a humanitarian saviour—which he denied. He cited the fact that UNHCR was clearly too slow to react to the Kosovo crisis and did not have the most competent personnel deployed to the field at the outset of the crisis. UNHCR had at one point estimated that 100,000 refugees could be externally displaced from Kosovo. But the assistance 'kit' prepared for them was in Belgrade, explained this official. It should have been foreseen that there would be difficulties in gaining access to distribute assistance to those refugees in the throes of the air campaign against Serbia. He noted that UNHCR had in 2000 again estimated that there could be as many as 100,000 refugees displaced if there were an armed Serbian incursion in Montenegro.

It is not clear whether humanitarian crisis response will be an important element of NATO activities in the future. While NATO has given itself a mandate to undertake such endeavours, it has yet to organize a substantial capacity to provide such services, according to an official at the EADRCC in 2000. The ongoing efforts are overseen by a relatively junior-level planning committee, and staffing and resources are meagre. This reflects the continued uncertainty about whether or not humanitarian action is a proper mission for this military organization.

Also, coordination at the working level with interlocutors in the European Union has sometimes proved difficult. For example, when France held the EU presidency in 2001, it insisted that there be no contacts initiated by

NATO until a broader political arrangement had been made between NATO and the European Union. Since then, more communications are reported to be occurring at the working level. But the nuances of different positions among EU member states continue to complicate discussions about apportioning humanitarian action roles between the EU, NATO, and OSCE.

Europe is a fertile setting for the development of regional capacities that can blend military and civilian responses to humanitarian crises, both within and outside Europe. No other region of the world is similarly endowed with such a complex overlay of capable entities. Nevertheless, difficulties of coordination and uncertainty of mission and purpose pervade these European structures in the conceptual disorientation of the post-cold war era. Overall, while the discussions are promising, Europe is not much more advanced than either the US or the UN in preparing to conduct new forms of humanitarian action. The result is hesitancy and is illustrated well by a French intervention after the 1994 genocide in Rwanda.

INTERVENTION IN AFRICA: OPERATION TURQUOISE

Other regional capacities around the world pale in comparison with Europe. There have been efforts over the past several years, particularly by France, the United Kingdom, and the United States, to strengthen African militaries and sub-regional organizations with training and equipment in order to build the capacity to undertake peacekeeping and humanitarian missions. Concerns about the appropriateness and the capacity of African interlocutors to absorb these resources have kept those efforts relatively modest, and lack of donor coordination has been an issue. As a consequence, direct international action by outsiders, albeit selective, remains the likely scenario in Africa.

The 1994 genocide in Rwanda inspired agonizing debates by policy makers about military intervention both during and after the fact. At the time, the UN Security Council was immobilized by the spectre of the recent fiasco in Somalia in which 18 US soldiers under UN command had been killed in pursuit of a Somali warlord and their bodies dragged through the streets of Mogadishu. This tragic event gave rise to what became known as the 'Mogadishu syndrome' of risk averseness in peace enforcement. The United States was particularly wary of another such deployment, and declined an invitation by France to join in an intervention in Rwanda in 1994.

This was a defining moment in Rwanda. Not only was the force level of the United Nations Assistance Mission for Rwanda not expanded, but all but 250 of 2,500 UN troops were withdrawn in the face of crisis following the murder of ten Belgian soldiers assigned to guard moderate Hutu Prime Minister Agathe Uwinlingiyimana.[20]

A discrete French military deployment ensued in June 1994. By June, however, much of the genocide had been accomplished. The mass killing was planned, and most of it occurred in April and early May. The Rwandan Patriotic Front (RPF) had invaded from bases in southern Uganda, and the government that had organized and presided over the mass killings of Tutsis and their supporters had fled from Kigali. Government troops and militia—the Interahamwe, or 'those who stand together'—were retreating in June, fighting rearguard actions.

It was in this context that the debate in France over intervention reached a high pitch, with foreign minister Alain Juppé advocating a response to the 'genocide'. On 13 June, South African President Nelson Mandela, attending a meeting of the Organization of African Unity, called for action to address the tragedy in Rwanda. This summons from the 'Anglo Saxon world', in the words of political scientist Gerard Prunier who was part of the French government's Rwanda crisis planning group, galvanized President François Mitterrand into action.[21] A frenzy of planning and diplomacy followed, with the result that on 23 June there began a deployment of 2,500 French troops supported by 100 armoured vehicles and an array of artillery, helicopters, and attack planes. The intervention began just hours before the UN Security Council passed Resolution 929, which authorized enforcement action under Chapter VII of the UN Charter.[22] The resolution specifically endorsed a mission of the member states to establish a temporary operation under national command and control 'aimed at contributing in an impartial way, to the security and protection of displaced persons, refugees and civilians at risk in Rwanda ... '. Resolution 929 limited the mission to a duration of two months.

The French forces entered southwestern Rwanda with considerable fanfare in June 1994, accompanied by an assembly of humanitarian agencies. The French quickly sought to provide security to about 8,000 Tutsis encamped in Nyarushishi. A smaller French force conducted reconnaissance in the northwest of Rwanda.

The French Safe Humanitarian Zone was thereupon established in a portion of southwestern Rwanda comprising approximately 5,000 square

[20] UK Home Office, 'Annex A—Chronology of Major Events—Rwanda—1899–2000', in 'Rwanda Assessment' (April 2001). At: http://www.ind.homeoffice.gov.uk/default.asp?pageid=51

[21] Prunier, Gerard, *The Rwanda Crisis: History of a Genocide* (New York: Columbia University Press, 1995), 281.

[22] Gerard, *The Rwanda Crisis*, 290.

kilometres. At the time French forces withdrew on 21 August, approximately 1.5 million persons had been accommodated in the zone.[23] The French deployment in Operation Turquoise is judged by a variety of commentators to have saved approximately 15,000–17,000 Tutsis.[24] But killings in the zone continued, and, upon the withdrawal, approximately 500,000 persons fled from the safe area to eastern Zaire.[25] There, many perished from an epidemic of cholera. Others continued their exile.

Perhaps the overriding question associated with Operation Turquoise is whether it was in fact a humanitarian endeavour. The deployment was expressly justified by the French authorities on humanitarian grounds. Circumstantial evidence, however, suggests the presence of important military and strategic considerations. Indeed, France's long history in Rwanda included support of the Kigali government and the provision of arms and military training for several years until at least the very outset of the genocide. In February 1993, French forces were used to halt an incursion by fighters of the RPF. Some of the French troops deployed in Operation Turquoise had served previously in Rwanda and trained the government's soldiers. Among the French soldiers were some who vowed specifically to punish the RPF.

Insights can be gleaned from one of the implementers of Operation Turquoise, Bernard Debré. Debré became an Africanist by virtue of the travel and work of his father, President Charles de Gaulle's first prime minister and the principal drafter of France's post-Second World War constitution. The author of a book on the Kingdom of the Tutsis, Debré the son was on the one hand a political ally of Prime Minister Edouard Balladur and Mayor of Paris, Jacques Chirac, and on the other hand President François Mitterrand's doctor. As such, he was uniquely placed to follow the internal political debates over intervention at the time of the 1994 genocide in Rwanda. Debré also served as a deputy in the National Assembly at the time of the onset of the crisis, and he was Minister of Cooperation in charge of development aid for several months just after Operation Turquoise was launched.

According to Debré, Operation Turquoise was a compromise between President Mitterrand, who wanted to have French forces occupy Rwanda and organize elections, which presumably would have re-established the

[23] Gerard, *The Rwanda Crisis*, 295.

[24] Des Forges, Alison, *Leave None to Tell the Story: Genocide in Rwanda* (New York: Human Rights Watch, 1999), 689.

[25] Prunier, Gerard, 'Operation Turquoise: A Humanitarian Escape from a Political Dead End', in Howard Adelman and Astri Suhrke (eds), *The Path of a Genocide: The Rwanda Crisis from Uganda to Zaire* (New Brunswick, NJ: Transaction Publishers, 2000), 301.

Hutu majority government, and Prime Minister Balladur, who wanted to stay out entirely. The compromise was a 'humanitarian' intervention to halt the 'genocide', or, as Debré puts it, a 'small' genocide—Tutsi killing Hutu—that followed a 'large' one—Hutu killing Tutsi.

Debré also places the intervention in the context of political rivalry in central Africa between the United States, which supported the RPF, and France, which supported the Hutu government. French fear of the development of a hegemonic regional policy by the US-backed English-speaking invaders from Uganda clearly influenced the policy course chosen. The United States did not join France in the June deployment, according to Debré, because to do so would have frustrated the war aims of the RPF.

While the French forces did not engage the RPF in 1994, it seems clear that the deployment had the effect of slowing the advance of the rebels, who then swept to victory after the French withdrawal. Whether this was the primary motivation of the intervention will remain the subject of historical debate. It seems clear, however, that decision makers were animated by an array of political and strategic factors in addition to the humanitarian consideration. The absence of a genuine multilateral character to the intervention—only Senegal contributed a modest contingent of troops—heightened the possibility and perception of the pursuit of political and strategic objectives in the guise of a humanitarian mission. Even the cover provided by UN Security Council Resolution 929 could not mask the reality of an essentially unilateral intervention.

However, even in humanitarian terms, the utility of Operation Turquoise was limited. This was not a sustained 'safe' area. While some 15,000–17,000 persons were saved by the intervention, others were killed when they were tricked in emerging from hiding in response to the display of French flags by Hutu extremists, and the safe zone itself harboured several former government officials who had planned and executed the genocide, and who then escaped to encampments in Zaire or even France. The Hutu fighters in the zone were not disarmed. Nor were those suspected of having organized the genocide arrested. In fact, an extremist radio station continued broadcasting for weeks from the Humanitarian Zone to the great embarrassment of the French forces, who finally had to silence the transmissions.

As a humanitarian intervention, Operation Turquoise was, according to Bernard Debré, 'not a success', which has been largely 'forgotten' by the French public and political elite in view of the modesty of the objectives and relative insignificance of the outcome.

Moreover, mixed motivations compromised the humanitarian effect. The transient nature of the arrangement permitted the gathering of displaced and vulnerable persons, but many then fled upon the French withdrawal.

The security threats ultimately posed by the encampments in Zaire near the border to Rwanda later prompted an attack upon those concentrations, leading to massive loss of life. The absence of a consensual arrangement regarding the safe area and the failure to fortify the area clearly diminished its utility. Indeed, in humanitarian terms, the best that can be said of Operation Turquoise is that it was more in the nature of a temporary staging and rescue operation, which, while it saved some persons, ultimately led to further displacement.

THE BROAD CONTEXT: INTERNATIONAL MIGRATION

Refugee movements must be appreciated in the larger context of international migration. The current educated guess is that there are nearly 170 million international migrants who reside outside their countries of birth.[26] This is a significant rise in numbers from 1965, when the United Nations Population Division counted 70 million long-term migrants. In terms of broad trends, international migration is expected to remain high during the new century while population growth continues to decline in the more developed region.[27]

While people move from all parts of the world and go to all parts of the world, the largest numbers of international migrants have relocated in Asia, followed by Europe and North America, and then Africa, Latin America, and Oceania. More than half of all international migrants live in developing countries. Yet the smaller share that lives in developed countries tends to represent a higher proportion of the overall population in those countries. These countries will continue to be net receivers of international migrants. The United States is by far the largest recipient of international migrants, with about 25 million foreign-born residents at the end of the 1990s. Among discernible trends, females among international migrants are a rising percentage; presently, approximately 52.5 per cent are male and 47.5 per cent are female.[28]

[26] Population Division of the United Nations Secretariat, 'Trends in Total Migrant Stock by Sex', Revision 4, UN Doc. POP/1B/DB/98/4. Estimates are derived assuming constant rates of growth during 1990–2000 with the addition of 10 million migrants resulting from the dissolution of the USSR.

[27] United Nations Population Division, *World Population Prospects: The 2000 Revision, Highlights* (New York: United Nations Population Division, February 2001), vii.

[28] International Organization for Migration and United Nations, *World Migration Report 2000* (Geneva: International Organization for Migration and United Nations, 2000), 7.

Broadly speaking, international migrants are either voluntary migrants or forced migrants. This is more of a continuum in motivations, however, than a clear distinction. Migrants may move abroad proactively for purposes of employment, study, family unity, or other personal factors. Forced migrants may have to leave their countries in response to persecution, conflict, repression, natural and man-made disasters, ecological degradation, or other situations that involve risks of serious harm. In reality, the motives of international migrants are often complex and mixed.

Many of today's international population movements began with the recruitment and employment of foreign workers. Some are recruited for seasonal work, often in agriculture. Others fill short-term labour shortages. Labour migration, itself a highly complex phenomenon, involves individuals who can be highly skilled or unskilled. National systems vary significantly for admitting labour migrants. Family unity is another major motivation for international migration. Many countries permit close family members of those already in the country to enter through legal channels.

Apart from legal avenues for entry, migration, of course, may be unauthorized. One of the difficulties in ascertaining the global dimensions of the movements of people is that statistics relating to unauthorized migration are elusive as such movements are generally clandestine. Unauthorized migrants nevertheless cross national borders for largely the same reasons as those who are authorized, namely, employment or family unity.

Social scientists have offered several models seeking to explain international migration. Economists focus on factors such as net differentials between countries in wages and employment conditions for individuals, economic opportunities and risks for households, the structure of modern industrial economies, and the impacts of economic globalization and market development. Sociologists identify social factors which can sustain and augment the economic underpinnings of voluntary movement. For example, networks or institutions customarily develop to support international migration. Political scientists focus on the policies of source and receiving countries. But whether one focuses on broad structural elements or on individual decision-making models, the enduring characteristic is the complexity of the phenomenon.

The effects of international migration can be both positive and negative on countries of both origin and destination. The economic impact in destination countries is largely a function of the way in which migrants are involved in the economy. If they are employed, they can make contributions, including to human capital—'brain gain'. But their contributions can be reduced if wages are low. If migrants are not employed, they may impose burdens on social programmes and the social safety net.

In terms of demographic impacts, international migrants add to a population base. If they have higher fertility rates, they may increase population growth. For that reason, immigration is sometimes offered as a way for societies in western Europe which have low birth rates and aging populations to remain internationally competitive and maintain relatively robust social welfare systems. Germany has recently made provision for 30,000 computer specialists in high technology in an attempt at designer immigration, but the response was lukewarm and only 8,000 permits were issued in 2001.[29] A government-sponsored Commission on Immigration and Asylum Policy recently recommended that 50,000 foreigners be allowed to come and live in Germany, and in November 2001 legislation on the issue was introduced.[30] The issue has even surfaced in policy debates in Japan in relation to the assimilation of some 640,000 Korean permanent residents.[31] But immigration by itself would require entry at levels that would be unprecedented to cancel these demographic trends fully, and is only part of the answer.

This is not only an economic issue. International migration can also change the racial, ethnic, and religious composition of the destination country. About 20 million foreigners live among the 383 million inhabitants of western Europe.[32] Extreme right-wing parties in Austria, Belgium, France, and Switzerland have begun to champion the anti-immigration cause. Diversity can result in conflict as well as creativity.

For source countries, migration can cost human capital—'brain drain'—but presumably only if employment opportunities at appropriate levels would have been available had the individuals remained in their home countries. Remittances from abroad can be a significant form of assistance to countries of origin. The International Monetary Fund estimates that in 1998 over $61 billion was sent back home by migrant workers, a figure that is probably understated given the vagaries in the collection and reporting of such information by governments.[33]

Broad trends relating to increased economic integration and globalization have important implications for the movements of people. Migration is an element of globalization, whether in terms of the movement of labour within a global economy or as a personification of the intermingling of

[29] Zachary, G. Pascal and Rohwedder, Cecilie, 'Germany Widens Door for Immigrants', *Wall Street Journal* (2 July 2001).

[30] Ibid.

[31] Tadokoro, Masayuki, 'Korean Minorities and Japanese Citizenship', *Correspondence: An International Review of Culture and Society*, 7 (Winter 2000/2001), 18.

[32] Münz, Rainer, 'Migration, Xenophobia, and the Future of Europe', *Correspondence: An International Review of Culture and Society*, 7 (Winter 2000/2001), 15.

[33] International Monetary Fund, 'Workers Remittances', Table B-19, *Balance of Payments Statistics Yearbook 1999* (Washington, DC: IMF, 1999), 54.

cultures and societies. But a basic dilemma results from the fact that while information and capital can move relatively freely, people cannot. Nevertheless, travel is often easy, and creates important sources of information and insight into countries in crisis, a proposition which can be verified by chatting with taxi drivers in many of the world's great cities.

National policy efforts to forestall the movements of people, particularly unauthorized migration, produce perverse incentives for the development of criminal networks and institutions designed to facilitate migrant smuggling. These trans-national criminal enterprises pose growing threats to states as they expand their nefarious activities to people. It is estimated by the United Nations Office for Drug Control and Crime Prevention that traffickers around the world move as many as 4 million people each year, generating $5 billion–$7 billion in a lucrative criminal enterprise.[34]

Refugees are a personification of the broader phenomenon of migration that has been an important dimension of the twentieth century and that will continue to grow in importance in the new century. There are more people in the world, it is easier for them to move, and more often now they can be facilitated and supported on their journeys. These population movements necessarily diminish the exclusive prerogative of nation states relating to border control in the modern world. Refugees cross borders. In that sense, refugees who secure protection from return to their home countries can be seen as the thin edge of a wider wedge comprising a forced dimension of the broader phenomenon of international migration.

In contrast to the multilateral consensus achieved with respect to refugees, governments have taken little more than hesitant steps to cooperate on international migration. Treaties concluded in 2000 on human smuggling and trafficking are perhaps the best example of emerging forms of international cooperation on the issue. Modest efforts are also reflected in the work of the International Labour Organization and a not very popular UN treaty relating to the treatment of migrant workers. For the most part, bilateral and unilateral policies and practices still characterize governmental responses.

The future of international migration is very likely to be a future of increased international cooperation and regulation of the movements of people. There will be concerted efforts to keep out the unwanted. But these efforts are not likely to work in any comprehensive sense, and the reality of such movements will cause policy makers to retreat to managing the phenomenon. On occasion, this pressure has produced, and will continue to

[34] Centre for International Crime Prevention (CICP), United Nations Office for Drug Control and Crime Prevention, at: http://www.uncjin.org/CICP/cicp.htm

produce, calls for an international arrangement on migration. However, a 1999 UN survey of governments about the desirability of a world migration conference elicited but a small number of responses with no discernible consensus on either the objective or the organization of such a conference. Despite the support of the ILO, many governments expressed reservations and some favoured a regional or sub-regional approach.[35] A greater degree of cooperation will depend on a deeper appreciation of the interests in and incentives for concerted action in the area of human migration, as discussed later in this book in the context of forced migration.

One clear interim result has been the pressure in developed countries to narrow the asylum remedy for refugees in order to ensure that it does not become an unmanageable exception to migration control. Constraints under international law, founded on moral considerations, serve as a countervailing force. How policy is formulated between this Scylla and Charybdis of perilous alternatives will be a measure of statecraft in the new century.

[35] The United Nations may well abandon its plans for an international conference on migration and development due to lack of support from member states. See 'Migration: UN Conference Likely to be Scrapped', *UN Wire* (15 August 2001). At: http:/ / www.unfoundation.org/unwire/index. For a summary of specific objections by member states, see 'International Migration and Development, including the question of the convening of a United Nations conference on international migration and development to address migration issues', Report of the Secretary-General, UN Doc. A/56/167 (3 July 2001), Sect. II.

6

Varieties of Refugee Concerns: The Beginnings of a Policy Toolbox

What will refugee arrangements look like over the next decades? While refugees matter, it is clear that they matter differentially to governments. This is particularly evident in the selectivity that has attended the innovations in humanitarian action described in earlier chapters. A refugee emergency concerning Haiti presents a different set of considerations from a displacement crisis in Chechnya. As a result, responses differ within the ambit of discretion permitted under international law.

By way of illustration, activities inside countries to protect and assist would-be refugees may be complemented by arrangements for asylum abroad. Asylum measures may be buttressed by relocation to third countries as exile becomes prolonged and local integration is unavailable. Repatriation may resolve exile, but only if return and re-integration are enduring. Efforts over the past decade to protect persons before they flee countries are innovations which have had mixed results and which have created new difficulties. Such responses, often motivated by the desire of states to contain would-be asylum seekers, can nevertheless provide effective remedies in lieu of exile.

The toolbox metaphor should carry with it no implication that any one remedy holds the answer to a particular refugee crisis. Rather, the combinations and sequence of responses are most often the crucial elements. The metaphor is meant to evoke the notion of managing the humanitarian consequences of chaos in the new century. New risks to civilian aid workers are among the unanticipated consequences which must be addressed.

This chapter opens with a vision of refugee arrangements in Africa in the Dadaab Camps in Kenya. The setting is sobering. In the absence of more effective humanitarian action, vast numbers of refugees will simply be condemned to wasted and fearful lives in like circumstances. The chapter then examines the various policy tools available to decision makers.

A NORM BY DEFAULT: THE DADAAB CAMPS IN KENYA

It was in Ifo camp in November 2000 where I met with Somali and Sudanese refugee leaders in north-eastern Kenya. The setting was similar to that of many long-staying refugee populations around the world.

The day was oppressively hot, and we sat in the UNHCR field office, discussing life in the camp. I mentioned that in 2000 Ifo looked more like a 'town' than the emergency encampment I had first observed in 1993. The refugee elders, however, patiently but firmly described to me the variety of ways in which Ifo was anything but a normal town. They discussed the pervasive violence, noting that people were afraid to leave their homes at night. They talked about restrictions on education and the impossibility of becoming part of Kenyan society. Refugees were confined to the camps, subject to special permission to reside outside if justified on humanitarian or medical grounds. They noted with hope a recent UN-sponsored peace initiative which raised the possibility of the return of refugees to Somalia. But that prospect remains uncertain. They also urged international support for the creation of conditions conducive to return. Above all, with understated dignity, they communicated an ardent and all-consuming desire to be somewhere, anywhere, other than Ifo.

I could not help noticing that the laments of the refugee leaders contrasted starkly to an idyllic mural painted on one entire wall of the UNHCR field office, titled 'Ifo Camp in Action'. The reds, yellows, and blues used by a refugee artist depicted scenes such as groupings of families at water wells, the provision of medical care, and school classes. The UNHCR female field officer who had commissioned the painting was prominently depicted as well in the mural. Notably absent from the mural were the armed police escorts, rapes, clan violence, and deprivation that the refugee leaders were earnestly describing to me in great detail. When I pointed out to the elders the contrast between their reports of hardship and the idyllic nature of the mural, they simply shrugged their shoulders, wearily recognizing their invisibility to the international community.

The camps

Dadaab is a small town of a few thousand inhabitants in northeastern Kenya, not far from the border with Somalia. The town is surrounded by three refugee camps, Ifo, Dagahaley, and Hagadera. As of November

2000, the camps had a total population of 127,629, the vast majority of whom are Somalis.[1] Largely nomads, the refugees also include farmers from areas along the southern Juba river valley as well as former civil servants and traders from urban areas. The small non-Somali population in the camps includes Eritreans, Ethiopians, Sudanese, and Ugandans. The camps were established in the early 1990s: Ifo in September 1991, Dagahaley in March 1992, and Hagadera in June 1992. Fighting in Somalia was the primary cause of the refugee influx.

When I first visited Dadaab in 1993, it was in the throes of an emergency. Violence and banditry were pervasive, and I stayed in a sandbagged tent in a fenced UNHCR compound. When I arrived by plane in November 2000, the emergency had long ago ended, and Dadaab was a 'care and maintenance' arrangement for this huge but largely invisible refugee population. This was the season of short rains in Kenya, and it had rained just the day before. The vegetation was a little greener than I remembered. However, by the next day a baking sun had dried the red sandy soil, and clouds of dust trailed the vehicles moving between the camps.

Questions of insecurity lingered in Dadaab, which has traditionally experienced a deficit of law and order. The UNHCR compound in which I stayed on this occasion was more established; it even had a lighted tennis court. But the security advice was a chilling reminder of my previous visit:

> As Dadaab is a high security location (Security Phase III) movements by all guests are restricted. All movements from and to Dadaab and the camps are to be done with armed police escorts in convoys. No movement is allowed otherwise, and the main gate of the compound is closed at 6:00 p.m. and not opened until the next morning.

Human insecurity is the defining characteristic in the camps around Dadaab. Banditry and violence remain pervasive between the complex network of Somali clans which are represented among both the refugees and the local community. A UNHCR field assistant described a spate of clan-related killings in early 2000. Indeed, Dadaab has achieved sufficient infamy within UNHCR to be used as a subject of a training videotape on security issues. In 1993 the security situation was dire; more recently it had improved somewhat. No convoy has been ambushed since 1998, when there was an attack on the road to Garissa.

[1] Information provided by UNHCR Sub-Office Dadaab, Kenya, November 2000.

Life inside the refugee camp remained disturbed, but the abnormality had achieved a perverse regularity. Bandits lurked and victimized those who dared to venture out. The harsh conditions and violence led a US State Department refugee official to brief me that Dadaab in 2000 was 'hell on earth'. To me, it seemed that Dadaab reflected the prolonged and indefinite character of refugee arrangements in Africa and elsewhere around the world: increasingly a norm by default.

The local Kenyan authorities have a difficult job to maintain security in the camps. The local police chief, who offered us a soft drink at a small table under a shade tree at his ramshackle headquarters, garrulously described the difficulties of his work. Often conflicts between the clans in Somalia were mirrored by conflicts in the camps. 'I am responsible for the physical protection of those in Dadaab', he explained. Police work relating to offences concerning refugees was complicated by the fact that generally Somali leaders preferred to handle the matters themselves through traditional justice practices, including the payment of compensation to victims.

The Dadaab police chief, who oversees the work of some 170 officers in the Dadaab area, was grateful for the support provided by UNHCR, which has funded salary incentives, equipment, vehicles, and buildings for the police. UNHCR's financing of the local police has buttressed both its own security and the security of the camps. As a result, relations between the police and UNHCR are good in Dadaab. UNHCR also provides finance to support a mobile Kenyan court, which convenes periodically in nearby Garissa to hear and decide cases pertaining to both refugees and local people.

The rape of women has become synonymous with the Dadaab camps. When I first visited the camps in April and May 1993, the issue was just emerging as a critical dimension of the insecurity in the camps. A UNHCR rape counsellor then reported 107 cases of rape in the two months before my visit.

As the issue garnered increased international attention, several measures were taken. In particular, live thorn bushes were provided in order to fence the camps to increase their security, a resource shared with the local community. In 1995, the US government funded an initiative to provide firewood to refugees. Many of the rapes occurred when women left the camps to search for firewood in the nearby territory. This initiative has since become a regular UNHCR budget item. When I was in Ifo camp in November 2000, I witnessed a mass firewood distribution.

The provision of firewood in the camps, however, is relatively expensive and funding is available to supply only 30 per cent of the current needs in the camps.[2] Nevertheless, the programme has apparently had an impact in reducing incidents of rape. According to a UNHCR protection officer, from January to October 2000 75 rapes had been reported in the Dadaab camps, up from 71 cases in 1999 but fewer than the 164 cases reported in 1998. Other measures had been taken apart from distributing firewood. The refugees in the Dadaab camps had themselves organized anti-rape committees, giving unusual prominence to an issue that afflicts many refugee camps around the world. UNHCR also refers rape survivors to Western countries for resettlement abroad.

A micro-credit lending programme financed by Ted Turner's United Nations Foundation and administered by Cooperative Action for American Relief Everywhere (CARE) has also been defended by its proponents, in part as a way to reduce sexual violence in the Dadaab camps. The lending programme, which targets vulnerable women, provides loans to groups of five women who undertake small-scale enterprises. These endeavours result in earnings which enable women to buy firewood without having to leave the camps, thereby avoiding exposure in the bush to rapists. By November 2000, nearly $1 million had been committed under this micro-lending scheme for women in the Dadaab camps.[3] Repayment rates were nearly 100 per cent. The women with whom I met were quite enthusiastic about the programme, although they allowed that there was some grumbling from men who complained that the women had been singled out for this benefit.

There are many situations around the world in which encampments of refugees supported by international assistance have inspired resentment on the part of local populations who may also be facing serious deprivation and insecurity. Such is the case in Kenya's northeastern territory, where refugee camps are situated in the midst of a local population which itself must cope with severe drought and poverty. This has resulted in a conscious effort by UNHCR in the Dadaab camps to address the needs of local people by digging wells for water and making medical services available without distinction as to whether the individuals were refugees or not. As a doctor from MSF-Belgium in Hagadera camp noted, 'We do not discriminate between refugees and the local community. Indeed, there is no real way to tell the difference between refugees and the local community and we do not check food ration cards.' In a similar manner,

[2] UNHCR Kenya Briefing Material, *Dadaab Refugee Camps: Highlights* (Kenya: UNHCR Sub-Office Dadaab, Kenya, November 2000), 3.

[3] Information provided by the UNHCR Sub-Office Dadaab, Kenya, November 2000.

UNHCR provides direct financial support to the local government health facility in Dadaab town.

The Kenyan doctor's point reinforces another characteristic of population displacements in Africa where movements often occur across borders imposed under colonial rule. International boundaries divide members of ethnic groups and host communities on one side receive those forcibly displaced from the other side of the border.

Environmental degradation is a typical impact of refugee camps on a host community in an ecologically fragile setting. Refugees in developing countries sometimes forage for firewood, cut down trees to build shelters, and otherwise deplete local resources. During the emergency phase when the Dadaab camps were built, little thought was given to such environmental impacts. Indeed, when the first camp, Ifo, was created, the area was bulldozed and levelled, depriving it of shade trees and natural foliage. The Ifo camp thus has a harsh, unsheltered character. Inhabitants have even been known to fight over spots in the shade in order to escape from the blazing sun.

When the later camps were created, first Dagahaley and then Hagadera, efforts were made to preserve trees and natural foliage, giving those camps a more normal appearance. Also, UNHCR has utilized the services of a German environmental NGO, and environmental working groups have been established in the camps comprising representatives from refugees and the local community to help regulate the use of local resources. A 'greenbelt' has been fenced around each of the three camps, and energy-efficient stoves have been distributed. The firewood distribution project, which uses local contractors, has an environmental as well as a security justification. Firewood is used at times as a form of payment for environmentally related work.

As the refugee emergency in Kenya gave way over the years to a more prolonged exile, there followed the establishment of educational programming and increased efforts to encourage self-sufficiency. However, these efforts are under threat as UNHCR has been forced to reduce its 2001 budget by 20 per cent, and further reductions are in prospect, much to the chagrin of the agencies responsible for implementing camp programmes. The aid workers I spoke with emphasized that this budget reduction would have a serious impact on the level of services provided to refugees, and particularly on programmes designed to enhance their self-sufficiency.

While large refugee encampments may have resource impacts in the immediate environs of where they are located, not all of the impacts are negative at the national level. Kenya has become a virtual regional centre for humanitarian and development agency activities. The streets and roads in the capital, Nairobi, are replete with the signs of literally hundreds of NGOs which are devoted to such endeavours and supported by international funds. They constitute a 'major industry', in the words of Bethuel A. Kiplagat, who directs the Africa Peace Forum and who had served in the Kenyan government as permanent secretary for foreign affairs from 1984 to 1991, and as ambassador to Great Britain from 1991 to 1993. Indeed, Kiplagat urges the Kenyan authorities to be particularly solicitous of NGOs given their willingness to invest resources and sustain activities in difficult times.

Kenyan refugee policy

By way of background, from the time it became independent in 1963 until the 1980s Kenya hosted refugees, mainly from Rwanda and Uganda. The numbers were relatively few, and refugees were integrated without much controversy into Kenyan society.

East Africa can be a tough neighbourhood, and the 1990s produced crises which transformed Kenya into a country hosting a vast refugee population. In 1991, the fall of the Mengistu regime in Ethiopia, along with the flight of Siad Barre and the dissolution of Somalia, added approximately 400,000 refugees to an indigenous population of some 30 million persons.[4]

The Somali influx in 1991 and 1992 was a singular event in Kenya. There were many reasons for this, according to Bethuel Kiplagat. This invasion of desperate people was shocking to both government and society in Kenya. When some who came by boat encamped around Mombasa, the outcry from the tourist industry prompted the authorities in 1995 to move the camps.

From the outset, the absorption of Somali refugees was resisted in Kenya. Intolerance can have complex roots. British colonial policies and history fuelled the resentment of Kenyans, according to Kiplagat, who explained that a British-imposed hierarchy of Europeans, Asians, and Africans was a relevant factor. The Somalis considered themselves to be the equivalent of Asians. Also, Northeast province, where the Somalis encamped, had been a closed territory during colonial rule, and its population was separated from Kenyan highlanders. Finally, the nationalist

[4] Carver, Richard, 'Refugees: The Problem of Security', in 'Kenya Since the Elections', WRITENET Country Papers, UNHCR RefWorld database (January 1994), Sect. 6, 14. At: http://www.unhcr.ch/refworld/country/writenet/wriken01.htm

aspiration for a greater Somalia created a lingering national security concern in Kenya. Indeed, Somalia had supported an armed insurgency in Kenya's northeastern territory, and relations between the two countries had been chilly for some time before Somalia imploded in the early 1990s.

In addition, the impacts of the Somali arrivals in the early 1990s on local people, who themselves were suffering from severe drought, aggravated this atmosphere of mistrust. While often a dilemma in refugee camp arrangements, this resource-driven dynamic was particularly sharp in this setting. A somewhat aggressive demeanour and propensity to bribe their way out of difficulties only complicated matters, said Kipligat, whose patrician demeanour was belied by his blunt assessments. 'Somalis are great survivors', he observed.

A deliberate choice was made by Kenyan government officials in the 1990s to largely cede refugee affairs to UNHCR. This has served to highlight problems in the agency's Nairobi branch office, which has long had a reputation for weak management. When I visited Nairobi in November 2000, rumours swirled about concerning bribery by refugees of UNHCR staff. Indeed, UNHCR then published an extraordinary public notice in Kenya's leading English language newspaper:

> UNHCR wishes to emphasize that any assistance given to refugees including protection screening and interviewing, the facilitation of repatriation or resettlement, counseling and medical services is free of charge. No refugee or asylum-seeker should pay for any services at the UNHCR offices in Nairobi or at the camps.[5]

The UNHCR representative in Nairobi, Daniel Tshitungi, confirmed that an investigation of the allegations of corrupt activities is ongoing. By June 2001 the investigation had resulted in five persons being charged criminally and 21 Kenyan employees being placed on involuntary leave without contract renewals.[6]

Kenya may be on the threshold of taking back its refugee responsibilities from UNHCR. According to senior government officials, a draft refugee bill, which had gone through several iterations since I last visited in 1993, may be submitted shortly to the parliament. This legislation to make provision for the recognition, protection, and management of refugees defines the term 'refugees' in accordance with UN and OAU treaty

[5] 'Public Notice', *Daily Nation* (10 November 2000), 5.

[6] 'Kenya: Two more UN Workers Charged in Refugee Corruption Scandal', *Associated Press* (12 June 2001).

standards. The bill would establish a National Council for Refugees to formulate and coordinate policy, which would include government officials responsible for foreign affairs, environment, health, education, domestic policy, refugees, and internal security. NGOs would be represented on the Council. A Refugee Trust Fund would be created and a Refugee Directorate would act as a secretariat to the Council. Other proposals concern the creation of a new refugee appeals body, as well as procedures and remedies, and provisions for family unity, refugee women, and refugee children.

There is no mention of UNHCR in the draft bill. But an exclusionary approach would be unwise, in Kiplagat's view, who believes that fashioning a sustainable refugee policy in Kenya will require joint action by the government, international organizations, and NGOs. Refugees in his view are 'opportunities for Kenya'. Of course, he allowed, rules of conduct under international law are necessary to clarify the rights of individuals and the responsibilities of the state. But, as Kiplagat elegantly put it, 'The [Refugee] Convention is not enough.' A calibrated set of policy tools is needed to deal with refugees.

TERRITORIAL PROTECTION ABROAD: ASYLUM

The term 'asylum' comes from a Greek word meaning 'without the right of seizure or arrest'. Asylum historically was synonymous with the refusal to extradite an individual to a requesting authority. It was a remedy in religious sanctuaries. With the emergence of nation states, territorial asylum evolved based on flight abroad to a receiving state. Today, asylum is cited in the foundational international human rights instrument, namely, the 1948 Universal Declaration of Human Rights. But the term is not defined.

In principle, there are two broad ideas embodied in the concept of asylum. The first is the notion of providing protection by way of admission into the territory of another state. The second is the permanent integration of the individual into the community of the asylum state. Asylum is most often considered an individual remedy for exile, but either idea can be extended to a broadened refugee concept to address mass population movements.

To state the obvious, for the asylum remedy to be effective, an individual must have access to the territory of an asylum state. Efforts by the authorities of a state to intercept unauthorized migrants thus can deny asylum seekers access to protection. Among the justifications used to limit the access of asylum seekers to protection are presumptions that they come from a safe country of origin or could find safety in a particular part of a territory of their home country. As well, asylum can be denied to individuals if they have transited through a safe third country where they are considered to have had an opportunity to find protection. In addition, some states have introduced limitations on access to protection, such as imposing time limits on the filing of asylum requests. Other barriers include the imposition of visa requirements and sanctions for common carriers who transport unauthorized migrants. Taken together, such measures, for example, constitute the policy walls around the new 'Fortress Europe' in relation to non-citizens seeking asylum.

UNHCR urges that returns to countries other than the home country should take place only in accordance with arrangements agreed upon in advance by the states concerned in order to determine which state is responsible for considering an asylum request. Formal bilateral re-admission agreements between countries provide the mechanisms for the return of asylum seekers to a state where a refugee protection claim can be lodged.

Asylum is an essential remedy for refugee exile. Most persons of concern today to UNHCR—12 million out of 21 million—are seeking protection outside their countries. Asylum is nothing less than a pragmatic exercise of individual will designed to seek safety abroad. Of course, the motives of asylum seekers may be mixed, and the effectiveness of the remedy depends in large measure on the ability and willingness of the asylum state to receive and accommodate arrivals. These problems may send policy makers looking for alternative remedies to asylum. But such options are often accompanied by their own complications, and these new complexities are producing the next generation of protection difficulties.

In exceptional circumstances, providing asylum can create serious political risks, as in 1991 in northern Iraq, and in 1999 in Macedonia. These risks may result in extraordinary efforts to find alternative protection remedies, such as the safe areas in Iraq or the relocation arrangements from Macedonia. But these innovations are clearly exceptions to the rule. Providing access to the territory of an asylum state will therefore continue to be the primary form of protecting refugees. But the quality of asylum is hardly uniform. Indeed, the differences are so dramatic at times as to be unconscionable.

The relatively lavish succour provided to the Kosovar refugees in Macedonia in the course of that great-power conflict stands in sharp contrast to the deprivations evident in camps in many parts of Africa, such as the complex of encampments surrounding Dadaab in northeastern

Kenya. There, women risk rape simply by venturing forth to collect firewood, and refugees fight over diminished food allotments. Enforced idleness, restrictions on movement, and detention are often aspects of asylum arrangements in developing as well as industrialized states. Governments, international organizations, and NGOs should do more to monitor the quality of asylum provided and report these findings publicly.

Refugees should more often be seen as opportunities rather than liabilities by host governments and societies. Experience teaches that more concerted and earlier efforts are necessary to include the local host community into relief-related development strategies. Refugees in situations of prolonged asylum should be seen as important resources in the building or rebuilding of societies riven by crisis. In Cambodia, for example, returned refugees are leading important indigenous NGOs and even serving in senior positions in government in a society still in transition. The situation of asylum should be the occasion for systematic investments by the international community in developing the human resources of refugee populations with a view to voluntary repatriation. But when refugee relief budgets are cut, it seems that the community assistance and self-sufficiency programmes are invariably put at the greatest risk.

In general, as noted earlier, states retain discretion over the procedures by which refugee protection claims are decided, including group coverage. This results in a myriad of differing interpretations of state responsibilities around the world. UNHCR by treaty is given a supervisory responsibility, but the agency has not been able to require states to accept a particular asylum seeker or to interpret the treaties in a uniform fashion.

A basic dilemma is that measures taken to control irregular migration may infringe on the ability of persons who are at risk of persecution to gain access to safety abroad. This could violate the prohibition under international law of return to a place of possible persecution. For that reason, UNHCR argues that the term 'protection' should be interpreted as involving, at a minimum, protection against return to a situation of persecution, serious insecurity, or other circumstances which would justify asylum.

The concept of protection also includes treatment during the stay of an asylum seeker in accordance with international human rights law as well as the law of the receiving state. Under this conception, refugees must be able to satisfy basic subsistence needs in a country of asylum, with assistance if necessary from the international community. This includes the provision of the basic necessities of life, including food, shelter, and basic sanitary and health facilities. If a determination of refugee status is to be made, the individual should be given access to a procedure with adequate safeguards. Legal assistance, trained and qualified interpreters, and minimally fair procedures are promoted by UNHCR. Unnecessary detention is opposed by the agency, which also urges that asylum seekers receive temporary identity documentation. UNHCR advocates standards for medical care, education, and employment opportunities, as well as family unity and special arrangements for children, including unaccompanied and separated children. Particular protection arrangements for women and the elderly are also advocated by the agency. Under general standards, family life and privacy are to be protected. Single men and women should be accommodated separately, and families should have the possibility to stay together in the same premises.

Asylum has proven to be a very effective and practical remedy in the implementation of refugee law. However, it is coming under increasing pressure by states which are concerned about the arrival of unauthorized migrants and the ability to distinguish them in a timely fashion from genuine refugees. There are widely varying criteria and procedures for granting individuals access to territory, and widely diverse conditions of stay. An undeniably arbitrary dimension has evolved in the practice of states providing asylum.

The closed centres that the United States hoped to establish in Caribbean countries as safe havens for Haitian boat people in the 1990s were a controversial asylum innovation. UNHCR worried that the designation of holding camps on the territory of third states may create a jurisdictional no man's land in which the rights of refugees may be compromised. Humanitarian measures increasingly have become instruments in the service of migration control priorities. According to UNHCR, '[t]hese safety zones should not be allowed to provide a distorted mechanism for offshore processing and detention, or one which consigns refugees to permanent lack of access to international protection with the blessing of the international community.'[7]

The process of economic and political harmonization occurring in the European Union presents a fundamental migration dilemma. Put simply, how can the visa-free movement of EU citizens within Europe be reconciled with regulating the arrival of non-citizens from outside of Europe? The uninhibited movement of people across internal borders is part of the concept of freedom embodied in the Union. Also envisaged in Europe is a common EU asylum and migration policy.

[7] 'Safety Zones: Executive Summary', UNHCR RefWorld database, Legal Information Section (1998), 2.

Not surprisingly, cooperation in matters of domestic law enforcement in western Europe focused initially on measures to replace the loss of internal frontier controls, such as the establishment of a fingerprinting system for the identification of asylum seekers. But more comprehensive approaches quickly evolved to include cooperation with developing countries from which asylum seekers originate. A High Level Working Group on Asylum and Migration was given the responsibility to implement action plans for Afghanistan, Albania, Morocco, Pakistan, Somalia, Sri Lanka, and certain western Balkan countries.[8] Also, 36 million euros, including 10 million for emergencies, were appropriated in 2000 for a European Refugee Fund to assist countries in improving reception facilities and promoting voluntary repatriation.[9] The fund, which was inspired by the need to manage the impact of the crisis in Kosovo, could help to develop common standards with respect to integrating refugees and immigrants into European societies. Indeed, the experience of the fund could be instructive on the ultimate prospects for effective forms of cooperation in Europe.

Currently, there is a policy convergence in Europe which involves making uniform the remedies for and the treatment of those seeking asylum. This includes determining which European state must decide an individual's claim for refugee protection, and achieving greater uniformity in the procedures and criteria for deciding whether an individual is deserving of status under a common refugee definition. Greater uniformity in the conditions of reception and the incidents of the status granted to individuals, such as the provision of social benefits, are also being discussed by policy makers.

Many of these components are the subject of already existing non-binding political documents negotiated by the EU states. Transforming them into binding legal obligations by 2004, as required by the Amsterdam Treaty, is a current policy challenge. Even if transformed in this fashion, it remains to be seen whether they will result in something other than the lowest common denominator of treatment, an outcome feared by many European asylum advocates.

[8] Council of the European Union, 'High Level Working Group on Asylum and Migration–Conclusions', 2206th Council–General Affairs, Press Release 296: Nr 11651/99 (Luxembourg: Council of the European Union, 11 October 1999). At: http://ue.eu.int/Newsroom/main.cfm?LANG=1

[9] European Commission, 'Proposal for Council Decision on European Refugee Fund', Press Release IP/99/982 (Brussels: 14 December 1999). At: http://europa.eu.int/comm/external_relations/news/12_99/ip_99_282.htm

THE TEMPORARY PROTECTION DEBATE

In 2001, the European Union ministers for justice, home affairs, and civil protection issued a policy on temporary protection for use in situations of mass influx of displaced persons in need of international protection. Under this directive, temporary protection can be obtained for up to three years, and would apply to those arriving spontaneously from a crisis as well as those admitted under a humanitarian evacuation programme.

In the late 1970s and early 1980s, the concept of temporary protection, then called 'temporary refuge', developed as a response to large-scale refugee movements in Indo-China. Most of the countries in that region had not acceded to the UN refugee treaties, and states were reluctant to receive asylum seekers into their territories. National practices vary. In the United States, for example, a temporary protection status is limited to certain persons already present in the territory.

UNHCR uses the term 'temporary protection' to refer to a provisional asylum arrangement in a situation of large-scale displacement in which a significant number of those displaced may be refugees. The purpose of temporary protection is to ensure reception in countries directly affected by a large-scale influx. The necessity of this provisional response is based on the impracticality of applying individual asylum-hearing procedures due to the size of the population movement coupled with the assumption that most of those affected are likely to need international protection. Temporary protection is synonymous with admission to safety, freedom from *refoulement*, adequate reception, and a right of temporary stay in accordance with minimum standards of treatment. According to UNHCR, these include adequate provisions for shelter, means of subsistence, basic health care, education for children, and respect for fundamental human rights, including family reunification. The limited duration of such temporary arrangements is the main attraction for government authorities, who are comforted by the prospect of early enforced return if the situation in the home country becomes safe.

If a crisis generating the need for protection is of a short duration, then the arrangement needs only to last until it has ended, when there would be an expectation that protected persons would return to their home country. However, UNHCR urges that persons who receive temporary stay should be given an opportunity to apply for protection under the UN refugee treaties if they still have a serious persecution claim. Return after fundamentally changed circumstances may be required under international refugee law.

In 1992, UNHCR urged that 'persons fleeing from the former Yugoslavia who are in need of international protection should be able to receive it on a temporary basis'.[10] Given the scale of the influx it was thought that individual asylum procedures were impracticable and temporary protection was seen as a suitable response, especially as it was hoped that the conflict would not last for a very long time. It was largely left to states to decide how to implement temporary protection remedies.

The international efforts over the past decade that have sought to assist or protect would-be refugees before they have fled from their home countries have been accompanied by restrictions on access to asylum abroad, particularly in the countries of western Europe and North America. These restrictive tendencies have been evident even where adverse foreign policy consequences may be caused, for example, by urging or even forcing asylum seekers to return prematurely to ravaged societies in places such as Bosnia and Kosovo. The aggravation of ethnic tensions and impact on devastated infrastructure produced as a result of premature return can make the already difficult enterprise of state building even more challenging.

Western Europe has become synonymous with antagonism toward asylum, now only heightened by new fears of terrorism. A particularly virulent and politicized debate regarding unwanted 'bogus' asylum seekers has occurred, for example, in the United Kingdom, where applications in 2000 were running over 8,000 per month, a trend which continued in 2001. A backlog of cases and appeals, coupled with costs of over $500 million in social assistance, have fuelled the controversy.[11]

Similar concerns have been expressed in Austria and Switzerland, where they have become part of the extremist rhetoric of right-wing political parties. In central and eastern Europe, countries are beginning to emulate their western neighbours. As people move from east to west, anti-asylum measures move from west to east.

The European asylum crisis is largely the product of an absence of a migration policy, coupled in practice with incentives for labour migrants to enter certain countries in Europe. Temporary protection has not proved to be synonymous with temporary stay. Western European countries often claim that they are not countries of immigration. Yet, in 1999, over

[10] United Nations High Commissioner for Refugees, 'A Comprehensive Response to the Humanitarian Crisis in the Former Yugoslavia', UN Doc. HCR/IMFY/1992/2 (24 July 1992), para. 12.

[11] Grose, Thomas K., 'Closing the British Door: Shunning the Roma', *US News and World Report* (17 April 2000). See also 'Time for Some Honesty on Asylum', *The Economist* (18 August 2001), 43; and Lyall, Sarah, 'Someone Has to Help. But Not Me', *The New York Times* (9 September 2001), Sect. 4, 4.

700,000 immigrants are estimated to have been received in European Union countries.[12]

Efforts to achieve a common asylum and migration policy are likely to be very difficult. Mounting economic and demographic pressures point to the need for more immigrants in order to maintain competitiveness and workforce levels in the face of ageing populations. New immigration initiatives have been designed to attract high-tech workers. Such moves could be the first step towards a more comprehensive EU immigration policy and the evolution of the notion of EU citizenship. But such issues present fundamental questions of national identity in many European societies, and are likely to prove controversial and provoke long and passionate debates.

GERMANY: AN ASYLUM DILEMMA

Germany faces an illustrative asylum conundrum. The Holocaust during the Second World War was the inspiration for modern refugee arrangements to provide remedies to persecuted exiles. Germany has received more asylum seekers than any other European country over the past decade. But this outcome has produced reactions, particularly after German reunification. Many Germans felt that the government was unable to manage the influx and to take measures to stem the abuse of the asylum system. After a spate of attacks against asylum seekers in 1992, such incidents decreased, only to surge again in 2000, including a notorious bombing attack against Jewish migrants.[13]

German interior officials preside over an asylum procedure that is rooted in the German constitution and UN refugee treaties. But the dirty little secret in western European asylum practice is that while relatively few are granted refugee status, very few rejected asylum seekers are removed. Instead, their stay is 'tolerated' and they subsist under uncertain circumstances without the possibility to integrate into society. In Germany, during 1990–2000, nearly 2 million asylum claims were filed, but the German authorities granted refugee status to only approximately 7 per cent of that total.[14] Yet, in 1998, only 9,286 aliens, including rejected asylum claimants, were deported; and 3,951 were removed in the first

[12] Lewis, Richard, Presentation at Wilton Park (3 October 2000), 8.

[13] 'Officials: Anti-Semitism possible motive in German train station attack', CNN website (28 July 2000). At: http://europe.cnn.com/2000/WORLD/europe/07/28/germany.blast.02/index.html

[14] Bundesamt für die Anerkennung ausländischer Flüchtlinge, *Asyl in Zahlen: Anträge Entscheidungen, Verfahren* (Nuremberg, 31 December 1999), 14, 26.

nine months of 1999.[15] Altogether, during 1990–7, only approximately 8 per cent of those rejected for asylum were removed.[16]

Those rejected for asylum are often nevertheless granted status under German law. In 2001, the government reported that approximately 7 per cent were granted asylum under the German Constitution, 9 per cent were granted refugee status under the 1951 UN refugee treaty, and 5 per cent were granted status under the Aliens Law. Approximately 57 per cent were rejected and 22 per cent of the cases were closed for reasons such as withdrawal of the application.

Foreigners who hold a so-called *Duldung*, or 'toleration permit', can be offered a temporary residence permit by action of the interior ministers of the German *Länder*. The last time this was done was 19 November 1999, when legal status was offered to those in a family, and those with at least one child, who entered Germany before 1 July 1993—singles before 1 January 1990—who can prove that they have sufficient income. As very few persons holding a toleration permit were granted a work permit, only approximately 6,000–7,000 persons were eligible for a temporary residence permit under this scheme.[17] Displaced persons from Bosnia and the Federal Republic of Yugoslavia, including Kosovo, were not able to benefit from this arrangement. Prior to 1999, the last legalization programme occurred in 1996.

The German asylum system is intricate and characterized by multiple levels of review and appeals. The authorities have sought to reduce the number of applicants through a variety of restrictive measures. Claimants are denied entry at airports, where they have fewer procedural rights. Also, claimants from certain designated 'safe' countries, such as Bulgaria, the Czech Republic, Ghana, Hungary, Poland, Romania, Senegal, and the Slovak Republic, are required by the German authorities to present more evidence of anticipated persecution than would otherwise be .required to obtain refugee status. The authorities also seek to return asylum seekers to countries with which Germany has negotiated formal re-admission agreements. Return arrangements operate among EU member states and with other states under re-admission agreements for asylum seekers. The outcome is the removal to a safe third country of

[15] Deutscher Bundestag, *Antwort der Bundesregierung auf die kleine Anfrage der Abgeordneten Ulla Jelpke, Petra Pau und der Fraktion der PDS*, Drucksache 14/2408 (15 December 1999), 1.

[16] Deutscher Bundestag, *Antwort des Parlamentarischen Statssekretärs Eduard Lintner vom 23. September 1997*, Drucksache 13/8596, 11.

[17] See generally Federal Ministry of the Interior, *Policy and Law Concerning Foreigners in Germany* (Berlin: Federal Ministry of the Interior, August 2000), 91–3.

persons whose protection claims have not been considered by Germany or the return of those who have been rejected for asylum. Germany has such arrangements to facilitate removal with all contiguous surrounding countries, and many others as well.

Apart from these procedural devices, the German supreme administrative court in the 1990s took a very restrictive view on the concept of persecution, building on earlier precedents that asylum applicants are not to receive refugee status if their claims are based on persecution by 'non-state actors' in situations of civil war, such as rebel groups in Afghanistan, Algeria, Somalia, or Sri Lanka. While precise statistics are unavailable, this restrictive interpretation has resulted in the rejection of thousands of claims since 1994.

An August 2000 decision of the German federal constitutional court may open new opportunities for refugees seeking protection from non-state persecutors.[18] The decision overturned two rulings concerning persecution alleged against the Taliban in Afghanistan. The constitutional court adopted a broad concept of what constitutes a 'de facto authority' for purposes of refugee protection. The court emphasized that persecution requires a coherent authority, and cannot be based on anarchy or state dissolution. Nevertheless, an entity in a civil war situation can be a persecutor, under the court's analysis. This new doctrinal development concerning persecution by de facto authorities awaits further refinement and interpretation in Germany to determine the precise scope of protection afforded.

Germany is a hard venue for UNHCR, according to the agency's representative in Germany, who calls Berlin a '51 Convention duty station'. UNHCR has a formal monitoring role in the German asylum process, but is not involved in decision making. The agency thus operates as an advocate. The UNHCR representative believes that refugee protection will remain problematic in Germany unless ways can be found to facilitate the voluntary return of properly rejected asylum seekers, an issue that would prove highly controversial among humanitarians. Nevertheless, UNHCR needs a presence in Germany in order to coordinate lobbying efforts in relation to the development of the common asylum policy envisaged in the political and economic integration under way in the European Union.

The German experience is reflective of an orientation by states away from asylum as a refugee protection response. State-oriented migration control policies are increasingly eroding the humanitarian and human rights dimensions of the asylum remedy for forcibly displaced persons

[18] Bundesverfassungsgericht, 2 BvR 260/98 / 2 BvR 1353/98 (10 August 2000). At: http://www.bverfg.de/entscheidungen/frames/2000/8/10

who arrive in Europe. The emerging intergovernmental consensus in Europe is clear: asylum should be a remedy of last resort, to be given grudgingly if at all. The real question, of course, is whether there are alternatives to asylum.

INTERNAL PROTECTION: SAFE AREAS, SECURITY ZONES, IN-COUNTRY PROTECTION, HUMANITARIAN CORRIDORS, ORDERLY DEPARTURE PROGRAMMES

Over the past decade, internal arrangements to protect would-be refugees have included proposals for the establishment in the midst of conflict of security zones or corridors in Rwanda, and the declaration of protected areas, safe areas, and safe havens by the UN Security Council in Croatia, Bosnia and Herzegovina, and Iraq. All of these efforts to secure internal protection, ordinarily with the consent of the local authorities, and occasionally without consent, reflect a more interventionist approach by the international community. They also reflect a restrictive trend toward allowing asylum seekers to enter another territory and a preference by states for arrangements which contain would-be asylum seekers in or near their country of origin. The ability to obtain asylum can be compromised, particularly if flight is restricted from in-country safe areas.

Internal protection strategies require ingenuity and creativity measured against a background of basic human rights principles. Such arrangements will generally be limited and should be coupled with the facilitation of evacuation in appropriate circumstances. For example, consent was instrumental for the operation of orderly departure programmes in Indo-Chinese countries of origin in order to ensure access to US resettlement by those claiming a well-founded fear of persecution in the 1980s and 1990s.

There are specific provisions of humanitarian law relating to the creation of 'safe havens' and 'neutralized zones', which permit the concentration of civilians in delineated areas established to furnish shelter and relief in the midst of armed conflict. For example, hospitals in safety zones may be established in order to protect the wounded, sick, aged, children under the age of 15, expectant mothers, and mothers of children under the age of seven. Such safe areas are established with the consent of the warring parties.

These new internal safety arrangements, however, do not necessarily require consent. Nor are they necessarily civilian in character. Moreover, they are not conceived of as temporary, nor are they automatically considered to have lapsed when their safety is compromised. Often, they blur the distinction between political and humanitarian action and can become targets.

In Bosnia and Iraq, the designation of safe areas was related to secessionist claims. The safety of such arrangements thus depends upon adequate enforcement capacity. This is what retired US Army General George Joulwan, who commanded forces in Bosnia and Rwanda, calls a 'pre-emptive' rapid reaction capacity, which he noted had been employed after Srebrenica had been overrun by Serb forces to discourage attacks upon the other declared safe havens in Bosnia. In northern Iraq, the maintenance of a strong US-led military deterrent has proved credible, although the area has been subject to incursions by forces from Iran, Iraq, and Turkey. Thus, while the arrangements in northern Iraq served as a precedent for the use of internal safe areas as a substitute for providing asylum to would-be refugees, the experience there has been problematic and at times unsafe. Nor did those involved in planning that response anticipate that an indefinite and prolonged engagement would be required to sustain the arrangement.

In general, workable internal safety arrangements have proved to be elusive and highly situational. The meaning of protection for displaced persons or would-be refugees in a situation of internal crisis must be based on tactics deeply rooted in local circumstances.

NORTHERN IRAQ: RECONCEIVING PROTECTION

After the end of the Gulf War in 1991, nearly 2 million Iraqi Kurds and Shiites fled their homes and sought safety in Iran, northern Iraq, Saudi Arabia, and Turkey. The extraordinary response to the refugee emergency in northern Iraq was the subject of political discussion and decision making at the highest levels. The searing photographs of men, women, and children stranded and perishing in the wintry mountains along the frontier between Iraq and Turkey galvanized the world's attention. The dilemma had been prompted by the refusal of the Turkish authorities to accept some 450,000 refugees into their territory and bring them down on the Turkish side of the mountains.[19] At the same time, some 1.3 million refugees fled into Iran.[20]

[19] United Nations High Commissioner for Refugees, *The State of the World's Refugees: Fifty Years of Humanitarian Action* (New York: Oxford University Press, 2000), 212.
[20] Ibid.

Turkey was concerned that an influx of Iraqi Kurds into Turkish territory would fuel instability in southeastern Turkey, which had been subjected to a low-level insurgency by Kurdish separatists for many years. Indeed, the then president of Turkey, Turgut Özal, telephoned President George H. W. Bush, according to Morton Abramowitz, then US ambassador to Turkey, and urged action to forestall the advance of refugees. US Secretary of State James Baker travelled to northern Iraq to observe the situation of the Kurds, and Operation Provide Comfort was thereafter launched by the military to encourage them to return down the mountains into Iraq. Turkey's refusal to admit Kurds into its territory prompted coalition forces to proceed to carve out 'safe areas' in northern Iraq. It was here that Fred Cuny, a legendary aid worker, helped to plan the movement of Kurds down from the mountains to the safe area in northern Iraq, which was accomplished relatively quickly by the military.

A memorandum of understanding was concluded between Iraq and the United Nations, establishing 'humanitarian centres' and governing the administration of humanitarian assistance. Coalition military forces were deployed on the ground and reinforced by a 'no-fly' zone, which has over time expanded in size.

The 'safe area' carved out in the north had problems. In 1995, Turkish army forces entered the area in pursuit of Kurdish separatist guerrillas. In 1996, as a result of a squabble between factions among the Iraqi Kurds, the Iraqi military entered the zone, prompting the flight and ultimately the resettlement to the United States of several thousands of those Kurds, some of whom had reportedly been linked with the Central Intelligence Agency.[21] Northern Iraq has over time evolved into a kind of staging area for asylum seekers and others to travel clandestinely onwards to western Europe, and a 'paradise for terrorists', in the words of one high-ranking Turkish parliamentarian in 2000.

Nevertheless, according to Abramowitz, overall it was 'a pretty safe area' and, more importantly, the least bad of several bad alternatives to address the 1991 crisis. The numbers were too large to utilize the approach later taken in the Former Yugoslav Republic of Macedonia, namely, 'humanitarian relocation', or temporary resettlement to a third country. Therefore, the creation of the safe areas in Iraq, still enforced and patrolled today by air power, was the option chosen.

[21] In September–December 1996, a total of 6,493 pro-US Kurds were evacuated from northern Iraq. For a breakdown, see website of the Federation of American Scientists, Military Analysis Network. At: http://www.fas.org/man/dod-101/ops/pacific_haven.htm, visited on 24 May 2001.

But the arrangement in northern Iraq had broad implications for humanitarian action. It was a 'watershed event' in the post-cold war world, bringing together humanitarian and peacekeeping activities in unprecedented ways, explained Anthony Zinni, a retired US Marine Corps general who oversaw Operation Provide Comfort in Turkey and northern Iraq. Coordination and cooperation among civilian humanitarians and the military were paramount issues.

Perhaps the overriding lesson of northern Iraq is that, when a capable state such as the United States is tested on refugee questions which have important national security implications, it will act robustly to find a remedy, even where asylum has been ruled out. The outcome in northern Iraq was in this sense reminiscent of the resettlement arrangements made for refugees in south-east Asia. Necessity, guilt, and revenge can be powerful motivations for a protective refugee policy. The United States owed a responsibility for protection to the Iraqi Kurds, as it did earlier to the Indo-Chinese refugees, and arrangements for their protection and resettlement followed. In the process, the asylum remedy was relegated to being but one among several methods of providing protection.

MITROVICA: A GLIMPSE OF INTERNAL PROTECTION

Mitrovica is the front line of a demographic confrontation in Kosovo. It seemed like a perfectly ordinary town as we drove into it on a crisp and sunny day in October 2000. The streets were full of people and cars on this early autumn day. The only hint of something amiss was a Kosovo military force (KFOR) checkpoint on the outskirts of town. But it was the KFOR tank in a fortified position guarding the Orthodox church on the road into town that gave away the secret of the ethnic conflict that gripped the town.

The city of Mitrovica in northern Kosovo has been effectively divided between a northern Serb portion and a southern ethnic Albanian section since 1999, when Serbian forces withdrew and ethnic Albanians returned to Kosovo. From Mitrovica north to the border with Serbia proper, Belgrade continues to have considerable influence and Serbs are in the overwhelming majority. To the south, the Albanians are in the majority, with a few mixed communities and enclaves of Serbs.

In September 1999, an abortive effort by United Nations Mission in Kosovo (UNMIK) and KFOR to return Albanians to northern Mitrovica resulted in rioting which injured over 150 persons.[22] The flashpoint for large demonstrations was the bridge on the Ibar river, over which we drove in October 2000, weaving between the fences and barriers which had divided the north and south ever since French troops laid barbed wire in June 1999. Serb 'bridge watchers', young toughs often equipped with hand radios, on occasion patrolled the northern end of the bridge.

After hostilities erupted in February 2000, which led to the displacement of 1,700 mainly Kosovo Albanians, KFOR created a 'confidence area' designed to serve as a buffer between the two sides. The centrepiece of this area is a set of three block-like buildings on the northern bank of the Ibar, into which several hundred Albanians were moved. They have access to the south over a footbridge constructed for that purpose. The confidence zone is protected aggressively by heavily armed French KFOR troops, who have been deployed to numerous fortified checkpoints. In late 2000, the zone was extended to the railway station in south Mitrovica. Insults, stone throwing, and occasional shooting and grenade attacks demarcate the boundary.

A few hundred Albanians live to the north of the confidence area. Home deliveries of food and medical care are provided to them when security conditions deteriorate. A handful of Serbs—16 as of September 2000—live under constant KFOR guard around the Orthodox church just to the south of the river.[23] UNHCR runs a bus service between north Mitrovica and Serb enclaves to the south. In February 2000, a UNHCR bus was attacked with a rocket-propelled grenade, killing three persons and wounding several others.

Protection work in a situation of inchoate conflict has to be innovative and pre-emptive in character. Approximately 260 Albanians who live isolated in the city have recently come under great pressure to leave their homes, which are then ordinarily occupied by Serbs, most likely themselves also displaced and returning from Serbia. UNHCR for some time provided metal bars and locks to reinforce the doors of apartments with inhabitants at risk. UNHCR and OSCE have facilitated discussions between Albanian and Serb families regarding arrangements under which the Serbs occupy the apartments and agree to protect the premises and its owner's belongings until the situation normalizes. But despite concerted efforts by UNMIK police and KFOR, including the use of

[22] SHAPE News Morning Update (12 September 1999). At: http://www.fas.org/man/dod-101/ops/docs99/mu12099.htm

[23] 'Ethnic Divide Between Serbs, Albanians Widens in Kosovo City', in Western Policy Center, *Regional Report: Yugoslavia*, 5, 3 (March/April 2000). At: http://www.westernpolicy.org/publications/reports/2000/c/yugoslavia/asp

24-hour teams ready to respond to emergency calls, those responsible for intimidation and threats have not been apprehended. As the pressures have mounted, families have been evacuated by UNHCR. Security remains unstable and sporadic outbreaks of violence and anonymous attacks still occur.

The situation of displaced Roma in Mitrovica remains bleak. UNHCR in April 2000 hosted a round-table meeting which resulted in a commitment to facilitate the voluntary return of the Kosovar Roma community. The Kosovar Albanian leadership subscribed to a written action plan, which 'welcomes the Kosovar Roma ... as part of the new Kosovo'.[24] The agency thereupon formulated a plan to return to their homes 275 Roma who lived in prefabricated housing near the railroad tracks in north Mitrovica. Most of these families were displaced from the Roma quarter in south Mitrovica, which was completely destroyed by the Albanians after the NATO air campaign ended and Serbian forces withdrew. The Albanians blame the Roma for allegedly having collaborated with Serbian forces in their repression.

When I viewed the old Roma quarter from the north bank of the Ibar in late 2000, it reminded me of a miniature version of the destroyed city of Vukovar in Croatia I had observed in 1993. UNHCR advocated the construction of a prefabricated transit centre in an area adjoining the quarter, which would allow the Roma to rebuild their homes. However, preliminary support by UNMIK and KFOR crumbled when the Albanian mayor of Mitrovica adamantly refused, according to William L. Nash, a retired US Army General who became the UNMIK regional administrator in Mitrovica in April 2000. The Roma of Mitrovica remain homeless.

REFUGEE RETURN

Voluntary repatriation is enshrined in refugee policy as the international community's preferred outcome. While repatriation was played down during the ideological confrontation of the cold war, it has emerged with renewed vigour over the past decade. Initially declaring 1991 as the year of repatriation, the UNHCR then declared the 1990s to be the decade of repatriation.

Refugee repatriation is associated with many positive images. Exiles return to their homes and land, take up prior positions, and resume normal lives. Contextually, conflict abates and repression ends. Functioning

[24] 'Declaration from Humanitarian Roundtable', Pristina (12 April 2000). At: http://www. unhcr.ch/world/euro/seo/protect/hrtdec.htm

government institutions emerge or re-emerge, providing basic services and opportunities for redress of grievances. In optimal terms, a reliable commercial context emerges, and the environment becomes promising for the realization of individual potentialities.

But this somewhat romanticized notion of repatriation is clearly the exception to the way it usually works. Refugees are changed by their exile. Sometimes women are empowered and children grow up in internationalized settings. Refugees acquire new capabilities because of the availability of education and necessity of coping with new challenges. The enduring refugee camps on the Thai-Cambodian border in the 1980s, for example, were the spawning grounds for many of today's NGO leaders in Cambodia.

There are many wasteful and negative outcomes as well. Refugees may have become vengeful and radicalized because of their deprivations, as has been the case recently in the former Yugoslavia and the Great Lakes region of Africa. They can become harbingers of conflict.

In addition, the situation in a refugee's homeland is often different when the time comes to return. Homes and lands may have been lost, with no real prospect for repossession or compensation. The economy may have been devastated, eliminating livelihoods. Repatriating refugees are thus often pioneers in their own lands, sometimes swelling the ranks of the dislocated urban poor, as was the case in Cambodia. The local population that remained behind often can be resentful, particularly if return assistance is given exclusively to repatriating refugees.

Even beyond these disorienting realities, there are many policy conundrums which plague even simple refugee return. Paradoxes and complications abound in relation to the concept of the 'durable solution' of refugee return.

Often there are lurking questions about whether or not individuals are, indeed, refugees. The passage of time may have dissipated the forces that gave rise to a claim of a well-founded fear of persecution or other needs for refugee protection under applicable legal standards. International protection and assistance can be withdrawn in these circumstances. But perhaps the key question is: who decides? The authorities of a weak host state may simply not be capable of making individual refugee determinations, nor do international organizations have the wherewithal to judge such matters in most instances. And treating whole populations as ineligible for protection and assistance risks wrongly abusing individual refugees.

Bureaucratic mandates can also come into play. An internal UNHCR document describes using a global positioning satellite in 2000 to determine whether or not Afghans had crossed the border into Tajikistan in the midst of a flood plain. UNHCR enjoys a mandate in practice to monitor the circumstances of refugee repatriation, but only for refugees who have initially crossed an international border and who wish to return home. Otherwise, an exceptional decision has to be taken to extend the agency's work to internal exiles, as discussed elsewhere in this book. As of 2002, no single UN organization has operational responsibility for internal displacement in Afghanistan.

The physical act of return itself, of course, is susceptible to objective verification. But simply crossing back over an international border is not repatriation. Refugees often return to become internally displaced. On occasion, individuals return briefly, even daily, to tend crops or visit their homes, simply to leave again to find haven across a border. Under these circumstances, there has not been refugee return in the sense of a lasting solution to the need for a new permanent home.

Whether return is indeed sustainable raises a whole host of questions concerning the interrelationships between short-term humanitarian aid and long-term development assistance. A genuine restoration of national protection and the establishment of viable social, economic, and political structures imply very significant and wide-ranging changes in societies. The funding of quick impact projects—now called 'small-scale projects' by UNHCR—which are a customary humanitarian contribution to filling this lacuna, may have negligible impacts or can even be counterproductive. No one really knows, as such efforts have not been systematically studied.

Perhaps the key conceptual question related to refugee return concerns the voluntariness of the return. One clear legal obligation frames the issue: in general, as discussed elsewhere in this book, a refugee may not be returned by the authorities of an asylum state to a place where he or she may experience persecution.[25] The corollary to this rule is that refugee return must be 'voluntary'. But the issue of voluntariness in the exercise of human will is analytically elusive and more in the province of philosophy and literature. Is the return of a refugee lawyer who cannot find comparable work in the country of refuge voluntary? Or the return of refugee youth who do not have access to secondary schooling? Or return because a refugee may risk loss of his or her home by reason of continued absence?

Perhaps the fundamental political question posed is: who decides about the appropriateness and quality of choice to be given to refugees

[25] Goodwin-Gill, Guy S., 'Non-Refoulement', in *The Refugee in International Law*, 2nd ed. (Oxford: Clarendon Press, 1996), 117–71.

in relation to return? If refugees are the decision makers, then prolonged stay may result. Exiles can put down roots and become de facto members of a new community. Ordinarily, an asylum state has a bias in favour of return. Governments sometimes seek to discourage stay through measures such as closed camps, and restrictions on movement and administrative detention, or by denying refugees and their families access to education or work. Sometimes social assistance is manipulated and reduced to prompt departure. Even a persecutor can have a role in facilitating return by granting an amnesty for political offences or by undertaking to build confidence on the part of prospective returnees.

UNHCR tries to act with delicacy on the question, but often finds itself favouring or disfavouring return in particular circumstances, more or less subtly. But the agency can offer help to returnees in either circumstance, largely through a semantic distinction. UNHCR can 'promote' return where it agrees with the outcome, or it can nevertheless 'facilitate' return where it does not agree with the outcome.

Particular dilemmas arise when refugees are placed under pressure by bad conditions in places of asylum and UNHCR feels obliged to make a judgment about whether remaining or returning would be better or worse for refugees. This sometimes grisly choice between the very bad and the bad has created difficult protection advocacy dilemmas, where mistakes can produce *refoulement*. UNHCR's acquiescence in the forced return of Rwandan refugees from Tanzania to Rwanda in late 1996 is a particularly poignant example.

Additional complications arise in the context of what are known as 'complex' peace operations, which are multi-faceted international operations involving not only a humanitarian response but also concerted political and military dimensions. Normally, these operations occur under the authority of a UN Security Council resolution and involve an inter-agency response in a country emerging from conflict or other forms of chaos to which refugees are returning. A basic conundrum is posed by the juxtaposition of political and humanitarian considerations. The needs of states and the needs of individuals can coincide or diverge.

Frequently, swift refugee return prior to internationally supervised elections has characterized these arrangements. The meaning of 'voluntariness' is qualified in these circumstances where repatriation is foreordained, and if at all relegated to the method and not the fact of return. The real issues concern the ensuing difficulties of re-integration, rehabilitation, and development.

Return, of course, should be lasting, and matters such as the techniques of re-integration and addressing the interrelationships between relief and development have proved challenging and difficult as repatriation has proliferated. Self-sufficiency can be difficult to achieve. Also, the issue of voluntariness increasingly is being questioned with arrangements made for refugee return in the context of comprehensive peace settlements and the use of mechanisms such as temporary protection, which can be terminated in order to require return to situations of fragile peace and presumed safety.

RETURN TO DEVASTATION: THE CASE OF AFGHANISTAN

Sadako Ogata was one of the longest-serving UN High Commissioners for Refugees, a position she held until the end of 2000. She has since agreed to co-chair a Commission on Human Security to which the Japanese government has committed over $100 million. In our meeting in Washington, DC, in November 2000, she spoke in a characteristically soft voice. I began our conversation by asking her about refugee return. During Ogata's tenure, substantial repatriation had occurred in Indo-China, Central America, and Africa. But on this occasion I drew her attention to 2.5 million Afghans, who form the largest conventional refugee population in the world and a cold war legacy that long pre-dated her tenure. Ogata, a distinguished Japanese international relations expert, had visited Afghanistan, Iran, and Pakistan in September 2000.

The Soviet intervention in 1979 in Afghanistan gave rise to a prolonged and highly politicized refugee emergency. After the intervention, an estimated 2.5 million Afghan refugees relocated in Pakistan alone.[26] A similar number fled to Iran. Mujahadeen 'freedom fighters' launched forays from Peshawar against Soviet forces until the latter withdrew in 1989. The ensuing situation of warlordism and factional fighting continued in Afghanistan with the Taliban and other groups.

Emphasizing the importance of avoiding such protracted displacements, Ogata recounted the series of political interlocutors that had frustrated peace in Afghanistan: the Russians, then warlords, and now Taliban. Wondering aloud whether there might be an opening with Taliban, which then controlled 90 per cent of the countryside, Ogata noted that the human rights situation, particularly discrimination against

[26] Zolberg, Aristide R., Suhrke, Astri, and Aguayo, Sergio, *Escape from Violence: Conflict and the Refugee Crisis in the Developing World* (New York and Oxford: Oxford University Press, 1989), 152–3.

women, had kept the United Nations from being able to deal with these de facto authorities. But, based on her visit in 2000, she was optimistic that it would be possible to have a dialogue with Taliban leaders about human rights issues.

According to Ogata, Afghans going to Pakistan were fleeing fighting, not persecution. Pakistan had just days before closed its border in the face of the influx, although the border was swiftly re-opened. International assistance has not been forthcoming and UNHCR has not been able to raise money to buttress the reception of asylum seekers in Pakistan. During the cold war, Pakistan was a very important ally of the United States and 'money was no object', said Ogata. Now, she noted, the remaining 2 million refugees are a problem. There are severe impacts on local communities in Pakistan, themselves afflicted by drought. Coupled with lack of assistance to the camps, people are leaving and migrating to urban slums.

Iran has also hosted large numbers of Afghan refugees, close to 1.5 million.[27] But, unlike Pakistan, Iran was given relatively little international assistance, a point that the Iranian authorities made repeatedly to me when I visited there in late 1991. Under pressure from the Iranians in early 2000, UNHCR began a joint programme with Iran to encourage the return of those Afghans who do not require refugee protection or who seek to stay on humanitarian grounds. Under this scheme, approximately $50 is provided to each returnee, who may also take any savings back to Afghanistan. In practice, some 30 per cent have been allowed to remain by the Iranian authorities under broad humanitarian criteria. 'The rest will have to go back', said Ogata.

In 2001, stark issues are presented by the notion of return to Afghanistan. Famine in Afghanistan has been caused by the worst drought in living memory in a country which has experienced over two decades of continuous warfare and destruction of infrastructure. Fleeing drought or conflict, or both, approximately 170,000 new refugees arrived in Pakistan during 2000.[28] That same year, over 500,000 Afghans were internally displaced, some 375,000 because of conflict and a further 140,000 primarily because of drought.[29] Some are stranded in camps; most others have joined the ranks of the urban poor. The UNHCR, World Food Programme, and other humanitarian agencies labour largely in isolation in a setting in which donor countries have withheld funding on political and human rights grounds. Fearful of US retaliation against

[27] US Committee for Refugees, *World Refugee Survey 2001* (Washington, DC: US Committee for Refugees, 2001), 3.

[28] US Committee for Refugees, *World Refugee Survey 2001*, 152–5.

[29] US Committee for Refugees, *World Refugee Survey 2001*, 152.

the attack, about 100,000 Afghans fled from Kabul in the week following 11 September 2001.

At the same time, pushed by increasingly reluctant hosts in Pakistan and Iran, UNHCR facilitated the return of approximately 80,000 Afghans from Pakistan and 135,000 Afghans from Iran, which the Taliban welcomed back.[30] Repatriation assistance in Afghanistan is far from uniform, with variations between returnees from Iran and Pakistan as well as between families and individuals. The result, as WFP noted ominously, was to encourage people to return and merge themselves with a starving population in Afghanistan. This effort at selective facilitation of return to places of relative safety occurred despite a worsening situation in Afghanistan. International scepticism continued to mount over organized return programmes. Such nice efforts at highly calibrated humanitarianism are difficult to manage and have foundered in the past.

A dire situation may only become worse. Terrorist attacks in the United States in September 2001 caused approximately 3,000 deaths and provoked military retaliation against terrorists operating in Afghanistan. As of that date, there were nearly 4 million Afghans exiled outside of their country and another 1 million internally displaced, out of a population of 26 million persons. Extensive conflict, or a descent into anarchy, would surely produce massive new displacement and a more severe humanitarian catastrophe, obliterating the prospect of refugee return, at least until there is a new government.

RELOCATION ABROAD: HUMANITARIAN EVACUATION, HUMANITARIAN TRANSFER, AND RESETTLEMENT

It was a late Sunday evening in November 2000 when our plane landed in Nairobi, Kenya. As I walked on the runway through the sultry air to the airport arrival hall, I became an unintended witness to the conclusion of the infamous journey of the 'lost boys of Sudan', some of whom I had visited in 1993 at the Kakuma refugee camp in northwestern Kenya. There, a remnant of some 17,000 children had come to rest after fleeing in 1988 from fighting in Sudan to Ethiopia, where they were attacked again after the regime of Mengistu Haile Mariam fell in 1991. This prompted a harrowing 600-mile trek by foot to Kenya, with many dying from attacks by wild animals and exposure.

[30] *World Refugee Survey 2001*, 152.

At the airport in Nairobi on this warm night, the first contingent of some 30 or so of those who were 17 years of age were waiting for a flight to the United States, where approximately 3,600, including 800 unaccompanied minors, were to be resettled as refugees, finally ending their exile. They had first been airlifted from Kakuma to Nairobi to avoid travelling over land through insecure territory. About 500 had been prioritized for relocation to the US before they turned 18 years of age so that they could be included as minors eligible for foster care under the US resettlement programme. The label 'boys', however, is a misnomer; given the passage of time, many were now adults and there were even girls among the group.

The Sudanese sat sprawled in plastic chairs in a hallway at the airport, wearing sweatsuits with shirts that were emblazoned on the front with the letters USRP (United States Refugee Program). They looked more like a travelling soccer team than a group of refugee survivors anticipating new lives in America. I could not help but think that this final leg of their decade-long journey, surrounded in a swirl of promise and disorientation, will lead inevitably to both new accomplishments and disappointments.

Resettlement is an important contribution to redressing refugee exile by immigration countries, notably Australia, Canada, and the United States. In 2001, for example, the US resettlement programme will provide for the admission of up to 80,000 refugees, more than all other countries combined, with some 20,000 coming from Africa.[31] Nevertheless, this represents a trend of decreased admissions over the past decade to the US from abroad. The reduction is due to a movement away from categorical offers of resettlement to case-by-case referrals by UNHCR of individual cases prioritized on protection grounds. But resettlement is often the only realistic option remaining for refugees who are in need of new permanent homes.

Refugee resettlement is an important policy tool for countries with immigration traditions to contribute to meeting international responsibilities to address the needs of refugees around the world. The rationale for resettlement is based on a blend of the capacities and preferences of the receiving country, as well as the protection needs of the individuals admitted. The immigration dimension of resettlement is shown by the fact that refugee screening has occurred in countries of origin, despite the fact that at least in theory the individuals have a well-founded fear of

[31] Bureau of Population, Refugees, and Migration, 'U.S. Refugee Admissions and Resettlement Program', Fact Sheet (Washington, DC: US Department of State, 1 March 2001).

persecution there. For example, special arrangements were made by the United States over the past decade for large-scale admissions from within Vietnam and the countries of the former Soviet Union.

Refugee resettlement became a preferred option during the cold war, when repatriation became incompatible with foreign policy objectives, but it nevertheless remains an important aspect of modern refugee responses. Increasingly, however, resettlement is coming under pressure because of the rise of anti-immigration sentiments. It is seen by some as comparatively expensive and a luxury among refugee policy responses. Apart from special bilateral resettlement initiatives, UNHCR now often serves as a kind of gatekeeper in terms of referring individual vulnerable cases to resettling countries. Such cases include the elderly, children, women, and disabled persons.

The 1999 Kosovo crisis inspired a new set of related responses—humanitarian evacuation and relocation—which, unlike resettlement, do not necessarily carry a connotation of integration and status as a permanent resident. Humanitarian evacuation involved an effort to ease the pressure of arriving Kosovars on Macedonia so that later arrivals would continue to have access to its territory. A Macedonian official who worked on crisis response issues in 1999 in the foreign ministry emphasized that the relocation abroad of some 96,000 Kosovars 'helped a lot'. Inter-ethnic relations between the Macedonian majority and its sizeable Albanian minority—22.7 per cent reported in a special 1994 census—is the most important national security issue in Macedonia, a point featured in the ethnic Albanian insurgency which burst forth in 2001.[32] The 1999 crisis in Kosovo caused 360,000 Kosovar ethnic Albanians to seek asylum in Macedonia, which has a population of 2.1 million persons.[33] Political stability was threatened in an atmosphere that this Macedonian official recalled as replete with 'fear', indeed, 'panic'.

The humanitarian evacuation programme was not envisaged as a resettlement programme, and UNHCR urged that resettlement procedures and criteria not be applied. Instead, the focus was to be placed on group protection. UNHCR sought to give priority to the most vulnerable Kosovars in the camps with the most difficult conditions. In order to facilitate eventual return, UNHCR urged that priority be given to evacuation to countries in Europe. Where evacuation outside Europe was necessitated by the deteriorating conditions in Macedonia, UNHCR

[32] Central Intelligence Agency, 'Macedonia, The Former Yugoslav Republic of', The World Factbook 2000. At: http://www.cia.gov/cia/publications/factbook/geos/mk.html

[33] US Committee for Refugees, *World Refugee Survey 2000* (Washington, DC: US Committee for Refugees, 2000), 255.

urged initially that it be limited to refugees with family links in the receiving countries.

Arrangements for refugee departures were carried out jointly by UNHCR and the International Organization for Migration (IOM). Lists of selected candidates were prepared and notices posted in camps along with descriptions of departure logistics. The lists included individual names, the country of destination, and the place and time for departure from the camp. The information was to be posted ordinarily a day before the time of departure, and, at the very least, the night before.

One of the concerns that emerged during the humanitarian evacuation programme in Macedonia was the problem of separating family members. As a consequence, the registration of refugees in Macedonia collected only essential information in order to facilitate rapid voluntary evacuation and to permit family tracing in the future.

Humanitarian evacuation related only to Macedonia. Albania permitted Kosovars into its territory there and thus no effort was made to arrange for humanitarian evacuation. Instead, a variant on the humanitarian evacuation programme was considered: humanitarian relocation from Macedonia to Albania. In part, this option was necessitated by obstacles to achieving the timely evacuation of sufficient numbers of asylum seekers out of Macedonia because of the selection criteria used by evacuation states, delay in organizing transport to receiving countries, and the need to keep families together. In some instances, there were delays to await the arrival of family members who were coming later from Kosovo or who had yet to identify themselves to authorities in the receiving countries.

Evacuation to Albania from Macedonia, however, was not popular. After a spate of forced relocations orchestrated by the Macedonian authorities, UNHCR insisted that the individuals at the very least 'not object' to relocation—or indeed to evacuation. For this reason, the individuals were to know the destination and that conditions in Albania were difficult and relatively deprived. Valid reasons to object to relocation included awaiting the arrival of family members in Macedonia, currently living with family members in Macedonia, wishing to ensure the protection of property in Macedonia, needing equipment or supplies available in Macedonia but not in Albania, and fear of specific protection problems in Albania. Relocation was thus not considered appropriate for unaccompanied or separated minors, female single heads of household, young girls who may be susceptible to trafficking, handicapped and disabled persons, and young men fearing recruitment by the KLA. Taken together, these requirements and concerns led to a predictable outcome: virtually no takers.

The humanitarian evacuation programme was conceived of as a burden-sharing endeavour, motivated by a desire to ease the pressure and impacts on Macedonia, and send a political signal that the international community was willing to help. Most of those relocated to European and North American countries did not return to Kosovo after the NATO victory there. Relocation abroad may make all the difference in the lives of the individuals affected. However, it proved to be an awkward instrument for use in responding to urgent political problems in the midst of an armed conflict.

RESOLVING INTERNAL DISPLACEMENT: GEORGIA AND DISPLACED PERSONS AS PRISONERS OF CONFLICT

Georgia is perhaps the most beautiful of the countries of the former Soviet Union. I was reminded of this as our plane descended to land at the airport outside Tbilisi in May 2000, and the sun danced off of the broken windows of abandoned factories that dotted the terrain. As we drove from the airport, the late afternoon sun played off the green hills surrounding Tbilisi.

The occasion of my visit was a meeting on internally displaced persons under the auspices of the UN Secretary-General's representative on the issue, Francis Deng. My first visit to Georgia had been in 1994, then accompanying George Soros, the financier, who was there to open his Open Society Georgia Foundation. As we drove through Tbilisi six years later, its beauty seemed unchanged. The other unchanging feature was the population of displaced Georgians who had fled conflict in 1993 in Abkhazia, many of whom continue to reside in hotels and with host families in Tbilisi. Hence the subject of this meeting: internal displacement. This is an old problem which has recently become somewhat more fashionable internationally.

By way of background, Georgia was one of the early sites of ethnic conflict after the spectacular implosion of the Soviet Union. Separatist conflicts in South Ossetia and Abkhazia afflicted Georgia in the early 1990s. While the status of Ossetia has yet to be resolved, the fighting has subsided and most refugees and internally displaced persons have returned to their homes. The situation with respect to Abkhazia, however, is still far from a solution. In November 1994, following heavy fighting in which Abkhaz separatist forces were militarily aided by Russia, a quadripartite peace agreement was reached between Georgia, the

Abkhazian authorities, Russia, and the United Nations. A Commonwealth of Independent States (CIS) peacekeeping force, really Russian troops, was deployed and monitored by a UN military observer mission. The conflict in Abkhazia resulted in the death of several thousand individuals, and displaced over 200,000 persons in Georgia.[34] In October 1999, after a referendum, Abkhazia declared independence and adopted a new constitution. While displaced persons return unassisted on occasion, insecurity in Gali, the principal place for such return which was almost totally populated by Georgians before the conflict, prompted some 40,000 persons again to flee violence in 1998.[35]

The political connotation of the term 'internally displaced persons' is highly charged in Georgia, as it is elsewhere. The Abkhazian authorities desire independence and have suffered economic blockades and hostilities for their separatist ambitions. They view the displaced Georgians as 'refugees' who have crossed a border by leaving Abkhazia. The government in Tbilisi, however, insists that they are internal exiles still resident in the sovereign territory of Georgia who wish to return to their homes in Abkhazia.

The reality in which this policy dilemma plays out in Georgia is sobering. Unresolved conflicts are dangerous, particularly to the thousands of ordinary people who could be put at risk upon the renewal of conflict. Ethnic groups abound in Georgia and other conflicts could emerge. In addition, unresolved conflicts can be dangerous to national leaders as the political fault lines in such a situation can be exploited by external forces seeking to manipulate the sides. Indeed, Russia has played this role in the past in relation to the Abkhazian conflict.

But the risk of unresolved conflict is highly differentiated. Georgia, and the Caucasus region more generally, are of diminishing strategic consequence to the West after the end of the cold war. There are, of course, familiar debates about oil and pipelines. Also, the European Union countries may be somewhat concerned about the arrival of unwanted migrants through the territory of weak states such as Georgia. The prospect of a substantial refugee outflow from Georgia itself is unlikely and seems remote. As a result, the response of the West has been predominantly in the nature of technical assistance and humanitarian relief. But

[34] Walker, Edwards, *No Peace, No War in the Caucasus: Secessionist Conflicts in Chechnya, Abkhazia and Nagorno-Karabakh*, CSIA Occasional Paper, Strengthening Democratic Institutions Project (Cambridge, MA: Belfer Center for Science and International Affairs, February 1998), 7–8. At: http://ksgnotes1.harvard.edu/BCSIA/Library.nsf/pubs/walker-cauc

[35] US Committee for Refugees, *World Refugee Survey 1999* (Washington, DC: US Committee for Refugees, 1999), 198.

external funding is decreasing, particularly in situations of prolonged humanitarian engagement such as Georgia. Nor can this loss be easily replaced. The capacities of the governments in the Caucasus region are meagre. These are impoverished states that still suffer grave economic distress.

The 'crisis' of forced displacement in Georgia is thus largely invisible. Decision makers in donor countries are not under immediate pressure by restive electorates to 'do something'. Georgia competes for resources with other emergencies such as Afghanistan, Macedonia, or West Africa.

What emerges then is a series of funding strategies packaged by international organizations and NGOs with the hope of maintaining the continuing engagement of donor countries. Whether called 'development' or 'prevention', these are strategies designed to take into account the decrease in resources and the possible withdrawal of humanitarian agencies in a post-conflict setting. Under these circumstances, inter-agency coordination and the development of a strategic plan become key necessities.

This funding imperative led to the recent UN proposal for a 'new approach' in Georgia. The innovation under discussion is a concerted effort to promote the self-sufficiency of internally displaced persons. This effort is explicitly justified, at least in part, as a way to address the gap between relief and development. Implicitly, it is a bid to encourage continued donor contributions to international programmes in Georgia. But the response has been modest. As of July 2001, only $1.3 million have been identified by donors to assist the internally displaced, a sum which reflects a mixture of both existing and new funding.

In a real sense, internally displaced persons in Georgia are 'prisoners' of unresolved conflict. This is precisely the term that was used at a small gathering of such persons that I visited in May 2000 in a one-room residence in a former resort hotel near the water reservoir outside Tbilisi. Indeed, these persons considered their lot worse than prisoners in the sense that they were being 'punished' without having committed a crime.

There may be other 'prisoners' in Georgia as well, including the national authorities, who are hostage to a political impasse that prevents any concessions which might imply recognition of Abkhazia as an independent entity. A corrupt government-in-exile reinforces the deadlock. One distinguished Georgian whom I met with noted that there was a need for a 'national debate' in Georgia on the question of Abkhazia. Most others I spoke with, however, believe that such a debate is unlikely in the foreseeable future.

There may even be other kinds of hostages in this situation, including those international organizations and NGOs that work exclusively within a humanitarian framework. UNHCR had a very unhappy experience with its effort in the mid-1990s to use refugee repatriation as a wedge issue to encourage political dialogue between Georgian and Abkhazian representatives. The agency organized a repatriation programme in which only a handful of the displaced ended up participating because the authorities in Abkhazia insisted on identifying those who may have committed war crimes and crimes against humanity in the course of the conflict. This ill-fated repatriation programme should serve as a warning to humanitarians about the inadvisability of venturing too far ahead of the resolution of a broader underlying conflict.

The hope in Georgia rests primarily in the independent sector. Whatever dialogue there is, and whatever efforts there are to promote understanding and exchange of information between populations in Georgia and Abkhazia, have been undertaken primarily by indigenous NGOs. This is perhaps the only way forward in the face of a political impasse in which the international community is fast losing interest. To harness the interests of affected individuals and assist them in advocating and realizing their interests is a customary activity of NGOs around the world. NGOs will remain long after expatriate aid and development workers rotate to the next crisis or transitional setting, and long after international organizations withdraw. The encouragement of their work and activities may be one of the most enduring contributions that the international community can make in Georgia.

IRRESOLUTE PREVENTION: THE FORMER SOVIET UNION

Refugee policy is fundamentally remedial in character. In that sense, its utility depends on a failure of prevention. Operational prevention in the context of forced migration is less a discrete option than an orientation that can be employed in addressing remedial strategies such as containment or intervention. A preventive approach in containment responses, for example, would seek to address the immediate causes of displacement so as to develop options for people to remain in their home countries or to seek asylum near their home countries. But this would require that conditions in those places meet basic standards of human dignity.

The past decade has been replete with calls for the need to prevent the causes of forced migration. The notion is that a small investment of resources now—an ounce of prevention, as it were—will avoid much greater expenditures later—saves a pound of cure. But the leading international refugee-related endeavour actually undertaken in the name of prevention, the 1996 CIS migration conference, dwindled into a marginal effort directed mainly at encouraging the growth of NGOs and strengthening state border controls in the region.

One of the most dramatic developments of the 1990s was the break-up of the Soviet Union, which resulted in vast population displacements. Forced migration attended ethnic conflicts in the region, and Russians and Russian-speakers returned from non-Russian former Soviet Republics to the Russian Federation. These movements of people prompted an international conference which was held in Geneva in 1996 to address migration-related issues under the auspices of the IOM, OSCE, and UNHCR.

The CIS migration conference attracted a relative pittance from donors, certainly no more than $50 million over the five-year life of the conference. Compare this effort with the estimated total of $66 billion in international assistance disbursed to Russia alone from 1991 to 1998.[36] Surely, the difficulty of assuring donors that funding would be used effectively would have been a serious barrier in any event. However, even the incremental and small-scale efforts envisaged in this migration initiative were not backed by significant sums. While a follow-up process to the CIS conference continues in name, the countries of the region and donor countries themselves have largely given up on this international gambit. Perhaps the single most tangible accomplishment of this endeavour was to seed a variety of NGOs in the region, which remain highly dependent on international funding.

Russia is a society in crisis. Whether the socio-economic distress has bottomed out or whether the trend line is slowly improving are questions that will have to be answered from a more distant vantage point sometime in the future. However, one measure may be the way that elements of civil society have begun to emerge and work together in the region. That is the promise of the CIS Research Council on Forced Migration, a group of social scientists who have come together after the fall of the Soviet Union to examine policy to address the scourge of human displacement.

I remember the conversation that gave rise to the birth of the Council when I met in late 1995 with Zhanna Zayonchkovskaya of the Russian Academy of Sciences in Moscow. Zayonchkovskaya, a geographer by training who has been publishing on migration issues since 1964, was

[36] This estimate excludes food aid loans, trade credits and debt roll-overs. See US General Accounting Office, *Foreign Assistance: International Efforts to Aid Russia's Transition have had Mixed Results*, GAO-01-8 (Washington, DC: GAO, November 2000), 9.

a fixture in the research community in the Soviet Union. We met in her small office in a dilapidated building situated in the outskirts of Moscow. The building was architecturally renowned for the sculpture of a gigantic human ear which is affixed to its facade.

Zayonchkovskaya was immediately enthused by the notion of a research council that would draw together researchers who had been isolated and dispersed by the dissolution of the Soviet Union. I was able to arrange for initial project financing from the Open Society Institute (Soros foundations) for the creation of the Council, which has now attracted substantial core funding from the Ford and MacArthur foundations. Specific project support has also been provided by IOM and UNHCR.

The fifth meeting of the Council was held in St Petersburg in September 2000 in an ornate meeting room of the European University. The building had been constructed at the time of Tsar Alexander II, and became the home of one of his mistresses: hence the flamboyant decor. Today, the building's restoration is a reflection of a new emphasis by international donors on reviving higher education in Russia.

The Research Council, with some 24 members drawn from all of the states of the former Soviet Union, was meeting to discuss the development of an information network. A slide presentation reviewed current migration trends, reflecting diminishing population movements to Russia from nearby countries. Migration primarily involved Russians and Russian-speakers coming to the Russian Federation, some 600,000 of the estimated 800,000 international migrants in the region. This was substantially lower than initial population movements in 1989, approximately by a factor of four, according to Zayonchkovskaya. Those who had wished to move at the demise of the Soviet Union, it seems, had already migrated.

But the number of persons from outside the region was on the rise, including persons from Asia and Africa seeking asylum and transiting onward to western countries. Russia's largest percentage of refugees and displaced persons in the region in late 2000 were from Azerbaijan, Armenia, and Tajikistan.

According to Zayonchkovskaya, the most dangerous places in the region currently are Tajikistan and the Ferghana Valley in central Asia, which could erupt at any time into violence and cause vast population displacements. Russia, with approximately 2 million refugees and displaced persons, had the largest absolute number of such persons, a total that was comparatively low in terms of percentage of population. But statistical record-keeping in the region is such that only estimates are possible at best. An Estonian expert at the meeting explained that this is because in Soviet times statistics were used to support ideologically oriented decisions and were not designed to illustrate actual circumstances. The task of introducing modern social science methods in the former Soviet Union clearly would be daunting.

The CIS Research Council is beginning to expand its work, seeking to recruit younger researchers in the constituent countries. Efforts to engage new researchers from outside Russia in the governance of the Council were also under way, largely at the behest of international donors. The fact of the meeting was nevertheless promising. Researchers were collaborating trans-nationally, discussing policy approaches in a region still in crisis.

The September 2000 discussions of the Council focused on a particular point. The disintegration of the former Soviet Union has been accompanied by the process of fortification of new borders, a dynamic still under way in this region. This trend has broad implications for freedom of movement and international migration. Just a few days before, the Russian Federation had withdrawn from the 1993 Bishkek agreement which had created a visa-free zone in the CIS. A Russian government official in attendance at the St Petersburg meeting explained that Russia's main concern was to curb criminality since a number of central Asian countries had visa-free arrangements with other countries outside of the region that could provide a place of entry into Russia for criminals and terrorists.

The initial inspiration for the 1993 Bishkek agreement had been western European arrangements, which had sought to regulate international travel from outside of Europe. But the CIS is not western Europe, and the withdrawal from the 1993 visa waiver agreement was the act of a relatively weak state to fortify its boundaries. It was also a device to pressure Georgia, many of whose citizens and families depend economically on travel to Russia to conduct business. While there were warnings by the experts in attendance in St Petersburg that such an arrangement was likely to simply encourage more Russians to migrate from the nearby countries of the former Soviet Union, the decision had already been taken, signalling yet another feature of dissolution in the region.

GETTING SERIOUS ABOUT PREVENTION

If genocide in Rwanda had been prevented, then the terrible refugee crisis of the mid-1990s would have been averted, and very possibly as well the inter-state conflict raging in central Africa at the outset of the new century. But the absence of resources to work on questions of encouraging and promoting prevention in the formulation and implementation of policy responses deprives decision makers of the advocacy of approaches that might over time reduce the need for expensive urgent crisis responses. The absence of resources dedicated to formulating proactive strategies necessarily leaves policy almost exclusively reactive. This is a basic rationale for the establishment of a new intergovernmental mechanism for Strategic Humanitarian Action and Research (SHARE), discussed later in this book.

Currently, the capacity to conceive of proactive approaches, much less to implement such policy, is ordinarily absent or horribly under-resourced in the structures for crisis response. For example, in the UN system, under the auspices of the Department of Political Affairs, a UN framework team has been established to share information and provide warning of impending humanitarian crises as well as make recommendations for preventive action to avert such crises. However, such recommendations have been lost in the uncertainty of the organization's decision-making process. While the Secretary-General's cabinet, comprising heads of departments and agencies which meets weekly, has taken decisions of consequence, the political constraints remain grave. The UN framework team is thinly resourced, with only one person dedicated to organizing periodic meetings. No resources are available for follow-up or collecting or analysing what has worked in the past for use in the future.

The problem is echoed even within national governments. In the US government, for example, there is a reluctance on the part of those in the intelligence community responsible for collecting and analysing situations to make recommendations about how to avert humanitarian crises. Oftentimes this is seen as infringing on the province of policy making, anathema to intelligence professionals who worry that making policy recommendations would risk politicization should the intelligence bureaucracy become aligned with particular policy outcomes. This could inject a bias into both collection and analysis.

The absence of resources, staff, and time devoted to developing strategies to mitigate crises, including post-crisis initiatives designed to minimize the likelihood of their recurrence, is a glaring deficit in humanitarian action. At the international level, a new strategic planning capacity outside of the UN system—SHARE—is needed to address these issues. Similar capacities need to be built in national structures, such as the new US Agency for Humanitarian Action (AHA), recommended in this book. Only by building the capacities of policy makers and their interlocutors to envisage and implement proactive approaches can responses seeking to mitigate refugee and humanitarian emergencies be made more intelligent, sustainable, and enduring.

MINIMIZING NEW CASUALTIES: AID WORKERS

The new trends in humanitarian action have produced many new complexities and unintended consequences. One of the harsh outcomes associated with the deployment of humanitarian workers in the midst of conflict has been the killing and abuse of aid workers. Humanitarian agencies are now often targeted by one or more of the sides in a conflict, or they become targets merely because of their resources and relative wealth.

There have been many notorious recent incidents. In September 2000, three staff members of the UNHCR were brutally murdered in Atambua, West Timor. In October 1999, two workers with UNICEF and the World Food Programme were killed in Burundi. The ICRC had six staff savagely killed in Chechnya in late 1996 in the hospital where they worked. In April 2001, six ICRC workers were shot and hacked to death in the northeast of the Democratic Republic of Congo, and an assault that month on the Médecins Sans Frontières compound in Mogadishu, Somalia, resulted in the death of twelve Somalis, including compound guards.

The trends, moreover, are ominous. Many aid workers have been killed, assaulted, or kidnapped with impunity over the past decade. While there is no comprehensive archive, an ad hoc compilation shows that in 1998, 48 civilian relief workers died and, after a brief downturn in 1999, in 2000 a like number perished.[37] In September 2000, the UN stated that a total of 198 of their civilian workers in the field had been killed since 1992.[38]

The exact dimension of the problem, whether abuses of aid workers are increasing or not, was not clear to Austen Davis of Médecins Sans Frontières-Holland, when we spoke in Amsterdam in 2000. He was unconvinced that the incidents are increasing. But this is distinctly a minority view. Marion Harroff-Tavel, with whom I spoke later at the ICRC in Geneva, believes that incidents are increasing, in part because of the changing nature of conflict. Armed conflict is increasingly intra-state in character, and the combatants have proliferated in unstructured ways. In one instance of internal conflict in central Africa, ICRC had 32 'interlocutors' to whom to relate, she said. 'Criminality, drugs and light weapons now move from conflict to conflict.'

[37] 'Chronology of United Nations and Humanitarian Aid Workers Killed in 2000', compiled by Dennis King, UNICEF Office of Emergency Programmes (15 January, 2001). At: http://www.reliefweb.int/library/documents/2001/chronology_15jan.htm Numbers for 1998 and 1999 obtained privately from Dennis King.

[38] 'UN Staff Protest Killing of Co-Workers', *Deutsche Presse-Agentur* (21 September 2000).

On occasion, in some places such as Somalia or Chechnya even the ICRC has had to arrange for armed escorts, despite a general policy to the contrary. Harroff-Tavel's passion on this issue was perhaps informed to some degree by the fact that, when we spoke in August 2000, two ICRC delegates were being held for ransom in the Republic of Georgia along with their driver. While they were later released, ICRC suspended its operations in the remote Georgian province adjoining Chechnya until appropriate security arrangements could be made.

Humanitarian workers customarily accept the sacrifice of personal comfort and safety in order to help others. Ironically, aid agencies are thus often embarrassed in some sense to champion their own security. But the result is an outcome deeply disruptive of the efforts to provide assistance in countries roiled with conflict and crisis. Access by agencies to minister to vulnerable populations can be effectively blocked by attacks on aid workers, which are tantamount to attacks on the system of humanitarian assistance itself. The international community must deal with this problem directly and robustly.

The current efforts to address it have been largely relegated to providing equipment—armoured vehicles, helmets, flak jackets—and training. Most large operating humanitarian agencies now have ex-military security advisers on staff. In February 2000, the UN Secretary-General appointed a senior official as United Nations security coordinator responsible for all policy and procedures relating to security in the UN system. But coordination, equipment, and training are not sufficient. The international community must ensure that there is an adequate legal framework to hold accountable those who kill or abuse humanitarian workers.

A United Nations treaty that entered into force in January 1999 provides universal jurisdiction to bring to trial offenders who have assaulted or murdered aid workers, and enjoins a duty on the part of signatory countries to prevent such abuses from occurring in the future.[39] As of April 2001, 51 states had become party to this treaty. While a good start, the UN safety convention leaves uncovered certain aid workers who are not associated with the United Nations, and there is a gap where the UN has undertaken peace enforcement activities and become itself a party to the conflict. Coverage in this circumstance is left to the province of international humanitarian law. These gaps have led some to call for an additional protocol to the safety treaty to extend coverage more broadly.

[39] Convention on the Safety of United Nations and Associated Personnel, adopted by resolution 49/59 of the General Assembly dated 9 December 1994, entry into force 15 January 1999, UN Doc. A/49/742 (1994).

The International Criminal Court, heralded by a multilateral UN treaty which 139 states including the United States, had signed as of February 2001, could provide another mechanism to safeguard humanitarian aid workers when it becomes operational.[40] But confining the jurisdiction of the court to 'widespread or systematic' infractions of international law in the nature of crimes against humanity could preclude application to individual abuses of aid workers. The court would have authority to remedy war crimes committed in the context of 'armed conflict not of an international character' as opposed to riots, sporadic acts of violence, or similar acts. That the court's jurisdiction would extend only to crimes against humanity and war crimes committed as a matter of 'policy' might also be held to limit its protection in relation to humanitarian workers. In any event, the capacity of the court will be inherently limited.

But the real challenges lay beyond legal mechanisms. What is needed is an international political campaign to bring such offenders to justice. The UN Security Council has recognized the crucial role played by humanitarian workers in complex emergencies. On several occasions recently, Security Council resolutions have cited the responsibilities to protect aid workers and to bring to justice those who commit offences against them.

But resolutions are not sufficient; the basic problem is impunity. Concerted efforts must be undertaken, including providing appropriate political and diplomatic incentives or disincentives in order to ensure that those who perpetrate offences against aid workers are arrested and either tried in a court of law or extradited to stand trial. This is a crucial adjunct to new efforts to assist vulnerable populations in the midst of conflict.[41]

Information is often a prerequisite to action. That there is no comprehensive archive cataloguing the abuses perpetrated against aid workers is the starting point for an accountability campaign. A systematic archive, ideally electronic, would inform all stakeholders of the dimensions and trends relating to the problem. The ReliefWeb website[42] would be an obvious candidate for this purpose, particularly its new advocacy site that is currently being developed, but other hosts should be considered as well.

If the international community is to find workable approaches to address humanitarian needs within countries that are riven by crisis and

[40] Rome Statute of the International Criminal Court. At: http://www.un.org/law/icc/statute.htm

[41] See 'Report of the Secretary-General to the Security Council on the Protection of Civilians in Armed Conflict', UN Doc. S/2001/331 (30 March 2001).

[42] See http://www.reliefweb.int

war, then much more has to be done to ensure that aid workers, this essential channel of access to humanitarian assistance, are protected. This is not just a plea not to harm the helpers; it is a recognition that the basic strategy of providing humanitarian aid in situations of internal strife and crisis depends upon achieving this measure of human security.

BEYOND TOOLS: DOING THE JOB

Concepts in the field of humanitarian action, as elsewhere, are easy to state but difficult to realize. Nothing is wrong if internal safety arrangements for would-be refugees are, indeed, safe. Nor is encouragement of seeking asylum in a nearby country a problem if the quality of asylum is adequate. Repatriation is acceptable if conditions are conducive to voluntary return. Humanitarian intervention and the use of force can be justified by necessity if the motivations are genuine and the involvement proportional. If law-enforcement power is projected on an extraterritorial basis, it must be accompanied by a responsibility to respect the rights of refugees.

A basic guiding principle should thus be followed in the conduct of humanitarian action. To the extent feasible, the choices of refugees and displaced persons should be respected. Not only is this the right approach, rooted as it is in notions of dignity and human rights; it is the most effective and workable approach. Dishonest policies may gain initial political advantage, but are liable to prove unsustainable over even the short term. Terrible hardships and profound political embarrassments can easily be produced by such policy blunders.

Tools, of course, can be used or misused. Humanitarian responses can be distorted by political considerations, and political and military action can be clothed in humanitarian rhetoric. Yet effective humanitarian action requires astute political insights in order to address the needs of both individuals and states. This is what Jan Eliasson, the ambassador of Sweden to the United States in 2000 and the first head of the UN Department of Humanitarian Affairs, calls 'humanitarian diplomacy'.[43]

[43] Eliasson, Jan, 'Outlook: Responding to Crises', *Security Dialogue*, 26/4 (1995), 409.

7

International Bureaucracy and the Debasement of Mercy

As I made my way across the plaza to the entrance to United Nations headquarters, I threaded through hundreds of tourists and students who were lined up for tours. Summer had finally come to New York in early May 2000, and it was a modest relief to enter the air conditioned hall. I made my way through the headquarters labyrinth, needing only once to ask directions to find the basement room where a monthly meeting was scheduled between the UN Office for the Coordination of Humanitarian Affairs (OCHA) and representatives of InterAction, a consortium of over 160 NGOs based in Washington, DC.

At the meeting, about 30 individuals were seated around a table. There were a series of reports, mainly by UN officials, on issues such as a plan of the Ericsson Corporation to provide telecommunications equipment for disaster responses, the status of the work of a high-level expert panel appointed by the Secretary-General to review UN peacekeeping operations, and the work of subcommittees of the UN's Inter-Agency Standing Committee on issues of security and the humanitarian impacts of sanctions. For the most part, the meeting was a series of status reports by UN officials, followed almost invariably by questions from the NGO representatives present about how they might become involved in the activities in question.

The measured pace of the meeting was broken, however, by a disturbing report on the current crisis in Sierra Leone: the 'crisis *du jour*' in the words of a senior OCHA official who was present. Over the past several days, fighters from the Revolutionary United Front (RUF) had reportedly killed four Kenyan peacekeepers. Several hundreds more were 'missing' and presumed captive, including an entire Zambian battalion that had been ambushed in a convoy and whose equipment had fallen into the hands of the rebel fighters. Ultimately, these captive peacekeepers, along with a contingent of 233 besieged Indian peacekeepers and unarmed military observers, regained their liberty.[1]

[1] 'UN Praises Sierra Leone Rescue', *Associated Press* (18 July 2000).

In their briefing on this occasion, OCHA officials made it clear that this was a preconceived military attack by the RUF against the UN peacekeeping force. Plans were being formulated and implemented to 'draw down' the UN and NGO personnel that had been deployed under the framework of a 1999 peace agreement. Approximately 8,700 peacekeepers of the 11,100 authorized by the Security Council had been deployed as of 7 May 2000.[2] The situation was quite fluid, and the outcome of the conflict between the UN and the RUF at the time was uncertain.

The coordination meeting had a particularly poignant moment. We were, after all, meeting in the headquarters of one of the combatants in Sierra Leone. The OCHA officials who were briefing us were clearly consumed by their concerns for the UN troops and civilian workers embroiled in the conflict. After the report on the military situation, a young representative from Médecin Sans Frontières took the floor to report that her agency's country headquarters in Freetown had not been able to communicate with staff in rebel-held territory in central Sierra Leone. She asked whether the UN had decided to 'block communications' in order to isolate the RUF. The senior OCHA person present, clearly angered by the query, called it 'a really sad question'. The answer, he said firmly, is 'no'. Another NGO participant noted that his agency's staff, which had received assurances of free passage from the rebels, had taken pains to dissociate itself from the UN, which was clearly the 'target' of the RUF fighters. The UN seemed at this moment to be small and oddly alone, as the Security Council dithered.

The UN has become a combatant in Sierra Leone, as it has on occasion in other places around the world. This circumstance can, of course, pose virtually insurmountable barriers to humanitarian coordination, with at least some NGOs becoming concerned about the loss of neutrality and being associated with one side in an internal conflict such as that in Sierra Leone. This is not a theoretical or abstract consideration; it may ultimately be a matter of life or death for aid workers and their beneficiaries.

I left this UN coordination exchange on that early summer day shortly before 1.00 p.m. when the headquarters plaza was relatively empty and before the predictable exodus of UN staff in search of lunch. A band of amateur musicians was tuning up, waiting for an audience on what promised to be a lazy summer day. But as I made my way onto the street, I could not help but wonder what would become of those peacekeepers and humanitarian workers who were caught up in the latest spasm of violence in a faraway place in the service of broad international ideals for a just and humane world order.

[2] 'UN Force in Sierra Leone Stands at 8,699', *Agence France-Presse* (7 May 2000).

INTERNATIONAL DISORGANIZATION

Coordination at its core is an inside bureaucratic game with profound outside human consequences. The term 'coordination' is defined as the harmonious functioning of parts for effective results. In the context of international humanitarian action, the stakes are particularly high. The mismanagement of humanitarian responses not only can waste valuable resources, it can translate into delay and inefficacy which can imperil the lives and well-being of refugees and displaced persons.

Uprooted persons need humanitarian assistance and are entitled to legal protection. The notion of international coordination arises particularly in circumstances where there is no adequate legal or institutional framework for policy formulation or implementation. Indeed, 'coordination' is often nothing less than a substitute for a multilateral consensus and enabling structure. Many treatments of international humanitarian action rue the lack of coordination.

Senior United Nations officials sometimes refer to coordination as the 'C word'. This is not particularly surprising given the amount of bureaucratic blood that has been spilt in UN reform efforts over the past decade. Nevertheless, the anxiety with which international agency heads still greet the term is revealing. Bureaucratic fights over money, personnel, and programmes are often masked by debates over 'coordination'.

Nor is there a common definition of the term in relation to its use in the humanitarian field, a circumstance that led one US State Department official involved in humanitarian assistance to plea that 'we should ban the word's use for a decade'. Coordination can mean control over resources and programming—anathema to many agency heads and NGOs—or merely sharing information and consultation, or something in between.

Coordination problems in refugee affairs have a long history, including the evolution of the fragmentary and overlapping sets of entities established to deal with displacement. This includes the squabbles that emerged after the International Refugee Organization, United Nations High Commissioner for Refugees, and Intergovernmental Committee for European Migration—predecessor to the International Organization for Migration—were established after the Second World War. But given the chronic nature of the problem, this old story bears retelling in a modern incarnation.

Coordination questions permeate the work of the international humanitarian sector. There is coordination within the UN system; between the UN system and other international entities, including the international financial institutions; between international organizations and governments and/or

NGOs as well as local authorities and indigenous 'civil society' actors; between the humanitarians and military-political planners in 'complex contingency operations', that is, emergencies; between relief and development agencies; between policy planners and operational programme managers; between headquarters and the field; between international entities that have universal mandates and those that have functional or regional mandates; between and among NGOs themselves, including relief agencies, human rights monitoring groups, and local actors; and between and among donors and recipients of funding. This list is not, of course, exhaustive. But duplication of efforts is endemic in the humanitarian 'new economy' that has emerged over the past decade, and gaps are more prevalent than structure in international humanitarian action. The imperative to 'coordinate' is the result.

Nevertheless, the formal framework for coordination of international humanitarian action has evolved significantly over the past decade. There are now more organizational links to promote communication, consultation, and data exchange between and among humanitarians. Whether and how the activities associated with this near blizzard of information affect local populations in the field is a different matter, which merits continuous assessment.

THE UN OFFICE FOR THE COORDINATION OF HUMANITARIAN AFFAIRS

In terms of the formal architecture of international coordination, the leading actor, at least nominally, is the Office for the Coordination of Humanitarian Affairs (OCHA), which is part of the United Nations Secretariat. Its mandate is to coordinate the provision of humanitarian assistance, particularly that of the UN system, in complex emergencies and natural disasters.

In 1991, there was a growing recognition that the UN system needed stronger coordination mechanisms to deal with innovative responses to humanitarian crises, such as the situation in northern Iraq. The humanitarian challenges there were singular in terms of their size and complexity. Duplication of efforts by humanitarian agencies and unmet needs among affected populations were rampant in that situation. While perhaps sometimes less aggravated, they continue to plague humanitarian efforts around the world.

There was much debate throughout the summer and autumn of 1991 between developing and industrialized nations, focusing on balancing the right of individuals to humanitarian assistance and protection against respect for national sovereignty. The outcome was General Assembly Resolution 46/182, adopted by consensus, which sought to set out guiding principles for UN humanitarian assistance for victims of natural disasters and other emergencies. The resolution provided for the designation of a single senior official to coordinate humanitarian relief efforts.[3] Under Resolution 46/182, it is no longer necessary that the affected country initiate a call for assistance. Noting that the 'sovereignty, territorial integrity and national unity of States must be fully respected', the resolution states only that 'humanitarian assistance should be provided with the consent of the affected country and in principle on the basis of an appeal by the affected country'.

The resolution underscores the importance of disaster prevention and preparedness and the need to deal with the root causes of disaster by addressing the needs of member nations for sustainable development. It reaffirms the UN's 'central and unique role to play in providing leadership and coordinating the efforts of the international community' and delivering humanitarian assistance to affected countries, and it provides for the appointment of the Emergency Relief Coordinator (ERC) to undertake this responsibility.

To support the ERC, the UN Department of Humanitarian Affairs (DHA) was established in 1992. The Inter-Agency Standing Committee (IASC), which has since become the primary coordination forum for humanitarian agencies in the UN system, was also established at that time. The purpose of the IASC is to facilitate inter-agency decision making in complex humanitarian emergencies. The IASC is also the forum in which programme responsibilities are allocated in situations where there are gaps in mandates or lack of institutional capacities.[4]

The next UN coordination milestone was the debate in 1997 over the UN Secretary-General's proposals to reform the UN system. The daunting challenges associated with the emergencies in Bosnia and Herzegovina and the Great Lakes region of Africa were in the minds of many UN officials. To address these issues, the Secretary-General entertained a proposal to integrate the DHA into the UNHCR in Geneva. In effect, this would have made UNHCR the permanent lead agency to deal with humanitarian

[3] 'Strengthening of the Coordination of Emergency Assistance of the United Nations', UN Doc. A/RES/46/182 (19 December 1991), Sect. 34.

[4] The members of the IASC are: FAO, OCHA (then DHA), UNDP, UNFPA, UNICEF, UNHCR, WFP, and WHO. Standing invitees are: ICRC, ICVA, IFRC, InterAction, IOM, the Steering Committee for Humanitarian Response, the Special Representative of the Secretary-General for Internally Displaced Persons, the Office of the High Commissioner for Human Rights, and the World Bank. See List of Abbreviations for acronyms.

catastrophes. In fact, this option came quite close to being realized, with UNHCR being asked by the Secretary-General's principal adviser on reform to prepare a plan to implement the consolidation. Much internal wrangling attended the proposal, with several donor governments and agencies expressing opposition. World Food Programme Executive Director Catherine Bertini and UNICEF Executive Director Carol Bellamy were notably outspoken in their opposition. The Secretary-General ultimately decided that, instead of creating an integrated institution, there would continue to be a separate Under-Secretary-General for Humanitarian Affairs. In furtherance of this decision, the DHA was re-named the Office for the Coordination of Humanitarian Affairs (OCHA). While most functions were retained, certain operational activities in which DHA had become involved, such as de-mining, were transferred from OCHA to other entities within the UN system.

There was high drama relating to the reform debates during this period at UN headquarters, with UN agency heads intensely lobbying governments and the Secretary-General with their respective views. But it is worth keeping in mind a field perspective. The reform outcome was in practice little more than a name change; the core mission of DHA remained the same. A UN staffer who was working in the field at the time confided recently that she was 'oblivious' to the changes. The reorganization simply made no difference in her day-to-day work.

Nevertheless, the reform debate revealed serious bureaucratic tensions in the UN system that continue today to influence the way humanitarian action is organized. By 1997, the UN's operational agencies had grown wary of DHA's 'mission creep', even though some of its ventures were designed to fill gaps in areas such as de-mining or demobilizing fighters. The office had become increasingly involved in field activities that competed with other agencies. The reform package which was finally adopted retained the policy development function in OCHA on issues such as the protection of internally displaced persons, although the criteria and procedures for developing authoritative policy were not explicitly addressed in the reorganization. As re-configured, OCHA was to have three basic functions: coordination of humanitarian emergency responses, policy development and coordination, and advocacy of humanitarian issues. This re-configuration, however, was not accompanied by budgetary authority over the resources of other agencies.

As currently configured, OCHA works in the field through UN resident coordinators who lead UN country teams. At the headquarters level, the head of OCHA has dual responsibilities as the Under-Secretary-General (USG) for Humanitarian Affairs and the Emergency Relief Coordinator who chairs the IASC. The IASC brings together the leading humanitarian entities, both within and outside the UN system. The USG head of OCHA is the principal adviser to the UN Secretary-General on humanitarian issues, and the convenor of the Executive Committee for Humanitarian Affairs (ECHA), which provides a forum for the humanitarian components and the political and peacekeeping departments at the UN Secretariat. Also, principals and heads of specialized agencies participate in weekly meetings—including via video conferencing—of the Senior Management Group, which serves as a functional cabinet for the Secretary-General, addressing humanitarian issues in a comprehensive context.

The ECHA is one of the four executive committees created in 1998 by the Secretary-General as a result of UN reform, which meets on a monthly basis in New York.[5] The Department of Peacekeeping Operations and the Department of Political Affairs, among others, are members of ECHA. This permits political and security perspectives to be integrated in the body's deliberations, and is perhaps the key, if not the only, feature that distinguishes ECHA from the IASC.

OCHA has a headquarters presence in both New York and Geneva. The USG/ERC is located in New York. OCHA in Geneva is the focal point for support to the field and hosts the offices that deal with natural disasters.

The 1998 UN reforms led the IASC to issue recommendations expressly addressing the coordination of humanitarian assistance. The recommendations draw a distinction between strategic and operational coordination. Strategic coordination is defined as the 'overall direction of the humanitarian programme'.[6] This includes setting the goals, allocating tasks and responsibilities, and ensuring that they are reflected in a strategic plan, in accordance with agency mandates. Also involved is the advocacy of humanitarian principles, negotiating access to the affected populations, mobilizing resources, monitoring and evaluating implementation, and 'liaising with the military and political participants of the international community'.[7] This is tantamount to humanitarian policy coordination but without the benefit of a cohesive structural framework at the international level.

Operational coordination is defined as interrelating a variety of matters in humanitarian operations, notably, specific technical sector activities, defined geographical areas, and particular beneficiary groups, as well as

[5] The members of ECHA are: UNDP, UNICEF, UNHCR, WFP, OHCHR, DPKO, UNRWA, the Special Representative of the Secretary-General for Children in Armed Conflicts, WHO, and FAO.

[6] United Nations, OCHA Orientation Handbook on Complex Emergencies (New York: UN, 1999), 20.

[7] Ibid.

the provision of common arrangements regarding security, communications, and logistics for humanitarian workers. In reality, the coordination of humanitarian functions on the ground in an emergency setting often evolves and works as a matter of necessity.

Put another way, strategic coordination is what humanitarian workers and agency officials talk about at headquarters meetings in New York or Geneva; operational coordination is what they talk about at meetings in the field.

The method of designating an international coordinator in an emergency situation is ad hoc. The IASC under the chairmanship of the ERC decides on the appropriate field coordination mechanism for each complex emergency on a case-by-case basis. This could include working through a resident/humanitarian coordinator, a representative of a lead agency, or, exceptionally, a humanitarian coordinator distinct from the office of the resident coordinator or lead agency. An international coordinator can also be appointed on a regional basis. Successful coordination, of course, depends to a great degree on the personal qualities and attributes of the person chosen for this position. Significantly, the IASC gives an assurance that the 'coordination arrangements will respect existing mandates of humanitarian organizations'.[8]

Normally, coordination arrangements are made on the basis of the 'resident coordinator system'. The resident/humanitarian coordinator is responsible to the ERC and 'should not be charged with operational responsibility to ensure *impartiality* in discharging coordination functions'.[9] As used in this context, the term 'impartiality' refers not to the provision of humanitarian assistance to needy persons without distinction as to which side of a conflict they are on, but rather to respecting the institutional mandates of the various UN agencies and an undertaking not to compete bureaucratically.

In terms of designating a lead agency, the factors to be considered include whether the sectors of assistance are closely related to the mandate of the agency; whether the agency in question has the capacity to coordinate, establish, and maintain common operational support and at the same time take action specific to its mandate; and whether the agency has sufficient personnel on the ground and/or the ability to deploy rapidly. An initial coordination response is to be provided by the UN resident coordinator—organizationally the UNDP country representative—in an

[8] UN Office for the Coordination of Humanitarian Affairs, Inter-Agency Standing Committee Recommendations Related to the Review of the Capacity of the United Nations System for Humanitarian Assistance (Geneva: OCHA, 14 August 1998), Sect. I.2.

[9] OCHA, *Inter-Agency Standing Committee Recommendations*, Sect. I.3.d ; emphasis added. See also UN Office for the Coordination of Humanitarian Affairs, *Complex Crisis and Complex Peace: Humanitarian Coordination in Angola* (New York: OCHA, February 1998), Ch. 1.2.

emergency situation, with a decision to be taken later as to whether or not a separate humanitarian coordinator or lead agency is to be designated. The terms of reference for a humanitarian coordinator are spelled out by the IASC.

With perhaps the exception of UNHCR, there seems to be diminishing enthusiasm in the UN system for lead agency designations in humanitarian emergencies. In 2000, UNHCR was designated to play a leading role with respect to Chechnya, based on the agency's prior involvements in the former Soviet Union. But it has proved difficult in practice for lead agencies to dissociate themselves from their mandate responsibilities. As one senior UN humanitarian official put it, 'in Angola [where the WFP has a leading involvement] the humanitarian challenge is seen largely as a food problem; in the former Yugoslavia [where UNHCR was the lead agency] it is seen as a refugee problem'. Neither is a fully accurate depiction.

The IASC endeavours to work 'by consensus'. When consensus is not possible, 'but where there is a convergence of views among a majority of IASC members', the ERC can decide on matters involving the implementation of already agreed-upon coordination arrangements. Other matters must be referred to the Secretary-General for decision. Significantly, the assurance is reiterated in the 1998 IASC guidance that 'all decisions will be taken in full respect of the mandates of individual IASC members'.[10]

One of the main tools at the disposal of OCHA for coordination is the consolidated appeals process. OCHA oversees this process, which provides a mechanism for UN agencies, international organizations, and NGOs to prepare an integrated appeal for funding and monitor the receipt and use of financial contributions. In practice, however, achieving a coherent approach has often proved difficult in the absence of budgetary authority. Sometimes consolidated appeals have been little more than wish lists. Optimally, the resources provided by donor governments could provide leverage to enforce concerted strategic action. As a World Bank official involved with post-conflict reconstruction noted: 'Coordination follows resources.'

DONOR COORDINATION: EUROPE AND THE UNITED STATES

A relatively small number of the world's governments—10 to 15 countries plus the EU structures—provide funding through multilateral mechanisms to address humanitarian emergencies. Notwithstanding the discrete number, however, there are five different channels for multilateral humanitarian

[10] OCHA, Inter-Agency Standing Committee Recommendations, Sect. VII.75(i) and (ii).

assistance. One route is through the formal governing boards of certain international organizations such as UNHCR. Second are informal coordination mechanisms for the multilateral organizations that do not have formal arrangements for donor input, such as ICRC. Third are formal bodies that deal with broad multilateral coordination of development assistance, but which have relatively weak mechanisms for dealing with humanitarian assistance—ECOSOC, Organization for Economic Cooperation and Development-Development Assistance Committee. Fourth are the numerous 'friends' or reference groups, mainly composed of senior non-elected officials, that have developed around specific country situations or humanitarian issues and that attempt to improve the coordination of humanitarian and post-conflict assistance programmes. Fifth is field level coordination among donor representatives in countries with ongoing humanitarian assistance programmes.

In terms of trends, informal groups are growing in importance as the relatively small group of major humanitarian aid donors finds international organizational governing boards to be too large and cumbersome to take quick and decisive action on important humanitarian issues. Information is exchanged in these settings often with no official records of decisions. In addition, much funding is now provided bilaterally without even a pretence at coordinated action. The United States, for example, provided $100 million in funding directly to NGOs in 2000.

A particular set of donor relationships—that between the US and the European Union—has been the subject of many international consultations. While the calculation of precise numbers is difficult because of variable methodologies, the EU is the source of over half of the humanitarian assistance around the world.[11] About one-half of this amount is distributed by the European Community Humanitarian Office (ECHO); the other half comes directly from EU member states. For example, Sweden, the Netherlands, Denmark, and the United Kingdom are important bilateral donors to UNHCR, and collectively give more than ECHO. They also often take policy positions on UNHCR funding and management questions which are very different from the position of ECHO. In that sense, EU member states act separately with the discretion to coordinate.

The US accounts for approximately 25–33 per cent of the world's assistance, depending on how food commodities are counted.[12] The programme

[11] See generally European Community Humanitarian Aid Office, *ECHO Annual Review 1999* (Brussels: ECHO, 2000).

[12] 'Global Humanitarian Assistance for 2001: Major Donors by Contribution', Reliefweb–Financial Tracking System, visited 6 June 2001. At: http://www.reliefweb.int/fts/reports/pdf/ocha_18_2001.pdf. See also 'WFP and Donors', World Food Programme website, visited 6 June 2001. At: http://www.wfp.org/info/Intro/donors/default.htm

mechanisms are 'tending to converge' and there is greater 'understanding of each other's system', in the words of a senior US humanitarian official. There are also certain differences: for example, ECHO's propensity to fund on a specific project basis as against the US propensity to fund on a more generic programme basis creates 'complexities' and adds to the challenges of coordination.

As to activities at the European level, ECHO allocated over 812 million euros in 1999—the equivalent of $717.6 million—primarily through the United Nations—20 per cent—and ICRC—15 per cent—with the remainder being used to finance NGO projects.[13] About half of the 1999 total was spent on the Kosovo crisis.

A premium is placed on donor coordination between the EU and US, which is evolving through the sharing of information and efforts to harmonize methodologies. ECHO's funding in 2000 is likely to be approximately $1 billion, with EU member states contributing approximately another $1.2 billion, for a total of over $2 billion. This compares with total US contribution of somewhat over $1 billion.[14] Other donors, including Japan, contribute approximately $500 million.

In 2001, ECHO's budget line is €500 million, with €208 million in an emergency reserve fund: equivalent to $468.85 and $195 million, respectively.[15] ECHO's funding decisions are taken by a management committee under normal Commission procedures, with a special provision for urgent disbursements for sums below €2 million—$1.88 million—which the staff can initiate, and with after-the-fact notification required for sums from €2 million to €10 million—$1.88 million–$9.38 million—which are needed on an emergency basis. Coordination by the Commission with the bilateral programmes of member states depends on disclosures by those states, which are not always forthcoming.

ECHO has sought to retain a relatively independent position and to use humanitarian principles to inform its funding decisions. This provides a degree of insulation from foreign policy objectives, at least to the extent that the policy objectives can be discerned in this collective EU setting. An evaluation in late 1999 considered the creation of an independent humanitarian agency, but decided to retain the ECHO structure. The review, however, recommended the consolidation of development assistance

[13] ECHO, Echo Annual Review 1999, 28.

[14] See generally ECHO, Echo Annual Review 1999.

[15] 'Forecast Budget for 2001' (ECHO's Finances–The Budget), ECHO Humanitarian Aid Office website, visited 19 July 2001. At: http://europa.eu.int/comm/echo/en/finances/finances2.htm. In 2001 the Commission committed €100 million to crisis assistance in Afghanistan.

programmes, resulting in the establishment of a new aid agency, Europe Aid, which began operating in 2001.

NON-GOVERNMENTAL ORGANIZATIONS

Much is said about 'civil society' and new roles for non-governmental organizations in discussions of new drivers in international affairs. Many commentators have recognized the increasing influence of NGOs in the public policy arena. There is frequent citation of the work of NGOs in recent years in relation to the promulgation of international treaties on the rights of children and banning of landmines as evidence of the impacts of independent sector actors in foreign affairs. Government officials and military leaders increasingly realize that they must take into account the self-assertions of special interests by NGOs in complex emergencies in order to help manage responses. To do otherwise is an invitation to surprise and frustration.

NGOs, of course, can be a negative as well as a positive force in humanitarian responses. NGO perspectives are often preoccupied with ethical concerns which may seem at times oddly inefficient in the midst of a crisis. Lack of accountability can mask institutional or political goals which are unrelated to the needs of individual refugees or displaced persons. Seeking to manage such disparate actors is akin to managing a thunderstorm; incoherence can reign. Nevertheless, NGOs are a customary feature of humanitarian responses. They must be taken into account in such operations. Decision makers ignore them at their political peril.

NGOs working in humanitarian, developmental, human rights, educational, and conflict-resolution activities are typically present in crisis situations. Sometimes they profess neutrality; at other times they declare sympathy with one or another of the sides in a conflict. This is a facet of new notions of sovereignty and humanitarian action. While such ideas remain controversial among states, for many years some NGOs have regarded national borders as little more than inconveniences in their work.

Often animated by grass-roots constituencies and decrying a state-centric orientation, humanitarian NGOs have sought to place an emphasis on human need and a 'rights-based' perspective. NGOs are increasingly the instrumentality by which humanitarian aid is provided as well as from which early warning and reconciliation endeavours emanate. Grass-roots contacts, small-scale projects, and access to local structures are typical features of these new civil society actors. NGOs can marshal rapid responses and promote empowerment. They monitor and advocate for human rights and the protection of minorities, and they seek to build local capacities. A 1998 US State Department unclassified cable concerning de-mining operations in Cambodia summarized a widespread donor perspective—and dilemma:

> NGO's provide a quality service that is very responsive to donor demands. They have low overhead, small staffs, and their expatriate leadership helps keep them above many of the political and cultural pressures that a national mine action center faces. Support to NGO's not only provides an incentive for the national mine action center to maintain international standards, but it reinforces the 'demining 2010' initiative to support NGO and private sector demining activities. If the goal of the USG [US government] program were not to create an indigenous capacity but rather to demine Cambodia as quickly as possible, then Post [the US Embassy] would recommend that the majority of our money be spent through NGO's.[16]

The most striking characteristic of the NGOs that work in humanitarian emergencies is their diversity. Perhaps this is inevitable in a category defined by a negative quality, being 'non-governmental'. The organizations literally come in all shapes and sizes. They include large relief or development agencies which have annual budgets of tens of millions of dollars. Others include small charities that mobilize in response to particular crises. Some are virtual subcontractors with substantial funding from governments or international organizations. Others have their own funding sources and insist fiercely upon independent action. Invoking the term 'coordination' in communications with certain NGOs can be tantamount to a declaration of institutional war.

Certain dynamics have structural underpinnings. NGOs compete for publicity in emergencies in order to raise funds in what one UNHCR official in 2000 called 'the new humanitarian market place'. These and other forces of disunity can be maximized in complex humanitarian emergencies.

Since 1997, through several agency networks the NGO sector has endeavoured to articulate standards and guidelines for work in humanitarian emergencies. The Sphere Project is a product of NGO collaboration that has published a humanitarian charter drawing upon precepts of international human rights, humanitarian and refugee law, and minimum standards for disaster response.[17] Published documents include an NGO

[16] Cable from US Embassy Phnom Penh to US Secretary of State (14 November 1998), Para. 10.

[17] Steering Committee for Humanitarian Response and InterAction, *The Sphere Project: Humanitarian Charter and Minimum Standards in Disaster Response* (Geneva: Steering Committee for Humanitarian Response and InterAction, 1998), 1–2.

field cooperation protocol as well as minimum standards based on key indicators in water supplies and sanitation, nutrition, food aid, shelter and site planning, and health services. Sphere documents are now being distributed through various NGO channels.

But this technical exercise is not without controversy. Médecins Sans Frontières (MSF) has led a group of agencies who have criticized this standard-setting exercise on the grounds that it will inhibit innovation and flexibility. MSF, which won the Nobel peace prize in 1999, has been a persistent critic of humanitarian coordination endeavours, expressing reservations about activities that may give rise to even a perception of compromise with respect to NGO neutrality and independence. MSF is the manifestation of NGO purity in the humanitarian field; or, as Austen Davis, General Director of MSF-Holland in 2000 described this role, 'being a pain in the ass'. Humanitarian endeavours should not be the province of 'technocrats', in his view; rather, they are part of a broader movement for change. The cardinal principles of impartiality and neutrality are implicated mainly to ensure access by groups to war-affected civilians to deliver humanitarian relief in the midst of conflict.

But humanitarian aid is not a technical exercise, at least exclusively, and whether NGOs can remain neutral in highly charged political settings, such as those which characterize internal conflicts, is the subject of fierce debate among humanitarians, some of whom call themselves 'political humanitarians'. MSF is 'not neutral', said Davis, who also cautioned against explicitly linking humanitarian and military-political objectives. He cited in this regard the 1999 conflict in Kosovo, where soldiers were called 'humanitarian workers' and the conflict a 'humanitarian war', a use of language that he found to be 'obscene'.

THE EXTERNAL EVALUATION OF UNHCR'S RESPONSE TO THE 1999 KOSOVO CRISIS

An external evaluation in 2000 of UNHCR's response to the 1999 Kosovo crisis is a revealing examination of coordination conundrums for a lead humanitarian agency in a complex emergency. The international intervention in Kosovo was, at least for humanitarian assistance providers, a singular event of a type that occurs relatively rarely in contemporary international affairs, involving the national interests of great powers, strong regional organizations, and military action in Europe. In this circumstance, refugees became virtual weapons of war. The objective to win the war was all-encompassing.

As the UNHCR evaluation notes, the population displacement issue in Kosovo was regarded by governments in some sense as simply too important to leave exclusively to UNHCR, even as nominally the lead humanitarian agency.

An after-action report in January 2000 of the US Department of Defense on the Kosovo operation, which addressed humanitarian assistance activities, highlighted the dilemmas caused by simultaneous combat and humanitarian operations. There was, according to the Defense Department's report, an 'inevitable competition for landing spaces, ground transportation, and other support assets'. There was 'demand by both operations [humanitarian and military]' for 'heavy lift aircraft, special communications and intelligence assets, and even military linguists'.[18] Issues relating to the establishment of refugee camps also occasioned unique military and humanitarian interactions.

The UNHCR Kosovo evaluation demonstrated graphically that the agency does not have the capacity to analyse potential 'hot spots' and envisage or plan for worst-case scenarios. This is due mainly to the reactive character of the way refugee work is organized at the international level. UNHCR is the primary international agency actor dealing with refugee emergencies and is highly regarded, having won the Nobel peace prize in 1954 and 1981. Yet, in Kosovo, UNHCR stumbled.

UNHCR's Kosovo response was characterized by unclear lines of authority, with much confusion about responsibilities between Geneva-based staff and relatively junior, inexperienced representatives working in Macedonia and Albania. These flaws were undoubtedly important factors in UNHCR's slow and inadequate response in late March to early May 1999. An earlier reorganization and reduction of UNHCR staff had contributed to this outcome. But this was, indeed, a unique event in which humanitarian responses were largely dictated by political and security imperatives outside of the control of the agency.

The report questions whether UNHCR's aspiration to be the 'lead agency' in the context of this military operation was appropriate or workable.[19] One lesson from Kosovo may be that the lead-agency model may have to be qualified to some extent by the exigencies of complex operations which involve military and political components. The dominant military-strategic framework and an overwhelming bilateralism, with governments directly

[18] US Department of Defense, *Report to Congress: Kosovo/Operation Allied Force After-Action Report* (Washington, DC: US Department of Defense, 31 January 2000), 105.

[19] Suhrke, Astri, Barutciski, Michael, Sandison, Peta, and Garlock, Rick, *The Kosovo Crisis: An Independent Evaluation of UNHCR's Emergency Preparedness and Response* (Geneva: UNHCR Evaluation and Policy Unit, February 2000), xiii, 109–15.

funding selected NGOs, posed a serious dilemma for many humanitarians used to working in a multilateral fashion.

The Kosovo evaluation report also treats issues associated with the new types of technology available to humanitarian actors which could have important implications for coordination. In this instance, the issue was refugee registration in Albania and Macedonia. Initially, there was a concern by the US State Department that Serbian forces were engaging in 'identity cleansing' through the destruction of documentation in order to deny the right of Kosovar refugees to return. While this scenario did not materialize upon the Serbian withdrawal in June, another problem was created by the failure to register refugees because of the difficulty of distinguishing between actual refugees from Kosovo and ethnic Albanians not originally from Kosovo. This could have important ramifications in terms of elections and the final status of Kosovo. UNHCR should have been able to make a contribution to the broader international framework in addressing those issues in ways that were consistent with the agency's protection responsibilities. Instead, UNHCR's efforts to be creative on the issue ended badly with an ineffective and ill-timed venture with Microsoft and several other high-tech companies, which offered mobile hardware and software systems to register refugees.[20] Much effort was expended by UNHCR in creating a database of refugees, but cases of expensive computer, camera, and printing equipment remained stockpiled while Kosovars began to stream home from Macedonia.

UNHCR and other humanitarian organizations should have ways to incorporate such technological advancements into their work. This includes development of a sound refugee registration system. Soft numbers and uncertainty characterize refugee statistics and can be manipulated by those wishing to either play down or exaggerate the gravity of a situation. However, at least a modest in-house research and development capacity would likely be needed by UNHCR to apply new technologies. It is obviously difficult to introduce such innovations in the midst of crisis.

Understandably, the UNHCR evaluation deals with the interrelationship of military and humanitarian action in Kosovo. This was a defining characteristic in that situation. But similar issues arise as well in other complex emergency operations that involve a military component. The notion that UNHCR should be precluded from 'close co-operation' and 'joint contingency planning' with military forces must be reconciled with the security components typically deployed in

[20] Suhrke *et al.*, *The Kosovo Crisis* , paras 358–64, pp. 71–2.

international arrangements such as those concerning Kosovo. The report states:

> This suggests that contemporary norms validate operational co-operation between UNHCR and a military that is a belligerent party only under two conditions:
>
> - when the military is engaged in a UN enforcement action under the Charter and authorized by the UN, or
> - there is no alternative way to avoid substantial suffering and loss of life.[21]

The first exception is implicitly a judgement about the legitimacy of the Kosovo intervention. The second exception provides little or no real guidance. Nevertheless, conflicts in which refugees are deliberately uprooted as part of political or military strategies are likely to be a feature of the new reality that policy makers must address. This suggests the need for a more constructive interaction between humanitarian and security perspectives.

If one clear lesson emerged in Kosovo, it was that military and political planners must understand the humanitarian implications of their plans. It may be that UNHCR should not be involved in providing such analysis. However, other resources must then be identified and capacities developed within governments. The most striking feature of the Kosovo emergency was the failure to anticipate the campaign of mass expulsions by the Serbian authorities. Better work by military planners to envisage scenarios relating to the humanitarian consequences of military action might have resulted in a greater degree of preparedness to respond to the external displacement.

Also, to state the obvious, relations with the military in humanitarian emergencies concern many civilian humanitarian actors apart from UNHCR. This would be an appropriate subject for a multi-party approach to designing appropriate methods of work, including international operating agencies and NGOs, along with the military, perhaps under the intergovernmental mechanism for Strategic Humanitarian Action and Research (SHARE) recommended in this book. More fundamental reforms or appropriate linkages with other institutions, both within and outside the UN system, would likely be required to foster a proactive capacity in the humanitarian components of the UN.

[21] UN High Commissioner for Refugees (UNHCR), 'The Kosovo Refugee Crisis: An Independent Evaluation of UNHCR's Emergency Preparedness and Response' (10 February 2000). At: http://www.unhcr.ch/evaluate/kosovo/toc.htm

MILITARY-CIVILIAN HUMANITARIAN ISSUES

The last decade has witnessed several international responses to humanitarian emergencies that have included military components. Violence and the degradation of public security in such settings have led to a rise in the involvement of the military. While more the exception than the rule in humanitarian action, these involvements persist and are sufficiently frequent to warrant examination. These mixed security and humanitarian operations have included relative short-term successes, like Haiti, and consensus failures like the ultimate outcome in Somalia after the initial success of the relief operation. Cooperation has been close in some venues, like Bosnia, and largely absent in others, like Rwanda.

Many lessons have been learned. While the military should not normally be the direct provider of aid, military and political cooperation and coordination can be essential to address humanitarian needs. While the role of the military has varied in settings from providing logistical support, such as heavy lift capacity, to deployment of ground forces with peacekeeping mandates under UN auspices—East Timor or Sierra Leone—or peace-related deployments under some other rubric such as NATO—Bosnia and Kosovo—or coalition forces in northern Iraq, there is often now a plan for a military element in such operations to address security issues. Indeed, public security and logistical support from the military has proved indispensable to civilian humanitarians in many international crisis responses.

Military personnel are thus more and more often involved in interactions with civilian humanitarian workers, and vice versa. This can result, in the words uttered in 2000 by a very experienced UNHCR logistics specialist, in a kind of 'culture clash'. Recognizing this, for some time the US military has invited humanitarian agencies to participate in training exercises, incorporated doctrine and procedures for civil-military planning, established training programmes to develop military staffs to liaise with relief agencies, and created streamlined funding channels to allow for more rapid military responses to requests for humanitarian support from NGOs; humanitarians have not reciprocated, largely for budgetary reasons. Yet, according to this seasoned UNHCR official, despite these efforts to interrelate working methods, military and humanitarian actors are still 'strange bedfellows' and 'not much more comfortable now despite several years of experience'. As he explained, the military mind-set is to view all civilians, even UN agency representatives, as NGOs. 'If you wear a T-shirt, then you are an NGO.'

Nevertheless, the exigencies of emergencies forced these strange bed-fellows together early in the decade. For example, according to an international humanitarian official, UNHCR and US forces collaborated in Operation Hotel in northern Iraq in 1992 to prepare materials and to plan to shelter Iraqi Kurds who might be uprooted by an Iraqi military attack. Such contingency planning between civilian and military actors was unthinkable not too long ago; and while accepted as a matter of doctrine and training in the military, this relationship remains untenable even today to many humanitarians.

The frictions between military personnel and civilian humanitarian workers are particularly evident at the outset of crisis. The military deploys and looks to hand over functions to civilians, and then the NGOs come with their variations of mandate and programme activities. Indeed, in many operations relief organizations are already in place and operating, requiring the military to rely on relief organizations both for immediate information and to continue humanitarian operations. While the military maintains contact procedures and planning processes with hundreds of relief organizations, there is little or no advance planning across the military-civilian humanitarian divide. For the most part, issues are sorted out after initial frictions, and operational coordination evolves in more or less workable ways in different settings.

The inherent tension between civil and military organizations can be attributed to a number of factors. The military and humanitarian communities are structured in very different ways and diverse organizational interests are at play. The military is hierarchical, while NGOs often have a grass-roots orientation in which authority is 'earned' and not imposed from above. These basic differences in organizational method and style can give rise to squabbles and inefficiencies.

Frequently, at least among the humanitarians, NGOs have a constituency of beneficiaries to serve. The military operates from a rigidly defined list of tasks, while NGOs often seek to react opportunistically in emergency situations without adhering to a strict agenda. Humanitarian NGOs engage in programme activities, generally pertaining to sectors such as food distribution, health, and education. The military seeks to accomplish tasks in as efficient a manner as possible, ordinarily in a discrete geographical setting. As one general officer in the United States Army knowledgeable about humanitarian operations noted in 2000, 'We say we own everything that occurs in a particular tactical area of responsibility.' This can be a bewildering assertion to NGOs.

The divide between the military and humanitarian sectors is reflected in the language they use. The military uses active terms such as 'we own the roads', while NGOs use more oblique language: 'We partner with indigenous actors.' They both have preconceptions and tend to see each other in monolithic terms: all NGOs are the same, and all elements of the military are the same. Greater familiarity, of course, leads to more subtle understandings.

In many settings, the military has come to accept the importance of relating to NGOs and civilians in the community in which emergency operations are undertaken. For example, US Army special forces personnel typically live in the community in which they undertake operations, such as Bosnia and Kosovo. They dress in fatigues and carry concealed weapons, learn the local language, and seek to achieve a non-intrusive image in order to facilitate relations with the community. This arrangement has proved very useful in connection with new policing responsibilities that the military has been required to perform in those locales.

New capacities to deal with peace operations are being given more attention in the military, including through training. In the US Army, for example, the civil affairs function has been strengthened after having been allowed to atrophy for many years. The golden age of civil affairs was the occupation of Germany and Japan after the end of the Second World War. Civilian experts in uniform participated in the efforts to reconstruct societies and economies which had been devastated by war. The function was situated in the army reserves, and it receded until it was energized by use in counter-insurgency operations in Vietnam. At that time, it became part of the US Army's special operations command, which is the current institutional host. Civil affairs was called upon in a wide range of operations in the early 1990s, from Panama to northern Iraq. It is now firmly part of US Army doctrine in such operations, albeit largely still in the reserves. According to one high-ranking US Army officer in 2000, until recently it had been a place for 'losers'. Now, civil affairs personnel are more capable and are drawn from reservists with a wide range of experience relevant to societal rehabilitation.

While the military currently undertakes training exercises involving NGO personnel and role playing, reflecting an awareness of the importance of cooperation with NGOs, more sustained interactions are needed to address the preconceptions and mistrust that still characterize relations between the military and civilian humanitarians. With humanitarian agencies and the military increasingly interacting in complex emergencies, personal contacts are growing, and more systematic ways should be found to accumulate such knowledge in order to use good practices to inform future operations. But liaison activities are likely to be controversial, given the reluctance of many NGOs to associate closely with the military, fearing loss of independence and compromise of neutrality and impartiality or moral perspectives in armed-conflict settings.

The humanitarian coordination challenges that are evident in emergency operations, including military and civilian humanitarian relations, are also present in post-conflict settings. The efforts to implement a peace agreement in Sierra Leone are illustrative.

SIERRA LEONE: A STRATEGIC FRAMEWORK FOR INTERNATIONAL HUMANITARIAN ACTION

The July 1999 peace accord signed in Lomé, Togo, sought to bring to an end nine years of armed conflict in Sierra Leone. This had been a horrific war characterized by grisly atrocities, including summary execution, and incidents of torture, amputation, rape, and sexual violence, which astonished and sickened the world. The Lomé accord, while not providing an adequate justice mechanism to deal with war crimes and crimes against humanity committed during the conflict, sought to resolve hostilities and provide immediate and unhindered access by humanitarian workers to populations in need. While access improved after the signing of the accord, leading to the deployment of aid and development personnel, the situation then deteriorated with the killing and abduction of UN peacekeepers in 2000.

A sustainable peace in Sierra Leone could provide an opportunity for the international community to address the needs of hundreds of thousands of war-affected Sierra Leoneans, but only if the widespread human rights abuses and massive displacement which characterize the conflict subside. Even then, however, the destruction wrought by the war will continue to affect the daily lives of most of the population. After an entire decade of war, most Sierra Leoneans find themselves in a nation without a formal economy and whose social infrastructure has been devastated. Sierra Leone has the highest infant mortality rate—170 per thousand—and the lowest life expectancy—37 years—in the world.[22]

In November 1999, OCHA issued a consolidated inter-agency appeal for Sierra Leone for 2000 premised on the Lomé peace agreement. The appeal sought funding to address the sectors of agriculture; child protection; coordination; education; food aid; health and nutrition; human rights; refugee repatriation, reintegration and resettlement; and water and environmental sanitation. While the coordination structures in government controlled areas were functioning, the continued occupation of most of the

[22] UN Population Division, *The World at Six Billion* (New York: UN Population Division, 2000), Tables 27–8. At: http://www.popin.org/6billion/t27.htm and http://www.popin.org/6billion/t28.htm

countryside by rebel forces, the Revolutionary United Front (RUF), inhibited humanitarian operations.

The efforts in Sierra Leone to provide humanitarian assistance in the midst of conflict inspired the drafting of a code of conduct. The code was introduced in 1997 and was developed as a foundation for humanitarian operations in 1998. The code sought to provide a basis for negotiating access by humanitarian agencies to needy populations located throughout the country. The code is divided into a statement of principles addressing issues of humanity, neutrality, impartiality, beneficiaries, accountability, human rights, and local capacity building. Specific operating guidelines address issues of cooperation and needs assessments. Guiding principles for states and non-state actors—that is, the rebels—are also included.[23]

The code of conduct became controversial in the negotiation of a Strategic Framework for Sierra Leone, the ongoing effort at UN headquarters to elaborate an integrated humanitarian and political peace-building plan. The Sierra Leone Strategic Framework is based on the optimistically formulated assumption that the 'UN System speaks with one voice and agrees to a set of principles and approaches toward the attainment of common goals'.[24] The possible objections to the Strategic Framework approach, indeed a cautionary advisory in virtually all multilateral coordination efforts, are acknowledged explicitly:

- To what extent are humanitarian principles safeguarded in the SF [Strategic Framework]?
- Is the SF an additional organizational layer in a country with already existing coordination mechanisms?[25]

The draft Strategic Framework notes that Sierra Leone is 'a successful example of close inter-agency coordination'. Several coordination mechanisms involving the UN and others already existed. These included relief and human rights fora as well as several technical committees. Policy making bodies such as a consultative forum and the executive committee for disarmament, demobilization, and reintegration were operating. There was thus considerable information exchange and consultation between and among humanitarian agencies regarding needs assessments and priorities. The dire situation in Sierra Leone, of course, demonstrates that the nominal

[23] UN Office for the Coordination of Humanitarian Affairs, 'Code of Conduct for Humanitarian Assistance in Sierra Leone', in *United Nations Consolidated Inter-Agency Appeal for Sierra Leone: January–December 2000* (Geneva: OCHA, November 1999), Annex I, 122–3.

[24] UN Country Team for Sierra Leone, 'Strategic Framework: Sierra Leone', Field Draft (14 April 2000), Sect. A.3.

[25] UN Country Team for Sierra Leone, 'Strategic Framework: Sierra Leone', Sect. B.6.

existence of coordination mechanisms is not sufficient to ensure a humane outcome.

The Strategic Framework concept which originated in Afghanistan sought to impose a common programming requirement whereby all programmes were prioritized for funding and implementation. The Sierra Leone version, however, would not impose this operational requirement. The Sierra Leone Strategic Framework would apply initially only to the UN system and set out a series of medium- to long-term goals with respect to peace building. Prioritization of programming would be the subject of a consultative process implemented through existing structures, such as the UN coordination forum chaired by the Special Representative of the Secretary-General for Sierra Leone and the separate UN agency heads forum chaired by the UN resident coordinator, as well as through national and regional coordination structures.

The UN's Department of Peacekeeping Operations initially expressed reservations to the inclusion of the code of conduct in the framework document, posing a basic question: are peacekeepers special or are they just another combatant in a conflict? The culture clash between humanitarian and military perspectives exists even in the context of UN peacekeeping operations. The fate of the Strategic Framework will surely depend upon the outcome of ongoing clashes between the rebels of the RUF and a coalition of UN and government forces in Sierra Leone. The arrest for trial of Foday Sankoh, the RUF leader, may herald a new peace on the horizon. A ceasefire agreement in November 2000 has enhanced this prospect.

The international response to Sierra Leone will, one hopes, soon switch from emergency relief to development, and the need for a strategic plan will again emerge. In any event, notwithstanding the lack of a UN system framework plan, the World Bank and donor governments moved ahead at a March 2000 donors' conference hosted by the British government in London regarding programmes related to the disarmament, demobilization, and re-integration of fighters in Sierra Leone. Clearly, the success of this programme is a necessary precondition for peace. The background to the World Bank's involvement in this exercise provides additional insights into the difficulties of international institutional collaboration in peace-building efforts.

BROOKINGS AND BEYOND

In January 1999, at the initiative of Sadako Ogata, then the United Nations High Commissioner for Refugees, and James Wolfensohn, President of the World Bank, a round-table meeting was held in Washington at the Brookings Institution. The subject was the international institutional arrangements and funding systems to deal with the frequently cited gap in post-conflict situations where emergency relief operations have ended and development projects have yet to be designed and implemented. This lacuna in sequence in humanitarian action can be seen as a facet of the lack of coordination between relief and development agencies, which act to some extent in isolation in terms of their respective mandates.

At the January 1999 meeting, the World Bank suggested the establishment of a post-conflict fund of $100 million to be made available to address the problem. The response to this proposal, however, was surprisingly cool. Considerable trepidation was expressed by a number of the donors represented, including various Nordic countries. Because of the lack of consensus on the need for such a fund, an 'action group' was established. It was composed of representatives of the World Bank, UNHCR, OXFAM, UNDP, OCHA, UNDPA, ECHO, the US, Netherlands, Germany, and Japan. The group, chaired by the Swedish ambassador for humanitarian affairs, met twice to prepare an options paper, followed by a second full round-table meeting.

Large and protracted arrears to international financial institutions are for many post-conflict countries a major obstacle to receiving assistance for reconstruction efforts. Mechanisms to clear the arrears of countries that adopt poverty reduction and growth policies after conflict are agenda items for both the World Bank and the International Monetary Fund. Inspired by the Brookings initiative, the World Bank sought to identify post-conflict situations in which to pilot new funding mechanisms. Four places were discussed by the action group: Burundi, East Timor, Kosovo, and Sierra Leone. Sierra Leone was considered an optimal choice by the Bank due to the inter-agency processes already under way there, including the Strategic Framework exercise. However, as the key UN agencies—UNDP, OCHA, and UNDPA—were already engaged, no new funding mechanism was deemed necessary. Instead, a joint tripartite assessment mission in which the Bank participated, along with UNHCR and UNDP, preceded the London donor meeting at which $158 million was pledged for disarmament, demobilization, and reintegration, conditional upon compliance with the Lomé peace agreement. The World Bank committed $25 million to the government of Sierra Leone for rehabilitation, to be disbursed in portions of $500,000 through community-based organizations.[26] All of these arrangements, of course, were suspended pending resolution of the crisis in Sierra Leone.

[26] 'Community Reintegration and Rehabilitation Project', World Bank Project Data website, visited 6 June 2001. At: http://www4.worldbank.org/sprojects/Project.asp?pid=P040649

The difficulties experienced with the Brookings initiative is a lesson in the politics of international organizational collaboration. The effort is seen in large measure as an attempted 'end run' on the part of Mrs Ogata and Mr Wolfensohn around the UN system, to address what many commentators have recognized for some time as a fault in the international architecture: the lack of an adequate interface between humanitarian assistance and long-term development. In the words of one senior US humanitarian official, it is more aptly described as 'the continuum from relief to nothing'. It usually takes upwards of 18 months or so before developmental planning is put into place after an emergency has ended, by which time UNHCR and other emergency-response actors generally have departed.

The stakes, of course, are high. In post-conflict settings, the failure of the international community to engage in a timely fashion can hinder progress in addressing the circumstances and factors that initially gave rise to conflict. While the Brookings effort in 2001 is largely 'institutionally exhausted', according to Mark Malloch Brown, Administrator of UNDP, one legacy is likely to be more joint programming efforts in the future with UNHCR on matters such as de-mining and demobilization in relation to refugee return.

THE WAY FORWARD: BUREAUCRATIC CONSOLIDATION

The need for coordinated action in humanitarian affairs is inevitable, given the gaps in the framework of the multilateral humanitarian system. Effective responses to meet the needs of refugees and displaced persons require more concerted efforts. In the largely unregulated environment of international humanitarian action, individuals and agencies can significantly affect the nature of the response to forced-migration emergencies.

The international system for delivering humanitarian assistance to needy populations around the world is badly fragmented. At present, the broad ethical imperative to meet the basic needs of vulnerable people around the world is carried out by a crazy quilt of bilateral and multilateral initiatives and entities. At the universal level, the United Nations system comprises a variety of offices that raise funds from donors, principally governments, and spend money, sometimes on direct operations or more often in subcontractual arrangements with NGO implementing partners. This is done frequently with little transparency in a circumstance in which no single official or entity can be held accountable for lapses in performance. The various international institutions involved in such efforts are divided by sector, comprising categories such as refugees, children, food, and health, among others. These groups populate a bureaucratic universe in which agency heads vie for attention and publicity, which translates into funding and which can dictate in important respects the quality of mercy offered to beneficiaries.

The deployment of humanitarian NGOs in high-profile emergencies can seem to be an overwhelming presence, often to the chagrin and frustration of local authorities. Catering to donors which have different agendas can result in duplication of efforts by NGOs. Yet institutional mandate limitations result in persistent gaps in both sequence and coverage in protecting and assisting needy populations. This frustrates effective policy coordination, as distinct from coordination at the operational level, which generally works, depending on the specific situation and personalities.

NGOs play a variety of roles, and, along with the media, some seek to bring a measure of accountability to a process that is fundamentally opaque. Other NGOs constitute a kind of labour roster that international organizations draw upon to undertake work on a contractual basis pursuant to institutional mandates. NGOs sometimes find themselves oriented morally toward beneficiaries, and contractually to funders, unless they have their own funding bases. Their own values and their sometimes idiosyncratic organizational mandates can create problems as well.

Not surprisingly, coordination problems are pervasive in a domain in which structures are disjointed; efforts are duplicated while important areas of human need remain unaddressed. Organizational and professional 'culture clashes' inhibit concerted action. Put another way, one could write a journalistic exposé on problems of coordination in virtually any complex humanitarian emergency.

Decisive reform is needed, and the bureaucratic trend is clear: consolidation of the varieties of entities and functions involved in the provision of humanitarian assistance in order to achieve greater efficiency. This trend should be promoted and institutionalized. If accountability can be secured through an organizational merger, then the quality of relief and protection to beneficiaries would be improved. This broad principle should inform the myriad of tactical and operational decisions involved in the organization of future humanitarian emergency responses.

As a first step, the UNHCR should be asked to oversee policy planning relating to internally displaced persons, a key under-served population in the world today, as discussed earlier in this book. UNHCR has a widespread field presence, unlike the smaller office of the High Commissioner for Human Rights, and it has integrated budgetary and programme activities, unlike OCHA. This would mean a well-informed coordinative role for UNHCR designed to ensure that the needs of vulnerable displaced persons are addressed comprehensively in international responses. UNHCR's reputation as one of the most capable agencies in the UN system buttresses such an arrangement. Advance designation of this role for UNHCR, as distinct from the current system of ad hoc assignments, would promote planning and preparedness.

The appointment in 2001 of a new High Commissioner, Ruud Lubbers, could be the occasion to make this change. In this fashion, it should be possible to identify who will do what for internal exiles in particular situations. Of course, care should be taken to ensure that UNHCR's refugee protection responsibilities are not diluted by adding these new policy coordination tasks. And it would require that UNHCR be given additional funding to undertake this catalytic role. While UN bureaucrats will undoubtedly yelp, giving UNHCR this new planning function would clearly strengthen humanitarian responses on behalf of internal exiles.

Ultimately what is needed is a consolidated UN humanitarian agency with a fully integrated budget and programme, an OCHA with budgetary and programmatic authority. But member states are likely to be lukewarm in response to a proposal to establish a new agency at the outset. Yet this is the unfinished business of UN reform, according to Maurice Strong, who at the behest of the Secretary-General oversaw efforts at reform in the mid-1990s. The impetus for such bureaucratic consolidation, however, would now have to come from outside the UN, most likely in relation to important real-world problems such as the need to address the plight of the internally displaced. Expanding the responsibility of UNHCR would be an initial move toward this end.

The coordinated framework envisaged here concerns only the UN system. Total consolidation of functions in the field of humanitarian action is neither likely nor desirable. Consolidation alone would not guarantee that the distribution of assistance is more responsive to actual needs. There should be ample latitude for differentiated responsibilities and roles by other actors, such as ICRC and NGOs, which will and should retain considerable independence and freedom of action in order to secure access to needy populations in the midst of conflict.

Other reasons buttress the notion of limiting consolidation to the UN system. If the humanitarian functions were consolidated, they would inevitably relate to political objectives in complex humanitarian emergencies involving UN missions. Certain elements of the NGO community would undoubtedly resist involvement in such circumstances. Yet, if the functions were instead situated in the independent sector, while the ethical values might be correspondingly purified, their divorce from the governing political framework could actually diminish the resources available or frustrate their deployment in some circumstances due to selective donor interest. A highly directed approach could be either irrelevant or even harmful if it is wrong, and usually there is no single right answer to such complicated problems. A measure of diversity in the system would provide a realistic safety net for vulnerable populations.

A discrete interim improvement would involve enhancing the quality of OCHA personnel. When asked in 2000 about the single most realistic step to improve UN coordination, one UN staffer did not hesitate: better quality 'staffing', she answered in with; OCHA's predecessor, DHA, was looked upon by some both in and outside the UN system as a kind of dumping ground to park those to whom political favours were owed. This is not to disparage OCHA's staff and leadership, which have included at times some of the most talented colleagues in the UN system. It is simply to underscore that staffing decisions matter.

The UN's Office of Human Resource Management in 2000 prepared proposals to reform the complex sets of UN personnel policies and rules, which many in the system regard as inhibiting flexibility and efficiency. While priority in this regard should be given to the humanitarian components of the system, it will not solve the problem. The special hiring rules and procedures foreseen in the creation of DHA never came into force. OCHA coexists with the relatively inflexible personnel regulations which inhibit both the speed and the ability to match the right people with positions at headquarters or in the field. But the fundamental defect is the absence of a strategic plan at the UN for humanitarian action which would permit the development of programme plans and budgets in order to design appropriate personnel capacities. 'We need the permission to get ready', explained a senior UN budget official in 2000.

Effective humanitarian action requires that decision makers understand the current system. Lessons learned and not learned as well as the personal experiences of the new cadre of humanitarian workers emerging in this new era of activism will inform humanitarian operations in the future. These operations will nevertheless continue to be somewhat messy and, yes, uncoordinated. However, to the extent that accountability and transparency may be enhanced even through relatively modest bureaucratic adjustments to address the internally displaced, then the disconnection between the bureaucracy and those in need will be narrowed incrementally. A broad system-consolidation option deserves consideration. Each crisis produces more institutional scar tissue. It is just a matter of time, therefore, before enough pressure builds for the creation of a more effective system to save lives and address the hardships associated with forced migration.

8

Reaction and Inattention Within the US Government

It was an uncharacteristically cold day in Washington, DC, in December 2000. The renaissance-style facade of the Old Executive Office Building was projected against the breaking dawn as I arrived for my breakfast meeting with Eric Schwartz, then Special Assistant to the President for National Security Affairs and Senior Director for Multilateral and Humanitarian Affairs at the National Security Council (NSC). Schwartz, whom I have known for many years, had worked on humanitarian issues at the NSC since 1993. He was already at the computer in his office when I arrived at 7.10 a.m. for our breakfast meeting. I sat in the waiting area outside his office, having made my way through the building which reflected an odd mix of grandeur and standardized office furnishings.

Schwartz's tenure at the NSC had coincided with a series of profound humanitarian challenges to the Administration of President Bill Clinton in the 1990s. Humanitarian emergencies in places such as Bosnia and Herzegovina, Cambodia, East Timor, Haiti, Iraq, Kosovo, Rwanda, Sierra Leone, and Somalia had shaken the US government bureaucracy. The office Schwartz directed had a staff of seven persons. In the prior Administration of President George H. W. Bush, one person at a lower level in the NSC had the brief on humanitarian and multilateral issues.

Schwartz explained that his office had become 'an outpost of concern on human rights and humanitarian issues' during the Clinton Administration. But his responsibilities had grown to involve as well traditional political and security issues relating to UN matters, which he believed made him much more influential in the policy arena. 'I go to so many more high level meetings with this brief', he noted. An exclusive focus on human rights and humanitarian issues risks marginalization in the foreign affairs bureaucracy, a dynamic that has been reflected, for example, by the difficulties in influencing policy experienced by the State Department's human rights bureau over the past several years.

Schwartz found the idea of a humanitarian response 'toolbox' to be an extremely important notion. Political will is often informed—indeed, on occasion fundamentally—by the responses that are available. Frequently, objections in senior-level government meetings on crisis responses are not stated in terms of high policy. The objectors do not say: 'Don't alleviate the horrible suffering of people.' Rather, they claim that such action is 'too hard to do'. Debates within government often swirl around issues of capacity and feasibility, and it can be crucial at Cabinet-level meetings to rebut the assertion that something is too hard to try. Of course, making the case can mean that you get the job as well. But it can make all the difference to show that there are skilled professionals, money, and accepted procedures in place and ready to undertake an initiative.

Crises arise in specific situations which demand a survey of feasibilities, in effect a rummage through the policy toolbox. Schwartz noted that it could be potentially a waste of time to agonize in advance over the general guidelines for humanitarian intervention: the proportionate use of military force for humanitarian reasons. The 1999 Kosovo conflict has given rise to several wide-ranging reviews of the legitimacy of such endeavours. But attempting to formulate broad policy is of limited value where the key issues are almost invariably operational: how to get from here to there in a particular crisis. 'I tell my staff they are not op-ed writers. We have a responsibility to make specific suggestions', said Schwartz.

Schwartz drew a distinction between those crises which are unanticipated and not of highest geopolitical concern and which are thus 'low on the radar screen' of decision makers, and those of long-standing duration. Prolonged crises such as the humanitarian emergencies in Bosnia and Herzegovina and Kosovo over the past decade are more amenable to a deliberate planning process. But even in these circumstances there can be important conceptual and institutional gaps. The oft-cited failure to integrate humanitarian considerations into military and political planning in relation to Kosovo is illustrative.

A toolbox notion could be particularly valuable in addressing unanticipated crises that are catapulted onto the agendas of decision makers. Political will in such instances can be informed significantly by having in hand operational options, such as the capacity to deploy troops or international police or to respond to requests for help by the training of indigenous forces in Africa or elsewhere. Also, having transitional administration capacities in the United Nations system can clearly encourage decision makers to undertake such daunting initiatives.

Schwartz, however, was sceptical given the obstacles facing the UN in this area. Turf squabbles are endemic. The UN Development Programme (UNDP) is reluctant to cede authority in this area to the Department of Peacekeeping Operations. But it is far from clear whether UNDP will be able to meet the challenges of becoming more operational and integrated into immediate post-conflict peace-building operations. The issue of UN reform and humanitarian action is increasingly bogged down in bureaucratic turf wars and in a long-standing debate between developed and developing countries on questions of intervention and national sovereignty. Nevertheless, Schwartz saw investing greater capabilities in international organizations as a key tool for the United States to address future humanitarian catastrophes around the world in a multilateral context.

Not only does the United States not need to act alone in formulating such responses; it normally should not act alone. International institutions can be indispensable mechanisms for mounting effective humanitarian action. In addition, while the United States will often have to play a key role, it need not play a dominant role: witness the intervention response to the East Timor crisis in 1999. US support was helpful in terms of military logistics, but the United States was relieved when Australia took the lead on the mission.

Within the US government, moreover, policy coordination can proceed along informal as well as formal lines. The Clinton Administration used Presidential Decision Directives (PDDs) to promulgate presidential decisions about national security, and Schwartz discussed PPD 56 which dealt with managing complex contingency operations. He noted that the planning procedures of PDD 56 had not been formally invoked in every complex humanitarian crisis. But the processes embodied in that document operated nevertheless. According to Schwartz, formally invoking a planning process could in some circumstances impose elements of bureaucratic paperwork and distract from effectiveness. Also, bureaucratic dynamics can become disruptive. PDD 56 suggests that planning should be under the aegis of a functional office, and the regional offices within the US Department of State and the NSC can be jealous and seek to guard their prerogatives. Planning can also pose diplomatic or security concerns if plans are leaked. Conversely, one can imagine a situation in which public revelation of a plan could also be useful in achieving a foreign policy objective.

The dynamics of crisis response described by Schwartz were echoed by Princeton Lyman, who has held leadership positions at the State Department in bureaux that are functional—refugees and international organizations—as well as regional—Africa. In his view, governmental humanitarian responses had been 'remarkably ad hoc' and often the product of bureaucratic rivalries. 'Very few decision makers have all of the options', he asserted. Lyman gave as an example his chairing of an informal inter-agency working group that sought to address a severe drought in Ethiopia in 1984 and 1985. In order to overcome reluctance by the NSC to aid the Mengistu regime, the working group organized a cross-border assistance effort from Sudan into Ethiopia to assist drought victims under the control of forces fighting the regime. While NGOs had used such an approach before, this was an innovation for the UN, which has since become a well-established humanitarian option. In the mid-1980s, agency turf battles could be avoided through such creative methods. But this flexibility seems 'less possible today; it's more bureaucratic now', according to Lyman.

Of course, a propensity for ad hoc approaches runs the risk of failing to appreciate what has worked in the past and what might work in the future. On the lack of institutional memory, Lyman cited the way policy makers apparently failed to embrace the safe-enclave option when Kosovar Albanians sought to enter Macedonia in 1999. A safe haven like that established in northern Iraq in 1991 could have changed the situation on the ground. If declared, it is quite conceivable that Serbian forces would have held back and the potentially devastating influx into Macedonia could have been averted through an arrangement to protect and assist the Albanians in Kosovo proper. But humanitarians have been wary of safe enclaves ever since the Bosnian city of Srebrenica was overrun in 1995. Faced with the influx, Macedonia closed its border to asylum seekers, and an extraordinary refugee relocation programme was undertaken by NATO countries. Similar experiences of relocating asylum seekers from Haiti and Indo-China could have helped guide policy makers to understand the political implications of this extraordinary resettlement effort. The controversial proposal, quickly withdrawn, to keep Kosovars at the Guantanamo Bay US naval base in Cuba was another product of the failure to appreciate fully prior political ramifications relating to refugee policy responses. The prospect of images of Kosovars in a US military compound behind barbed wire repulsed humanitarians within the Clinton Administration.

Knowing what has worked and what could be refined and used to respond to a future crisis could be quite valuable, in the estimation of Lyman, who also underscored the importance of seeing international organizations as important adjuncts in humanitarian action. He advocated an annotated policy toolbox, which would be useful, including for the next US presidential Administration.

The new political leadership in the United States is supported by permanent staff which functions effectively as an institutional memory, particularly in the refugee bureau of the State Department, according to Julia Taft, a self-described 'operational person', who headed that bureau during the second Clinton Administration. But this will not necessarily be true in the regional bureaux, she noted, nor at the Agency for International Development. There is only one person who remains at AID's Office of Foreign Disaster Assistance—which Taft characterized as a 'revolving door'—since she headed it during 1986–9. AID's Office of Transition Initiatives is entirely new and did not even exist when she was there. A toolbox that surveyed the international machinery, including NGOs and international organizations, as well as their respective capacities would be 'a great reminder' as policy makers confront humanitarian crises in the future.

For example, in Taft's view, the experience in northern Iraq indicated that safe havens, while rare, should be promoted under appropriate circumstances. In addition, refugee camp insecurity has bedevilled arrangements from Goma to West Timor over the past decade, and the efforts to respond to this persistent problem should be catalogued. 'We need a principles guide for donors', she said, urging the creation of a reference guide setting out the best ways to deal with such crises. This would promote coordination and be an invaluable resource for new policy makers coming onto the scene. Taft felt certain that the new Bush Administration would retain a significant function at the NSC on humanitarian issues. She noted that her colleagues in the regional bureaux covering the Balkans and East Timor are grateful to this day for her bureau's efforts. The reason is basic: in her view, the end of the cold war had fundamentally changed perspectives and expectations. Humanitarian action is deeply political and now firmly part of the new national agenda. There is no choice: 'It will have to exist. And this is some of the hardest stuff in the world to do.'

My conversation with Schwartz in December 2000 turned, as one might have predicted at the end of a presidential Administration, to prospects and possibilities. The White House mess where we had breakfast that day was crowded, and there was a buzz of conversation. Occasionally, I could overhear a reference to the US Supreme Court argument, scheduled later that morning, concerning the legality of a recount ordered by the Florida Supreme Court in the disputed presidential election between George W. Bush and Al Gore. But our world seemed strangely insulated from this political controversy, and more enduring.

We hurriedly finished our breakfast in time for Schwartz to return to his office and participate in an 8.30 a.m. conference call on UN arrears owed by the United States for peacekeeping operations. I departed, leaving him to conduct his business at the end of the Clinton Administration on that cold and dreary December morning, wondering who would be the workers in the next Administration who would reach for a refugee policy toolbox.

As of May 2001, after the first 100 days of the Administration of George W. Bush, the question remained unanswered. The size of the NSC contingent working on multilateral and humanitarian issues had been reduced to an Acting Senior Director and four professionals, all career personnel. The reduction in size of the office is reflective of a general reduction in NSC staff and an approach designed to decentralize operational decision making. The NSC's role is to broker inter-agency disputes and fill the gaps in governmental structures in this Executive Branch. Political appointments have been made at the NSC and are on the horizon at the State Department.

Following the issuance of National Security Presidential Directive 1, two directly relevant policy coordinating committees were set up at the Under-Secretary/Assistant Secretary level. One committee, Democracy, Human Rights, and International Operations, is to be chaired by the NSC, and will be responsible for rapid-onset humanitarian emergencies. The other, International Development and Humanitarian Assistance, is to be chaired by the State Department, and will be responsible for longer-term development and humanitarian relief issues. This structure could be seen as seeking to formalize the type of inter-agency coordination that occurred during the 1999 Kosovo crisis. The regional policy coordinating committees are also likely to play important roles, as is the case with the humanitarian crisis in Afghanistan, given the customary regional emphasis in the foreign policy bureaucracy. While the new bureaucratic structure is largely untested, the humanitarian crisis in Afghanistan in late 2001 has presented an early challenge.

ORGANIZING HUMANITARIAN POLICY

> If asked to design from ground zero an institutional structure for delivery of our civilian humanitarian assistance, few would come up with our current structure.
>
> —From a January 2000 Executive Branch review of humanitarian assistance programmes.

The past decade has presented a series of new challenges to US decision makers as they have tried to organize responses to global refugee emergencies, denominated 'complex contingency operations' in the bureaucratic language of the Executive Branch. These challenges resulted in a series of dilemmas which were addressed in the Clinton Administration by three Presidential Decision Directives, issued to provide guidance to US government agencies and departments involved in such operations. Such directives are customarily reviewed by an incoming Administration, which may or may not decide to retain them as guidance.

There is no single inter-agency forum in the US government to formulate international humanitarian policy. By default, the White House—National Security Council—plays a coordination role; indeed, in the words of a senior NSC official in the Clinton Administration, at times 'too great of a coordination role'. A presidential directive was considered but not issued on international migration policy. According to this same NSC official, the lack of attention to this substantive issue is simply another example of urgent matters precluding attention to important matters. Nevertheless, the considerations that animated the issuance of three Presidential Decision Directives on humanitarian operations over the past decade are enduring, and they thus merit discussion here.

EXECUTIVE BRANCH

The proliferation of peacekeeping deployments at the end of the cold war, coupled with the misadventure in Somalia, prompted an inter-agency review in 1993 by the Clinton Administration of US peacekeeping policies and programmes. This review resulted in a 1994 Presidential Decision Directive—PDD 25—which sought to improve the way the US government manages and coordinates such operations in a multilateral context. A public White Paper summarizes the rationale for PDD 25:[1]

> During the Cold War, the United Nations could resort to multilateral peace operations only in the few cases when the interests of the Soviet Union and the West did not conflict. In the new strategic environment such operations can serve more often as a cost-effective tool to advance American as well as collective interests in maintaining peace in key regions and create global burden-sharing for peace.
>
> Territorial disputes, armed ethnic conflicts, civil wars (many of which can spill across international borders) and the collapse of governmental authority in some states are among the current threats to peace. While many of these conflicts may not directly threaten American interests, their cumulative effect is significant.

[1] 'White Paper on the Clinton Administration's Policy on Reforming Multilateral Peace Operations' (May 1994).At: http://library.whitehouse.gov/WH/EOP/NSC/html/documents/NSCDoc1.html

The White Paper specifically identifies what value is added by working collectively in such operations:

> UN and other multilateral peace operations will at times offer the best way to prevent, contain or resolve conflicts that could otherwise be more costly and deadly. In such cases, the US benefits from having to bear only a share of the burden. We also benefit by being able to invoke the voice of the community of nations on behalf of a cause we support. Thus, the establishment of a capability to conduct multilateral peace operations is part of our National Security Strategy and National Military Strategy.

Building on the intervening experiences of military and civilian deployments in Haiti and the former Yugoslavia, a further Presidential Decision Directive—PDD 56—concerning the management of such 'complex contingency operations' was issued in May 1997. Its rationale is detailed in another public White Paper:[2]

> In the wake of the Cold War, attention has focused on a rising number of territorial disputes, armed ethnic conflicts, and civil wars that have posed a threat to regional and international peace that may be accompanied by natural or man-made disasters which precipitate massive human suffering. We have learned that effective responses to the situations may require multidimensional operations composed of such components as political/diplomatic, humanitarian, intelligence, economic development and security: hence the term complex contingency operations.

PDD 56 also requires that a 'political-military implementation plan' be developed for each operation. The plan is to include a comprehensive situation assessment, mission statement, agency objectives, and the desired 'end state'. An 'after action review' involving those who participated in or monitored the operation is to be prepared at the conclusion of each mission.

Following the experience of the deployment of NATO forces in Kosovo, another Presidential Decision Directive—PDD 71—was issued in February 2000 to strengthen criminal justice systems in support of complex peace operations. While rule of law issues have been implicated in humanitarian operations throughout the decade, from Cambodia onwards, the stark situation of impunity in Kosovo in late 1999 gave impetus to this new policy review. PDD 71 surveys an array of existing US government initiatives, focusing on rule of law issues, and seeks to facilitate inter-agency cooperation to deal with issues of international civilian police, development

[2] 'White Paper on the Clinton Administration's Policy on Managing Complex Contingency Operations' (May 1997). At: http://library.whitehouse.gov/WH/EOP/NSC/html/documents/NSCDoc2.html

of indigenous police forces, and the establishment of justice systems in transitional settings.

THE BUREAUCRATIC ARCHITECTURE OF US RESPONSES

Below the presidential realm in the US government there is a complicated administrative framework that deals with forced migration emergencies. There are two broad categories of agency actors. One set of activities deals with refugee protection, resettlement, and asylum, principally undertaken by the State Department and the Justice Department's Immigration and Naturalization Service. The other broad category of agency actors—namely, USAID's Bureau for Humanitarian Response and Office of Foreign Disaster Assistance—deals with humanitarian assistance. The NSC provides the mechanism at the presidential level to bring both sets of actors together for coordination in complex humanitarian emergencies, including to identify the contribution that the military may be uniquely situated to provide, for example by airlifting large quantities of relief supplies. Together, the combined budgets of these US government offices total upwards of $2 billion annually.

The main offices in the State Department that deal with migration-related humanitarian operations are the Bureau of Population, Refugees and Migration (PRM), established originally in 1980, which offers assistance to refugees and conflict victims primarily by providing funding through multilateral international organizations like the UNHCR or the ICRC; and the Bureau for Democracy, Human Rights and Labor (DRL), which publishes annual country reports on human rights conditions that can address refugee issues.

At the Agency of International Development, the Bureau for Humanitarian Response serves as a focal point for the development of humanitarian policy. USAID's Office of US Foreign Disaster Assistance (OFDA) provides urgent humanitarian assistance as well as undertakes prevention, mitigation and preparedness activities in cases of natural or human-made disasters abroad. OFDA's assistance is usually provided in the form of grants to NGOs or international organizations, and addresses population displacements in the context of disasters. USAID's Office of Food for Peace (FFP) provides food assistance in crises through the World Food Programme and other agencies; its Office of Transition Initiatives (OTI) focuses on assisting the return to normal governance and development of capacities in countries that have been riven by crisis.

The legislative framework for complex humanitarian operations has evolved over the past 40 years. In particular, the Migration and Refugee

Assistance Act of 1962 (MRA) provides the basic authority for US government assistance for refugees and migrants. The current annual budget for programmes managed by PRM is approximately $700 million.[3] Of this total, 70 per cent goes to 'Overseas Assistance' programmes for refugees and migrants, channelled primarily through international agencies such as the UNHCR and ICRC.

The Foreign Assistance Act of 1961, which authorizes OFDA's activities, provides a general statutory framework for assisting displaced persons, with specific authority to assist disaster victims. Significant assistance may also be provided to displaced persons under Title II of the Agricultural Trade Development and Assistance Act of 1954, commonly referred to as 'P.L. 480' or the 'Food for Peace Act'. Title II programmes provide agricultural commodities to foreign countries to address famine, malnutrition, and the alleviation of hunger.

The culture of a bureaucracy clearly affects the quality of its work product. In terms of perceptions, humanitarian officers are often viewed by senior policy makers as technical implementers, and not as experts who should be present and heard when foreign policy is discussed and formulated. Humanitarian programmes are seldom seen as policy instruments that require prior strategic analysis, contingency planning, and policy advocacy. Instead, emphasis is placed on the management of relations with operational partners, including NGOs. As a consequence, both within the State Department and USAID, humanitarians have relatively weak influence as compared with those in regional and even other functional bureaux.

This is not a new dynamic. Within the State Department and the National Security Council, regional perspectives predominate. In the words of a former senior NSC official involved in humanitarian affairs: 'Policy will always be regionally focused.' Functional offices such as PRM or the humanitarian directorate at the NSC normally react to regional initiatives, and seek to ensure a measure of consistency in response. Internal tensions between functional and regional offices are often present in decision making in the foreign affairs bureaucracy.

While perhaps obvious, another important factor is the quality and stature of leadership. Competent and credible leadership adds weight to the advocacy of a policy option. Considerations are heard and listened to which might not otherwise have emerged from the debate. This is a crucial matter which can make virtually all the difference in crafting humanitarian policy.

[3] US Committee for Refugees, 'Congress Approves $700 Million Budget for Refugee Aid', Press Release (Washington, DC: 26 October 2000). See also US Department of State, *The Budget for Fiscal Year 2002*, 731, 732. At: www.whitehouse.gov/omb/budget/fy2002/sta.pdf

Bureaucratic biases are often intertwined with substantive considerations in Executive Branch decision-making on the issues. The political process often requires responses with short-term perspectives and an emphasis on immediate responses. In the words of one seasoned bureaucrat, 'it is a luxury to ask the question: What is the best way to solve the problem?' Nevertheless, that is precisely the question that was posed in an interagency review of humanitarian activities completed at the end of the Clinton Administration in late 1999.

THE JANUARY 2000 EXECUTIVE BRANCH HUMANITARIAN REVIEW

The Kosovo crisis in 1999 frightened US officials. They had stared into an abyss and felt fortunate that a victory had been snatched from the jaws of a potential quagmire. Among the lessons they learned from the emergency was the importance of considering humanitarian dimensions in military and political planning. When the crisis had ended, and the vast majority of Kosovars had returned, the Clinton Administration initiated an Interagency Review of US Government Civilian Humanitarian and Transition Programs.[4] The basic objective was to encourage a more coherent policy and unified leadership in such situations. A wide range of options was considered, and three broad approaches emerged in the review. But no decision on the options was taken during Clinton's tenure, and while the report has no status in the new Bush Administration, the issues are endemic. For that reason, the substance of the report remains highly relevant.

The Interagency Review report, which was initiated by Morton H. Halperin, then Director of Policy Planning at the State Department, characterizes the current administrative architecture as '[a] less than logical structure, with unclear lines of accountability'.[5] 'Overlapping mandates' and 'duplication of efforts' are particularly noted in the report. In extraordinary circumstances, such as the humanitarian crises relating to Hurricane Mitch or Kosovo, high-level political appointees become involved in decision-making. Otherwise, such crises are normally handled by officials below sub-cabinet rank who interact without assignment of lead responsibility or formal

[4] US Department of State, *Interagency Review of US Government Civilian Humanitarian & Transition Programs* (Washington, DC: US Department of State, January 2000). At: http://www.gwu.edu/~nsarchiv/NSAEBB/NSAEBB30

[5] US Department of State, *Interagency Review*, 10.

coordination procedures. The review made recommendations on humanitarian and transition assistance policy, and identified organizational options for making this assistance most effective.

The rationale for the review is articulated as follows:

Since the end of the Cold War, the foreign policy stakes of US civilian humanitarian programs have risen significantly, driven by profound changes in the complex crises themselves . . . and the prominent place these now occupy in our overall foreign policy. The humanitarian factor has become central to senior policy makers' deliberations over US foreign policy priorities and possible diplomatic, economic or military interventions to ease crises and facilitate humanitarian relief.

As our global humanitarian interests have become more complex and vital to our national policy, the need has grown for the USG [US government] to have unified, coherent humanitarian leadership. This is not to imply that humanitarian considerations will or should dictate foreign policy outcomes. Rather, USG leadership is needed to guarantee that humanitarian considerations are present and an active force within the foreign policy-making process. As we've witnessed in Rwanda, Bosnia, Kosovo, Timor, Sudan and elsewhere, major foreign policy challenges typically feature, at their very center, complex humanitarian emergencies that demand coherence in our policy responses.[6]

The review report noted significant gaps in programme capacity to deal with issues such as internal exiles,[7] and framed the problem in the following terms:

Our humanitarian achievements notwithstanding, we can and should do better to empower the humanitarian agenda and overcome the fragmentation of USG humanitarian affairs. Internal conflict victims now figure as a major and growing humanitarian challenge, yet they have traditionally been a secondary or indirect priority for both State and USAID. Neither agency has a clearheaded responsibility for addressing this humanitarian problem, even though it now exceeds that posed by refugees ... Increasingly, complex emergencies generate a complex mixture of refugees and internally displaced. However, neither [USAID's Bureau for Humanitarian Response] natural disaster competencies and primarily bilateral response nor PRM's multilateral emphasis and refugee response provide the basis for a comprehensive approach...

[6] US Department of State, *Interagency Review*, 3.

[7] The absence of overall policy and of a lead office on issues of internal displacement was again recognized in August 2001 in a report of the US General Accounting Office. There are six offices within the State Department and USAID that directly assist internally displaced persons, plus several other agencies and offices involved in related functions. See US General Accounting Office, *Internally Displaced Persons Lack Effective Protection*, GAO-01-803 (Washington, DC: GAO, August 2001), 30.

Overall, the current split between State and USAID's civilian emergency programs has impeded coherent leadership on humanitarian issues, domestically and abroad, and complicated the coordination of civilian and military humanitarian efforts. The humanitarian voice in Senior USG policy-making has often been absent at critical moments, such that the humanitarian implications of political-military choices in crisis situations do not receive adequate consideration. Overlapping bureaucratic mandates and duplication of effort hinder both the operational efficiency of our humanitarian programs, especially with respect to internally displaced persons, and the inter-linkage of programs.

... [T]he central aim of creating unified leadership is to strengthen consideration of the humanitarian implications of political-military choices in crisis situations, including the mandate and role of external military interventions. This essential step will not, it must be said, necessarily guarantee there is always adequate high-level political will to take the appropriate political-military decisions necessary to advance USG humanitarian interests. Ultimate decision responsibility rests with political authorities above the officials who manage our humanitarian programs. This reality notwithstanding, our top political authorities will be far better equipped to reach decisions that must advance US humanitarian interests when they are served by unified humanitarian leadership.[8]

The review concluded that:

The current structure results in less than coherent leadership on complex humanitarian issues in our foreign policy making process.

We do achieve effective operational coordination, but only through significant effort in a context of continued mandate overlap and some duplication of effort.

We do not optimally leverage our humanitarian influence abroad, in proportion to the level of effort and resources expended and the general prestige attached to our programs.

There is inadequate interlinkage among emergency, transitional and development programs.

The report is succinct in its ultimate assessment:

Given these conclusions, the present status quo is not an optimal basis for promoting US humanitarian interests. We can and should do better.[9]

The report identifies three approaches to enhance US leadership in humanitarian action. The review report's first option, called by one State Department official the 'can't we all live together better?' variant, calls for closer consultation, communication, and cooperation. Formally denominated as 'discrete measures', this option would call for the creation of 'a senior humanitarian

[8] US Department of State, *Interagency Review*, 3.
[9] US Department of State, *Interagency Review*, 3–5.

policy seat' at NSC meetings and a 'joint State–USAID Policy and Planning Task Force'. Collaboration in training and evaluation activities is advocated, as is outreach to Congress and the media. These efforts would be undertaken within the existing structures. One legacy of the US response to the Kosovo crisis is that this collaboration may already be happening to some extent. However, the Interagency Review sounds a note of caution:

> Since this approach works within the current division of responsibility between State and USAID, it does not answer the question of each responsibility or eliminate overlapping mandates and duplication of effort and may even increase duplication.[10]

The second approach, called by the same State Department official the 'who is in charge?' option, is a designated lead agency model. In each emergency situation, a particular agency would be designated to manage and coordinate the response. The method of designation is the subject of an additional array of choices. One variation is based on the current system, in which the USAID Administrator, who is also the President's Special Coordinator for International Disaster Assistance, would make the decision. While this is the current arrangement, it has not been implemented in practice. This choice, therefore, would be to strengthen the role of the USAID Administrator in order to make this approach real.

Another proposal is for the designation to be made on a case-by-case basis, with the National Security Council serving as the mechanism, subject to the Secretary of State's ultimate direction, for choosing the lead agency depending upon the character of the emergency and the relative advantages of the agency in question.

A further option would be to promulgate in advance a rule for decision making, with PRM taking the lead in complex humanitarian emergencies, and USAID's Bureau for Humanitarian Response addressing natural disasters such as famines or floods, unless the Secretary of State decides that a higher leadership level is warranted in a particular case. Of course, an overall coordinator for the US government humanitarian response could be named by the President in exceptional cases. Consultation with Congress would be required, but no modification of statutory authorities would be necessary. Each of these choices would be accompanied by the creation of a senior humanitarian advisory council.

In comparing the last two options—case-by-case or by-rule designations of the lead agency—a case-by-case approach might act as a disincentive for US government agencies to develop their own specialized comparative advantage because they would never be sure on what basis they would be chosen

[10] US Department of State, *Interagency Review*, 13.

to act as the lead. A rule-based approach in advance, on the other hand, might encourage pre-designated agencies to enhance planning capacities.

A third variant identified in the Interagency Review is the administrative consolidation of US government humanitarian activities. This outcome would clearly require legislation. One institution and one senior official would be accountable. The function could be located in one of three places: within the State Department, within the Agency for International Development, or in a separate foreign affairs agency reporting to the Secretary of State. As the review explains:

> Central to deciding among the three possibilities is what priority is attached to competing policy goals: to integrate humanitarian affairs into foreign policy; to create an empowered single-focus humanitarian entity; and to integrate relief, transition and development assistance.[11]

Situating the function in the State Department would promote humanitarian and foreign policy integration. Refugee situations are caused by political situations and are often linked to political solutions. If USAID were the location, this would encourage the integration of relief and development perspectives. This could address the customary gap between emergency response and longer-term development. A separate office would enhance the focus—as well as, perhaps, promote the marginalization—of humanitarian policy formulation. No consensus was reached in the review on which option to recommend to the Secretary of State. In any event, the humanitarian review came too late in the Clinton Administration to result in reform. The problem of bureaucratic fragmentation thus remains to be unearthed again in future crises.

THE POLITICS OF BUREAUCRATIC REFORM

The State Department's Bureau of Population, Refugees and Migration can be seen as 'a guardian' of humanitarian sensibilities that can foresee problems coming in the formulation of foreign policy initiatives within the State Department. As a senior humanitarian official at the State Department who served in the Clinton Administration explained, 'AID is never involved in these questions. As a different agency, they never find out soon enough.' Some would also question whether there would be a loss of 'leverage' in multilateral relations by moving the $700 million budget out of the State

[11] US Department of State, *Interagency Review*, 14.

Department, which would likely serve to dissociate the funding from foreign policy goals.

'AID does not take direction from State', said Julia Taft, who characterized the provision of humanitarian assistance as 'the human face of foreign policy'. To buttress this point, she cited several conversations with foreign ministers of donor countries who longed for a budget, which was situated in the development bureaucracy of their country, to implement humanitarian policy. Moreover, she noted, somewhat ruefully, that 'NGOs do not want to be stuck with just one interlocutor'. They like to shop among different policy and funding entities, whether it be AID, NSC, or the State Department.

A contrary position has been taken by J. Brian Atwood, former Administrator of USAID during the Clinton Administration, who recommended in connection with the 1999 humanitarian review that relief assistance be consolidated and located at AID in order to encourage consideration of development impacts and perspectives. Atwood sees such an outcome as a step toward the organization of a cabinet-level agency on development and humanitarian responses, which he proposed after leaving government in 2000.

During much of the Clinton Administration, USAID was fending off a proposed merger of the State Department and USAID advocated by US Senator Jesse Helms.[12] For USAID, therefore, the issue is one of 'institutional survival', in the words of a former AID staff member. The reform question is necessarily 'very political' as it involves an agency that is in a 'struggle for its life'.

For instance, the establishment of the OTI could be seen as an effort to become more relevant in an era of diminished resources for development and in the course of the tussle with Congress over the fate of the agency. USAID, recognizing the attraction of an integrated approach to economic, political, and social rehabilitation in post-conflict situations, established OTI as a response to working in countries emerging from conflict. Located in the Bureau for Humanitarian Response, OTI has been featured in US government responses in many post-conflict situations, such as Angola, Bosnia, Guatemala, Haiti, Liberia, Rwanda, Sierra Leone, and more recently in Colombia and Nigeria.

A former AID official noted the 'politicization of humanitarian assistance', with increasing involvement by the White House—that is, the National Security Council—during the Clinton Administration in directing the day-to-day management of relief activities. She attributed this development in part to a post-cold war lack of conceptual clarity. Humanitarian

[12] Republican, North Carolina.

assistance can be a relatively easy tool to employ in response to the political imperative to 'do something'.

The new administrator of USAID, Andrew Natsios, has a reputation for dynamism and candour. He testified at an April 2001 Senate hearing that the agency's 'career officers are demoralized and frustrated' and that efforts to reform AID have been 'too slow, and neither innovative nor sweeping enough to get the job done'.[13] He made a pledge: 'things are going to change.' Natsios, who worked at AID from 1989 to 1993, is familiar with military and civilian humanitarian issues, and he sees the return of refugees and displaced persons as an essential objective of the agency's work in post-conflict situations. But whether his energetic expressions of intention will translate into broader bureaucratic reform remains to be seen.

For Mort Halperin, the initiator of the 1999 review, it is less important which institutional arrangement is chosen. Indeed, he suggested that a single official could wear dual agency hats and be housed in one of the agencies. The most important point is that just one person be responsible. When humanitarian crises emerge, 'no one knows who is in charge', he concluded. Nevertheless, Halperin leans toward consolidation within AID in order to retain the speed of bureaucratic responses to crisis and to avoid the cumbersome clearance processes that operate within the State Department. Halperin noted that, ironically, AID's assistance is often more closely linked to foreign policy objectives as it is deployed through NGOs at the behest of US ambassadors in embassies abroad, while PRM's funding is mostly given through multilateral channels which are somewhat more insulated from US political direction.

A PROPOSAL FOR A NEW US AGENCY FOR HUMANITARIAN ACTION (AHA)

Recent experiences, particularly the Kosovo crisis, have pushed the humanitarian components in the US government to work together more closely, including through information exchange and a greater degree of joint engagement in the planning, implementation, and evaluation of programmes. But much more needs to be done to improve the coherence of US government responses to humanitarian and refugee emergencies. This would include such matters as designing protection strategies for internal exiles or improving the capacity to deploy rule-of-law expertise in

[13] Natsios, Andrew S., *Statement before the U.S. Senate Committee on Foreign Relations* (25 April 2001). At: http://www.usaid.gov/press/spe_test/testimony/2001/an_conf_stmt.html

post-crisis situations. A place is needed to forge and collect the new conceptual tools to deal with new forms of humanitarian action. These activities are not handled adequately in the current structure.

The 1999 inter-agency humanitarian review pointed to three ways to organize US responses more effectively. But no consensus was achieved in the deliberations in terms of the direction of bureaucratic reform, leaving the options: location of the function (1) within the State Department in order to relate humanitarian considerations to foreign policy objectives, (2) within USAID to relate the considerations to longer-term development strategies, or (3) in a separate agency reporting to the Secretary of State.

Given the continued fragmentation in the governmental structures for humanitarian responses, fundamental reform is warranted. In particular, a new separate civilian agency reporting to the Secretary of State, here called the Agency for Humanitarian Action (AHA), should be created to discharge US government functions in this field. This proposed agency, foreshadowed in the 1999 humanitarian review discussed earlier, could retain appropriate linkages to foreign policy objectives by virtue of oversight by the Secretary of State. As it stands now, the policy preferences of regional bureaux at the State Department can smother the perspectives of a functional bureau like PRM, even with its substantial budget. Also, appropriate linkages between humanitarian action and development work could be retained as well through the Secretary's oversight of USAID. The arrangement would also preserve the comparative speed of crisis response that characterizes AID's work.

But the primary point is that just one entity and person would be in charge.[14] Location in an agency such as AHA could help profile the humanitarian voice in Executive Branch deliberations. The principal critique of the separate agency outcome—that distancing humanitarian issues from foreign policy and development imperatives might marginalize the humanitarian voice—could be remedied by ensuring that the person appointed to administer the new agency has political stature and relates closely to the Secretary of State and the President of the United States. The increasing importance of this area of governmental action in fashioning international humanitarian responses would justify the appointment of just such a person of stature. This person should also have deep expertise on the issues in order to relate humanitarian policy appropriately to diplomatic and developmental perspectives. The executive office of AHA should be

[14] The absence of budgetary and programme authority was a fatal institutional weakness of the US Coordinator for Refugee Affairs, a position which was created within the State Department in 1979 and abolished in 1993.

physically located at the State Department to ensure a presence at key high-level meetings, as proximity is often half the battle in bureaucratic deliberations.

There is a further justification for the establishment of a new civilian agency, one that the 2000 humanitarian review simply did not address: finding an appropriate mechanism for civilian-military planning in advance of responses to complex humanitarian emergencies. The US military is a key player in foreign humanitarian and refugee operations. In 1999, the US Department of Defense estimated that it expended 864,239 staff days on such operations.[15]

The overarching lesson from Kosovo was the recognition that humanitarian considerations have to be better integrated into military and political planning. But little has been done to realize this received wisdom, and there is a growing recognition that there will be more of these kinds of operations over the next years. More capacity is needed within the US government to plan to undertake them. This realization recently has prompted the new Bush Administration to consider organizing separate military forces and specialized headquarters units to handle humanitarian missions such as refugee emergencies. The military would swiftly hand over operations to civilians and NGOs 30 days after being deployed. This would seek to remedy a customary disjunction between the time when the military deploys in complex operations, establishes basic security, often accompanied—if not preceded—by civilian humanitarian agencies providing immediate relief, and the time when activities are undertaken to provide policing, basic human security, and the rudiments of law and order.

Experience teaches that more needs to be done, however, to strengthen headquarters structures in the US military to relate to civilian humanitarians. The most ambitious outcome would be a dedicated headquarters structure for humanitarian and peace operations, including appropriate liaison relationships with NGOs. However, a new structure would have to overcome the current political and bureaucratic reluctance to see military capacities develop in this direction, including force structure and funding constraints, as well as congressional scepticism on the issue. But if a dedicated structure were created, it would become a bureaucratic advocate, seeking to maximize available budgetary resources. The development of the special operations and space commands are examples of such arrangements within the US military.

[15] US General Accounting Office, *Military Personnel: Full Extent of Support to Civil Authorities Unknown but Unlikely to Adversely Impact Retention* (Washington, DC:GAO, January 2001), 7.

A less dramatic, but perhaps somewhat more realistic, outcome would be to identify personnel in the planning and operations components of headquarters structures responsible for being the liaisons and points of contact for humanitarian operations. These personnel would be expected to remain knowledgeable about international organizational and NGO activities before, during, and after deployments in such situations. This is what retired US Marine Corps General Anthony C. Zinni, who oversaw military force deployments in northern Iraq and Somalia, calls a 'virtual organization' in headquarters: one that exists on paper and which can be activated to deal with an emergency situation. One weakness in such an approach is that this function could be crowded out by the perceptions and realities of other priorities.

Any integrated civilian and military mechanism to plan and implement programmes of reconstruction and rehabilitation in post-crisis settings could involve international institutions, such as the United Nations at the universal level, or the EU, NATO, or OSCE at the regional level. But as US Army retired General George Joulwan has noted, the US government needs an internal capacity as well to plan such transitional responses. 'There must be a better way of doing these things', he said. Joulwan, who commanded US military deployments in Bosnia and Rwanda, has seen many instances of lack of coordination and cooperation between the civilian and military sectors. As a result, he urges that a joint military and civilian mechanism be created to plan for crisis responses involving the United States: a possible function for the new AHA which could provide an authority to interrelate military and humanitarian perspectives.

The military is familiar with operational coordinating mechanisms such as Civil Military Operation Centers. But this broader humanitarian coordination function should not be situated within the military. Many NGOs will be understandably wary of close involvements with the military, and vice versa. AHA would thus be an appropriate integrated civilian umbrella to associate those NGOs which are willing, or could be persuaded, to engage with the military in crisis management planning.

The Administration of George W. Bush will inevitably confront the need to mount responses to refugee emergencies, and the new cadre of officials would be well advised in advance to address the question of the optimal agency architecture to provide adequate humanitarian responses. To fail to address the issue will simply condemn the bureaucracy to repeat the mistakes and inefficiencies of the past. And such an outcome would have profound human costs. Bureaucratic delay in this area translates into loss of life and terrible hardships.

Ultimately, the value of such anticipatory planning efforts will have to be demonstrated in the real world. But lack of preparedness is not a defensible option. Rather, it is itself a decision to disfavour involvement. As General John Abizaid of the US Army warned when I met with him in Germany in 2000, 'muddling through is not good enough.' The ultimate truth is simple: the US government needs more capacity to plan comprehensively for effective humanitarian action.

A FIRST TASK: CONTRIBUTING TO RULE OF LAW INITIATIVES IN POST-CRISIS SETTINGS

An obvious place for AHA to start its work would be to assemble the currently fragmented efforts within the US government to deal with threshold issues of human security and refugee return in post-conflict settings. This is a problem at the international level, discussed later in this book, but it also poses a policy coordination challenge within the US government.

The February 2000 White Paper relating to Presidential Decision Directive 71 recounts relevant recent experiences:

> In Somalia, for example, the police simply left their posts in 1991 when a new government failed to emerge after the Siad Barre government was deposed. In Haiti and Bosnia, the police were involved in the conflict and consequently were viewed as biased combatants rather than public servants by large segments of the population. Even before the conflict arose, the public safety forces in Haiti, as in many areas where peace operations are conducted, were the primary instrument for state-sponsored repression of the citizens.[16]

PDD 71 was premised on the notion that indigenous law enforcement and criminal justice frameworks are a prerequisite to achieving a sustainable peace in post-crisis situations. Among the US national interests in the establishment of a workable rudimentary justice system are the 'successful completion' of peace operations and the deterrence of criminal activities. As the White Paper notes, '. . . such wrongdoers often include organizers of terrorism, illicit drug and arms trafficking, and international criminal syndicates'. Finding a workable methodology for disengagement is viewed by many in the Executive Branch as a prerequisite to undertaking such military/humanitarian deployments in the future. The new focus on addressing a bundle of these basic rule-of-law issues early in a post-conflict setting may provide such a methodology.

[16] 'White Paper on the Clinton Administration's Policy on Strengthening Criminal Justice Systems in Support of Peace Operations' (February 2000), 1. At: http://www.fas.org/irp/offdocs/pdd/pdd-71-4.htm

The political and military plan developed in each operation is to address public safety and the restoration of the criminal justice system. The process currently used to recruit, train, and deploy civilian police officers in such operations is not adequate, and there is a need to improve the speed of deployment as well as to enhance the discipline and accountability of those deployed.

The Office of International Narcotics and Law Enforcement (INL) in the State Department has been identified to take the lead on these issues. As the White Paper explains:

> This office shall be responsible for policy development, all aspects of provision and oversight of US CIVPOL [civilian police] to field operations, development and implementation of training and technical assistance plans and programs for foreign police forces, and priority setting and coordination among other US activities relating to the criminal justice system, among other tasks.[17]

INL has a budget of $10 million for Fiscal Year 2001 to organize a 2000-person standing roster of civilian police[18] and is hiring staff to develop training for police candidates and reach out to local police authorities to facilitate recruiting. As of August 2001, no political decision had been made on how to establish the US CIVPOL programme on a permanent basis, and discussions are ongoing between the State Department and the Department of Justice on these issues. USAID's Center for Democracy and Governance focuses on the justice system issues, which a State Department official characterized as 'much more complex'.

Apart from the capacity to train and develop foreign police forces, arrangements are needed as well to develop assistance in judicial and penal matters. In the words of the White Paper:

> When such systems break down or are destroyed, the damage is felt in a variety of ways, ranging from economic interests, to humanitarian concerns, to the physical safety of American citizens. We must therefore continue to expand and improve cooperation and development activities with other countries, especially those emerging from periods of instability where havens of criminal impunity might otherwise develop.[19]

[17] 'White Paper on the Clinton Administration's Policy on Strengthening Criminal Justice Systems in Support of Peace Operations', 3.

[18] In 2001, approximately $1 million a week was being spent on the US CIVPOL contingent in Kosovo.

[19] 'White Paper on the Clinton Administration's Policy on Strengthening Criminal Justice Systems in Support of Peace Operations', 5.

The White Paper specifically recognizes the value of a multilateral approach to build such capacities:

> ... US government capabilities should not become the international community's instrument of first resort whenever CIVPOL-related requirements arise. Many other countries and organizations have similar interests and responsibilities and should share the burden of these activities. Therefore, the US government shall seek to enhance the capacities of non-US entities including those of other countries, international organizations, and non-governmental organizations.[20]

The PDD 71 White Paper refers specifically to 'constabulary forces and paramilitary forces present in other countries to conduct crowd control and basic law and order functions' and to the expertise of the United Nations as well as the OSCE in Europe in the deployment of international police. The White Paper emphasizes that, in general, civilian police are not to 'exercise executive authority' except in exceptional circumstances such as 'Kosovo and East Timor where the international community is responsible for the administration of a territory...'[21]

PDD 71 is in effect the product of a survey of current US government local capacity building efforts which are highly relevant to the management of forced migration emergencies. It seeks to address the 'public security gap' by enhancing US capabilities to recruit, train, and deploy police officers, and provide the necessary criminal justice resources. The directive reflects the notion that a discrete set of measures designed to enhance the rule of law can promote normality and refugee repatriation preliminary to the much more ambitious objectives of reviving economies, rehabilitating societies, or building Western-style democracies. These justice system issues are a discrete package of human security elements in the context of a much more complex and long-term endeavour that would ultimately require greater indigenous support and participation to succeed in fostering the rule of law.

A more coherent structure within the US government such as AHA to address such problems in the future would facilitate the development of doctrine and mechanisms at the national level. This could be the first step toward contributing most usefully to a model rule of law 'service package' to be assembled under a framework of international standards for deployment in post-crisis situations.

[20] 'White Paper on the Clinton Administration's Policy on Strengthening Criminal Justice Systems in Support of Peace Operations', 6.

[21] 'White Paper on the Clinton Administration's Policy on Strengthening Criminal Justice Systems in Support of Peace Operations', 10.

A cautionary note is in order, however. Having been involved in efforts to build the capacity of legal systems in Bosnia, Haiti, and Rwanda, Ian Martin, who oversaw UN efforts in these places, expresses concern about the poor performance of bilateral donors in building criminal justice institutions. They are, in his words, 'badly coordinated'. Donors concoct projects with no real idea about the justice system in the country in question. 'No one does it well', he said ruefully. Oftentimes, the bilateral donors are influenced mainly by their own judicial systems. There simply is no forum for international policy coordination—a possible role for the intergovernmental mechanism for Strategic Humanitarian Action and Research (SHARE) described in this book.

CONGRESS

The complexities of the US legislative process have produced reams of scholarship and commentary, although relatively little has been written in terms of Congress and the formulation and implementation of US government humanitarian responses. How the process is organized, however, may not be the most salient factor. Senior congressional staffers on both the Democrat and Republican sides emphasized that perhaps the most significant considerations are the 'politics and personalities involved'. It is also notable just how few staff persons, a mere handful, address refugee issues in Congress. Nor is there any single member who has made generic humanitarian action his or her top issue currently. Thus, refugees in general do not have what can serve as a powerful engine for action: a congressional champion. Nevertheless, certain dynamics and trends are discernible.

The manner in which the US government responds to international refugee emergencies is shaped at least to some extent by how Congress is organized in relation to the Executive Branch. This relationship concerns funding and policy oversight. 'We are concerned with the bottom line, not the details of policy', explained one senior Democratic staffer. The committee structures of Congress in some ways mirror the work of the foreign policy bureaucracy in the Executive Branch. In other respects, the interface is less obvious.

Like many policy areas, several congressional committees deal with refugee issues. In terms of substantive policy oversight, where the admission of refugees to the US from abroad is concerned, the House Committee on the Judiciary, particularly the Subcommittee on Immigration and Claims, has jurisdiction. On the Senate side, the Subcommittee on Immigration of the Committee on the Judiciary has responsibility. These involvements flow from the fact that those committees oversee the Immigration and Naturalization

Service, a sub-agency within the Department of Justice, which implements refugee admissions programmes under US immigration law. International refugee protection policy, however, implicates other sets of legislative actors.

Where the international response involves humanitarian relief, on either a multilateral or a bilateral basis, the congressional committees overseeing foreign policy and international development have jurisdiction. In the House of Representatives, this is the Committee on International Relations, notably the Subcommittee on International Operations and Human Rights. On the Senate side, it is the Committee on Foreign Relations, particularly the Subcommittee on International Operations. These committees relate directly to the work of the State Department and the USAID. However, as in the Executive Branch, since the staff of the International Operations subcommittees are oriented more around regions than functions, thematic issues such as refugees can receive relatively low priority.

Sometimes international financial institutions seek to address funding issues in post-conflict reconstruction and rehabilitation efforts. In these instances, the House Committee on Banking and Financial Services and the Senate Committee on Banking, Housing and Urban Affairs are interested.

When a military deployment is an aspect of a US government response to a humanitarian crisis, then the House Armed Services Committee and the Senate Armed Services Committee have substantive policy oversight. Recent experience suggests that the Armed Services committees have little interest in refugee issues, and they have exhibited a bias against the military's preparation for and participation in refugee-related missions, what has been referred to somewhat derisively as 'nation building' since the 1993 withdrawal of US forces from Somalia. This hostility stems from a variety of causes, including the drain on defence resources, which is a persistent complaint voiced by some military leaders and their supporters in Congress. In recent times, the committees' deliberations have reflected the reluctance of the Pentagon to have the US military become engaged in non-traditional humanitarian activities such as peacekeeping or peace-building operations for which the record has been mixed.

Aside from policy oversight, congressional committees also are deeply involved in funding the responses to international refugee emergencies. Indeed, as one senior Republican staffer noted, funding appropriators are often more important to legislative outcomes than the policy authorizers in Congress, except perhaps when substantive committees with considerable political influence are involved, such as Armed Services. As a foreign policy committee staffer bemoaned in relation to the dynamics of Executive Branch and congressional Appropriations Committee negotiations: 'They try to pretty much ignore us'.

Refugee issues are often considered somewhat obscure and they frequently arise episodically, thus 'falling between the cracks' even for policy authorizers. This is compounded by the fact that refugee issues in broad terms have not had congressional advocates in recent times. More often, particular ethnic groups have been championed, said one senior Democratic staffer involved in appropriations. His explanation was pointed, 'There is no real political pay off at home.' This results in a situation where there is no incentive to develop expertise on refugee issues and provide a counterweight to the Executive Branch. Nevertheless, in general terms, refugee programmes have done 'better than most', this staffer said; both Democrats and Republicans like humanitarian aid more than long-term development aid.

Refugee-related issues frequently end up being raised as reactions to Administration initiatives. Also, because there was not much consensus over the substance of foreign policy during the Clinton Administration, Congress focused its energy on considering the annual budget, which is primarily the domain of the funding appropriators. To the extent that refugee issues are embodied in budget considerations, the members and staff who are appropriators became the key actors.

In the House and Senate Committees on Appropriations, for example, a powerful Senator or Representative, or even a strong staffer on the Subcommittees on Commerce, Justice, State and Judiciary or the Foreign Operations Subcommittees, can do more to shape a policy outcome than the committee responsible for substantive policy. The substantive authorizing committee has to take the initiative to prevail; as one Republican staffer puts it, 'we have to legislate.'

The dynamics of interactions between Congress and the Executive Branch in this policy area are illustrated by recent congressional efforts to grant US resettlement to Vietnamese refugees. One of the signature modern events of refugee exodus concerned Indo-China after the end of the Vietnam war. The first refugees from Laos reached the Thai border in early 1975, followed shortly thereafter by Cambodians after Phnom Penh collapsed. The end of the Vietnam war in 1975 marked the beginning of a refugee emergency which was characterized by a flotilla of boat people, brutal high-seas attacks by pirates, and summary rejection of asylum seekers as well as their harsh treatment in nearby countries in south-east Asia. The peak period for arrivals was between 1979 and 1981, when some 640,000 arrivals from Vietnam, Laos, and Cambodia were registered for asylum in countries in the region.[22]

[22] Minot, Michael, 'Refugees from Cambodia, Laos and Vietnam, 1975–1993', in Robin Coven (ed.), *The Cambridge Survey of World Migration* (Cambridge: Cambridge University Press, 1995), 452.

An international conference in Geneva in 1979 sought to guarantee reception for these arrivals in return for a promise of resettlement in the West, mainly in Australia, Canada, France, and United States. The US then led one of the most generous resettlement programmes of all time to rescue allies who had assisted the war effort. Over the next 20 years, more than 1.4 million Vietnamese were admitted to the US; 900,000 gained entry into other countries.[23] An extraordinary pact was struck: countries of resettlement, notably the US, would accept refugees in return for a guarantee that they would be permitted to land and stay in countries of asylum.

As the years passed, the need for the resettlement commitments by the US and other countries was increasingly questioned. Some policy administrators were concerned that the admissions scheme had become a magnet for economic migrants instead of refugees with a fear of persecution. Forced return was introduced in 1989 under the aegis of an internationally-agreed Comprehensive Plan of Action (CPA) in order to discourage Vietnamese and others in the region from undertaking unauthorized, risky journeys. Refugees were to be screened in nearby countries of asylum. Those who were found to have a well-founded fear of persecution upon return were to be resettled abroad. Those who failed to qualify were to be sent back to Vietnam. This proved to be a prolonged exercise. The last Vietnamese asylum seekers under the CPA were released and expelled from a detention camp in Hong Kong only in 2000.[24]

Concerns over the accuracy of the screening process established under the CPA prompted action by House Republicans in 1995, led by Congressman Christopher Smith,[25] then the chair of the Subcommittee on International Operations and Human Rights of the House Committee on International Operations. Representative Smith introduced a bill which would have mandated a second case examination for Vietnamese who had been rejected under the CPA procedures. This approach was strongly opposed by the US State Department and UNHCR, among others, on the grounds that it would undermine the deterrent effect of the CPA. While this re-screening provision was part of a broader foreign aid bill that ultimately was vetoed for a variety of reasons by President Clinton, it was clear that the provision was likely to emerge again in subsequent legislative efforts.

[23] US Department of State, 'East Asian Refugee Admissions Program', PRM Fact Sheet (Washington, DC: US Department of State, 18 January 2000). See generally 'Flight from Indochina', in United Nations High Commissioner for Refugees, *The State of the World's Refugees: Fifty Years of Humanitarian Action* (New York: Oxford University Press, 2000), 79–103.

[24] 'Vietnamese Migrants', Enforcement and Liaison Branch, Hong Kong Special Administrative Region, Government Information Center. At: http:/www.info.gov.hk/immd/a_report/right4.htm

[25] Republican, New Jersey.

The legislative incentive coincided with a debate within the Executive Branch about the proper course of action. 'This was an NGO proposal that we argued, that we agreed with', explained a senior humanitarian official at the National Security Council during Clinton's tenure, who acknowledged that there were 'significant screening errors' under CPA procedures which rendered the outcomes of cases uncertain. 'We wanted to make peace with Congress and avoid a diplomatic train wreck, since our ASEAN [Association of South East Asian Nations] partners would not have accepted a re-screening requirement.' An initiative to provide additional opportunities for resettlement to Vietnamese previously rejected under CPA procedures was thus 'imposed by the NSC on an acquiescing State Department'.

The result of the negotiations was an administrative programme of Resettlement Opportunities for Vietnamese Refugees (ROVR) for those refugees deemed of special interest to the US who return to Vietnam under the terms of the CPA. The new interviews were to occur in Vietnam as part of an in-country refugee programme that had existed for many years. Despite some delays in implementation by the Vietnamese authorities, after 1996 approximately 20,000 Vietnamese were admitted to the US as refugees under the ROVR programme, which ended only in 2000.[26]

The saga of the ROVR programme is a lesson in power politics between the leaders of a Republican Congress and a Democratic Administration. The Administration's position was negotiated by a handful of foreign policy officials. The legislative effort was led by a highly committed individual member who garnered leadership support. The outcome was an Executive Branch reaction to a congressional initiative, although an NSC official cautioned that 'if we had decided to oppose instead of co-opting the initiative, we may well have succeeded'. Instead, the result was a last spasm of generosity for a discrete group of Vietnamese refugees.

There are many other forms of policy leverage in the legislative process. Appropriations generally and, on the Senate side, nominations and confirmations can provide a passive form of pressure. There are numerous examples. An initiative in 2000 by US Senator Judd Gregg,[27] who chaired the Appropriations Committee's Subcommittee on Commerce, Justice, State and the Judiciary is illustrative. Senator Gregg unblocked funding for UN peacekeeping to Sierra Leone in return for an agreement by the Administration to exclude the leader of a rebel group from a power-sharing

[26] 'Relating to Continuing Human Rights Violations and Political Oppression in Socialist Republic of Vietnam', Congressional Record, 146, 3 (May 2000), p. H2421. At: http:/www.access.gpo.gov/su_docs/aces/aces150.html

[27] Republican, New Hampshire.

arrangement negotiated in a peace agreement signed by the combatants in July 1999, and to assist in reconstituting a more effective peacekeeping force. Upon the accommodation with the Administration, Senator Gregg agreed to release $50 million to fund the US share of peacekeeping expenditures in Sierra Leone.[28]

The impact of the system of congressional committees on the legislative agenda can be summarized as follows. The involvements of the appropriations committees and strong substantive committees such as Armed Services can be determinative. Ironically, the substantive foreign policy oversight committees have in recent years largely been talk shops and not very consequential in the legislative mix.

This pecking order is illustrated well by the lack of even informal consultation concerning the 1999 review of humanitarian assistance undertaken by the Executive Branch. Some of the options set forth in the review, particularly those regarding the consolidation of functions at the State Department and USAID, would require legislation. But as a key senior staffer involved in international operations noted in May 2000 in relation to the review, 'I did not even know about it.' His ignorance of the exercise illustrates graphically a lack of consensus and communication on humanitarian issues between important policy overseers in that Republican Congress and Democratic Executive Branch.

Of course, certain unique dynamics are at play in a situation where one political party holds the White House and the other the Congress. Ordinarily, in such a circumstance, a great deal of legislative business gets done at the end of the year in omnibus spending bills, in which the authorizers may have only a limited role. A veteran Republican staffer repeatedly noted in 2000 the 'reactive' posture of Congress, with a Democratic Administration undertaking policy initiatives which it negotiates with the Republican leaders. 'In the end it very much depends on what the Republican leadership thinks', observed this staffer, who cited the military deployment in Kosovo as an example. 'The Administration usually gets what it wants.'

It remains to be seen whether this disjunction will be repaired in a situation where one party has captured both Congress and the Executive Branch, particularly with a Congress so finely divided that a change in party affiliation by one Senator propelled the Democrats into the majority in the Senate in June 2001.[29] But a senior NSC staff person in the new Bush

[28] 'Amnesty International USA Applauds Senator Gregg's Release of Sierra Leone Funds', Press Release (Washington, DC: Amnesty International–USA, 7 June 2000).

[29] Dewier, Helen, 'Jeffords Staged a "Coup of One," Angry Lott Says', *Washington Post* (31 May 2001), A8.

Administration noted in May 2001 that old 'bad habits' in Congressional and Executive Branch relations are hard to break. He was referring to a vote in the House of Representatives that day, over the Administration's opposition, to block part of the payment of UN dues in reaction to the US not being re-elected to the UN Human Rights Commission. Whether new political leadership will change these dynamics remains to be seen.

9

Imagining Better Refugee Policy

You can only predict things after they have happened.
—Eugène Ionesco, *Le Rhinocéros*, Act III.

The future of refugee policy is contingent upon a myriad of decisions within and outside of officialdom. Circumstances in the real world will impose constraints and create opportunities for policy development. The present is an inherently inadequate vantage point for prognostication. But it is the difficulty of foreseeing the future that demands a concerted effort to think about possibilities: to prepare to be astonished. Prediction in the realm of social affairs is often an exercise in futility. Uncertainty and unintended consequences are increasingly recognized as key aspects of designing and implementing policy. In this sense, leadership is indeed an art and not a science. Yet leaders and thinkers must attempt to see forward: to expect the unexpected. Scenario analysis, the method employed in this chapter, is increasingly a tool for decision makers in an era of uncertainty.[1]

The objective of this chapter is to provoke thought about policy directions and tools, not to forecast the most likely outcome or to promote an ideal world. Rather, the rationale for scenario analysis is to encourage creative thinking about how to address future contingencies which range from the likely to the remote. It is a device designed to make explicit the assumptions we make about possible future policy directions. Innovative discussion is encouraged by seeking to minimize the fear of 'being wrong' which can inhibit creativity, whether it be within government, the academy, or elsewhere.

Presented in this chapter are three possible forced migration policy futures over the next decade: international cooperation, containment, and proactive policy. None of the policy scenarios articulated below is necessarily likely. Indeed, as elaborated later in the chapter, the policy framework that emerges is likely to contain elements of each future scenario. The chapter closes with a discussion of the likely policy future, and urges promotion of certain outcomes, notably international cooperation.

[1] See Schwartz, Peter, *The Art of the Long View: Planning for the Future in an Uncertain World* (New York: Currency-Doubleday, 1996).

SCENARIO 1: INTERNATIONAL COOPERATION

This is a world in which arbitrary population displacement is a diminishing phenomenon. Many of the causes of forced migration, such as armed conflict and state dissolution, are on the wane. The forces of globalization, particularly trade and capital movements associated with multinational business, have resulted in the continued strengthening of free markets as well as increased economic well-being more generally. New democracies are emerging, particularly in Eurasia and Africa, but the predominant characteristic of this world is stability.

While the benevolent effects of new economies are most pronounced in the developed world, particularly in North America and western Europe, there are widespread positive effects elsewhere. Clear concentrations of wealth and military power are evident, and the United States remains the world's pre-eminent military power, and the strongest single economic power. The European Union has expanded and now includes the Baltic states, the Czech Republic, Hungary, Poland, and Slovenia. Other regions, notably Asia and Latin America, have experienced significant economic prosperity. China is economically ascendant and becoming more democratic, and it aspires to have more regional influence.

There are clear winners in this world, but the sea of well-being is generally rising for others as well. Only a few countries and sub-regions are left out of the new prosperity, notably several countries in South Asia and sub-Saharan Africa. Climate change and population growth continue to stabilize. Inter-state wars are increasingly rare, and even internal and ethnic or identity-based conflicts have decreased in number and intensity.

This scenario is characterized by an unprecedented process of international treaty making on a wide variety of issues, including the environment, water management, health care, and education policy. Successful arrangements to curtail the small-arms trade have been implemented, modelled on the achievements of several years ago regarding containment of the funding of armed conflict in Africa by the diamond trade. Debt arrears have largely been forgiven through initiatives of the World Bank and International Monetary Fund, as well as their regional counterparts. International development efforts have become increasingly effective. Famine is rare, in part due to the increasing prevalence of genetically modified crops which has resulted in a substantial food surplus, and to efficient international warning and food delivery mechanisms.

To address displacements and damage caused by natural disaster, the International Disaster Relief Organization (IDRO), an intergovernmental body, was created in 2008. The IDRO administers an emergency low-interest loan fund to assist with quick recovery projects as well as maintains rosters of logistical resources, including military capabilities, civilian police, and disaster workers, who can be deployed on short notice.

In these good times, global student groups have begun to agitate over the Internet for the establishment of an international court of historic and cultural injustices, arguing for compensation to a variety of indigenous peoples and others for wrongs in the past. This era has witnessed several technological advancements which have had positive social impacts, such as the development and distribution of low-cost medicines to treat AIDS.

Episodic forced migrations are dealt with through new international arrangements designed to spread the risks among affected states. The most developed treaty-based arrangements exist at the sub-regional and regional levels and operate in ways analogous to insurance schemes. By investing resources and making commitments in advance, states undertake to offer assistance and international relocation to refugees and displaced persons once a crisis occurs. Commissions have been established under the aegis of an intergovernmental mechanism for Strategic Humanitarian Action and Research (SHARE) which was founded in 2005 to design and implement these arrangements. These commissions have been established to create specific formulae for apportioning tasks and responsibilities developed by experts with respect to potential crisis and post-crisis situations.

The Caribbean Initiative for Responsibility Sharing (CIRS) is illustrative. CIRS signatories promise to receive and host any displaced persons who arrive at their shores or territories. Furthermore, signatory states to CIRS agree to temporarily shelter and provide for such individuals for up to 60 days under universal minimum standards of care. If displacement continues beyond 60 days, the nearby states agree to admit individuals and their families as temporary residents for up to three years with provision for primary and secondary education for minors as well as access to employment in the labour market for adults. An admissions quota formula based on a variety of economic and social indicators has been fixed in advance by a technical expert body established under CIRS. If the causes of displacement persist beyond three years, provisions are made for permanent residence and ultimately naturalization. CIRS has been used to accommodate persons displaced by reason of natural disaster as well as political crisis. Similar sub-regional arrangements currently exist in southern Africa, the Mediterranean region, south-east Asia, and Central America.

When the UNHCR was re-organized in 2010, a Division of Human Security was created to promote intergovernmental burden-sharing agreements and provide a forum for the promulgation and oversight of minimum standards. Based on these practices and experiences, a world conference on migration and free international movement has been scheduled by the UN General Assembly in 2015 to consider a Convention on the Amelioration of Forced Migration, which seeks to promote regional responsibility-sharing arrangements, with an aspiration of universal coverage in the foreseeable future. The proposed treaty defines forced migration to include all persons subject to arbitrary displacement, including those defined as refugees and internally displaced persons under previously negotiated international treaties. Decision-making on individual and categories of cases is to be lodged in a treaty-based new International Organization for Forced Migration. The prospects for the establishment of this new treaty regime appear to be good.

SCENARIO 2: CONTAINMENT

In this world, forced human displacement has increased to well over 100 million persons. Ethnic conflicts are increasing in number and intensity in south-east Europe, the Caucasus region, and central Asia. Secessionist movements in Africa and Asia have declared independence and civil wars are raging. Inter-state wars have also broken out in those regions, and biological and chemical weapons have been used. Riots have occurred in Beijing and several large cities in China. Twelve states around the world now have nuclear weapons, and threats have been made by a few 'rogue states' to use them.

The growth of population—7.2 billion globally—is increasing in some parts of the world, despite a global AIDS epidemic. Rates of increase are highest in developing countries, particularly in swiftly expanding urban areas. Rapidly ageing European and Japanese populations have fuelled internal political tensions over maintaining levels of social services and increasing immigration.

International efforts to regulate the environment and to protect endangered species and rainforests have been seriously undermined by a growing group of developing countries who believe that they cannot afford to invest in environmental protection activities at the expense of economic survival. Local conflicts have emerged over water scarcity. Natural disasters seem to increase in frequency and intensity. Malaria, tuberculosis, and other infectious diseases have mutated and become resistant to antibiotics.

Growing global economic disparities in wealth characterize this world. IMF programmes are not receiving funds. The prosperity of a few 'islands' of relatively rich countries, mainly North America and western Europe, stands in stark contrast to the rest of the world, where infant mortality rates are rising and life expectancy is falling. Africa is rife with famine, disease, and conflict, and the continent is considered largely a lost cause among development experts.

International criminal syndicates have proliferated, particularly as government structures have weakened in many countries. Human trafficking now rivals the drug trade as the most lucrative activity of organized crime. Loose networks of terrorists are present in many countries and they engage in occasional but spectacular acts of random destruction and mayhem as well as cyber-terrorism. Very substantial resources have been invested by developed countries in high-tech border controls, including technical assistance and capacity building on border-management programmes for developing countries.

In response to population pressures and movements in the world, developed countries have created a formidable set of barriers to the arrival of unwanted migrants. These measures include at their core a wide network of re-admission agreements negotiated by developed countries that oblige countries of transit to receive back unadmitted non-citizens. In addition to creating a '*cordon sanitaire*' to forestall the arrival of asylum seekers, developed countries generally incarcerate those individuals who manage to traverse access barriers in order to facilitate their swift removal and to deter the arrival of others. Also, financial arrangements and sanctions have been designed by relatively wealthy countries of arrival with countries of origin, whereby the arrival countries pay substantial sums of money to encourage pre-departure enforcement and manage visa programmes to facilitate the return of unwanted migrants. Many technologically proficient countries have introduced a trans-national DNA-based identification system and shared database to control the admission and stay of non-citizens.

Those states that are parties to the UN refugee treaties retain the discretion to determine who is and who is not a refugee entitled to the specific political and social rights proclaimed under the treaties. While the vast majority of states remain signatories to the refugee treaties, they are nevertheless able to deny asylum in most cases because of this discretionary prerogative. This includes the restrictive application of treaty criteria concerning refugee status for those who have a well-founded fear of persecution upon return to their home countries. However, a few states, mainly in Europe, formally renounced their treaty obligations when it became clear that their national legal systems demanded more generous interpretations under the treaties or forbade certain deterrent or non-entry measures.

A new international treaty on temporary protection has been concluded and over 100 states have acceded to this new instrument which provides for temporary stay and swift return of non-citizens after a crisis causing displacement abates. The lower priority given to refugee protection by international organizations and states has been accompanied by the growth of NGO monitoring organizations in a loosely affiliated Refugee Watch network. Many refugee protection activities have thus been largely privatized.

In order to encourage would-be refugees to remain in their home countries, even though riven with crisis and conflict, humanitarian assistance strategies have been developed and refined, including for internal exiles. UN humanitarian agencies have finally been consolidated into one entity and re-named the UN Office for Humanitarian Responses (UNOHR) and substantial research and development has been invested in the provision of 'smart aid' and mechanisms for its swift delivery and monitoring. New coordination structures have been established in several donor countries to increase the effectiveness of humanitarian action. In the United States, for example, a new Agency for Humanitarian Action (AHA) was established in 2004.

Concerted international efforts have been launched to apprehend and prosecute those who have killed or abused aid workers, a phenomenon that has reached unprecedented levels. These enforcement efforts are designed to facilitate the delivery of humanitarian relief. This is so despite the fact that the International Criminal Court treaty has yet to enter into force because of intense counter-pressures by anti-globalization NGOs.

Regional interventions to forestall migration emergencies have occurred. Italy has deployed forces again in Albania under the auspices of the OSCE; and the US has deployed forces in Colombia and again in Haiti under the aegis of the Organization of American States. But most of this action is occurring in a privatized security sector. Well-armed private security forces have been hired by UNOHR to set up and administer 'safe' enclaves and zones as well as regional safe havens in situations of crisis and conflict. Composed of ex-military personnel and financed largely by major transnational corporations who have decided that stability and security are good for business, such internal safety arrangements have been established in Africa, Asia, and South America.

SCENARIO 3: PROACTIVE POLICY

Basic socio-economic indicators are rising in this world. While there is significant inequality in terms of wealth and prosperity, basic indicators around the world are positive, including infant mortality and life expectancy. Globalization is expanding, although there are many places in the world that are unaffected and that remain impoverished and unconnected. Nevertheless, it is a world in which the dominant approach is to 'buy into' the expansion of well-being and prosperity reflected in the international movement of persons, goods, and information.

The guardians of this new prosperity, the Group of Seven (G7) nations with big economies, have developed mechanisms to anticipate problems that might threaten these positive international trends, and permit responses before matters get out of hand. In this connection, a well-supported network of NGOs has been established to give early warning of impending crises around the world to a variety of regional organizations and the United Nations. Preventive action efforts, involving coalitions not only of diplomats but also of international businesses and NGOs, seek to ensure the maintenance of stability that promotes prosperity. As an adjunct to this new international organizational architecture, an Organization of African Unity High Commissioner on African Ethnic Affairs (HCAEA) has been established in Nairobi, Kenya. The mandate of the HCAEA, inspired by the successful earlier work of the OSCE High Commissioner on National Minorities in Europe, focuses on quelling potential ethnic conflict in Africa, where interstate and internal wars have persisted.

The World Bank and the International Monetary Fund have made substantial progress in clearing debt arrears in transitional countries, and development programming has been considerably refined. The United Nations Development Programme (UNDP) has been reformed and is amply funded. UNDP is undertaking effective new approaches around the world to encourage sustainable economic development and good governance. The United Nations High Commissioner for Human Rights has also developed effective technical assistance programmes, partly as a result of the establishment of a new training facility in Geneva, which has catalogued the best practices and experts at building and maintaining rights-respecting state structures around the world. Considerable expertise has been accumulated in techniques to reconstruct inter-group relations in post-conflict societies.

In this world, developed states with extraordinary capacities involve themselves selectively in the internal situations of less capable states in order to forestall the flight of would-be refugees. This includes deploying troops as peacekeepers and peace enforcers, primarily but not exclusively under multilateral auspices, as well as undertaking efforts to build state structures in those countries that have failed or that are in the process of imploding as states.

International organizations in this world are well-funded and quite efficient. They engage in monitoring, reporting, and fact-finding activities in places of potential intervention. Economic sanctions have been refined through experience and made 'smart' in the sense that they are designed to fall exclusively on abusive leaders and targeted individuals, *inter alia*, by curtailing their ability to travel and seizing their ill-gotten fortunes. In this connection, bank secrecy provisions in various countries have been reformed and relaxed.

Military doctrine and capabilities have evolved to the point where modern military forces can deploy around the world and undertake peace operations rapidly and effectively at short notice. For some years now, the United Nations has had standing military and police forces that can be deployed anywhere in the world in a matter of hours, supplemented as necessary by rapid reaction forces pre-identified by France, the United Kingdom, and the United States. There is a consensus among political leaders in the US and other democratic states that such peace-enforcing military deployments are workable and supported by their respective electorates.

While military deployments for humanitarian purposes can be undertaken often in a matter of days, public criticism continues to be levelled against the UN system for even short delays in responding to emergencies. As a result, a new grass-roots organization, Humanitarians Without Borders (HUWOB), has been organized in several developed countries. HUWOB forms citizens brigades who call themselves 'Road to Hell Gangs', referring to the title of a book popular in humanitarian circles that was published in the late 1990s.[2] Using the Internet to organize 'direct actions', these groups seek to go immediately to the scene of humanitarian emergencies, with or without the consent of the local authorities, in order to render help to needy persons in whatever way they see fit.

The International Criminal Court has now tried and passed judgment on several former officials and even former heads of states who have been implicated in genocide, war crimes, and crimes against humanity. The notion of sovereignty as a form of states' responsibility to ensure the general welfare of their inhabitants is well established in the thinking of many political theorists. Even intellectuals and political leaders in developing countries have largely accepted notions of military interventions relating to genuinely humanitarian concerns.

To promote multilateral endeavours, the Security Council has been reformed, and Brazil, Japan, Germany, South Africa, and India have joined as permanent members. The veto of the Permanent Five in the Security

[2] Maren, Michael, *The Road to Hell: The Ravaging Effects of Foreign Aid and International Charity* (New York: The Free Press, 1997).

Council has been reformed to require a majority of three of the five in order for a veto to be sustained.

Use of force for humanitarian purposes by military forces has been facilitated by the continued development of precision weaponry, which permits air campaigns and near-certain targeting anywhere in the world with little or no risk of battle casualties. In this sense, virtual war has become a doctrinal norm, which but a handful of very capable states are able to prosecute. These states have often combined in practice to utilize their impressive military capacities to ensure peace.

In particular, Europe has a functioning rapid reaction military capacity, which has deployed to pre-empt conflict in south-east Europe and the Caucasus region. Also, regional peacekeeping capabilities have been developed in Africa with substantial coordinated investments by France, the United Kingdom, and the United States, which permit the deployment of up to 30,000 troops from contributing African nations, most of which are presently deployed in operations around the continent. A doctrine of preventive deployment has resulted in troops and paramilitary police being deployed in the Mediterranean region, south Asia, Africa, and Indonesia in order to forestall possible separatist conflict.

Concomitantly, precision peace-building techniques have been developed, and packages of programmes can be deployed internationally on issues such as the rule of law, including policing, and the establishment of legal systems and courts in order to quickly address situations of anarchy and power vacuums where international military involvements have occurred. Internationalized concepts of temporary martial law for peace building have been perfected to ensure quick transitions to secure environments. The peace-building capacity of the UN has been strengthened, and 100,000 troops and civil administrators are currently deployed under the auspices of the renamed UN Department of Peace Building.

An international centre for the training of peace builders has been operating at The Hague now for several years, and has graduated several thousands of troops, police, and international civil administrators who have been deployed in various locales around the world. Outside of the UN, an intergovernmental mechanism for Strategic Humanitarian Action and Research (SHARE) has been established to develop doctrine and to marshal expertise relating to state building. Operations designed by SHARE are under way in several regions around the world.

At the United Nations headquarters, a separate Office of Preventive Initiatives has been established within the Department of Political Affairs, with a substantial staff that includes technical advisers to a variety of governments seeking to strengthen governance systems. In many governments, including France, the United Kingdom, and the United States, similar centres for preventive action have been established in the agencies responsible for foreign affairs and/or development aid.

While governments continue to support prevention initiatives modestly, notions of corporate social responsibility have become ascendant. An Ounce of Prevention Foundation has been established by a trans-national consortium of billionaires, and over $10 billion has been pledged to support conflict prevention activities around the world. This money is used to fund project proposals by international organizations and NGOs to address the underlying and immediate causes of human insecurity.

WHICH WAY?

We are on the cusp of a new humanitarian enterprise and the direction taken will have critical consequences for both individuals and states. The causes and circumstances of human displacement have evolved and are both qualitatively and quantitatively different now. Ethnic conflict, nationalism, and tribalism fuel secessionist movements and state destruction. Weak states permit the operation of criminal and terrorist enterprises which pose national security threats. Populations are increasingly at risk and demands to deal with them are growing. The traditional tools of humanitarian response—provision of basic material assistance, asylum, and resettlement—are just the beginning of a set of policy tools which decision makers need to respond to new complexities in this environment.

The difficulty of envisaging the future is no excuse for not thinking about possible outcomes. Indeed, it is just the opposite. Leaders must embrace creative forms of guesswork if they are to fulfill their responsibilities, including to anticipate a wide variety of contingencies. The aim of the above policy scenarios is to promote preparation by encouraging just such constructive surmise.

To separate the strands of policy direction is analytically and intellectually useful for our purposes. Here, we imagine the future of refugee policy because to imagine its future is to help understand its present direction and how we might get from here to there—or, indeed, to help us realistically assess whether we can get from here to there. Policy is most often reactive and driven by a variety of forces. But it is very much a human endeavour, and it matters greatly which policy choices are made and implemented.

Yet the underlying assumptions in these scenarios are sobering. The cooperation scenario depends upon the fact of a diminishing primary problem in terms of the scope and gravity of forced displacement. A growing group of countries need to have the economic wherewithal and political interest to provide help. As the problem becomes more manageable, cooperation serves to spread a measurable degree of diminishing risk. And the leaders of like-minded capable states have accepted the development of international institutional frameworks with capacities that in some respects rival governments. If this is too much good news, then that simply means it is a rather unlikely scenario.

The containment scenario seems the closest to the trajectory of current trends, although clearly somewhat aggravated. Problems persist and are magnified by continuing conflict and population growth. Economic disparities remain and organized criminal and terrorist enterprises become an even more serious problem. States eschew cooperation, instead hoping that they can be insulated from refugees who are to be contained elsewhere. Humanitarian responses have been made more effective in lieu of asylum seeking and addressing the underlying causes of displacement.

The proactive scenario reflects a workable hegemony by a group of like-minded leading states that are willing in certain circumstance to invest treasure and, if necessary, blood in dealing with refugee and humanitarian emergencies. The primary methods for dealing with these needs are strengthened international organizations and enhanced security capacities. A well-functioning United Nations system with the ability to engage in state building and civil administration is part of the equation. Regional structures with this capacity exist as well, particularly in Europe. An underlying assumption is that the social and economic climate is relatively positive, with problems confined to particular places. Again, scepticism about whether these objective circumstances are likely to exist would indicate that this scenario is not likely to be realized, at least not fully.

Taken together, the scenarios' assumptions present a paradox. A worsening situation in terms of forced displacement would seem to make international cooperation and proactive policy even more important objectives. Yet, bad circumstances can militate against achieving cooperative arrangements in the midst of crisis or undertaking international initiatives when the domestic situation is dire. Witness the lack of a response in the 1990s to the calls for burden sharing by Germany in the face of displacements from the former Yugoslavia or by the United States in relation to Haitian boat people. On the other hand, in a relatively benign world the impetus is diminished to make the effort to achieve cooperation or craft proactive policy. Policy reform may thus depend upon marshalling and promoting a variety of counter-intuitive factors and motivations: in other words, astute leadership which appreciates the recurring and escalating nature of the risks and the incentives for cooperation.

In relation to refugee policy, the underlying economic, social, and political factors will be highly influential in terms of the nature of the policies that evolve. The numbers and character of the movements of people, the needs that they have, and the problems and opportunities they present will be key determinants in the nature of the international responses to refugees. Yet the policies that emerge are likely to differ in terms of the places, population, and capacities of the states involved. Elements of cooperation, containment, and proaction are thus likely to be reflected in different places around the world at different times.

The world has become relatively effective at reacting to crises by addressing the basic needs of individuals in distressed circumstances for food, clothing, and shelter. But such a narrow humanitarian approach necessarily condemns to repetition such charitable impulses in situations where proximate and underlying causes are not also mitigated. A new willingness by the international community to intervene has run up against frustrations and uncertainties about the use of the developed world's resources to attempt to address what sometimes appear to be perpetual quagmires of chaos and human insecurity. The obviously desirable preventive and cooperative approaches founder on the difficulties of realizing these broad prescriptions in specific situations.

For humanitarianism to contribute to human security, it must come to grips proactively with larger issues relating to sovereignty and trends in the movements of people. Strategies are difficult to realize, and some of the dilemmas created may, indeed, be insoluble in the present circumstances. But that is no excuse for not finding a way forward to address more than the immediate needs of individuals in distress, and to try to cultivate human security in situations of potential and actual crisis. A stronger capacity within the international community to think and do something about such situations is key to making progress.

There are many reasons for decision makers to embrace such an approach. But chief among them is a value indisputably coveted by states: stability in the system. This is a fundamental self-interest by which decision makers should justify longer-term approaches that strengthen guarantees of human security. The values associated with promoting human rights and humanitarianism, of course, are in and of themselves critically important. But foreign policy realists appreciate the abiding importance of stability, order, and prosperity. This in a basic sense is why refugees matter as well as the meaning of dealing with them.

The current political incoherence is reflected in policy incoherence in the United Nations system. For that reason, the UN is not likely to be a very useful setting for the development of these new capacities. NGOs are more likely to be the source of creativity and inspiration. Like-minded groupings of states pushed by their citizens to address the issues will then emerge as the bridge for change. These are the conceptual pillars for the recommendations made in the following chapters.

BETWEEN THE LIKELY AND THE DESIRABLE

As noted, the future is likely to contain elements of each of the above scenarios. In some circumstances, cooperation among states will be reflected in the responses to refugee emergencies. In others, containment strategies will be utilized. On occasion, political and military interventions will characterize the international response. In relation to all of these approaches, preventive orientations will emerge at times. But selectivity in response will be evident.

Containment as a trend in international responses is discernible in a variety of unilateral state responses, such as the current US programme to intercept at sea and return Chinese, Cubans, Dominicans, and Haitians to their home countries. Italy does the same with Albanians. The interrelationship of containment and international cooperation is illustrated particularly well by recent developments in the European Union to achieve a harmonized asylum policy. European politicians often decry abuse in asylum procedures. Yet, ironically, the use or misuse of asylum procedures to come to Europe is attributable largely to the absence of an explicit European migration policy. People migrate for many reasons, but chief among them are the desires to join family members or find employment. They undertake such journeys, sometimes with the aid of smugglers. If the asylum mechanism is the only one available, then they seek asylum. A market-driven transnational criminal enterprise emerges. The official response is usually a broad deterrence strategy, where population movements are generally discouraged and refugees are encouraged to seek asylum at the first available place where they can lodge a protection request. A harsh policy environment results which can deny refugee rights.

The new intervention trend was prefigured by UN Security Council Resolution 688, which created safe areas in Iraq for Kurds and Arabs. Resolution 688 was a seminal document in relation to the way the international community organizes responses to humanitarian emergencies. This extraordinary arrangement, motivated by political considerations and a sense of obligation to the Kurds who rose up after the defeat of Saddam Hussein in the Gulf War, prompted coalition forces to carve out a safe area in northern Iraq once Turkey had denied entry to asylum seekers at its border.

Intervention and containment interface where there are efforts to assist and protect internal exiles. On the one hand, providing such assistance and protection can forestall the departure of would-be asylum seekers. On the other hand, such an approach depends on access to the territory of a country, even perhaps without the consent of the governing authorities.

The preoccupation with the plight of internally displaced persons is a species of this new attention to the erstwhile internal affairs of states. The territorial barriers associated with sovereignty can no longer shield from attention the predicament of uprooted populations. Efforts are ongoing to find an appropriate legal framework and effective institutional mechanisms to help persons in these situations. However, such efforts must proceed against growing scepticism by developing countries about the erosion of national sovereignty and their suspicion that humanitarian motives could mask the political agendas of powerful states seeking to involve themselves in their internal affairs.

A containment strategy is not likely to be very effective unless it also addresses the proximate causes of displacement. Similarly, an intervention strategy is not likely to succeed unless sufficient time and resources are committed to building an enduring peace that addresses the underlying causes of displacement. This is where the notion of prevention comes into play. But the notion of introducing preventive action into reactive humanitarian responses has been largely a theoretical exercise, and little concrete action has resulted. An international conference concerning the former Soviet Union was undertaken in 1996 in the name of prevention, but the lack of engagement by key international institutions, most particularly the international financial institutions, precluded significant investment of resources in this endeavour. Small-scale information campaigns over the past decade to discourage unauthorized departures by Albanians, Romanians, and Vietnamese have been justified as tactical preventive measures. But prevention of the causes of forced displacement, or crisis and conflict more generally, has proven an elusive objective. The reactive character of the humanitarian system has meant that very little has been done or even thought about in this connection.

Emergency responses to humanitarian crises are not susceptible to single pre-formed answers. Humanitarian action after the cold war has become largely a management exercise founded on the unique characteristics of each situation, and informed, if at all, by broad principles relating to human rights, which for the most part have not been articulated in anything approaching operational guidelines. In part, this is due to the fact that humanitarian action is based on the notion of immediate reaction, perhaps seasoned with a pious hope that future disasters will not occur. This precludes investment in more systematic efforts to conceptualize new approaches. The last humanitarian response largely informs the next, and very little happens in terms of the accumulation of a body of doctrine to inform future action. But if this circumstance is not remedied by achieving more concerted proactive approaches, then the future of refugee policy is likely to remain largely a series of ad hoc responses characterized by situational frenzy.

FOSTERING INTERNATIONAL COOPERATION

International cooperation has long been an aspiration in refugee arrangements. Cooperative efforts have emerged in situations over the past decade involving particularly strong and capable states which have significant interests in solutions to refugee problems. This is so whether the solution is in the nature of resettlement, as illustrated in the cases of Indo-China and Macedonia, or in the discouragement of the arrival of asylum seekers and efforts to keep them closer to their home countries, as in the case of western Europe.

The resettlement of Indo-Chinese refugees, initially under an international compact concluded in 1979 and then re-conceived in 1989, involved a high degree of cooperation. The compact involved not only the countries of asylum to which refugees had fled but also the countries of origin from which they had fled. Cambodia, Laos, and Vietnam were thus party to these arrangements along with all of the surrounding countries of asylum. But the key actors were the countries of resettlement, led by the United States. These countries established generous programmes to find new permanent homes for Indo-Chinese refugees who had fled from the communist regimes that had emerged after the conflict in Indo-China ended. But these resettlement countries grew weary of what seemed to be an indefinite commitment that seemed increasingly unrelated to the refugee population of concern. They worried that the generosity of the relocation offer was luring asylum seekers to take dangerous journeys by boat with the hope of settling abroad, even if the individuals involved were not refugees with a well-founded fear of persecution. For that reason, the 1989 Comprehensive Plan of Action introduced screening and repatriation, including enforced return, into the policy mix.

Ultimately, some two million Indo-Chinese refugees were resettled. But this generosity was in some measure coerced. Large-scale resettlement followed from the willingness of the local authorities in the asylum countries to deny the rights of refugees by refusing to permit boat people to land, and either forcibly returning asylum seekers to their home countries or exposing them to hardships and dangers by redirecting them out to sea. Resettlement countries thus stepped in to fortify access to protection.

An even more recent example of international cooperation involved the relocation in 1999 of some 96,000 Kosovars from the former Yugoslav Republic of Macedonia to European and other countries outside the region, including the United States. This extraordinary programme was undertaken in order to lighten the political risks associated with demographic changes in that country in crisis. This resettlement effort, motivated mainly by political concerns which arose in the course of the NATO bombing campaign, helped to dissipate this threat. While some of the evacuated Kosovars have returned to Kosovo, most have remained abroad and are now rebuilding their lives in new home countries.

The political and economic harmonization in Europe provides another example of efforts to achieve international cooperation relating to refugees, perhaps the most ambitious such endeavour to date. The attempt to formulate a common immigration and asylum policy under the aegis of the European Union reflects this new concerted effort. Cooperation, of course, is not necessarily synonymous with generosity. In western Europe, it has been directed mainly at enforcement measures designed to frustrate the arrival of asylum seekers and to encourage them either to remain in their home country or locate in a nearby country of asylum. These European barriers are spreading eastward as western European states strike deals with their counterparts to the east requiring that they accept back nationals and foreigners who transited through their territories in return for financial and technical assistance.

These efforts in south-east Asia, Macedonia, and western Europe to apportion humanitarian responsibilities have benefited both states and individuals. In addition, while there are clear problems, the practice of states to protect and assist refugees is widespread. And virtually all states have an interest in limiting their exposure to unanticipated refugee arrivals. These are the ingredients out of which to forge a greater degree of international cooperation in refugee policy.

But states have not yet made general commitments in advance to share the burdens and responsibilities associated with the uprooted. Over the past decade, such schemes have evolved in specific situations when other options were not available, such as the Indo-Chinese resettlement programme, the humanitarian evacuation programme from Macedonia, and even the internal safe areas created in northern Iraq.

In large part, international cooperation has foundered because it is not clear to what extent it is actually a 'burden' to accept refugees. Immediate impacts on localities can be serious. In relatively rare circumstances, a country's political stability or national security can be threatened. However, over time, newcomers who integrate into new home countries generally contribute to the societies in which they arrive, including economically.

Additionally, states consider themselves as already contributing in a variety of ways to addressing humanitarian and refugee emergencies, whether through the provision of material relief, contributions to peace operations, or undertaking military or diplomatic initiatives. Even allowing access to the labour market and the resulting moneys sent home by migrant workers in the form of remittances might qualify in this regard. There is, however, no consensus on how to calculate the contributions already made. For this reason, models of refugee burden-sharing schemes premised narrowly on the redistribution of people have remained in the province of academic theory, and are not likely to be realized in the foreseeable future.[3]

A broader recognition by states of the utility of cooperating to limit the risks of adverse impacts associated with the reception of asylum seekers, or to maximize the positive contributions newcomers can make to a society, will have to await a greater appreciation of the value of a more regular migration scheme in a world with a burgeoning population and increased movements of people. International cooperation will likely play a greater role in future responses to humanitarian and refugee emergencies, as international migration grows and population displacements become larger. This realization is likely to be forced incrementally by continuing humanitarian catastrophes and population displacements. While it may be difficult to implement cooperative schemes in the throes of crisis, the continuing occurrence of emergencies of increasing magnitude, coupled with the inadequacy of other responses, will inevitably encourage a greater degree of responsibility sharing and agreements in advance of crises.

Are there lessons in terms of how to foster international cooperation concerning forced migration that can be learned from other sectors of human endeavour? Undoubtedly. Cooperation, while embryonic in relation to human displacement, is a well-established feature in other sectors. These include the realms of finance and trade, environment, health, and international law enforcement. While generalizable insights must be necessarily tentative, given the wide diversity of factors involved, it is clear that international cooperation can result either from responses to rapid-onset crises or the evolution over time of structures to perceived threats. Participants

[3] See, for example, Hathaway, James and Neve, R. Alexander, 'Making International Refugee Law Relevant Again: A Proposal for Collectivized and Solution-Oriented Protection', *Harvard Human Rights Journal*, 10 (1997), 115–211. See also Schuck, Peter H., 'Refugee Burden Sharing: A Modest Proposal', *Yale Journal of International Law*, 22 (1997), 243–97.

join such compacts in order to limit exposure to risks and to derive measurable benefits. In order to foster international cooperation on refugee arrangements, a mechanism like the intergovernmental Strategic Humanitarian Action and Research (SHARE) entity proposed in the book is needed to map these interests and incentives in the area of refugee protection.

The development of a scheme for states to share the responsibilities associated with forced displacement would require a clear assessment of the varieties of interests and incentives which will vary in particular settings. For that reason, a process is needed, not a model or fixed formula. Research and policy discussions are needed, whether on universal, regional, or sub-regional bases. The SHARE mechanism could be a catalyst for these inquiries. SHARE also could facilitate regional or sub-regional negotiations on issues of responsibility and burden sharing. Such deliberations would require both a comprehensive examination of trends and issues of international forced migration and a more precise calibration of the contributions made by affected governments and their societies in response to emergencies, through activities such as providing humanitarian and development assistance, military deployments, or remittances from abroad. Out of this practice by states, a norm may emerge as well as ultimately a sense of international legal obligation.

10

Achieving Comprehensive and Proactive Refugee Policy

> Over the last decade, the United Nations has repeatedly failed to meet the challenge: and it can do no better today. Without significant institutional change, increased financial support and renewed commitment on the part of Member States, the United Nations will not be capable of executing the critical peacekeeping and peace-building tasks that the Member States assign to it in the coming months and years.
>
> —From the 17 August 2000 'Report of the Panel on United Nations Peace Operations' (Brahimi Report)

Today's refugee crises take place in a new challenging global context. The increased dimensions of human displacement and the higher costs of humanitarian responses, the prominence of internal conflicts, a new willingness by certain like-minded states to become involved and deploy military forces, evolving concepts of sovereignty, searching media coverage, and the changing nature of warfare are all factors which have altered the landscape for humanitarian action. These elements, coupled with bureaucratic inertia, the emergence of an international human rights agenda, increased risks to aid workers, the convergence of humanitarian and political objectives, new military roles, and the relationship between relief and development, will combine to animate humanitarian policy in the new century.

International forced migration is on the rise, and increasingly is seen as a source of insecurity to both states and individuals. In 2001, there were 19 'complex emergencies', a term coined in Mozambique in the latter half of the 1980s to signify conflict-related crises.[1] Some 44 million persons were affected, and the aggregate costs of responses are rising.[2] For example,

[1] OECD-Development Assistance Committee, *Guidance for Evaluating Humanitarian Assistance in Complex Emergencies* (Paris: OECD, 1999), 5.

[2] United Nations Office for the Coordination of Humanitarian Affairs, *Humanitarian Action in 2001: A Mid-year Review for 19 Complex Emergencies* (Geneva: OCHA, 22 May 2001).

annual humanitarian assistance from the United States government alone exceeded $2.5 billion in 1999 during the Kosovo crisis.[3]

Among the causes of conflict, issues of ethnic or communal identity have become prominent, as witnessed by conflicts over the past decade in Africa, Asia, south-east Europe, and the former Soviet Union. A basic pattern emerges: a dominant ethnic majority represses a minority. This in turn engenders and reinforces group identity and perceptions of injustice. Resistance follows, and all too frequently leads to armed conflict, usually internal to a country. There have been recent crises in Africa, the southern Balkans, and Indonesia which could erupt again and spread. Indeed, a large number of states, particularly in Africa and Eurasia, have the makings of such conflicts. Whether they occur depends upon a myriad of factors.

The changing nature of warfare shapes policy responses. Most, but not all, humanitarian crises stem from internal ethnic and separatist wars in which combatants seek as a deliberate strategy to engage in displacement by design. Added to the continuing phenomenon of internal conflict, new kinds of external conflicts are likely as well, particularly occasional international military expeditions to fight terrorist networks, which may result in population displacements.

The conflict-related internally displaced are now estimated to number approximately 25 million persons worldwide. While there is some evidence indicating that the number and intensity of internal conflicts are decreasing, the quantitative aspects are not determinative. It takes only one high-profile emergency to divert all the time and attention of decision makers away from other important business. Indeed, a situation of fewer crises to which to respond might actually encourage more international involvements. A focus will therefore remain on such humanitarian catastrophes, which will continue to be a driving factor for the foreseeable future.

At the same time, new trends of humanitarian action are evident. For example, while still exceptional, military deployments motivated by humanitarian reasons are now sometimes seen as necessary to advancing important national interests and values. Such forcible interventions have ramifications that will undoubtedly shape responses to future conflicts.

New forms of humanitarian action correspond as well to the erosion of certain state prerogatives because of the forces of technology and globalization. Information and capital move without regard to territorial boundaries. But this dynamic is not limited to the realm of electronic signals. Border

[3] US Department of State, *Interagency Review of U.S. Government Civilian Humanitarian & Transition Programs* (Washington, DC: US Department of State, January 2000), 6.

controls, for example, are increasingly frustrated by the ease of international migration.

In addition, emergency responses now occur in the glare of intensified media coverage, which is characterized by accelerated and real-time communications directly from inside crisis situations. The harsh realities of mass human suffering are transmitted directly to the homes of aroused electorates in democratic states. Such constituents then call upon decision makers for effective responses. These visual images stimulate intense domestic political pressure to act quickly and effectively.

The increased willingness of states to become involved and intervene is a consequence of the human rights agenda in the post-cold war era. Complex emergencies often force the international community to confront urgent human rights issues, including how to cope with evidence of war crimes and genocide, as well as how to ensure that humanitarian relief does not become an instrument of abuse in situations of conflict. Peacekeeping has sometimes evolved into peace enforcement, as reflected in Sierra Leone, as well as state building, as reflected in Bosnia, East Timor, and Kosovo. Complicated questions concerning how or whether NGOs can remain impartial and neutral in the midst of complex operations with a military component have emerged in the debates of humanitarians.

Civilian humanitarian responses over the past decade have become increasingly dependent upon military capabilities, including for logistical and security assistance. There are many hard lessons learned in places like eastern Zaire—now the Democratic Republic of Congo—Rwanda, and Somalia, where humanitarian implications and issues were not adequately factored into military and political decision making. Indeed, political-military operations designed and executed in isolation from humanitarian ramifications have on occasion had catastrophic unintended consequences, with Kosovo being the paradigmatic case.

Governments also increasingly interrelate humanitarian and foreign policies. High-profile cases over the past decade demonstrate that actions to address humanitarian crises have become interlinked with foreign policy goals, such as democratization, respect for human rights, regional stability, control over weapons of mass destruction, preservation of development investments, and consolidation of societal transitions from war to peace. Emphasis is often placed on conflict prevention, although this goal remains elusive and difficult to realize in practice.

International institutional responses are evolving incrementally, but fundamental reform is not likely in the near future. A programmatic distinction between refugees and internally displaced persons, founded on the UN refugee treaty regime, is no longer viable. The UN

Secretary-General's special representative has done much to profile the issue, and an inter-agency review within the UN system on internal displacement programming was undertaken in 2001. In practice, UNHCR and many other agencies, such as the UNICEF, WFP, and IOM, as well as a wide variety of NGOs, often deal with populations beyond the category of refugees. A focus on internal exiles is a central feature of the work of the International Committee of the Red Cross. Because the legal and institutional frameworks dealing with internal displacement are not adequate, coordination becomes a paramount consideration. This highlights the activities of the UN Emergency Relief Coordinator and the UN Office for the Coordination of Humanitarian Affairs. But this problem is a policy wound which is sure to grow and which will produce pressure for more effective concerted action.

Furthermore, the link between responses to complex emergencies and longer-term development objectives is being increasingly highlighted, particularly in post-conflict settings. This results in efforts to find new funding strategies in a general climate of diminishing resources. How these issues are addressed will say much about the nature of humanitarianism in the new century.

The 2000 Brahimi report on reform of UN peace operation, introduced earlier in this book, emphasized the need for clear, credible, and achievable mandates for international action. Honesty by the bureaucracy is seen as a key ingredient to workable mission deployments: 'The Secretariat must tell the Security Council what it needs to know, not what it wants to hear, when formulating or changing mission mandates . . . ', the report urges.[4]

Of course, peace operations mandates should be clear. But it is unrealistic to suggest that diplomats hold up peace agreements until clarity in the terms of a peacekeeping mandate is achieved. Ambiguity is often key in diplomatic efforts to finesse differences and postpone resolution of difficult issues in order to consolidate progress toward a final settlement. While they can be decried, imperfections in these circumstances are likely to be the norm, and it is naive to suggest that the United Nations can 'just say no' to powerful member states. Instead, what is needed is a more capable international system to undertake these responsibilities.

As this book demonstrates, the current system for international humanitarian action is fundamentally flawed. Whether the UN system can rise to the occasion will tell the tale of humanitarianism in the new century. UNDP, for example, has ambitious plans to expand its Emergency

[4] 'Report of the Panel on United Nations Peace Operations' (Brahimi Report), UN Doc. A/55/305-S/2000/809 (21 August 2000), x.

Response Division and establish a post-conflict recovery fund. Indeed, the Brahimi report observes that UNDP has 'untapped potential' in the implementation of peace-building strategies.[5] Some commentators familiar with international humanitarian action admit to being baffled by this reference. Brahimi himself explained in late 2000 that this did not mean that 'new functions' would be given to UNDP but that the UN agencies 'would work together a little better'.

The Brahimi report also makes a proposal, without specifics, 'for the United Nations to reach out to civil society and to strengthen relations with non-governmental organizations, academic institutions, and the media who can be useful partners in the promotion of peace and security for all'.[6] Many of the innovations proposed in the report, moreover, are hardly radical. 'It could have been bolder', said a serving Special Representative of the Secretary-General of the report's recommendations. It will not be enough to tinker with the system.

BACK TO BASICS AND ON TO THE FUTURE: UNHCR

The primary international institution involved with refugees is the United Nations High Commissioner for Refugees (UNHCR), which was established in 1950 to protect and assist refugees and supervise the implementation of the UN refugee treaty regime. In the 1990s, UNHCR grew into an agency with staff exceeding 5,000 employees and an annual budget of more than $1 billion.[7] Conceived of initially as a temporary office to deal with residual displacement in the aftermath of the Second World War, UNHCR has become an ordinary and necessary facet of international responses to refugee and humanitarian emergencies. The recent course of UNHCR's evolution, moreover, says much about the development of the modern humanitarian order.

UNHCR was created in large measure to consolidate the international effort to resettle displaced persons from Europe after the Second World War and upon the rise of the cold war. The refugee treaty definition, with its individualized persecution requirement, was designed to facilitate resettlement by avoiding the need for the ad hoc categorization of displaced

[5] 'Report of the Panel on United Nations Peace Operations', 8.

[6] 'Report of the Panel on United Nations Peace Operations', 45.

[7] 'UNHCR and Refugees'. At: http://www.unhcr.ch/un&ref/what/what.htm#Finding the funds. See also 'What is UNHCR?'. At: http://www.nato.int/sfor/indexinf/84/ogata/t000327a.htm

persons. UNHCR was thus linked instrumentally to the refugee definition and the post-Second World War East-West confrontation. The agency, for example, became a key player in the post-1956 Hungarian refugee exodus which followed the abortive revolution there.

After helping countries to receive and resettle Hungarian refugees, UNHCR's focus shifted to areas outside Europe. 'UNHCR is an African, a Southeast Asian, a Central American agency', said an experienced UNHCR programme official in 2000. The involvement of UNHCR in Eurasia after the dissolution of the Soviet Union was thus difficult, said this official, who worked on relief programming in Tajikistan and Afghanistan. UNHCR's protection mandate has sometimes been distended by these new realities. Before 1991 in the mountains of northern Iraq, it was 'heresy to work in a country of origin'. The operational imperatives in such exercises had profound consequences on how UNHCR interpreted its protection responsibilities. 'I wanted to get people warm', said this UNHCR programme colleague of his logistical work in northern Iraq, 'doctrine to follow'.

The question of UNHCR's relevance has been a continuing debate. Donor governments, principally the European Union, Japan, and the United States, which together accounted for more than 80 per cent of UNHCR's budget in the 1990s, have pressed UNHCR to deal with the variety of humanitarian emergencies that have arisen over the past decade.[8] In this regard, UNHCR has been asked by donors to play an increasing role in the home countries of would-be refugees, thus avoiding the arrival of uninvited asylum claimants. UNHCR officials often equivocated in the face of such requests, citing mandate limitations and responsibilities under the UN treaties to offer legal protection to asylum seekers. The frustrations caused by the failure of a meeting of the minds between UNHCR and donor governments inspired continuing concerns about UNHCR's role in relation to new directions in humanitarian action. On the other side of the debate, NGOs have criticized UNHCR for a weakened commitment to conventional refugee protection. The agency has often been the voice of voiceless refugees around the world. But, over the past decade, the agency has on several occasions been criticized for having fallen silent in the face of violations of refugee protection, as with the forced return of Rwandan refugees in 1996 from Tanzania.[9]

A recent dramatic example of UNHCR's new internal deployment as a humanitarian response was in 1992 in Bosnia and Herzegovina, which

[8] UNHCR, 'UNHCR Seeks 953.7 Million to Help Uprooted, Press Release' (Geneva: UNHCR, 15 December 2000). At: http://www.unhcr.ch/news/pr/pr001215.htm

[9] Loescher, Gil, *The UNHCR and World Politics: A Perilous Path* (Oxford: Oxford University Press, 2001), 311–12.

the agency justified initially with the phrase 'protection by presence'.[10] UNHCR air drops and truck convoys delivered assistance to two million persons in Bosnia who were affected by the war, including being forced from their homes. Negotiations by UNHCR staff with Serb forces to enable the delivery of assistance or provision of protection were often excruciating. This was coupled with a concomitant call by UNHCR for 'temporary protection' arrangements in Europe outside the ambit of the UN refugee treaties, which states found attractive in order to maximize their discretion to require return after the crisis had abated.

UNHCR came to regard its deployment in Bosnia as a misuse of humanitarian aid as a substitute for decisive political or military action. The notion of 'humanitarianism' itself as a response came to be discredited in the eyes of many commentators.

Many at UNHCR with whom I spoke in 2000 described it as a tired agency. The past decade has buffeted around the agency and its unique mandate to protect refugees and ensure that their basic rights are respected. In the face of concerns by states about UNHCR's relevance to the new realities of human security and forced migration, the agency has embarked on a broad programme of consultations on issues of refugee protection on the occasion of the 50th anniversary of the 1951 UN refugee treaty. This will involve the first meeting ever of state parties to the UN refugee treaties. But NGOs worry that the impact of this assemblage on principles of refugee protection will be negative.

In addition, a financial crisis is looming. The future of UNHCR as the institutional centrepiece of refugee protection has been drawn into question by budgetary pressures. Unreliable and diminished funding has caused UNHCR's 2001 budget to be cut by $130 million—14 per cent—and 939 posts to be eliminated, many in Africa.[11] There has been a particularly steep decrease in contributions from the European Commission to the agency: from $95 million during the height of the Kosovo crisis in 1999 to $38.4 million in 2000, in part reflecting disenchantment with the agency's below-par performance during that crisis.[12]

But the problem runs deeper. While 1999 was a recent peak in terms of funding by ECHO related to Kosovo, even in that year it did not represent a significant overall increase in contributions by the Commission to UNHCR.

[10] Statement by Mrs Sadako Ogata, United Nations High Commissioner for Refugees, at the ICRC/UNHCR meeting in Geneva (19 February 1992).

[11] UNHCR, 'Under-Funding Forces UNHCR to Cut Back, Refocus', Press Release (Geneva: UNHCR, 1 June 2001).

[12] Bacon, Kenneth H. and Freih, Loubna, 'Europe is Turning Its Back on the World's Refugees', *International Herald Tribune* (20 June 2001).

The relatively high level of Commission contributions from 1992 to 1995—an average of over $200 million a year—during the wars of secession in the former Yugoslavia and after the genocide in Rwanda is not likely to be replicated anytime soon. The funding downturn is thus the product of systematic reductions by the Commission and several 'under performing' EU member states, in UNHCR's view. According to ECHO staff, the total contribution in 2000 to UNHCR from the European Union—member states and ECHO—was $251 million, compared with $245 million from the US.

As a consequence of funding shortfalls, UNHCR has had to undertake a 'right sizing' exercise to identify UNHCR's core activities, slash expenditures, and identify additional revenue sources. On 26 June 2001, UNHCR proposed an $828 million budget which the High Commissioner characterized as 'the absolute minimum', urging a more regular budget process and calling for donors to continue to contribute one dollar or one euro per citizen.[13] That same day, the agency requested $17.5 million to cope with the growing consequences of conflict in Macedonia.[14] By October 2001, UNHCR had received an additional $26 million to prepare for an emerging humanitarian crisis in Afghanistan.[15]

While many UNHCR staff are upset, refugees will feel more acute pain. Most unprotected internal exiles are likely to remain outside UNHCR's work. In addition, efforts to strengthen the self-sufficiency and promote the re-integration of refugees in situations of prolonged exile, particularly in Africa, are likely to wane under budgetary pressure.

A NEW HIGH COMMISSIONER FOR REFUGEES

Ruud Lubbers never wanted to be UN High Commissioner for Refugees. Lubbers, a professor of globalization in the Netherlands and that country's prime minister for twelve years until 1994, was surprised when Kofi Annan, the UN Secretary-General, asked him in late 2000 to take this position. The Secretary-General's selection process was decidedly opaque, with rumours of names circulating for several months before Lubbers was tapped.

In early 2001 in New York, Lubbers began a round of consultations with several governments and NGO representatives. In February, he visited West Africa, where UNHCR was grappling with the forced displacement of

[13] Lubbers, Ruud, United Nations High Commissioner for Refugees, Statement at the Standing Committee (Geneva: UNHCR, 26 June 2001).

[14] 'UNHCR Concerned over Deepening Refugee Crisis', UNHCR News Release (Geneva: 26 June 2001).

[15] UNHCR, 'Afghanistan Humanitarian Update—No. 13' (Geneva: 4 October 2001), 1.

some 250,000 persons. Of course, this was but the first of what will be many crises and emergencies on his watch, some of which will be much higher in profile and imbued with more powerful geo-political interests.

When we met in Geneva on an early Friday morning in January 2001, Lubbers, craggy-featured with distinctive bushy eyebrows, talked at length about the challenges he would face. We sat in his elegantly furnished seventh-floor office at UNHCR headquarters, a modern grey stone and glass atrium building. The weather was clearing after a night of cold rain, and it was one of those occasions in Geneva when you could see the wall of mountains surrounding the city. The World Economic Forum was opening that day in Davos, but Lubbers had decided not to go, opting instead to begin work at UNHCR, including interviewing several candidates for the position of Deputy High Commissioner for Refugees. The deputy position, with just a brief recent interruption, has traditionally been reserved for a US national.

Lubbers explained that he plans to adapt UNHCR to contemporary global developments. His ambition is for UNHCR to become a genuine multilateral institution. This includes expanding universal coverage of the refugee protection regime by promoting the signing of the UN refugee treaties by states, particularly in the Middle East and Asia.

But more than formal treaty arrangements are on Lubbers's mind. The impetus for UNHCR came initially from a number of western European states, a kind of 'coalition of the willing', in today's parlance of humanitarian action, and the agency has become a mechanism through which a discrete group of relatively wealthy donor states seek to help refugees and displaced persons on a somewhat selective basis. Lubbers noted that in the decade of the 1990s, 'We did a lot, and UNHCR expanded according to these ambitions.' But support for such initiatives was not sustained and was available only on a case-by-case basis, depending upon the selective interests of the governments involved; indeed, perhaps 'a little bit too selective' in his view. 'We did good, but not enough', said Lubbers, indicating that what he means by 'globalizing' the agency is to marshal support for the refugee regime in the future from a broad array of states.

Lubbers said that he must consider the concerns of governments on whether the refugee treaties were still relevant. Previewing his thinking, though, he admitted that he is likely to find they are still 'good'. But the treaties clearly do not address all of the issues, which is the rationale for a meeting of states to reaffirm and perhaps elaborate upon the 1951 UN refugee convention on its 50th anniversary in December 2001.

Noting that UNHCR's core activity is to protect refugees, Lubbers also sees a role for the agency in the broader arena of humanitarian action.

Specifically, he cited the interrelationship of humanitarian as well as diplomatic and peacekeeping endeavours, and the need for 'good cooperation with politicians and the military'. Within the UN system, this particularly means a relationship with the Department of Peacekeeping Operations and the emerging security structures in the European Union, 'which does not realize that we are partners or at least has a problem to translate that into action and financial support'. He cited as an example the fact that the European Union is internally investing huge sums on its asylum systems and immigration control systems, but has spent relatively little, and not in a coherent way, to address forced displacement in broader and more effective ways.

Dealing with the needs of people in post-conflict settings clearly requires cooperation with other international organizations. Lubbers referred to the Brookings process, an effort discussed in detail elsewhere in this book and led by UNDP, UNHCR, and the World Bank, which has the goal of narrowing the gap between emergency humanitarian assistance and long-term development in devastated post-conflict societies. He was, however, sober in his assessment of what could be done. 'My impression is we should see what we can do within concrete categories and be very practical in how we assist specific groups with projects.' Often development is discussed in macroeconomic terms and not in terms of empowering people; these should not be considered 'abstract' issues, he emphasized.

On the issue of helping internally displaced persons, Lubbers noted problems with respect to how such persons had been dealt with in the past, but he was cautious. He recalled UNHCR's established criteria, which are set forth in a 1993 policy statement and which identify as crucial such factors as the numbers of persons affected, a request for involvement by the UN Secretary-General, the consent of the home country, and the availability of donor funds for such operations.

His preference in terms of UNHCR involvement on issues of internal displacement is for a pragmatic, case-by-case approach. He was pushed on the issue in his brief meeting with Ambassador Richard Holbrooke, then the US representative to the UN, when he visited New York in January 2001. Holbrooke asked him whether he was committed to the cause of internal exiles and assured him that 'we are partners'. But Lubbers was clearly sceptical about whether the resources would be forthcoming from governments for such work.

Lubbers recognizes that the need for better legal and institutional arrangements to assist and protect internally displaced persons will continue to be featured in ongoing debates. The issue is being addressed conceptually in the 'human rights tradition' with the elaboration of guiding principles under UN auspices, and bureaucratically through an inter-agency review of the activities of various UN agencies. He cited repatriation schemes that served to encourage refugees to return to situations of internal displacement, and the continuing responsibility of the international community for those dislocated people.

Lubbers understandably focused on the need for additional financial resources to discharge his responsibilities. Clearly, UNHCR has to streamline itself and find ways to outsource activities among other UN agencies—notably UNICEF and WFP—as well as NGOs. On exactly how the size of the agency would be reduced, he said: 'Come back next year.' Of course, a humanitarian catastrophe could intervene which would require urgently increasing its size once again. The need for a surge capacity in the agency was a lesson drawn from a 1999 review of UNHCR's experience in Kosovo.

UNHCR in Lubbers's view should play more of a role as a coordinator and author of protection standards. 'We can lecture countries about human rights', he allowed, but as it stands now he is afraid that the budgetary shortfall will mean that minimum standards relating to humanitarian assistance are likely to be compromised, a prospective outcome which he finds 'not acceptable, and an outrage'.

Lubbers hopes for support from a group of emerging philanthropists like Ted Turner and Bill Gates, whom he planned to invite to work with UNHCR. As a student of globalization, Lubbers was particularly keen to see new links with business enterprises and NGOs to help address refugee problems. He sees globalization as having built great wealth, but with an underside that fosters instability and deprivation. A comprehensive approach is needed to build the capacity to look after people in misery, whether they be refugees or internally displaced persons. And this is not a problem just for politicians. The wealth of the world should be made available more systematically, working in tandem with new interlocutors in the NGO and private sectors.

Lubbers was keenly aware of the fact that some NGOs have charged UNHCR with being 'arrogant' and duplicating work that they believe they have adequate resources to do more efficiently. Indeed, at a January 2001 round-table meeting in New York there were representatives of three NGOs, which together had budgets equalling that of UNHCR. He also noted that UNHCR had been charged by NGOs with not giving sufficient priority to its core protection functions. But he was mystified by this criticism. Lubbers describes himself as a 'no-nonsense' former prime minister who seeks to be a 'no-nonsense' High Commissioner. In this regard, he is drawn to practical answers to particular problems. When NGOs ask him to do more on protection, he wants to know what it is that he is specifically being asked to do. What precisely is the problem?

When Secretary-General Annan offered the appointment to Lubbers, he sought assurances that Lubbers would have time not only for UNHCR but also for its sister agencies and the UN system more generally. Lubbers explained that the Secretary-General places great value on teamwork and an 'open attitude'. It is the success of the UN system and its components, and not just UNHCR, which is at issue, an attitude which some observers have found lacking in UNHCR's approach in the recent past. Lubbers's political acumen and experience with compromise should go some way toward repairing inter-agency tensions, which reached a crescendo during UN organizational reform efforts over the past decade. But he admitted that other UN agencies and offices were still 'a bit concerned' about UNHCR's non-collaborative style.

Lubbers contrasted his responsibilities with those of the 'world of power' which was meeting not so very far away at Davos as we spoke that day; 'I am very much in that world', he explained. He describes his primary role as simple: to protect refugees. But the context is very challenging. Globalization has been criticized by protesters in Seattle, Davos, and Genoa as neither good nor fair. Refugee work is a concrete way to address the misery of people by investing resources in the weakest and empowering them. This means not just organizing charity but also the need for more enduring structural reforms. 'We must live and act as an example for others', said Lubbers.

THE PROPOSAL: AN INTERGOVERNMENTAL MECHANISM FOR STRATEGIC HUMANITARIAN ACTION AND RESEARCH (SHARE)

This book urges the creation of an intergovernmental mechanism for Strategic Humanitarian Action and Research (SHARE), which would be a policy research centre designed to add value to the international humanitarian system by promoting proactive approaches before crises erupt, advocating comprehensive protection for uprooted persons through appropriate policy responses, and planning human security strategies to encourage the lasting return of refugees and displaced persons. The activities of this entity correspond to the gaps in the field of international humanitarian action demonstrated in the cases and circumstances examined in this book.

SHARE would have a deep conceptualizing capacity with a small core staff which could draw upon expert consultants. It would be a repository of expertise related to humanitarian management issues before a crisis erupts, during an emergency, and after a disturbance abates. Put another way,

SHARE would be the international locus for the manufacture and refinement of the tools necessary for new forms of humanitarian action. A myriad of possible initiatives are suggested by the experience of the past decade; from encouraging sub-regional dialogues on reform of property and citizenship policy in the former Yugoslavia to ease the voluntary return of refugees and dislocated persons, to promoting strategies designed to strengthen the sustainability of indigenous NGOs in Cambodia, Haiti, and East Timor. Its exact functions would depend upon the specific situation and the stage of the crisis in question, as detailed below.

SHARE would complement the work of others and have linkages with specialized agencies in the UN system, notably UNDP, UNHCHR, UNHCR, and UNICEF, as well as in the UN Secretariat, notably OCHA, DPA, and DPKO. There would also be appropriate linkages with the Bretton Woods institutions, ICRC, relevant regional organizations, as well as NGOs and the private sector. SHARE could even be conceived of as an advisory mechanism serving the UN Secretary-General.

SHARE is really a category of activities under which there are several bundles of tasks which could be addressed depending upon donor and recipient country interests. Indeed, it is an expression of the ultimate objective of making humanitarian action more capable, including by infusing refugee policy with a preventive orientation and using the humanitarian imperative to promote earlier and more effective political action. Even partial progress on these points would result in important policy improvements.

As envisaged here, SHARE would be an expert entity and an intellectual resource, not a political body. In UN peace operations, it would provide services under the authority of the United Nations, including where appropriate a Security Council resolution. Where relevant, SHARE could be called upon by a Special Representative of the Secretary-General to provide a strategic resource in peace operations on humanitarian issues not adequately addressed by existing institutions.

The placement of SHARE outside the UN system would avoid having these initiatives smothered by a cumbersome and often dysfunctional bureaucracy. The creation of this new mechanism could also escape the increasing political polarization between industrialized and developing countries in the UN, which has surfaced repeatedly in relation to recent debates on humanitarian policy. Many in the developing world are sceptical of the motivations behind recent humanitarian initiatives. In the words of Lakhdar Brahimi in 2000, peace operations are often seen as 'a kind of conspiracy by developed countries to infringe on their sovereignty'. Establishing a new entity is warranted and is likely to be easier than seeking, for example, to reform existing institutions or to revitalize the UN's Trusteeship Council or mandate arrangements, which have unfortunate connotations related to the era of colonialism. SHARE would provide an intergovernmental forum for a like-minded coalition of states, whether wealthy or impoverished, to work together to address issues of human security in the context of forced migration.

If possible, the UN system should be reformed and made to work. But it is not at all obvious that such reforms can be made and sustained in the field of humanitarian action. For example, even relatively modest adjustments in UN personnel rules designed to better match staff with emergency needs have not been effectuated. If the proposal for SHARE is seriously pursued, it might actually provoke more effective UN action out of a sense of bureaucratic threat and institutional self-preservation.

Another reason to situate SHARE outside the UN is that much of the action is outside the UN: witness NATO and the Office of the High Representative in Bosnia and Herzegovina, or crisis-management facilities in Europe, discussed earlier in this book. To place such an effort within the UN would risk depriving it of important interlocutors. By way of illustration, because the High Representative in Bosnia is not in the UN system, he was not asked to contribute to the Brahimi peacekeeping report despite the obvious relevance of his work.

International agencies may assert that they are already doing some or all of these things, and some critics will decry the establishment of what they may characterize as yet another layer of bureaucracy. But this is not the case. SHARE is envisaged as a small and flexible collection of expertise. Moreover, the decade of experience surveyed in this book shows the existence of indisputable and critical gaps in the capacity of the currently configured international system to undertake effective humanitarian action, which this new entity would be designed to address.

Indeed, SHARE should appeal to international and regional organizations, which could use it as a mechanism to support and enhance their work. This new centre should also appeal to governments as an intellectual resource to draw upon in order to plan concerted strategic humanitarian action. Governments are, of course, already engaged in humanitarian initiatives, albeit increasingly on a bilateral basis. SHARE would provide a forum for more effective donor coordination and collaboration with recipient countries.

SHARE ought to be intergovernmental in character in order to ensure both political legitimacy and a sufficient funding base from donor governments that are increasingly reluctant to support UN peace operations. High-level support from important governments would be crucial. Even a modest initial budget of $10 million should permit a sufficient repertoire of pilot projects and activities—some of which are detailed here—to show the worth of the new approach.

An analogy to such a mechanism is provided by the history of the International Organization for Migration (IOM), which was established originally as a committee of governments in 1951 and which as of June 2001 was governed and financed by a group of 86 member states.[16] IOM is not treaty-based but rather reflects the collective interests of state members. IOM, however, is not a candidate for the new function proposed here because it is primarily operational and not a research entity. IOM has been involved in 25 emerging and post-conflict situations in the 1990s, ranging from assistance to demobilizing combatants to the electoral registration of Kosovars outside Kosovo. Indeed, one of its highest-profile activities was the assistance which the agency provided in repatriating 150,000 stranded foreign nationals during the Gulf crisis in 1990 and 1991.[17]

Initial efforts along the lines of SHARE are likely to emerge first from NGOs and researchers.[18] Indeed, this mechanism would amplify and not supplant these independent sector efforts. SHARE would work ordinarily as an inside provider of advisory and technical services, and not as an outside critic, a role particularly appropriate for NGOs.

What could be a work programme for SHARE? The Brahimi report urges the achievement of 'a preventive orientation in UN operations', a theme picked up in the June 2001 Report of the Secretary-General on the prevention of armed conflict.[19] A preventive course requires not only diplomacy in the narrow sense but often a mixture of political, social, and economic elements dictated by the particular circumstances of the specific situation. In one venue, language or citizenship policy may be crucial; in another, education policy or cultural revival for minorities or ethnic groups; and in still another, general human rights protection and ensuring accountability in order to curtail impunity for violations. This is by no means an exclusive list. What is missing in the UN system is a coherent approach to developing preventive strategies in situations where missions are deployed.

[16] 'IOM Members and Observers'. At: http://www.iom.int/iom/Mandate_and_Structure/Mem_&obs_engl.htm

[17] 'A Brief History of IOM's Fifty Years'. At: http://www.iom.int/iom/ Mandate_ and_ Structure /entry.htm

[18] Such as the work of the International Crisis Group, see: http://www.crisisweb.org, or the proposal for a Strategic Recovery Facility by the NYU Center on International Cooperation at: http://www.cic.nyu.edu

[19] 'Prevention of Armed Conflict', Report of the Secretary-General, UN Doc. A/55/985–S/2001/574 (7 June 2001).

In the period before crisis, therefore, SHARE would draw upon existing information and resources to develop proactive strategies to avert or mitigate emergencies in possible 'hot spots'. Information is abundant and there is no need to build a new collection system. But what is known is not often fashioned into realistic policy options. Another function of SHARE would be to advocate ameliorative strategies to decision makers. As this book has demonstrated, the humanitarian system, including conventional refugee policy, is deeply reactive. SHARE would assemble expertise to formulate proactive strategies which are sensitive to local situations. This could include, for example, appropriate advance burden and responsibility-sharing arrangements relating to asylum seekers, like those explored unsuccessfully by the US in the throes of crises involving Haitian boat people in the 1990s. The objective would be to give decision makers more humanitarian response options.

Refugee policy should surely be more than the administration of misery. Human displacement calls for more proactive efforts to forestall or mitigate humanitarian catastrophes. In some instances, the prospect of a refugee emergency adds weight to the need for more effective political action. In early 2001, when Macedonia began to haemorrhage refugees, a proactive approach would have featured a peace-building plan then to deal both with immediate security issues and with more enduring issues related to equity and justice. A pre-emptive military and police deployment of EU forces under a nascent European crisis-response mechanism, like that which occurred in 1991 under UN auspices, could have been used early on to help promote and enforce peace. Strategies would have followed to manage the inter-ethnic dialogue in Macedonia in an effort to counter trends toward polarization. In fact, a NATO effort emerged along these lines later in 2001, hopefully in time to stem a conflict. Having the capacity to act early in the face of brewing crisis can help to manage these conflictual tendencies and avert their adverse humanitarian consequences.

A recent African refugee crisis makes the point even more clearly. In early 2001, refugees were pushed by fighting from Sierra Leone and Liberia into the Parrot's Beak area of south-west Guinea. As the conflict spread, they were joined in this locale by dislocated and vulnerable Guineans, for a total of 250,000 individuals.[20] Ultimately, they were evacuated under the auspices of UNHCR. But a more fundamental response is needed to manage the crisis.

[20] 'Towards a Comprehensive Approach to Durable and Sustainable Solutions to Priority Needs and Challenges in West Africa', Report of the Inter-Agency Mission to West Africa, UN Doc. S/2001/434 (2 May 2001), 11.

In particular, a broad international plan of action could have been prepared under the auspices of the United Nations, the Organization of African Unity, and the Economic Community of West African States (ECOWAS) to deal with the economic, social, and political dimensions of the crisis. Recommendations along those lines were made in the report to the UN Secretary-General of an inter-agency mission that he dispatched to West Africa in March 2001.[21] To come up with a specific package of policies designed to supplant the destructive impacts of conflict, diamonds, and wartime economies would require a strategy rooted deeply in the situation of these countries. Such a planning process would identify the bundles of 'sticks and carrots' necessary to diminish the power and influence of those responsible for promoting conflict in the region and to strengthen those seeking peace. But a wariness of prolonged and unmanageable involvement has kept outside governments away from exploring such approaches. A carefully calibrated plan on how to get from here to there could encourage engagement, and SHARE could provide a framework for the development of a plan rooted in specific local circumstances.

Anticipating crises, SHARE could focus on developing and advocating protection strategies for needy populations, with a particular emphasis on forced migrants who are not covered under the currently limited mandate of UNHCR or some other international organization. This residual responsibility could include developing doctrine and identifying who will do what for internal exiles. In this fashion, SHARE could serve as a planner and catalyst for action by other operational agencies.[22]

For post-crisis settings, SHARE could develop doctrine on issues of crisis management and rehabilitation. It could prepare protocols and checklists for those responsible for organizing mission deployments, and provide a forum for planning and digesting experience in the wide variety of situations where missions may deploy. It would be both a strategic planning resource and an archive of lessons learned. This would help repair a customary weakness in international peace operations: the seeming inability to plan or to learn lessons. As detailed earlier in this book, for example, there is very little cross-learning between the Cambodia and East Timor transitional missions despite the obvious similarities and mutual proximity.

Specific suggestions are given in the Brahimi report for the use of 'quick impact projects' (QIPs) to help establish the credibility of a new mission.[23]

[21] See, generally, ibid.

[22] If the role of UNHCR in relation to internal displacement is expanded or if the UN system humanitarian components are consolidated, as recommended earlier in this book, then SHARE would not need to undertake these tasks.

[23] 'Report of the Panel on United Nations Peace Operations', 7.

But, as the experience in Cambodia reflects, the efficacy of QIPs is largely unstudied. Sometimes they risk being little more than a temporary palliative or, worse yet, undermining longer-term development strategies. Nor is there an adequate institutional mechanism to design such projects or to arbitrate between competing interests. This could be an activity for SHARE.

The Brahimi report also urges that elections be viewed as part of a broader effort to strengthen governance institutions. This point is made presumably to avoid recent hard lessons where elections were an exit strategy which served to ratify a tyranny in Bosnia or were overturned by force after the departure of the UN mission in Cambodia. The holding of elections without effective security provisions produced the crisis in East Timor. Optimal electoral timing is a function of the specific context. Responsibility for tactical planning to achieve these ends could also be a function of SHARE.

If state building is to be an important function of the United Nations, there has to be both a new conceptual framework as well as enhanced institutional capacities. SHARE could provide technical support in achieving these improvements. It would craft responses to fill the gaps that regularly emerge after humanitarian relief has been provided and, for example, military security has been established, but before the emergence of a functioning state: what US Army General John Abizaid calls 'everything in between'.[24]

Fundamentally, there is no doctrine of state building, no strategic vision of such an endeavour, and no authority to plan for such an outcome in the UN system. This is an important rationale for the creation of the capacities embodied in SHARE. These deficiencies must be repaired if the international community is to launch effective peace operations and provide real solutions to returning refugees and displaced persons in post-crisis settings.

In noting the challenges of transitional civil administration, evident in Kosovo and East Timor, the Brahimi report found a conundrum:

> The Secretariat faces an unpleasant dilemma: to assume that transitional administration is a transitory responsibility, not prepare for additional missions and do it badly if it is once again flung into the breach, or to prepare well and be asked to undertake them more often because it is well prepared.[25]

Civil administration may well be a recurring if exceptional responsibility in peace operations. It is an endeavour that has already been featured in many missions relating to refugees over the past decade. It will continue to

[24] See Chapter 3.

[25] 'Report of the Panel on United Nations Peace Operations', 14.

be an aspect of international peace endeavours. Nor should it be a surprise that preparedness for such responsibilities will occasion the greater use of the United Nations in such situations. This is not 'an unpleasant dilemma' but rather a new reality, underpinning the need for calibrated options of international action to address the plight of refugees and displaced persons. Patience, resolve, and creativity, coupled with new capabilities such as SHARE, will be required to accomplish these difficult and daunting tasks.

DEVELOPING AN INTERNATIONAL JUSTICE PACKAGE FOR POST-CRISIS SETTINGS

The Brahimi report makes specific recommendations relating to the development of 'a common United Nations justice package' for use in post-crisis situations. Such a package would address the need for an interim legal code while the question of the applicable law was finally resolved. The report cautioned, however, that 'no work is currently under way within the Secretariat legal offices on this issue'.[26] The report noted that issues of property law would not be addressed in any such justice package.

An early activity of SHARE could be to work on applying rule of law concepts in post-crisis settings. This could include addressing recurring issues such as land and property rights. But perhaps the most obvious needs that have emerged concern criminal justice issues such as recruiting, training, and rostering civilian police, police leaders, legal experts, judges, prison officials, and other personnel who could be assembled into transitional 'packages' to operate legal systems in the early period of post-crisis settings. But while these needs are obvious, a variety of political and bureaucratic constraints have kept them from being met—a rationale for involvement by SHARE.

What precisely do we mean when we speak of the 'rule of law?' The term evokes a cascade of images and ideas ranging from lofty ideals of social and economic justice to notions of fair and non-discriminatory procedures and pragmatic goals of predictability in human interactions and commercial transactions. Ask lawyers what the rule of law is and you will evoke a surprising variety of answers, just as you will from politicians, development experts, philosophers, and entrepreneurs. Indeed, the range is so great that it is clear that there is no one answer. Also, there are many instances where adverse unintended consequences have arisen from the imposition of external concepts on indigenous cultures and societies. Yet, despite the

[26] Ibid.

opacity of the concept, enhancing the rule of law was a declared long-term objective of international peace operations in virtually all of the venues discussed in this book.

Creative approaches will be needed to avoid fighting the proverbial last humanitarian 'war' in the highly contextualized situations likely to confront decision makers in the future. These applied rule of law efforts would be designed from the outset to contribute to the development of indigenous legal systems in post-crisis transitions. International efforts have had enduring if unintended effects in Cambodia, for example, where the laws introduced by UNTAC are still operative.

Establishing a functioning judicial system in post-crisis settings is crucial to achieving a measure of security. Tentative explorations are under way in the UN, the EU, and the US government, and efforts are emerging as well in the independent sector.[27] But a bridge is needed between NGOs and the world of governments and international institutions—a rationale for such work by SHARE. A UN lawyer who has worked in Bosnia, Kosovo, and East Timor suggests that international standards should govern for at least six months while locally based structures are put into place. But this assumes the existence of model codes and standing organizational arrangements to deploy pre-identified experts, resources which currently do not exist. The Brahimi report argues for a 'doctrinal shift' in the use of the United Nations police monitors as well as the use of 'international judicial experts, penal experts, and human rights specialists' who could be deployed in sufficient numbers to address rule of law issues.[28] But no indication is given in terms of possible doctrinal direction.

A rule of law service package for a multi-faceted peace operation involving civil administration responsibilities would have at least three distinct functions which could be designed and tested in pilot projects in a new entity like SHARE. The first is the international military deployment, when basic security is imposed. Hostile forces are suppressed, and crowd control and basic public order are guaranteed. At this time, military forces or paramilitary constabulary groups, such as the French Gendarmerie, Italian Carabinieri, or Spanish Guardia Civil, would be responsible for security. Prison and judicial functions during this period would be undertaken by the military under United Nations standards.

In this connection, a model criminal code and criminal procedure law could be developed under UN auspices, with the assistance of an entity like

[27] For example, an ambitious effort has been launched at the United States Institute of Peace on peacekeeping and the administration of justice. See http://www.usip.org

[28] 'Report of the Panel on United Nations Peace Operations', 7.

SHARE, for use in advance of mission deployment and drawing upon work relating to the International Criminal Court to harmonize common and civil law traditions. International judges, prosecutors, and defence lawyers would be pre-identified and rostered for quick dispatch as well. These military and police functions should be exclusively international and carried out by the military under the authority of an appropriate UN Security Council resolution. The duration of this first phase should be governed by the state of security or insecurity in the place in question, whether it be the whole or a part of the territory of the operation.

The second function—international civilian mission—would involve the transfer of the relevant functions, including police, prison, and the judiciary, to pre-designed international organizational mechanisms developed under uniform standards. This would involve a pre-identified roster of police, which could be called up on short notice. The number of national contingents would be limited in any particular deployment to avoid the operational cacophony that now customarily attends multilateral policing efforts, as detailed in the cases in this book. Pre-identification would permit screening for qualifications and training as well as an orientation, including on cultural issues, prior to deployment. In failed or failing states, the international police would presumably be armed and have full authority and responsibility for law enforcement during the tenure of the UN mission. In less extreme settings, where government structures still function to some extent, they would have a monitoring and capacity-building role.

This is not just a human resources issue. Much technical work remains to be done to develop a supporting framework for international police deployments. As of 2001, for example, despite a decade of experience, the UN has yet to develop a uniform manual for international police operations.

But this is only the beginning of the endeavour. International police have now been deployed on many occasions in post-crisis settings only to discover that no prisons or courts exist to detain and place offenders on trial. While the policing issue has received limited attention in terms of lessons learned, the broader criminal justice challenges have received virtually no attention by those responsible for formulating future crisis responses. International prison administrators, seconded from governments and operating under yet-to-be formulated UN standards, would be identified for use in such operations.

These resources, taken together would constitute the core of an international criminal-justice system service package developed in advance and available for deployment in multi-faceted operations in which state building is an objective. The absence of such a mission capacity can seriously undermine the credibility of a UN mission, as was the case in Kosovo. The duration of this phase would be the duration of the international civilian mission.

There would also be an explicit development component of the mission which would have the assignment to prepare as soon as feasible a plan to build the capacity of local legal institutions. A general problem with UN operations in places such as Kosovo and East Timor is the difficulty of handing over law enforcement to indigenous actors and structures. This transitional planning phase is where the issue of applicable law would be situated, a question which early on vexed the UN missions in Kosovo and East Timor. Nevertheless, the primary functions during this second phase would be discharged by international personnel.

The third function—rule of law development phase—would be undertaken in an open-ended manner, reflecting both the elusive nature of the concept and the patience and resolve required to invest capacity in willing but often untutored students in such endeavours.[29] International action here would connect with broader ongoing efforts undertaken by governments and institutions such as UNDP and the World Bank to reform and restructure legal systems in order to introduce the rule of law.

Conceiving of international mission justice-system deployments in these three functional categories provides a rationale for action without mixing methods and objectives in a self-defeating exercise. Efforts to discern and enforce applicable law in the military security phase, or to build indigenous legal institutions before the international civilian mission achieves basic law-and-order functions, can work at cross-purposes and render already difficult challenges nearly impossible. This confusion can cause immense frustration and undermine the basic credibility of international post-crisis initiatives. A segmented approach would promote clarity and greater effectiveness in creating or restoring legal systems in the context of international peace operations and other transitional settings.

More thinking is needed on the application of legal concepts in humanitarian action. Legal policy arrangements in post-crisis settings should encourage individual interests to be asserted and disputes resolved in a wide variety of circumstances. This should include issues regarding the ownership of houses and land, which often rise to the fore after a crisis has abated and refugees and displaced persons are returning, and which should be addressed earlier and in the context of formulating state-building strategies. Litigation and compromise will result, establishing a workable legal

[29] This justice package-development exercise is distinct from questions of transitional justice involving the prosecution of violation of international human rights and humanitarian law, discussed earlier in this book, for which there are evolving models of international and special tribunals as well as less formal truth and reconciliation commissions.

architecture. The accretion of norms and indicia of accountability and reliability that evolve in local legal systems must be fortified by a legal profession and judiciary that become increasingly independent and proficient. This architecture, spanning both the governmental sector and civil society more generally, is fundamental to the building of a modern, rights-respecting state.

In his Millennium Report, the UN Secretary-General summarized the need to strengthen UN peace operations in the following terms:

> With the end of the cold war confrontation and the paralysis it had induced in the Security Council, the decade of the 1990s became one of great activism for the United Nations. More peace operations were mounted in that decade than in the previous four combined, and we developed new approaches to post-conflict peace-building and placed new emphasis on conflict prevention.
>
> While traditional peacekeeping had focused mainly on monitoring ceasefires, today's complex peace operations are very different. Their objective, in essence, is to assist the parties engaged in conflict to pursue their interests through political channels instead. To that end, the United Nations helps to create and strengthen political institutions and to broaden their base. We work alongside governments, non-governmental organizations and local citizens' groups to provide emergency relief, demobilize former fighters and reintegrate them into society, clear mines, organize and conduct elections, and promote sustainable development practices.[30]

A more capable international system would better protect the uprooted and assist them in finding solutions to the need for permanent homes. Finding ways to realize this objective in the context of the Secretary-General's vision will be a principal task for policy makers over the next decades.

[30] 'We the Peoples: The Role of the United Nations in the 21st Century', Millennium Report of the Secretary-General of the United Nations (2000). At: http://www.un.org/millennium/sg/report/full.htm

Conclusion

Over the past decade, the plight of the uprooted has become an integral part of new concepts of humanitarian action. From the mountains of northern Iraq in 1991 to the tropical landscape of East Timor in 1999, refugees have inspired vigorous debates on foreign intervention and been popularized in the mass media. They have become linked inevitably to broad conceptions of foreign affairs.

Informed by this multi-faceted political context, this book demonstrates that refugee policy must be more comprehensive and proactive. To this end, it is necessary to reform how policy is organized, both internationally and nationally. The need for these changes is evident from several policy disasters over the past decade.

In 1990, the trends in refugee policy around the world were as uncertain as the newly emerging framework for international relations. The Indo-Chinese refugee crisis was waning. A peace process in Central America heralded the prospect for large-scale repatriation. The Soviet Union was disintegrating, with outbreaks of ethnic violence in its former constituent regions. Western European policy makers debated a fearful scenario involving the arrival of large numbers of asylum seekers from the East. We could not know it for certain, but we were on the threshold of what turned out to be a decade of human displacement with massive upheavals in the Balkans, Africa, and Eurasia.

The end of the cold war loosed a variety of geo-political inhibitions, and a new propensity emerged over the past decade to address the needs of would-be refugees within their home countries. This includes growing efforts to protect and assist the world's 25 million conflict-related internal exiles. Motivations, of course, have not always been altruistic. Many wealthy countries preferred selfishly to keep away and contain asylum-seeking populations in or near their home countries, and this created daunting new complexities for decision makers.

These efforts to deal with forced migration have forged new but often uncomfortable alliances between politicians, soldiers, bureaucrats, and aid workers. Basic questions were raised about national security and human need. The singular events of the past decade pose a formidable question: can a deeply reactive humanitarian system be transformed into one that is more anticipatory and effective? Whether called humanitarian diplomacy or something else, a new form of statecraft is clearly needed in order to conduct effective humanitarian action.

But what would a comprehensive and proactive refugee policy look like? Such an approach would seek to develop calibrated options for decision makers to respond to crises. It would encourage earlier attempts at preventive action to forestall or mitigate crises. But very little thinking and less action on these issues seems to be coming from governments or international organizations. This is the kind of policy planning activity for which an organization such as the intergovernmental mechanism for Strategic Humanitarian Action and Research (SHARE) proposed in this book could be a catalyst. A few cases illustrate the point.

If preventive action is to be among the repertoire of policy responses, it must be decisive and come early in the dynamics of a conflict. The establishment at the beginning of the last decade of a Balkans stability pact to promote economic activity in the region could have served as a counterweight to discourage the secessionist violence which then followed. The belated effort which was made has not attracted significant funding. Instead, international engagement in the Balkans has now become synonymous with the notion of managing ethnic separation. Severe discrimination and reverse ethnic cleansing have become features of faltering efforts to encourage the emergence of new states. Political changes in Serbia and Croatia raise hopes for a broader peace. But frustrations with the slow pace of reform in Croatia, pressures for independence in Montenegro, and a smouldering insurgency in Macedonia raise alarms. An earlier effort, say in 1992, to create a Balkans stability pact could have dampened the conflagration.

The 1994 Rwandan genocide provides a further example of how preventive action might have averted or mitigated the gravest humanitarian disaster of the past decade. Obviously, the magnitude of the genocide could have been diminished substantially by augmenting instead of reducing the numbers of UN peacekeeping troops present. A conservative assessment is that a military intervention early in the genocide could have saved tens of thousands of lives if not more.[1] It might also have been more cost-effective.[2]

[1] By some estimates, a major intervention would have saved 275,000 Tutsi, compared with the 150,000 who actually survived. See Kuperman, Alan J., 'Rwanda in Retrospect', *Foreign Affairs*, 79/1 (2000), 94–118.

[2] A Carnegie Commission study estimated that the total cost of the augmented peace operation would have been $500 million annually and that preventive action in Rwanda would

Once the genocide had occurred and Hutus had regrouped into ominous large encampments just outside Rwanda's borders, a serious international effort to police the camps and separate for trial the killers from innocent civilians, even if only partially successful, might have built enough confidence in Rwanda to have avoided the ensuing attacks on the refugee camps. The incapacity and ultimate unwillingness of Zaire to undertake this endeavour, coupled with the reluctance of the international community, immobilized by the ghosts of Somalia, to field a mission with this objective opened the way for the broader inter-state conflict that followed.

Even as late as mid-1996, a concerted international effort to address African refugees in the Great Lakes region, involving political and financial as well as humanitarian actors, and comprehensively addressing issues of refugee protection, justice, and security, in return for substantial commitments of foreign aid, could have made a difference. This presumably would have included concerted efforts to isolate armed elements in the camps in Zaire. A central African refugee conference might have been able to achieve a workable plan to assemble and deploy sufficient international resources to provide security and supplant the war economies and vested interests that have kept the region at war. But the humanitarian agencies were alone in these settings,[3] and no comprehensive political framework was available in which to undertake such endeavours. The lack of engagement by the international community thus removed this potential brake to descent into war in Africa.

There are also circumstances where anticipatory refugee policy responses can forestall the need for costly and dangerous military deployments. The 1994 invasion of Haiti by US forces was motivated primarily by the objective of migration control. Regional safe-haven arrangements had not been made, and there was no international framework under which they could be quickly established. The only control measure left was the direct refugee-return policy, which, while it had withstood legal challenges in the US courts and the condemnation of UNHCR, was not politically sustainable. Policy experts foresaw that the resulting loss of control in the situation might prompt a US military intervention, but, as in so many other

probably have cost $1.3 billion; in the end, the overall assistance to Rwanda in the wake of the genocide had a price tag of $4.5 billion. See United Nations Security Council, 'Prevention of Armed Conflict: Report of the Secretary-General', UN Doc. S/2001/574 (New York: United Nations Security Council, 2001), 6.

[3] The high water mark of international efforts during this period was a meeting in February 1995 in Bujumbura, Burundi, sponsored by UNHCR and OAU and driven by humanitarian considerations, that focused on assistance to returnees and displaced persons.

instances, decision makers had no real choice given the paucity of options available in the heat of the moment.

In retrospect, US policy responses would likely have evolved very differently if, when President Clinton relaxed the summary return policy in May 1994, regional facilities had been available to accommodate the outflow of boat people. If the exodus had been managed and an equilibrium achieved, then the United States probably would not have proceeded so aggressively to deploy military forces to restore democracy. Whether the democratic outcome actually achieved in Haiti is enduring is another matter. But, whatever the ultimate outcome, the elaboration of regional schemes to manage a refugee or migration emergency humanely could give decision makers new tools for responses short of a military deployment.

Specifically, a Caribbean regional forced migration planning centre could monitor circumstances that may prompt displacements and engage in contingency planning in order to promote preparedness to deal with future emergencies. Optimally, this humanitarian response planning office should be organized under the auspices of a regional international organization such as the Organization of American States in order to ensure that policy expertise is integrated at the political level. This kind of anticipatory approach would help policy to escape the excessively reactive posture that precludes cooperation in the throes of crisis.

Over the past decade, ambitious designs to build and strengthen governance structures within states and create the conditions conducive to refugee return have taught the need for humility by outside actors. New states cannot just be built. An initial objective of fostering basic security and stability in an international mission deployment should be followed by effective policies oriented toward creating the conditions for sustainable refugee return, including inculcating the rule of law and preventing the recurrence of crisis. Nor is this endeavour the exclusive province of governments. Civil society elements are key components, including both international and indigenous NGOs.

For refugee policy to become more comprehensive and proactive, moreover, basic reforms are needed in the way policy is organized. While there have been many laudable efforts by well-intentioned officials and other individuals, overall the current system lacks the capacity consistently to achieve even modest expectations in relation to the demanding new terrain for humanitarian action.

Internationally, this book proposes to consolidate the fragmented humanitarian components in the UN system, including those related to protecting and assisting internal exiles (see Chapter 7). Initially, policy coordination would take place under the aegis of the UNHCR, with a view toward full programmatic and budgetary consolidation. The book also recommends the creation of an intergovernmental mechanism, SHARE, outside the UN system, which would be a technical, expert resource for like-minded developed and developing states to work on filling the gaps in humanitarian action (Chapter 10). These lacunae include re-conceiving refugee policy to have a preventive orientation, designing plans to protect and assist the internally displaced, and fostering post-crisis capacities in international mission deployments to enhance human security and the rule of law.

Within the US government, a new organization, the Agency for Humanitarian Action (AHA), is recommended (Chapter 8). This would not only help rationalize the bureaucratically fragmented character of US humanitarian policy, but would provide an appropriate authority for military and civilian planning to prepare for future humanitarian catastrophes. AHA would also provide an effective way to marshal the capacity within government to contribute usefully to international efforts to introduce legal systems in post-crisis settings.

These new directions, of course, cannot be taken without adequate funding. Indeed, as the new High Commissioner for Refugees has recognized, a substantial increase in global funding is needed even to maintain the current regime of refugee protection. But a targeted global investment from donor governments and private sources of even an additional $100 million a year to craft comprehensive and proactive policies concerning forced migration would likely forestall the need to pay much larger costs later. This would be a proportionate and modest sum to devote to this end given the current levels of humanitarian expenditures.[4]

The policy options available in the future will in many respects be similar to those that have been at the disposal of decision makers in the past. But a greater focus on international cooperation and preventive approaches would refine and amplify the tools available to those who formulate and implement policy. The amalgam of approaches and options that emerge, and that are described in this book, will constitute the new toolbox to address human displacement and humanitarian action in the new century. Much is at stake. The neglect or misuse of these tools would result in human misery and political instability. However, success in this humanitarian management endeavour would surely mitigate the refugee problem and help us to avoid paying the high human, economic, political, and security costs—the price of indifference.

[4] In addition to UNHCR's current budget of approximately $800 million discussed in an earlier chapter, the World Food Programme expended $1.49 billion in 2000, and UNICEF was funded at $1.12 billion in 1999. See: http://www.wfp.org/aboutwfp/facts/2000.htm, and http://www.unicef.org/ar00/ar00eng_part3.pdf

Bibliography

Allard, Kenneth, *Somalia Operations: Lessons Learned* (Ft. McNair, Washington, DC: National Defense University Press, 1995).

Annan, Kofi, *Renewing the United Nations: A Programme for Reform*, UN Doc. A/51/950 (New York: United Nations, July 1997).

—— *We the Peoples: the Role of the United Nations in the 21st Century*, Millennium Report of the Secretary-General of the United Nations (New York: United Nations, April 2000).

Barber, Ben, 'Feeding Refugees, or War?', *Foreign Affairs*, 76/4 (1997), 8–14.

Byman, Daniel L., Lesser, Ian, Prinie, Bruce, Bernard, Cheryl, and Waxman, Matthew, *Strengthening the Partnership: Improving Military Coordination with Relief Agencies and Allies in Humanitarian Operations* (Santa Monica, CA: RAND, 2000).

Carothers, Thomas, *Aiding Democracy Abroad: The learning curve* (Washington, DC: Carnegie Endowment for Peace, 1999).

Cernea, Michael M. and McDowell, Christopher, *Risks and Reconstruction: Experiences of Resettlers and Refugees* (Washington, DC: The World Bank, 2000).

Childers, Erskine, and Urquhart, Brian, *Strengthening International Responses to Humanitarian Emergencies* (New York: Ford Foundation, 1991).

Clark, Jeffrey, 'Debacle in Somalia,' *Foreign Affairs*, 72/1 (1993), 109–23.

Clark, Wesley K., *Waging Modern War: Bosnia, Kosovo, and the Future of Combat* (New York: Public Affairs, 2001).

Clarke, Walter and Herbst, Jeffrey, 'Somalia and the Future of Humanitarian Intervention,' *Foreign Affairs*, 75/2 (1996), 70–85.

Commander-in-Chief United States Atlantic Command, *Operation Uphold Democracy: Joint After Action Report* (Norfolk, VA: US Department of Defense, 1995).

Cohen, Roberta and Deng, Francis M., 'Exodus within Borders', *Foreign Affairs*, 77/4 (1998), 12–17.

—— *Masses in Flight: The Global Crisis of Internal Displacement* (Washington, DC: Brookings Institution Press, 1998).

Council on Foreign Relations, *Bosnia: What Went Wrong?*, A Foreign Affairs Reader (New York: Council on Foreign Relations, 1998).

Crisp, Jeff and Mayne, Andrew, *Review of the Cambodia Repatriation Operation*, EVAL/CAM/13 (Geneva: UNHCR, September 1993).

Crocker, Chester A., Hampson, Fen Osler, and Aall, Pamela (eds), *Managing Global Chaos: Sources of and Responses to International Conflict* (Washington, DC: United States Institute of Peace Press, 1996).

Daalder, Ivo H. and O'Hanlon, Michael E., *Winning Ugly: NATO's War to Save Kosovo* (Washington, DC: The Brookings Institution, 2000).

Des Forges, Alison, *Leave None to Tell the Story: Genocide in Rwanda* (New York: Human Rights Watch, 1999).

External Review of the Humanitarian Response to the East Timor Crisis: September 1999–May 2000, on behalf of UNTAET/HAER (24 May 2000).

Forman, Shepard and Patrick, Stewart (eds), *Good Intentions: Pledges of Aid for Post-Conflict Recovery*, Center on International Cooperation, Studies in Multilateralism (Boulder, CO: Lynne Rienner Publishers, 2000).

Ghosh, Bimal (ed.), *Return Migration: Journey of Hope or Despair?* (Geneva: International Organization for Migration and United Nations, 2000).

Glenny, Misha, *The Balkans: Nationalism,War and the Great Powers, 1804–1999* (New York: Viking, 2000).

Goodwin-Gill, Guy S., *The Refugee in International Law* (Oxford: Clarendon Press, 1996).

Gourevitch, Philip, *We wish to inform you that tomorrow we will be killed with our families: Stories from Rwanda* (New York: Farrar, Straus and Giroux, 1998).

Gurr, Ted Robert, 'Ethnic Warfare on the Wane', *Foreign Affairs*, 79/3 (2000), 52–64.

Hayes, Margaret Daly and Gary F. Wheatley, *Interagency and Political-Military Dimensions of Peace Operations: Haiti—A Case Study* (Washington, D.C.: National Defense University, 1995).

Helton, Arthur C., 'The Comprehensive Plan of Action for Indo-Chinese Refugees: An Experiment in Refugee Protection and Control', *New York Law School Journal of Human Rights*, 8/1 (1990), 111–48.

—— 'Legal Dimensions of Responses to Complex Humanitarian Emergencies', *International Journal of Refugee Law*, 10 (1998): 533–46.

—— 'Establishing a Comprehensive Scheme for Refugee and Migration Emergencies in the Caribbean Region: Lessons from Recent Haitian and Cuban Emergencies', in Max J. Castro (ed.), *Free Markets, Open Societies, Closed Borders? Trends in International Migration and Immigration Policy in the Americas* (Miami: North-South Center, University of Miami, 1999).

—— 'Forced Displacement, Humanitarian Intervention, and Sovereignty', *SAIS Review*, 20/1 (2000), 61–86.

—— 'Protecting the World's Exiles: The Human Rights of Non-Citizens', *Human Rights Quarterly*, 22/1 (2000), 280–97.

—— 'A Call for an Accountability Campaign', in Yael Danieli (ed.), *Sharing the Front Line and the Back Hills: International Protectors and Providers: Peacekeepers, Humanitarian Aid Workers and the Media in the Midst of Crisis* (Amityville, NY: Baywood Pub. Co., 2001).

—— 'Bureaucracy and the Quality of Mercy', *International Migration Review*, 35/1 (2001), 192–225.

—— and Voronina, Natalia, *Forced Displacement and Human Security in the Former Soviet Union: Law and Policy* (Ardsley, NY: Transnational Publishers, Inc., 2000).

Henkin, Alice H. (ed.), *Honoring Human Rights and Keeping the Peace: Lessons from El Salvador, Cambodia and Haiti* (Washington, DC: Aspen Institute, 1995).

—— (ed.), *Honoring Human Rights, from Peace to Justice: Recommendations to the International Community* (Washington, DC: Aspen Institute, 1998).

Holbrooke, Richard, *To End a War* (New York: The Modern Library, 1998).

Ignatieff, Michael, *Virtual War: Kosovo and Beyond* (New York: Metropolitan Books, 2000).

Independent International Commission on Kosovo, *The Kosovo Report: Conflict, International Response, Lessons Learned* (Oxford: Oxford University Press, 2000).

Inter-Agency Standing Committee, *Protection of Internally Displaced Persons*, An Inter-Agency Standing Committee Policy Paper (New York: Inter-Agency Standing Committee, December 1999).

Judah, Tim, *Kosovo: War and Revenge* (New Haven, CT: Yale University Press, 2000).

Kälin, Walter, *Guiding Principles on Internal Displacement: Annotations*, Studies in Transnational Legal Policy, No. 32 (Washington, DC: American Society of International Law and The Brookings Institution, 2000).

Krauthammer, Charles, 'The Short, Unhappy Life of Humanitarian War', *The National Interest*, 57/Fall (1999), 5–8.

Kumar, Radha, 'The Troubled History of Partition', *Foreign Affairs*, 76/1 (1997), 22–34.

Kuperman, Alan J., *The Limits of Humanitarian Intervention: Genocide in Rwanda* (Washington, DC: Brookings Institution Press, 2001).

Kwiatkowski, Karen U., *African Crisis Response Initiative: Past, Present and Future?* (Carlisle Barracks, PA: US Army War College, 2000).

Lavenex, Sandra, *Safe Third Countries: Extending the EU Asylum and Immigration Policies to Central and Eastern Europe* (Budapest: Central European University Press, 1999).

Loescher, Gil, *Beyond Charity: International Cooperation and the Global Refugee Crisis*, A Twentieth Century Fund Book (New York and Oxford: Oxford University Press, 1993).

——*The UNHCR and World Politics: A Perilous Path* (Oxford: Oxford University Press, 2001).

Macrae, Joanna, *Aiding Peace ... and War: UNHCR, Returnee Reintegration and the Relief-Development Debate*, New Issues in Refugee Research Working Paper No. 14 (Geneva: UNHCR, December 1999).

Maguire, Robert, Balutansky, Edwige, Fomerand, Jacques, Minear, Larry, O'Neill, William, Weiss, Thomas, and Zaidi, Sarah, *Haiti Held Hostage: International Responses to the Quest for Nationhood 1986 to 1996*, Occasional Paper No. 23 (Providence, RI: Thomas J. Watson Jr. Institute for International Studies, 1996).

Mandelbaum, Michael, 'A Prefect Failure', *Foreign Affairs*, 78/5 (1999), 2–8.

—— 'Foreign Policy as Social Work', *Foreign Affairs*, 75/1 (1996), 16–32.

Minear, Larry, Clark, Jeffrey, Cohen, Roberta, Gallagher, Dennis, Guest, Iain, and Weiss, Thomas, *Humanitarian Action in the Former Yugoslavia: The UN's Role 1991–1993*, Occasional Paper No. 18 (Providence, RI: Thomas J. Watson Jr. Institute for International Studies, 1994).

Minear, Larry, Cortright, David, Wagler, Julia, Lopez, George A., and G. Weiss, Thomas, *Toward More Humane and Effective Sanctions Management: Enhancing the Capacity of the United Nations System*, Occasional Paper No. 31 (Providence, RI: Thomas J. Watson Jr. Institute for International Studies, 1998).

—— van Baarda, Ted, and Somas, Marci, *NATO and Humanitarian Action in the Kosovo Crisis*, Occasional Paper No. 36 (Providence, RI: Thomas J. Watson Jr. Institute for International Studies, 2000).

Moore, David, *Humanitarian Agendas, State Reconstruction and Democratisation Processes in War-torn Societies*, New Issues in Refugee Research Working Paper No. 24 (Geneva: UNHCR, July 2000).

Moore, Jonathan (ed.), *Hard Choices: Moral Dilemmas in Humanitarian Intervention* (Lanham, MD: Rowman & Littlefield Publishers, Inc., 1998).

Müller, Joachim (ed.), *Reforming the United Nations: The Quiet Revolution* (The Hague: Kluwer Law International, 2001).

National Intelligence Council, *Global Humanitarian Emergencies: Trends and Projections, 1999–2000* (Washington, DC: National Intelligence Council, August 1999).

—— *Global Trends 2015: A Dialogue About the Future with Nongovernmental Experts* (Washington, DC: National Intelligence Council, December 2000).

NATO, *Kosovo One Year On: Achievement and Challenge* (Brussels: NATO, 21 March 2000).

Nicholson, Frances and Twomey, Patrick (eds), *Refugee Rights and Realities: Evolving International Concepts and Regimes* (Cambridge: Cambridge University Press, 1999).

Nye, Joseph S., 'Redefining the National Interest', *Foreign Affairs*, 78/4 (1999), 22–35.

Oakley, Robert B., Dziedzic, Michael J., and Goldberg, Eliot M., *Policing the New World Disorder: Peace Operations and Public Security* (Washington, DC: National Defense University Press, 1998).

Office of the High Representative, *Bosnia and Herzegovina: Essential Texts* (Sarajevo: Office of the High Representative, January 1998).

Ombudsmen of the Federation of Bosnia and Herzegovina, *Report on Human Rights Situation in the Federation of Bosnia and Herzegovina for 2000, Sarajevo* (Sarajevo: March 2001).

OSCE Office for Democratic Institutions and Human Rights, *Kosovo/Kosova As Seen, As Told: An Analysis of the Human Rights Findings of the OSCE Kosovo Verification Mission, Parts I and II* (Warsaw: OSCE Office for Democratic Institutions and Human Rights, 1999).

Plender, Richard (ed.), *Basic Documents on International Migration Law*, 2nd edn (The Hague: Martinus Nijhoff Publishers, 1997).

Project on Internal Displacement, *Handbook for Applying the Guiding Principles on Internal Displacement* (Washington, DC: The Brookings Institution, 1999).

Prunier, Gerard, *The Rwanda Crisis: History of a Genocide* (New York: Columbia University Press, 1995).

Ratner, Steven R., *The New UN Peacekeeping: Building Peace in Lands of Conflict after the Cold War* (New York: St Martin's Press, 1996).

Rieff, David, 'Case Study in Ethnic Strife', *Foreign Affairs*, 76/2 (1997), 118–33.

—— *Slaughterhouse: Bosnia and the Failure of the West* (New York: Simon & Schuster, 1995).

Roberts, Adam, 'NATO's "Humanitarian War" Over Kosovo', *Survival*, 41/3 (1999), 102–23.

Rodman, Peter W., 'The Fallout from Kosovo', *Foreign Affairs*, 78/4 (1999), 45–51.

Rohde, David, *Endgame: The Betrayal and Fall of Srebrenica, Europe's Worst Massacre since World War II* (Boulder, CO: Westview Press, 1998).

—— 'Kosovo Seething', *Foreign Affairs*, 79/3 (2000), 65–79.

Rubin, Barnett R. (ed.), *Cases and Strategies for Preventive Action* (New York: The Century Foundation Press, 1998).

Shawcross, William, *Deliver Us from Evil: Peacekeepers, Warlords and a World of Endless Conflict*, revised edn (London: Bloomsbury, 2001).

Solana, Javier, 'NATO's Success in Kosovo', *Foreign Affairs*, 78/6 (1999), 114–21.

Steering Committee for Humanitarian Response and InterAction, *The Sphere Project: Humanitarian Charter and Minimum Standards in Disaster Response* (Geneva: Steering Committee for Humanitarian Response and InterAction, 1998).

Stremlau, John, *People in Peril: Human Rights, Humanitarian Action, and Preventing Deadly Conflict*, Report to the Carnegie Commission on Preventing Deadly Conflict (New York: Carnegie Corporation of New York, May 1998).

Suhrke, Astri, Barutciski, Michael, Sandison, Peta, and Garlock, Rick, *The Kosovo Crisis: An Independent Evaluation of UNHCR's Emergency Preparedness and Response* (Geneva: United Nations High Commissioner for Refugees, Evaluation and Policy Analysis Unit, February 2000).

Traub, James, 'Inventing East Timor', *Foreign Affairs*, 79/4 (2000), 74–89.

United Kingdom Ministry of Defence, *Kosovo: An Account of the Crisis*, UK Ministry of Defence (1999).

United Nations, General Assembly Resolution 46/182 on Strengthening of the Coordination of Humanitarian Emergency Assistance of the United Nations, UN Doc. 46/182 (1991).

—— 'Code of Conduct for Humanitarian Assistance in Sierra Leone', in *United Nations Consolidated Inter-Agency Appeal for Sierra Leone: January-December 2000* (Geneva: United Nations, November 1999), Annex I, 121–124.

—— 'Report of the Secretary-General on the United Nations Interim Administration in Kosovo', UN Doc. S/2000/177 (3 March 2000).

—— 'Report of the Panel on United Nations Peace Operations' ('Brahimi Report'), UN Doc. A/55/305 and S/2000/809 (21 August 2000).

—— 'Report of the Secretary-General Pursuant to General Assembly Resolution 53/35 (1998)' ('Srebrenica Report'). At:http://www.un.org/news/ossg/srebrenica.htm

United Nations High Commissioner for Refugees, *The State of the World's Refugees: The Challenge of Protection* (Oxford: Oxford University Press, 1993).

United Nations High Commissioner for Refugees, *Working in a War Zone: A Review of UNHCR's Operations in Former Yugoslavia*, EVAL/YUG/14 (Geneva: UNHCR, April 1994).

—— *The State of the World's Refugees: In Search of Solutions* (Oxford: Oxford University Press, 1995).

—— *The State of the World's Refugees: A Humanitarian Agenda* (Oxford: Oxford University Press, 1997).

—— *The State of the World's Refugees: Fifty Years of Humanitarian Action* (New York: Oxford University Press, 2000).

United Nations Office for the Coordination of Humanitarian Affairs, *Guiding Principles on Internal Displacement* (New York: OCHA, 1998).

—— *Manual on Field Practice in Internal Displacement: Examples from UN Agencies and Partner Organizations of Field-based Initiatives Supporting Internally Displaced Persons*, Inter-Agency Standing Committee Policy Paper Series No. 1 (New York: OCHA, 1999).

United Nations Transitional Administration in East Timor, *Official Gazette of East Timor*, Vol. I and onward (Dili: UNTAET, 2000).

United States General Accounting Office, *Humanitarian Intervention: Effectiveness of UN Operations in Bosnia*, GAO/NSIAD-94-156BR (Washington, DC: United States General Accounting Office, April 1994).

United States Mission to the United Nations, *Global Humanitarian Emergencies, 1996* (New York: United States Mission to the United Nations, February 1996).

—— *Global Humanitarian Emergencies, 1997* (New York: United States Mission to the United Nations, April 1997).

—— *Global Humanitarian Emergencies, 1998–99* (New York: United States Mission to the United Nations, September 1998).

US Department of Defense, *Report to Congress: Kosovo / Operation Allied Force After-Action Report* (Washington, DC: US Department of Defense, 31 January 2000). At: http://www.defenselink.mil/pubs/kaar02072000.pdf

US Department of State, *Interagency Review of US Government Civilian Humanitarian & Transition Programs* (Washington, DC: US Department of State, January 2000). At: http://www.gwu.edu/~nsarchiv/NSAEBB/NSAEBB30/index.html

—— *Kosovo Judicial Assessment Mission Report* (Washington, DC: US Department of State, April 2000).

Zolberg, Aristide R., Suhrke, Astri, and Aguayo, Sergio, *Escape from Violence: Conflict and the Refugee Crisis in the Developing World* (New York and Oxford: Oxford University Press, 1989).

Index